Target: Italy

Target: Italy

THE SECRET WAR AGAINST MUSSOLINI, 1940–1943

The Official History of
SOE Operations in Fascist Italy

Roderick Bailey

FABER & FABER

First published in 2014
by Faber and Faber Limited
Bloomsbury House
74–77 Great Russell Street
London WC1B 3DA

Typeset by Donald Sommerville
Printed in England by CPI Group (UK) Ltd, Croydon, CRO 4YY

A CIP record for this book
is available from the British Library

ISBN 978–0–571–29918–8

2 4 6 8 10 9 7 5 3 1

Contents

Plates

Plates

20. General Bedell Smith signs the Italian Armistice. *National Archives, Kew*
21. Inscription in the former Gestapo prison, Via Tasso, Rome. *Author's photo*

Map

SOE personnel sent into Italy, 1940–3.

Prologue

At two minutes past ten on the evening of 13 August 1943, a single British aircraft – a four-engined Halifax bomber – took off from a desert airfield in Allied-occupied Algeria. At the controls was a Canadian, Alfred Ruttledge, a 29-year-old flight lieutenant with a reputation as a fine pilot, who now set a solitary course across the Mediterranean for enemy territory. Cap Matifou, the last of North Africa, was passed ten minutes later. Menorca was skirted at half past eleven. The Îles d'Hyères, off the south coast of France, were reached at one in the morning. Then the Halifax was over Italy.

At two o'clock, Ruttledge and his crew picked up in the moonlight a river junction north of Alessandria. Turning for the hills and peaks north of Milan, taking care to stay out of range of the city's anti-aircraft guns, they took a fresh bearing as they recognised Lodi. The Halifax finally reached its target at half past two on the morning of 14 August, when it arrived, growling and low, over Lake Como.

Hidden, fjord-like, in the foothills of the Italian Alps, Lake Como is one of the most striking stretches of water in Europe. Lush wooded slopes drop steeply to the shore. Ochre-roofed villages and villas dot the edge. For centuries it has inspired artists, writers, composers and poets, from Virgil and Pliny to Verdi and Byron. 'A more charming path was scarce ever travelled than we had along the lake of Como,' the poet William Wordsworth wrote to his sister in 1790, recalling hillsides of 'large sweeping woods of chestnut spotted with villages, some clinging from the summits of the advancing rocks, and others hiding themselves within their recesses. Nor was the surface of the lake less interesting than its shores; part of it glowing with

1

the richest green and gold the reflexion of the illuminated woods, and part shaded with a soft blue tint . . . At the lake of Como my mind ran thro a thousand dreams of happiness which might be enjoyed upon its banks.'[1]

With the dark mass of Wordsworth's summits looming uncomfortably on either side, Ruttledge ran the Halifax down the length of the lake, turned, and returned. Then, as the crew's subsequent sortie report records, 'at 0248 hrs, [on a] bearing [of] 240° [and from a height of] 2,000 ft,' a man parachuted from the aircraft straight into the water.[2]

Nestling on Como's banks is the little medieval commune of Carate Urio. It was from here that a baker, Fulvio Borghi, heard the Halifax appear and, in the moonlight, saw the parachute snap open. Borghi hurried to the village's cobbled quay. With him were three other local men – Giovanni Abate, who had also heard the plane, Emilio Rusconi and Domenico Taroni – and a soldier on sick leave by the name of Morandotti. Taking the oars of a rowing boat, they pushed out onto the lake. Finally they made out in the gloom a figure paddling a small rubber dinghy. They shouted at him to stop. '*Amico!*' ('Friend!') he shouted back, still paddling.[3]

According to one account of what happened next, the rowers fired a warning shot. The figure stopped paddling. An awkward standoff ensued. The man in the dinghy boldly demanded to know if those shouting and shooting at him were fishermen. When they failed to respond, he put his question again. This time he sounded annoyed. Yes, they said eventually, they were indeed fishermen. And who was he? An Italian, the man replied: an airman who had bailed out of an Italian aircraft. He scrambled aboard their boat and together they made for the shore.[4]

By the time the rowers returned to the quay, the sun was up and a crowd had gathered. One little girl among them was Emilio Rusconi's daughter. Sixty-seven years later she recalled the excitement of that curious morning and how, gathered on the road that still overlooks the quay, she and the other children had peered down at the parachutist as he was led to someone's home to warm up.[5]

Before long he was under guard in the commune offices, his compromising kit having quickly betrayed his claim to be an Italian airman. Beneath a rubber diving suit he wore civilian clothes. Strapped to his leg was a watertight bag, inside which, so the Italian authorities would record, were 'thousands of Italian lire in L.1000 notes, identity cards and permits, driving licences, and military discharge papers, all perfectly forged, as well as spare parts for a wireless set and cryptographic negatives, all carefully concealed in boxes, [plus] a book entitled *Italia mia* by Giovanni Papini.'[6] Closer inspection of his belongings was to reveal more rolls of money and some photographic negatives concealed in two hollowed-out torch batteries, a wireless aerial disguised as a washing line, and the crystal for a wireless set hidden in the handle of a shaving brush. Pages 185 to 188 of *Italia mia* were sealed together; when they were sliced open, more negatives were found.

At about this moment the captive declared in fluent Tuscan-accented Italian that he was Lieutenant Richard Norris, a British officer of the Parachute Regiment. Later that day he and his kit were put in a truck and driven along the lake to Como town, the journey apparently preceded by his first beating, this one at the hands of a plume-helmeted officer of the elite Bersaglieri who, unhappy with the prisoner's answers, hit him twice in the face. Incarcerated in Como, Norris was soon under the scrutiny of Italian counter-espionage officers. 'An enemy parachutist has been captured,' read a report that evening to the Italian Army's Chief of Staff and the War Ministry in Rome; 'of British nationality, [he] is wearing civilian clothes and speaks perfect Italian. He is now being interrogated.'[7]

⊙

Richard Norris's real name was Richard Dallimore-Mallaby. Known to friends as Dick Mallaby, he was a British secret agent. A head-and-shoulders photograph pinned to a declassified file shows a fresh-faced, good-looking young man with straight blond hair combed back. Details in other documents add blue eyes, weight eleven stone, almost six feet in height, permanent scars on his right elbow, shins and right cheekbone, a heart tattoo on his left forearm, and an age: when plucked from Lake Como he was twenty-four. Plenty of papers testify to his courage and coolness. '[E]veryone is very impressed with him,' wrote a colleague at headquarters as Mallaby was preparing to jump into Italy. 'He is a very likeable fellow . . . unassuming and well disciplined.'[8] Mallaby 'at no time showed any signs whatsoever of nerves' recorded the officer who saw him off at the airfield; 'given the necessary amount of luck, I consider he will do a first-class job'.[9]

Dick Mallaby was a member of a secret British organisation called the Special Operations Executive, the principal Allied force engaged in encouraging resistance inside Italy since Benito Mussolini, the country's dictator, had declared war on Britain and France in 1940. Today, the public image of SOE is dominated by the work of its agents in Nazi-occupied France, a picture itself distorted by exaggerated claims as to their effectiveness and by a book market unbalanced by stories of the thirty-odd women that it trained and sent in. In fact, from humble beginnings, SOE became active in every theatre of war, dispatching thousands of trained operatives – of dozens of nationalities and almost all of them men – to harass enemy garrisons, attack important instal- lations, and encourage, arm and fight beside movements as diverse as communist partisans in the Balkans and headhunting tribes in Borneo. What follows is the first full account of SOE's clandestine endeavours at striking at Italy between June 1940, when the Italians entered the Second World War on the side of Nazi Germany, and September 1943, when they finally signed an armistice with the Allies.

Commissioned by the Cabinet Office, this is an official history, the sixth about SOE to be published. The series began in 1966 with the publication of M. R. D. Foot's *SOE in France*.[10] Foot's commission was partly a response to public and private calls for clarity about SOE's French operations, which were fast becoming shrouded in controversy and myth. Partly it was born from an official desire to correct foreign impressions of Britain's contribution to wartime resistance movements. In time, ongoing concern for accuracy saw more commissions. Official histories of SOE's work in the Far East and Scandinavia appeared in the 1980s.[11] A fourth volume, dealing with operations in the Low Countries, was published in 2001.[12]

An early case for an official history of SOE's work in Italy was made in Whitehall in 1969. When asked to explore the pros and cons of further volumes to follow Foot's, a Foreign Office mandarin, Dame Barbara Salt, herself once a member of SOE, argued that several grounds existed that made Italy worthy of formal attention. One was that it offered an opportunity to high-light unique challenges that SOE had met when getting to grips with Mussolini. Another was that it could permit recognition of the post-armistice exploits of British personnel who had fought side-by-side with Italian partisans in German-occupied Italy.[13] An official history was eventually commissioned, but acknowledgement of the fundamental differences between SOE's early work against Fascist Italy and its later role with the partisans saw a decision taken later to divide it into two. The fifth official SOE history, David Stafford's study of SOE activities in German-occupied Italy between 1943 and 1945, was published in 2011.[14]

As for each of its predecessors, the brief for what follows was to produce a fluent account that discerns, as far as possible, the facts, warts and all, of what SOE had done and had tried to do. With a view to accessibility, I have tried to tell the story with a modern readership in mind. Principal among the primary sources are SOE's own files and additional British military and government records, most of which are open today at the National Archives at Kew. These sources have been complemented by the memories of men and women who witnessed or took part in some of the events related here. Seventy years on, very few were still around to share their testimonies directly with me; some, though, told their stories to the Imperial War Museum, or deposited penned accounts in the museum's archives, or wrote or spoke to Christopher Woods, a British diplomat-turned-historian who began researching SOE's Italian operations in the late 1980s and whose own Italian background began in 1944, when, as a young SOE officer, he parachuted into northern Italy to work with the partisans.[15]

Most of SOE's official histories have made scant use of foreign records. Here, however, I have sought to produce a rounded account by drawing upon declassified files from a series of overseas archives. Records of the counter-espionage branch of Italy's wartime military intelligence service, the Servizio Informazioni Militare (SIM), proved especially rewarding.[16] Also of considerable value were the files of SOE's American equivalent, the Office of Strategic Services, and those of the FBI.

Another unique feature of this book – focused, as it is, on the underground war waged within Italy's borders as opposed to that fought in Italian-conquered lands – is that this is the first in-depth account of SOE's efforts to cause trouble inside an enemy country as opposed to an enemy-occupied one.[17] As such, it may be read as a study of the dangers and obstacles that foreign agencies can encounter when trying to encourage domestic resistance to secure, if unpopular, authoritarian regimes. Conventional Allied forces may have found themselves better disciplined, led, motivated and equipped when meeting their Italian adversaries on the battlefield, but clandestine penetration of Fascist Italy proved a formidable proposition. When SOE began that task in 1940, the cautious policies of pre-war British governments meant that it had few foundations on which to build. Overconfident and impatient as it tried to forge ahead, it could also be careless with the slim resources that it had to hand. It could be uncaring, too. Often it felt hamstrung by the conflicting priorities of policy-makers reluctant to provide the backing that it felt was necessary for success, and its alliance with its similarly secret cousin, MI6, Britain's Secret Intelligence Service, was uneasy. But its greatest difficulties stemmed from the reluctance of many Italians, both inside and outside Italy, to engage in resistance, coupled with the efficiency of Mussolini's regime in crushing and dispersing most organised opposition.

'The [overall] aim of SOE work in Italy', recorded one of its senior officers in 1942, 'is to assist the [Allied] armed forces to bring about the defeat or withdrawal from the war of this weak link in the Axis in a shorter time and with fewer casualties.'[18] A weak link on the battlefield, certainly. But Italy was fundamentally different to almost every other country where the Allies tried to encourage resistance. True, the Fascists had intimidated or defrauded large sections of the electorate and, in 1940, burdened Italy with a costly and ill-starred war that it was poorly equipped to fight. But this did not mean that its population was very inclined to confront those in charge. Nor did it mean that the Italian people were especially pro-Allied. The officer running SOE's Italian desk at the end of the war would remark ruefully that it had been very wrong to believe, as the British had believed at the beginning, 'that because Fascism was not universally popular in Italy, anti-Fascists would betray their country to its enemies'.[19] Once Italy had thrown off Fascism and become German-occupied, that changed. Italian units of a new co-belligerent army started fighting alongside the Allies. Behind the German lines, countless Italian civilians assisted thousands of Allied ex-prisoners on the run. SOE itself would dispatch dozens of elite teams to work hand-in-hand with Italian partisans: the subject of David Stafford's book. But before that break it struggled along with very little knowledge of local conditions and found few Italians who were ready and able to help it.

Although it may help to shed some light on why so few of Mussolini's enemies in Italy came to be harnessed effectively to the Allies' fight against him, this is not a study of the Italian anti-Fascist Resistance. Rather, it is an account of how a foreign organisation, with scant resources and little experience, attempted to grapple with its task of targeting an enemy country by covert means. With conventional Allied forces never close to landing on Italian soil until well into 1943, SOE was confined to doing this from the edges, groping its way in the dark. On foot and by parachute and submarine, a small but select band of agents was sent in to work secret wireless sets and seek out underground contacts. Explosives and other subversive stores were smuggled over the border from neutral Switzerland. For a time, SOE hoped to ignite a revolt in Sardinia that might spread to the mainland and bring Fascism down. In Sicily it wanted to work with the Mafia. In 1943, when the then Allied commander in the Mediterranean, General Dwight Eisenhower, landed two armies in Sicily, a dangerously exposed SOE team went ashore to search for more sympathisers beyond the frontline. One scheme long-hidden in the files saw steps taken to send a man to assassinate Mussolini.

Taking these operations in turn, showing how SOE sought to go about its task, what follows seeks also to illuminate the agents who were prepared to go clandestinely into Italy in spite of the obvious risks. It was a level of commitment to the Allied war effort and the anti-Fascist cause that deserves recognition and, for some, proved fatal. Dispatched in ones and twos, all of these agents risked brutal treatment and the harshest penalty if caught. Half were killed. The deaths were lonely and squalid. Official histories of SOE operations in other countries have had much larger casts of agents; here, the fact that only a handful went into Italy allows their lives and fates to be explored and documented in some depth, although the first-hand stories of some are inevitably muted or missing. For those who never came back, training assessments written by British instructors and observers can provide glimpses of an agent's personality and motivations, but these are the opinion of foreigners who could be partial, brusque and prejudiced. Bursts of fraught testimony can sometimes be found among reports drawn up of Italian interrogations, but these are the statements of men who were facing a firing squad.

SOE's war on Mussolini's Italy was a desperate business. Errors were made. The obstacles were immense. The difficulties included enemy intelligence officers skilled and experienced in counter-subversion, complemented by varying degrees of ignorance and naïveté on the part of the British, and reveal an important world of Italian accomplishment and British inferiority that a modern audience may find entirely unfamiliar. When significant success was had by SOE, it resulted more by accident and from clever quick-thinking than from any established anti-Fascist activity or carefully laid plan. The supreme instance of this – an episode that Barbara Salt would later highlight as further cause to record SOE's contribution to the war against Italy – was the remarkable solo role that Dick Mallaby was destined to perform in the events that led to the Italian surrender in September 1943. Events, wrote Dwight Eisenhower in his memoirs, 'that, if encountered in the fictional world, would have been scorned as incredible melodrama'.[20]

I

'Useless wishful thinking'

July 1937. An MI6 officer calling himself Mr Constable is waiting by the ticket barrier at London's Waterloo Station. A train draws in, and the final passenger to disembark is a tall, blond, blue-eyed man of twenty-nine years of age. From the barrier the pair leave the station and cross the Thames to the Strand Palace Hotel. They exchange pleasantries – they have not met before – and then talk of more serious matters. Speaking fluent English with a pronounced Italian accent, the young man explains that he holds a British passport, has an English wife, and is a prominent member of an underground organisation of Italian anti-Fascists. He tells Mr Constable that he wants money from the British to help spread anti-Fascist propaganda inside Italy.[1]

The young man's name was Max Salvadori. Probably he was the most outstanding Italian asset within easy reach of British Intelligence in the years running up to Italy's entry into the Second World War. Destined to leave an indelible mark on the history of Italian anti-Fascism, he was a toughened and dedicated activist whose hard-won knowledge and experience of underground work gave him rare insight into the ways, means and difficulties of opposing the Fascist regime from within. Later, while attached to SOE as a commissioned officer in the British Army, he would take part in the invasion of Sicily, land on the mainland at Salerno and Anzio, be wounded by a landmine on the banks of the Garigliano, parachute into the German-occupied north, work closely with some of the most senior members of the Italian resistance, rise to the rank of lieutenant-colonel, and be decorated by the British with the Distinguished Service Order and Military Cross. 'This officer was in constant danger of capture in civilian clothes,' reads the recommendation for his DSO; 'his courage and determination in these circumstances were of the highest order.'[2]

But in 1937 that military record lay far in the future. So, too, did an appetite among policy-makers in Britain for anything more than the most oblique approach to confronting Italian Fascism: a lack of appetite at that time that helps explain why British plans for taking clandestine action against Italy were virtually non-existent when war with Mussolini eventually came. It was an approach perfectly illustrated by the course of British dealings with Salvadori up to June 1940.

Born Massimo Salvadori-Paleotti in London in June 1908, Max Salvadori was brought up in Florence in a freethinking and liberal home in which both parents found Fascism repellent. His father was Guglielmo dei Conti Salvadori-Paleotti, a philosophy professor descended from protestant landowners on Italy's Adriatic coast. His mother was Giacinta Galletti di Cadilhac, whose English mother was the daughter of Sir Robert Collier, a lawyer and Liberal politician under Gladstone. It was by his father's side on an autumn afternoon in 1922 that Salvadori first saw Mussolini in the flesh. A crowd had filled the piazza facing Florence's railway station. Then, to cheers and flanked by black-shirted Fascists, an open-topped car drove slowly through the throng. Standing inside was Mussolini, the blacksmith's son, ex-journalist, ex-socialist and ex-soldier who was destined to become, a few weeks later, Italy's premier. 'Looks like a gorilla,' Salvadori heard his father say.[3]

Salvadori's own loathing of Mussolini's regime was forged, with blood, at an early age. In March 1924, an article by his father entitled 'Fascismo and the Coming Elections' appeared in Britain's *New Statesman*, drawing attention to the Fascists' use of violence in Italy's electoral process. Publication was dangerous and Salvadori's father knew it. 'We were warned that if we put his name to his article he might be murdered by the agents of Mussolini,' the *New Statesman* reported the following month; 'but as a brave man, he wished his name to appear, and so we decided to print it.'

We now learn, not from the Professor himself but from some of his English relatives who can speak without fear of further reprisals, that he has been punished most brutally for the honest expression of his opinions. A band of armed Fascisti visited his house and demanded an explanation. This he offered to give at their headquarters. He went there and was received by a dozen or so Blackshirts, first with gross insults and menaces and then with blows. They hit him repeatedly in the face and head and turned him out bleeding, to be struck again – this time with leather-covered canes – by another band at the door. His young son, who was waiting outside, rushed to his father's rescue, and he, too, was hit and thrown to the ground. The two got away, but were followed by their tormenters, who presently came up with them and once more beat them over the head with their sticks. Policemen looked on without interfering. They were only saved by a passing officer, who deputed two soldiers to escort them home.[4]

The Fascist headquarters in Florence sat in a piazza with a monument in its middle to the dead of the Risorgimento, the great nineteenth-century struggle for national unification that culminated in the creation of the Kingdom of Italy in 1861 and made famous the names of Garibaldi, Mazzini and Cavour. Salvadori would vividly recall the square's evening stillness being 'shattered by yells and curses' as 'black-shirted *squadristi* carrying clubs and daggers' burst from the building's doors. Seeing his father, 'silent, his face covered in blood', in their midst, Salvadori had hurled himself at the gang, striking one in the face as hard as he could. An 'avalanche of blows' descended. Semi-conscious, he felt someone lift him, then drop him, and heard a voice say, 'He's dead.'[5] Soon afterwards, on foot and by sleigh, he followed his father into Switzerland and exile.

In Switzerland Salvadori finished his schooling and enrolled at the University of Geneva for a degree in economic sciences. It was also in exile that his anti-Fascism matured. In Paris in 1929 he joined Giustizia e Libertà, literally 'Justice and Liberty', a movement of Italian anti-Fascists, mostly socialists and liberals, whose members tried to oppose and undermine the new regime in Rome. Propaganda was their primary weapon. Few other means of action seemed remotely within their grasp: money was short; weapons were few; and no foreign states were interested in backing them. Those in charge in Paris included the charismatic scholar and thinker Carlo Rosselli. With Rosselli's encouragement, Salvadori returned to Italy and began three years of underground activity. It was a period that saw him gain a sobering introduction to the challenges faced by anyone tempted to rebel in Mussolini's Italy.

As with all groups that tried to oppose Italian Fascism, Giustizia e Libertà was a tiny band – a few thousand sympathisers at most – with a mountain to climb. Although helped by a strategic use of violence, typically in the form of rampaging Fascist thugs, Mussolini had not seized power: Italy had chosen to forgo democracy in favour of the authoritarianism and strident nationalism proffered openly by his new Fascist Party. Fuelled by domestic unrest, economic crisis and terror of the communist spectre that stalked most of Europe after the First World War, a popular fear of socialism had been key to Fascism's success. So had the disunity, ineptitude and ineffectiveness of the Fascists' rivals. Liberalism in Italy looked weak and incapable. Fascism offered action, discipline and direction, and promised to revive the fortunes of a war-worn country whose dead between 1915 and 1918 came to well in excess of half a million. Parliament, the police, the civil service and the courts all viewed the nascent Fascist Party with sympathy. Ultimately Italy's governing elite decided that the only acceptable means of containing the party's militant, street-fighting, strike-breaking edge was to invite Mussolini to form a government. The support of other parties then allowed him to form a coalition cabinet, secure the reforms needed to fill parliament with Fascists, and take long-term control.

The foundations of Fascist rule became more concrete as the regime worked hard to win more popular support. A great many Italians were more concerned with more pressing matters, like enduring the day-to-day grind of life in inter-war Italy, especially rural inter-war Italy, than with whatever political changes were occurring in Rome. Of those who were more interested, plenty accepted and tolerated Mussolini more than they supported or liked him. But a good number were won over by his charisma alone, while the Fascists' promises of improved order and prosperity were certainly effective, accompanied as they were by a refreshing degree of political stability, an apparently revived economy and the fast-declining ability of Fascism's opponents to seem an attractive alternative. Care was taken to keep big business, the Catholic Church, the monarchy and the courts onside. Posters, film and radio were mobilised to bolster the notion of a strong state, with *Il Duce*, 'The Leader', at its heart. Propaganda also began to bombard the public with Italy's supposed claims to greater territory overseas, together with tales of the iniquitous imperial influence of rival nations, especially Britain, gained at Italians' expense.

All of this also helped to ensure that domestic opposition to the regime was kept to a minimum. What also helped was the fact that there was precious little room for organised dissent. To tighten Fascism's grip, a flurry of laws saw Italians deprived of their rights to free speech and free association: spontaneous meetings and demonstrations were banned; strikes were outlawed; Fascist editors were installed on all main newspapers; Fascist prefects took charge of local government; anti-Fascists living abroad were deprived of their citizenship; and so on. Meanwhile Fascist thugs pursued their dirty work of intimidation and worse. One infamous method – juvenile and designed to degrade – was to ambush their victims, force open their throats, and make them drink laxative castor oil. They could be much more brutal. The most prominent early target was Giacomo Matteotti, the leading Socialist deputy and a vocal critic of the regime. In June 1924, while walking in central Rome by the Tiber, he was bundled into a car by a Fascist gang, then beaten and stabbed to death with a carpenter's file. His body turned up in a shallow grave two months later. A year later it was the turn of the liberal politician and journalist Giovanni Amendola, who, in 1924, had accused Mussolini publicly of responsibility for Matteotti's death and, at the head of a liberal coalition, tried to stand against him in Italy's general election. Brutally bludgeoned by a Fascist gang who stopped his car on a road in Tuscany, Amendola never recovered from his injuries: he died in gangrenous agony in a clinic in Cannes in 1926. Dozens of other opposition deputies were beaten up, arrested or otherwise maltreated. Many went into exile. Hundreds of their followers were murdered.

Also in place in Italy was a robust judicial and security system. One element was the Tribunale speciale per la sicurezza dello Stato, the Special Tribunal for the Defence of the State. Set up in 1926 after a run of attempts on Mussolini's life, it was presided over by military judges, applied military law, and could hand down the death penalty, which was reintroduced – having been abolished in 1889 – for crimes of espionage and armed rebellion. Much is made today of the fact that formal death sentences under the Fascists were comparatively rare, which was true. It is also the case that the Special Tribunal and smaller courts imposed prison sentences or *confino* – confinement to a penal island or some other form of forced isolation – with comparative abandon. Among the first to come before the Tribunal was the head of the Italian Communist Party, Antonio Gramsci. Arrested in 1926, he was sentenced to twenty years' imprisonment. The cells took their toll and a decade later he was dead.

Another victim was Carlo Rosselli. Arrested in 1926 for underground activities and given ten months in prison, he completed his sentence but was promptly interned, for the same crime, on the penal island of Lipari, the largest of the volcanic Aeolian

Islands off Sicily's northeast coast. In 1929, in a dramatic and daring escape reported in newspapers worldwide, Rosselli and two friends swam out to a waiting motorboat under the noses of the guards and were whisked to the safety of North Africa. It was then that he went to Paris and co-founded Giustizia e Libertà. 'Fascism has been in power for seven years,' Rosselli told an audience at London's Liberal Club later that year. 'It has now all the prestige of success, duration, and strength. Its adversaries are beaten down, driven into exile, or constrained to silence in the prisons or on the islands of deportation. Nothing is left of the former democratic regime.'[6]

Also at work in Italy was the OVRA. A secret, ruthless and efficient force of political police, it had been set up at about the same time as the Special Tribunal and was dedicated to rooting out sedition and subversion. Some debate remains over quite what the acronym meant. Probably it was short for the Organizzazione di Vigilanza e Repressione dell'Antifascismo, the Organisation for Vigilance and Repression of Anti-Fascism.[7] Insidious and skilled, it could be brutal in its methods and was able to inflict plenty of punishment, from physical torture to stretches of *confino*, without prisoners needing to be tried. It has been said that the OVRA served as Himmler's model for the Gestapo. Mussolini's police chief, Arturo Bocchini, was in charge.

Entering this world in 1929, Salvadori, still only twenty-one, based himself in Rome and began spreading anti-Fascist propaganda and forming and coordinating groups of supporters. Propaganda, he wrote later, ranged from 'leaflets dropped unseen in letter-boxes in the hope of kindling a new spark' to 'the stamp-sized emblems of G.L. – a red flame flanked by an 'I' (Insurrection) and an 'R' (Resurrection) – stuck on walls and in places where people would notice them (in trams, on mail-boxes, on theatre posters, even in public urinals)'. It was small-scale work, he knew, but the most that could be done in the circumstances.

It was absurd to think of a revolution against the well-armed, well-organized fascist regime ... Under a dictatorship there is not much that can be done to rouse people's minds and consciences, and every opportunity had to be grasped. It was worth doing even if it did no more than spread the knowledge that an organized opposition existed.[8]

To appear above-board and divert suspicion, Salvadori enrolled for a doctorate at the University of Rome and found work at the Institute of Foreign Trade. He allowed himself to be conscripted into the Bersaglieri for seven months and underwent officer training in Milan. But carelessness, spies and tortured confessions saw arrests among his colleagues grow, and his own turn came in July 1932.

Arrested at his mother's home in the Marche, Salvadori was imprisoned in Rome in the main prison of Regina Coeli, on the banks of the Tiber, in a stinking, windowless, bug-infested cell measuring six feet by three. He was spared the tortures inflicted on others. Although the police, it seems, failed to realise the full extent of his activities, the strain of incarceration still had an effect, for he scribbled to Mussolini a letter appealing for clemency. Later Salvadori would write of his 'humiliation' at penning those 'words of self-abasement'.[9] Recently re-discovered in Italian archives, the letter has been described by one modern Italian writer as Salvadori's 'failure' and 'act of submission to fascism'.[10] It ought to be seen as a human response to a system designed purposely to break men down. On scrutiny, the text of his *letterina* shows that he had played down his past and kept the full extent of his real work secret, claiming to have 'walked away from the straight path' only a few months before.[11]

Half a year in Regina Coeli was followed by a stint in jail in Naples. Then Salvadori was transported to the penal island of Ponza to see out a sentence of five years' *confino*. In every place were graphic examples of what the regime was capable of meting out to its subjects. In Rome he met a young communist who had had needles driven under his fingernails, his testicles crushed, his cheeks burnt with an oil-lamp and his heart damaged by repeated beatings with a sandbag; also a girl who had had her breasts and genitals slashed with razor blades. In Naples he spoke to 'a tall emaciated ghost of a man' with shrunken body and transparent skin who had spent eleven months in an underground cell for supposedly plotting to kill Mussolini. Another man met in Naples was a courier of Giustizia e Libertà leaflets whose torturers had applied burrowing insects, beneath a glass, to his navel.[12]

After serving a year of his sentence, Salvadori was removed from Ponza and placed instead under house arrest at his family home in the Marche. A cousin in Britain's Foreign Office, Laurence Collier, grandson of the biologist Thomas Henry Huxley, had intervened by reminding Rome of its prisoner's place of birth. Finding house arrest as frustrating as prison but easier to escape, Salvadori decided to go once more into exile, setting off for Switzerland and successfully crossing the border by showing the borrowed passport of another British cousin to whom he bore a good resemblance. From Switzerland he made his way to Britain where he settled down to a job at a prep school in Buckinghamshire and resumed his anti-Fascist activities, giving talks and writing articles. In 1934, to earn a living and perhaps evade the attentions of Fascist agents and officials visiting London, he left to farm in Kenya. His young English wife, Joyce, whom he had married a few months before, went with him. In 1937, three harvests later, they returned to Europe.

Salvadori had reached Geneva, where he had been offered a university post, when news reached him of the murder in France of Carlo Rosselli. Recently returned from the Spanish Civil War where he had shared command of a column of Italian anti-Fascists, Rosselli had been staying in a hotel in Normandy with his younger brother, Nello, when Fascist assassins stalked and killed them. Salvadori renewed his connection with Giustizia e Libertà and rejoined the struggle. It was in London that summer that Laurence Collier, his Foreign Office cousin, helped put him in touch with British Intelligence.

When he met 'Mr Constable' that July, Salvadori was eager to work with the British. 'I was not interested in the UK as such nor in the British Empire,' he would recall of his thinking at the time:

[What] mattered [was] the British contribution to modern progressive civilisation (priority of the rule of law, of reason over non reason and over all dogmatisms and fanaticisms, of tolerance . . . moral equality . . . parliamentarianism [and] economic liberty . . .) [What] mattered [was] Bacon, Locke and Newton, J. S. Mill, Herbert Spencer and A. Toynbee.

What I believed in was threatened by totalitarianism, in the interwar period red, black and brown, all three born from a socialist matrix made explosive by nationalistic frenzy . . . In 1937–39 I was convinced that the French had suffered and lost too much to face another war; that only imbeciles could trust Stalin and (national) communism, national socialism's rival twin; that Americans knew little and understood less (except a few, among whom fortunately the President and his wife) about what happened beyond their borders, and were totally absorbed in their own problems.

[What] remained [were] the British, badly wounded in WWI but not as badly as the French, deeply attached to their institutions even when not knowing what they meant, who in long drawn-out conflicts had saved enough of the Western community from inquisitorial Spain, absolutist France, Jacobin-Bonapartist dictatorialism, to enable modern civilization to survive and advance.[13]

If Salvadori thought that Fascist Italy was now beginning to worry the British, he would have been right. Where he was to be disappointed was in his hope that they were prepared to do something about it.

'The impression created by the new Prime Minister is essentially one of strength,' had been the cautious reaction of *The Times* in 1922 when, at the age of thirty-nine, Mussolini had become Italy's youngest premier; 'he smiles but rarely, speaks slowly and says little but without hesitation. His eyes are black and very expressive ... and [he] answers to the description "A Napoleon turned pugilist".[14] Left-wing British newspapers would consistently loathe him. Conservative opinion in Britain tended, early on, to view his drive, determination and uncompromising anti-socialism with a degree of respect, even admiration. Churchill, speaking in Rome in 1927, was one of many public figures to praise him.

By the mid-1930s, sympathy for the regime had mostly evaporated. Tolerance had been tested by stories of Fascist efforts to suppress internal opposition, while Mussolini's imperial ambitions, aggressive tendencies and gradual drift into the arms of Hitler were causing British governments growing unease. In 1935, keen to acquire an image as a conqueror and imperialist, Mussolini sent forces to invade Abyssinia, better known today as Ethiopia; the Italians' use of gas against Abyssinian tribesmen was met with worldwide revulsion. In 1936 Mussolini concluded a treaty of friendship with Germany, spoke for the first time of a Rome–Berlin 'Axis,' and dispatched aid, aircraft and men to back Franco's fight in Spain. But with slim and shrinking resources with which to protect their country's interests, and an electorate still traumatised by the First World War, British statesmen had little appetite for international confrontation or threatening sabre-rattling. The remit of MI6, meanwhile, was strictly limited to gathering intelligence. Listening in the Strand Palace Hotel in July 1937 to Salvadori's appeal for help, 'Mr Constable' broke the news that the British were not in the line of sponsoring anti-Fascist propaganda.

Salvadori left the meeting disappointed and empty-handed. But he had made an impression. 'Mr Constable' worked for Claude Dansey, a senior MI6 officer who was running a European network of agents known as the 'Z' organisation.[15] Based in an office in Bush House on the Strand, a stone's-throw from where Salvadori and 'Mr Constable' had their chat, this was a top-secret set-up that paralleled the work of MI6 stations whose existing networks the Germans were suspected of having blown. Shrewd and experienced, the sixty-year-old Dansey had been MI6's man in Rome from 1929 until 1936 and felt he saw in Salvadori a man who might have much to offer if the right opportunity came along. Later that year, when Salvadori left for war-ravaged Spain in a similarly unsuccessful effort to seek help from Spanish socialists – he particularly wanted assistance with a plan to drop propaganda leaflets over Italy from aircraft flying from Spain – he went with a false identity that Dansey helped arrange. And in early 1938, when Salvadori left for the United States to give a series of anti-Fascist talks, Dansey urged him to keep in contact. 'I should be extremely sorry to lose touch with you,' Dansey wrote to him in a letter that survives among Salvadori's private papers. 'I feel quite certain that there are ways and means for continuing an association.'[16]

Such an opportunity came that summer, when Salvadori, back in Britain, participated in his first clandestine job for the British. Germany, not Italy, was the target but he agreed to take part all the same. The plan was for a tiny group of European exiles to sail a small boat close to the German coast and, from there, broadcast anti-Nazi propaganda. A British trawler, the *Girl Beatrice*, was found, hired and sailed to Boulogne. A wireless transmitter was brought up from Paris, carried aboard and installed. Then, in August, with the boat still berthed in Boulogne's inner harbour, there was an explosion. Petrol was being pumped into the tank at the time and Salvadori was down below. 'I heard a terrific crash,' reads an account among his papers. 'I saw flames all round me. I ran as quickly as possible up the stairs, which had been half destroyed, to the deck and jumped thence on to the quay. The whole of the forward part of the deck was on fire. I helped the Captain, who appeared to be badly injured, to get on to the quay, where I also found the cook, who was badly burned on the face and hands.'[17] The boat was wrecked, the cause was never discovered, and the project was over before it began.

In subsequent weeks, in letters heavy with security-conscious euphemism, Dansey kept Salvadori informed of the potential for another 'yachting' expedition. But progress was slow – in the end no fresh 'yachting' came off – and in October 1938, with nothing else on the table and now a young family to support, Salvadori left for the United States to take up a teaching post at St Lawrence University in upstate New York. By now, however, it was becoming obvious that war in Europe was approaching fast, and he and Dansey kept in regular touch. 'I think it looks like being a hot summer,' Dansey wrote to him in June 1939. 'You must always let me know where you are [to] be found by cable so that if any opening suddenly appeared, I could communicate with you quickly.'[18] In August he added: 'The temperature increases and I always have you in the back of my mind.'[19] Six days after that, with war with Germany imminent, Dansey telegraphed: 'Come [to] London as quickly as possible.'[20] Salvadori dropped everything and sailed for Britain.

⊙

In September 1939, when Nazi Germany invaded Poland and went to war with Britain and France, Italy proclaimed itself neutral. In Britain, though, there were few doubts remaining as to Mussolini's likely allegiances. In 1938, Italy had introduced new laws to persecute Jews and offered no objection to Hitler's *Anschluss* with Austria. Nor had Mussolini objected in March 1939 to the betrayal of the Munich Agreement when, to international outrage, German troops marched into Bohemia and Moravia. That April, Italian forces invaded and annexed Albania, while in May the 'Pact of Steel' had established a military and diplomatic bond between Italy and Germany that implied mutual support in any forthcoming conflict.

When he arrived in Britain from the United States, however, Salvadori found himself in a country still clinging to a policy of keeping Italy non-belligerent. Great care was being taken by the British to avoid doing anything, or being caught doing anything, that could create an excuse for an Italian entry into the war on Nazi Germany's side, thereby creating serious problems for Britain's ability to defend itself and its host of worldwide commitments. 'On Italy's inactivity depended ... the free use of the Mediterranean and, it was believed, the Red Sea for our shipping,' explains the official history of British wartime strategy. 'For these reasons the British Government deliberately avoided giving Italy provocation.'[21] As Salvadori quickly discovered, one consequence was that Britain's clandestine organisations were banned from engaging in anti-Italian activity or even preparing for a showdown.

One such organisation was Military Intelligence (Research). A shadowy department of the War Office from which SOE would partly spring, MI(R) had evolved from an earlier section, GS(R), established in 1938 to research matters of military significance such as tactics, training and lessons to be learned from contemporary conflicts like those in China and Spain. GS(R) had been required to be 'small, almost anonymous', one senior officer had instructed. Its men should be permitted to 'go where they like, talk to whom they like', but their existence was to be 'kept from files, correspondence and telephone calls'. In charge at its office in London was the deep-thinking Jo Holland, a lieutenant-colonel in the Royal Engineers. In the summer of 1939, with Holland in command, MI(R) was given an expanded role, which included the task of preparing the ground for irregular operations in countries that might come under the control of real or future enemies. In September, one MI(R) officer studied a few files and drew up a report on roads and railways in northern Italy with a view to hindering any future Italian moves against France. The only action taken was to pass a copy to the French Deuxième Bureau. Aside from some thin research into the possibilities of causing trouble in Italian possessions like Albania, the Dodecanese and Abyssinia, nothing more on

Italy was done. Until the eve of Mussolini's declaration of war, most of MI(R)'s slim resources were devoted to the possibilities of creating difficulties for Nazi Germany. As MI(R)'s war diary explains: 'The scope of preparation to meet active Italian hostility was limited by the British Government's fear of offending Italian susceptibilities.'[22]

Another organisation, a little more active and energetic, was Section D. This was an offshoot of MI6 and would be another of SOE's forebears. Set up in 1938, it had been envisaged, as SOE would be envisaged, as much more aggressive than MI6, which was traditionally devoted to the quieter processes of intelligence collection. Section D's job was to help counter the intentions of enemies and potential enemies in countries that seemed likely to become hostile or fall under enemy influence. Its methods ranged from printing propaganda to gunrunning.

In charge of Section D was another Royal Engineers officer, Major Lawrence Grand. Rarely seen without a red carnation in his buttonhole or a cigarette holder in his hand, Grand was a dapper and likeable man of drive and imagination. Among Section D's surviving files are his handwritten recollections of the interview at which Hugh Sinclair, head of MI6, offered him the job. At one point Sinclair had wondered if Grand had anything to ask. 'My first question was "Is anything banned?" He replied "Nothing at all."'[23] But resources would always be slight and its expertise slim; even its own in-house history described Section D as 'a relatively unsupported body of amateurs bent on the crudest forms of sabotage'. Slim, too, was the degree to which it was officially permitted to act without regard to the main priorities of higher policy.[24] Well into 1940, even the approach governing underground work into Italian-occupied Albania was to 'do nothing that might cause Italian resentment and thus tempt Italy into war on the side of the Axis'.[25]

It was for Section D, housed in London offices at 2 Caxton Street and in rooms next door at the St Ermin's Hotel, that Max Salvadori was first invited to work. Aware of the prevailing British policy of tiptoeing round the Italians, he quickly set down his thoughts on what could and should be clandestinely done. '[U]nder the Fascist regime, initiatives from the inside of the country are extremely difficult, unless they come from leading personalities,' he began. 'Those who talk today of a possible internal revolution, of a coup d'etat by the Army or the Crown, or organised opposition on the part of the Catholic Clergy, indulge in a [sic] useless wishful thinking.' Propaganda, he urged, was the best way forward. It should seek to turn Italian opinion against Nazi Germany and be aimed at 'responsible people, or people who are capable of initiative, and enjoy prestige, influence or power'.[26]

As for how to put that propaganda across, Salvadori proposed four methods: letters, leaflets, radio broadcasts, and something that he termed the 'personal approach'. Letters could be sent to carefully selected addresses: he recommended those of 'political leaders (from Secretaries of local *Fasci* [political groups] up), military leaders, civil servants, the clergy, professional and business people, etc.' Leaflet distribution would be small-scale, more costly and less practical, but nevertheless possible with the assistance in Italy of surviving anti-Fascists such as socialists and members of Giustizia e Libertà. Broadcasts, Salvadori felt, perhaps thinking back to his *Girl Beatrice* days, could be transmitted to Italy from a boat off the coast of a neighbouring territory, like Corsica, Malta, Dalmatia or Tunisia. As for the propaganda content, he stressed that this had to avoid being seen as anti-Fascist; instead, it should be 'strongly patriotic, monarchical and Catholic and contain only violent attacks against Germany', while giving the impression that those responsible were Italians acting in Italy's interests. The purpose of Salvadori's last proposed method – the 'personal approach' – was 'to get close to people in key positions' and 'win political and other leaders to the cause of the Allies'. This might be achieved, he suggested, by spreading doubt about Germany's ability to win the war, for example, or by the offer of political 'advantages' or wealth.[27]

Presented in a paper read as far as the Foreign Office, Salvadori's proposals were dismissed out of hand. 'I do not say that such propaganda would not produce results,' wrote the Foreign Office's Sir Andrew Noble, Second Secretary in its Southern Department, 'but it would certainly be dangerous and I think at the moment unnecessary and unwise.' Noble's reasoning provides a good snapshot of how anxious the Foreign Office was at that time to keep Italy neutral. No Italian of much importance seemed keen on war with Britain, Noble firmly asserted, before reasoning feebly that the unwillingness of the Italian Army 'is sufficiently shown by the fact that a little while ago – about the middle of September – soldiers attacked [Fascist] militiamen in the streets of Turin, calling them "tedeschi" (Germans) and other rude names'. Mussolini, Noble conceded, remained 'the enigma in the Italian political jigsaw', but it was possible that even he was 'coming down more on the side of neutrality'. Some 'cautious' propaganda might do 'considerable good', he went on, if 'designed to explain to the Italians what we are fighting for and thereby show them that our interests are theirs, and to bring home the fact that though this war does look rather queer, we are really going the right way about winning it'. But Salvadori's 'more adventurous policy' would involve 'very great risks': 'Signor Mussolini would certainly come to learn soon or later what we were up to and he might be expected to hold very strong views about it.' There was also the possibility that pro-German Fascists would be given a 'weapon' to attack more moderate ones. 'Time is on our side,' Noble concluded hopefully, before echoing the appeasement arguments of the 1930s: '[I]f we can also make it profitable for the Italians to remain neutral we are likely to achieve the results we desire without running the dangerous risks involved in Mr Salvadori's scheme.'[28]

This was a time when Italy's protestations of neutrality were encouraging even British diplomats in Rome to believe that Mussolini might stay out of the fighting for good. The Italian press, Fascist editors all, had started to adopt a less pro-German tone. In October a reshuffle of Mussolini's Cabinet seemed to sideline some of the most pro-Nazi sabre-rattlers. In December the Fascist Grand Council, the state body empowered to approve policy and elect party leaders, reaffirmed Italy's official attitude of non-belligerency. Italy still seemed willing to sell Britain warlike goods, allowed escaped Polish soldiers to cross Italian territory unimpeded, and, in the face of an apparent warming in Russo-German relations, expressed sympathy for the Finns when they were attacked by the Soviet Union. This was also a time, as one MI6 officer recorded in early 1940, when the quality of British intelligence on Italy was 'lamentable'.[29]

⊙

What Salvadori did next has been recently and publicly interpreted as a reason to explode his reputation as an honest and whole-hearted anti-Fascist. Documents unearthed in Italian archives in 2004 revealed that in 1939 Salvadori had offered his services to the Fascist regime. His first move had been that autumn, when, prior to leaving the United States for Britain, he had presented himself to the Italian ambassador in Washington, DC, to explain that he was poised to proceed to Britain and that, because war between the British and Italy seemed possible, he felt it his 'duty' to make his services available to Italy. In October, after news of this move reached Rome, Arturo Bocchini, Mussolini's police chief, responded. Salvadori, who by then had reached London, was given a confidential address to which he should send all future correspondence, together with instructions to address everything to 'Adriano' and refer always to Bocchini as 'Mr H. G. Roberts'. Salvadori was also informed that Switzerland might make a convenient place for a face-to-face meeting.[30]

In December 1939, so the Italian documents show, Salvadori then travelled from London to Switzerland and, in a Geneva hotel, met an emissary whom Bocchini had sent from Italy. At this meeting, so the emissary recorded in a report that survives in the OVRA archives, Salvadori insisted that he remained anti-Fascist but explained again that he felt compelled to 'do everything possible' for the good of Italy. He added that he was willing to develop pro-Italian propaganda and would give his 'full commitment to Fascism' if only the regime allowed greater free speech. He asked, too, for the opportunity to return to Italy to speak with the authorities there. On returning to Britain and with Bocchini's encouragement, Salvadori struck up correspondence with Italy's ambassador in London, Giuseppe Bastianini, to whom he repeated his keenness to visit Italy and his willingness to encourage understanding of Italy's foreign policies in the 'political and intellectual circles' he frequented and in newspaper and magazine articles.[31] These statements, it was claimed in 2004–5, provided grounds on which to challenge Salvadori's credentials as a constant anti-Fascist and support the belief that he had suffered a moment of 'political crisis'. The title of one newspaper article neatly sums up the thrust of the claims: 'L'uomo che visse due volte: prima al servizio del Duce, poi di Sua Maestà' ('The man who lived twice: first in the service of the Duce, then of His Majesty').[32] It was considered 'valid' to conclude that Salvadori had kept the British in the dark and his OVRA contacts to himself, fooling the former into believing that he was entirely committed to the cause against Italy.[33]

There is no doubt at all that Salvadori was in contact with Fascist officials. It is also true that he had offered them his services. But a collection of his contemporary papers, dating from his time with Section D and SOE, which Salvadori passed to the British historian Christopher Woods in the early 1990s, and which were unavailable to other researchers in 2004–5, show that there was rather more to this picture than has been supposed. Ranging from incoming letters and telegrams to copies of his own reports and outgoing correspondence, these documents shed important new light on the real nature of Salvadori's dealings.

Particularly instructive is surviving paperwork for Salvadori's trip to Switzerland to meet Bocchini's emissary. This was a trip that Lawrence Grand, the head of Section D, had in fact recommended. '[W]rite yet another letter to your friend [Adriano] suggesting that Mr Roberts should meet you,' reads one instruction from Grand.[34] 'I can see what I can get from an interview with Mr Roberts,' Salvadori wrote in reply, according to a surviving draft. 'For that I shall have to go to France and arrange a meeting.'[35] It is also a trip documented among Salvadori's papers down to the costs incurred, since Section D paid his way and required an account of his expenses. With an exit permit and visa provided by Section D, Salvadori had left for Paris at the end of November. From the Elysée Palace Hotel he drafted a message to 'Adriano' saying he wanted to meet. He then proceeded via Lyons (train ticket: 320 Francs) to wintry Geneva (return train ticket: 685 Francs) where, from the Hotel Cornavin by the city's railway station, he sent 'Adriano' a letter.[36] Salvadori scribbled a copy on the hotel's headed notepaper: 'please let me know as soon as possible, if possible by telegram, in what locality in France, Switzerland or Germany we can meet and when'.[37] Also among Salvadori's papers is a copy of the later report he submitted to Grand about the conversations that had followed. Its title ('My meeting with an agent of the OVRA') is perhaps enough on its own to demonstrate that Salvadori was not deceiving the British, while his account of what was discussed matches almost exactly the Italian report, by Bocchini's man, found recently in the OVRA archives.[38]

In his report for Lawrence Grand, Salvadori sought to record verbatim the key points covered when he and the OVRA agent spoke. 'I come with orders directly from the Chief, Bocchini,' the agent had announced at their first meeting. 'We would like you to give us information concerning your political friends who live as exiles in foreign countries. I am authorized to pay as much as you ask.' To this, Salvadori replied:

I am afraid that you are looking in the wrong direction. My relations with the exiles have been reduced to a minimum, because I do not approve of their extremists' views. I have no intention to betray them or to act as an agent provocateur. As for your monetary offer, my teaching job provides me amply with the little I need and I could not renegate [sic] my past by accepting your money.

Salvadori had then explained what he *was* prepared to do:

My attitude towards your Government remains what it has always been. I am willing to recognise what good it has done to the country, but I still maintain my conviction that freedom is indispensible in a State. I believe that a nation can prosper, increase its authority and bring a contribution to the civilisation of mankind, only if its members enjoy certain liberties. A nation in which there is little or no political freedom can attain certain achievements under exceptionally good leadership, but is bound to lose later on more than it has ever gained.

I am glad however that you came here. We live in a particularly difficult time and, apart from every question concerning the internal politics of your government, I believe that an effort should be made in order to bring about a better understanding between the country from which my family came and the country in which I was born. If there is anything which I can do in that field I am perfectly willing to do it.

If I can find a situation in England, I will remain there a few more months. Otherwise I will go back to the United States at the beginning of the next month. In either country I have a large circle of acquaintances and friends. I can do my best to explain [to] them the point of view, the grievances, eventually the claims of Italy.

Salvadori also requested permission and safe passage to enter Italy and speak with its Ministers of Information and Education:

There are two questions which I would particularly like to ask to one or both ... 1) Is there a possibility of seeing one day in Italy greater freedom and tolerance than they exist at present? 2) What are approximately the aims which the Italian government would like to attain? Once I am clear on that point, I can try to interpret either in England or America or in both countries your claims, many of which are probably justified.

'Italy needs intelligent people,' the OVRA agent told Salvadori in response,

I will report to the Chief and you can be sure that responsible elements will greatly appreciate your offer ... I will speak to Bocchini, who will have to discuss the matter with the Head of the Government [i.e. Mussolini] before taking any decision ... We will be very glad to see you in Italy.[39]

Talks over, the two men said their goodbyes and went their separate ways. Salvadori returned to London at the end of December and at once filed his report with Section D. He finished it on a high note: 'I believe that after the two interviews and ... [unless] the Fascist Government adopts a more strongly accentuated pro-German policy, I could go more or less safely to Italy.'[40]

In subsequent months, Salvadori continued his correspondence with 'Adriano' and cultivated a similarly duplicitous relationship with Giuseppe Bastianini, the Italian ambassador in London. Again Salvadori kept the British informed about what he was doing. In April 1940 he would tell Claude Dansey of recent suggestions by 'my excellent friend' (a security-conscious reference to 'His Excellency' Bastianini) that Britain start 'conversations' with the Italians about control in the Mediterranean and a thirty-year pact of friendship.[41]

Such was the real nature of Salvadori's contact with Fascist officials in Geneva and London in 1939–40. He and the British seem to have wished to win their trust in order to exploit it, by seeking insight into Italian intentions and perhaps exerting a little influence: a tactic with obvious parallels to the 'personal approach' that Salvadori immediately recommended when he arrived in Britain in September 1939.[42]

By the spring of 1940, British observers were increasingly certain that the Italians would enter the war at the moment most likely

to secure, quickly, a place on the winning side with the minimum of risk and effort. That meant Germany's side. In February, Mussolini had ended negotiations over an economic agreement with Britain. In March, Joachim von Ribbentrop, the German foreign minister, had been warmly welcomed on a flying visit to Rome that suggested keen German interest in Italy's intentions. Days later, in a snowstorm at the Brenner Pass on Italy's alpine border with Austria, Hitler had stepped from his train to speak briefly with Mussolini.

Details of what transpired on that occasion were not immediately known in London (Mussolini had in fact pledged to enter the war at an opportune time). But film, photographs and the fact of the meeting were widely publicised and, from that point onwards, Italy's press became stridently anti-Ally. '[T]he word "Axis" creeps back into the journalists' vocabulary,' observed Sir Percy Loraine, the British Ambassador in Rome; '[A]ll pretence on the part of the press of holding the scales evenly between the belligerents falls away; on each occasion the German case is vehemently defended.'[43] In April, after Germany's invasion of Denmark and Norway, Rome began to fill with growing numbers of German officers.

In May, when Germany struck at France and the Low Countries, Italian attitudes became still more extreme, as Loraine recorded:

[T]he walls of Rome were plastered with placards obnoxious to Britain, bands of Fascist hooligans marauded in the streets . . . and there were a few cases of molestation of British officials and subjects . . . And, of course, the press and propaganda services poured out a shriller and yet more strident jazz of boastful vituperation . . . All the taps were turned on in order to make Italy war-minded and anti-British – Italy's poverty, her land hunger, her strangulation in the Mediterranean, British arrogance towards her, British decadence and inefficiency in war.[44]

'Is it too late to stop a river of blood from flowing between the British and Italian peoples?' wrote Winston Churchill, Britain's new Prime Minister, to Mussolini that month. 'We can no doubt inflict grievous injuries upon one another and maul each other cruelly, and darken the Mediterranean with our strife. If you so decree, it must be so . . .' Mussolini's reply sought to justify what was to come. He wrote of 'grave reasons of an historical and contingent character which have ranged our two countries in opposite camps'. He highlighted Britain's decision in 1935 to apply sanctions against Italy for invading Abyssinia, when his country, as he put it, had merely sought 'a small space in the African sun without causing the slightest injury to your interests and territories or those of others'. He pointed to 'the real and actual state of servitude in which Italy finds herself in her own sea': an allusion to Britain's prominent presence in the Mediterranean, a central theme in Italian anti-British propaganda. Finally he told Churchill that, in view of the fact that Britain had declared war on Nazi Germany to honour its treaty commitments to Poland, 'you will understand that the same sense of honour and of respect for engagements assumed in the Italian–German Treaty guides Italian policy today and tomorrow in the face of any event whatsoever'.[45]

By then, the ban on British planning for conflict with Italy had at last been removed. Orders had been issued for aerial reconnaissance of Italian ports. The Admiralty began to reinforce the Royal Navy in the Mediterranean and re-route merchant shipping. There was even a little movement when, in May, Max Salvadori submitted another set of proposals on how the British should seek to keep Italy neutral. His paper included another dark and prophetic analysis of the difficulties of finding Italians who were able and willing to help. 'Responsible people, or people who can take initiative, enjoy prestige, possess influence or exercise power, form a very small fraction of the population,' he pointed out. 'The majority [of people] . . . are always ready to applaud those who are strong and successful [and] will not lift a finger to defend those who have not many chances of succeeding . . .' Once again he urged that any effort to keep Italy out of the war had to focus on anti-German propaganda and 'personal approaches'.[46] Days later, on 23 May, with British and French forces on the Continent now reeling from the German onslaught, Salvadori was given a passport, a laissez-passer, 2,000 francs, and instructions to board a Paris-bound flight leaving Hendon the following morning. His mission was to put the British in touch with old colleagues from his Giustizia e Libertà days.

Salvadori arrived in a city already terror-struck by the German advance. A week earlier, when Churchill had flown in, the French Government was already burning its files and preparing for the evacuation. 'When you reach Paris ring Mr Beresford at Invalides 1881,' reads a handwritten note from Section D that survives among Salvadori's papers; 'He is au fait with the situation and will accompany you to your friends. Bon Voyage!'[47] 'Mr Beresford' was really Willie Berington, a 36-year-old Englishman employed in Section D's Paris office whose civilian occupation is recorded in its files as 'Lord of the Manor, Little Malvern'.[48] Berington also spoke some Italian, having travelled and studied in Italy, and, on 25 May, he accompanied Salvadori to a meeting with three Italians: Alberto Cianca, Emilio Lussu and Aldo Garosci. Cianca was a lawyer, journalist and former editor of the liberal newspaper *Il Mondo* who had been forced into exile in 1925. Lussu, a prominent Sardinian socialist, had escaped from Lipari with Carlo Rosselli. Garosci was a journalist and liberal socialist who had fought and been wounded in Spain. All now discussed an alliance wherein Giustizia e Libertà would assist Section D in drafting and distributing in Italy propaganda directed against Germany. Later that day, Salvadori and Berington spoke to two more Italian anti-Fascists: Alberto Tarchiani, former editor of Italy's one-time leading liberal newspaper, the *Corriere della Sera*; and Vincenzo Nitti, son of one of Italy's former prime ministers. A week after that, on 1 June, Berington gave Cianca £20,000 and said that Section D would try to deliver 11,000 leaflets to a contact of Cianca's in Turin.[49] Then all contact with Cianca and his friends was lost. With the Dunkirk evacuation well under way and the German Army bearing down on Paris, Berington joined the rest of the Section D office and left the city, finally scrambling aboard a boat leaving Bordeaux for Plymouth.

As for Salvadori, he had flown home from France at the end of May and resigned himself to the fact that he had little future in Britain. Making propaganda was one thing, but he had always wanted to do more active work. Since arriving in London the previous autumn he had tried repeatedly to secure a British Army commission. Every attempt had been knocked back: there were long waiting lists; there were concerns about the implications of his Italian background. Also, as a family man who, since turning up from the United States in September 1939, had always worked for the British on an occasional and temporary basis, he needed a regular income. Frustrated, he contemplated a return to the United States to resume his university duties and fight Fascism from there. 'I feel that the place for those who are fit for active service is in the Army,' he explained to Section D in May 1940. 'Civilian work, including propaganda, can be carried on perfectly well by those who, being elderly, in bad health or foreigners, are unfit for active service . . . My family and employers [in the United States] would understand [if] . . . I remain in Europe as a member of the fighting armies. But after eight months of absence, there is no justification for my permanence in this country if I am simply doing [propaganda].'[50]

One last-ditch appeal for help was to Claude Dansey. 'Because of my foreign accent, a commission in a unit exclusively composed of 100% English people would be out of the question,' Salvadori wrote to him in early June. 'I wonder if I could not be of some use in a colonial unit. The little Swahili which I used to know would still be handy . . .'[51] Dansey regretted that he was unable to help, 'much as I should like to . . . [P]ersonally I know you would make an excellent officer.'[52]

35

On 11 June, hours after Italy had finally declared war on Britain and France, Salvadori sailed from Liverpool for New York. He would not return for two and half years.

2

'Pottering about'

At a quarter to five on the afternoon of 10 June 1940, the British Ambassador in Rome, Sir Percy Loraine, arrived at the Palazzo Chigi, a grand sixteenth-century palace overlooking the Via del Corso and the Piazza Colonna. He was there to speak with Italy's Foreign Minister, Count Galeazzo Ciano. At that moment Britain and France had been at war with Nazi Germany for nine months. French collapse seemed imminent. Italy had remained estranged from the conflict but seemed unlikely to stay out for long. Days earlier, Ciano, who was also Mussolini's son-in-law, had openly told Loraine that his country was poised to enter the war on Germany's side and the only doubt remaining was the date. Now they met again, shook hands, and sat down; and this time Ciano announced to Loraine that Italy and Britain would be at war from midnight.

The urbane Loraine was nicknamed 'Ponderous Percy' by unkind underlings but was not a man easily wrong-footed. 'In the previous months everything had been said and done to make clear Britain's disinclination for war with Italy,' he told the Foreign Office afterwards, 'and enough had been said to show that though we did not seek war, we did not fear it thrust upon us. The moment was not one for covering the ground again [and] ... dignity forbade a retort.'[1] Instead he took cold and careful note of the declaration, scribbled the details on a sheet of headed paper from a pad on Ciano's desk, double-checked that Italy was declaring war also on France, then left to return to the Embassy and make arrangements for his journey home. Ciano wrote in his diary that Loraine had been 'laconic and inscrutable. He received my communication without batting an eyelid or changing colour.'[2]

An hour later, Mussolini spoke from the balcony of Rome's Palazzo Venezia to an excited crowd below. 'This is the hour of destiny for our country – the hour of irrevocable destiny,' he declared. 'We are going to fight the democracies of the West . . . Run to your arms, show your stubbornness, courage and valour . . .'[3] Radio and loudspeakers carried his words across the country. London, meanwhile, heard the news from Loraine. 'Mussolini decided to come into the war, and we had to wake up Winston from his afternoon slumber and tell him,' reads the Downing Street diary of Jock Colville, the Prime Minister's assistant private secretary. 'All Winston said [was] . . . "People who go to Italy to look at ruins won't have to go as far as Naples and Pompeii in future".'[4]

'At least it was not unexpected,' Colville continued in his diary. 'There has never been such a flourish of trumpets to announce a grand entry; but the Italians have a sense of the melodramatic.' Certainly Britain had had forewarning. Where Colville was less accurate was in adding that it had 'given us time to make our dispositions'.[5] Declassified British files from this period reveal some very obvious facts: the paucity of preparation for Italy joining the war; the shallow and amateurish nature of the clandestine resources on which Britain could draw when the gloves came off; and the subsequent snail-like pace of progress towards targeting Italy clandestinely, despite the creation of a fresh organisation, the Special Operations Executive, in July 1940 with subversive action against the Italians as one of its priorities.

A sense of that under-resourced amateurism can be found among documents charting the near-farcical course of one of the few anti-Italian schemes – besides the limited dealings with Max Salvadori and Giustizia e Libertà – to engage much of Section D's attention before Italy entered the war. This was a plan to disrupt the rail traffic between Germany and Italy that ran through neutral Switzerland. Trains snaking into Italy along that route imported goods of vital importance to the Fascist war effort. Coal coming from Germany, for example, which the British estimated in 1940 to be at least a million tons a month, met most of Italy's industrial needs.

Section D's first step towards targeting that traffic was to make contact in London in the autumn of 1939 with a friendly Austrian railway engineer by the name of Strauss. In the past he had worked on the Swiss railways. Latterly he had been employed in London as foreign editor of a British weekly called *Modern Transport*. Sponsored jointly by French Intelligence, Strauss was then dispatched on an exploratory mission to Switzerland. He returned with a few useful contacts in the form of some anti-Nazis and trade unionists employed by the Swiss Federal Railways.

Next, Section D decided to recruit, train and send out to Switzerland a British agent to develop those contacts with a view to beginning sabotage. A candidate was found, interviewed and selected. Soon he was being put through a course in basic sabotage techniques and signals. By now there was growing urgency to the business. By April 1940, with Italy becoming more anti-British by the day and the ban on anti-Italian planning lifted, Rome and Berlin were known to have reached an agreement whereby the Germans undertook to provide Italy's entire coal requirement and send all of it overland, a commitment that would mean coal-trains reaching Italy from the Reich at a rate of one every twenty minutes.

The name of the British agent now poised to leave for Switzerland was Cuthbert Hamilton Ellis. It is fair to say that the decision to select him for such a covert job was ambitious. Educated at Westminster and the universities of Oxford and Munich, Hamilton Ellis had worked before the war as a journalist on *The Railway Gazette*, a popular read among schoolboys and train-spotters. He had also written a few children's books and liked to paint pictures of steam trains. Noting that he spoke fluent German and adequate French 'including technical terms', Section D thought that he stood a good chance of settling into the Swiss railway milieu on the strength of his claim to be 'a good mixer' having 'lived amicably with a Scandinavian engine-driver for some time'.[6] A friend and fellow railway enthusiast would later recall that 'Cuthie' in uniform cut 'hardly a striking figure' but could be roused under pressure, 'as when we were standing together in the corridor of a London-bound train one morning when it was attacked by a German aircraft just south of Polhill Tunnel. He had spent some time in Germany after Oxford and occupied much of our journey through the tunnel conjuring up choice remarks to direct at the hostile pilot.'[7]

When he joined Section D, Hamilton Ellis was thirty years old and had recently become a private soldier in the Royal West Kent Regiment. In the end, delays in securing his discharge from the Army (the War Office lost his papers) and problems arranging a visa (the Swiss raised eyebrows when his application said he was a railway engineer) saw him spend weeks kicking his heels at his home in Sevenoaks before the call to go eventually came. Finally leaving London on 5 June, he reached Switzerland on 8 June armed with a ten-day visa, a false passport, a false job as a correspondent for *Modern Transport*, and the rather eccentric pseudonym of Elmer T. Rudd. 'The travelling was not bad,' he reported happily on arrival, having checked in to Berne's Hotel Bären.

[T]he Swiss railways are a treat after those of England and France under wartime conditions. The weather has been perfect ever since I left home; there was a bit of a thunderstorm in the mountains today, but that merely made the scenery look more imposing and laid the dust. Were it not for the damned war, this would be a most enjoyable job, in a lovely city like Berne with no black-out.[8]

As Section D recorded later, Hamilton Ellis had arrived on a Saturday, 'which prevented him from making any contacts over the weekend'. Sunday, which happened to be his thirty-first birthday, he spent 'watching the traffic on the Berne–Simplon line from which he could confirm the considerable volume of traffic between Italy and Germany. He obtained a certain amount of railway information while pottering about, but it was purely of academic interest.'[9] On Monday Italy entered the war.

After a few hastily arranged and unproductive meetings with three or four of Strauss's contacts, Hamilton Ellis consulted the British Legation in Berne and was advised to leave immediately for Britain. He decided to follow that advice. A slow train took him from Geneva to Bellegarde, just inside the French frontier. France, in the final throes of defeat, was not a healthy place to be. Sensing that it was unlikely that any trains would be running that could take him west or north, he abandoned his luggage, save for a briefcase containing his papers, jumped on a bicycle, and pedalled all the way to Marseilles, a distance of some 250 miles. From there he proceeded by collier to Gibraltar where he boarded another boat and sailed home.

On his return, thought was briefly given in London to employing Hamilton Ellis as an agent on other projects. It was noted that he was 'very keen on going out again'.[10] Someone wondered if he might be suitable for a mission to Spain. It was also noted that he must have shown 'considerable initiative during his escape' and that 'there is no doubt that on the subject of railways his character assumed a decisiveness that was not apparent in his ordinary manner'.[11] Ultimately it was decided that his talents lay elsewhere and he was signed out of the secret world in November 1940. After the war he continued to devote himself quietly to all things rail and was widely published, his books including such titles as *The Splendour of Steam*, *The Trains We Loved*, and *Rapidly Round the Bend*.

◉

'There seems little doubt that Ellis would have been better advised to have remained in Switzerland rather than run for it,' observed

Section D after he made it back to London. 'It must, however, be said on his behalf, that, as a new and untried agent, he was put in an extremely difficult position, particularly since he had no contacts in any British intelligence organisation [there].' It was also noted that the Legation's advice that he should abandon Berne 'was given without any knowledge that Ellis was engaged on other than purely journalistic activity'.[12] A perceived need to prevent future cases of poor coordination – there had been plenty of instances more serious than this – was one reason why, in July 1940, the British War Cabinet agreed to establish something new: a single secret body devoted to sabotage, subversion and supporting popular resistance inside enemy territory.

'This organisation will be known as the Special Operations Executive,' announced its founding charter, signed off by Neville Chamberlain, the former Prime Minister, in his final government role as Lord President.[13] Deniable, free from parliamentary control and financed from secret funds, it was formed from an amalgamation of Section D, MI(R) and a third organisation, Electra House, which had been concerned with subversive propaganda, and was placed under the control of the Minister of Economic Warfare. In 1940, this was Hugh Dalton, Labour Member of Parliament for Bishop Auckland. Hugely enthusiastic about the possibilities of irregular warfare and the potential of occupied populations to contribute to the British war effort, Dalton had lobbied hard for SOE to be created, for it to be divorced from military control, and for himself to be put in charge of it. His job was not to direct its operations but to act as the political head to whom all major issues of policy would be referred, speak for SOE when relevant matters were discussed at ministerial level, and liaise with the Foreign Secretary, the Chiefs of Staff and other government and military bodies whenever its activities touched on their interests. It was Dalton who recorded in his diary Churchill's famous injunction that he should now 'set Europe ablaze'.[14]

Today, SOE is rarely mentioned without some reference to that command. But in 1940 the reality was that it was a fledgling organisation scarcely capable of setting fire to anything at all. Before it could function properly a great deal of groundwork was required, ranging from the establishment of headquarters offices and training schools, to the recruitment of prospective agents, to the setting up and staffing of the sections and desks assigned to the various countries and tasks with which it was to involve itself. Even when progress began along these lines, SOE found itself struggling to secure essential support from the Air Ministry, for example, which proved reluctant to divert valuable aircraft from what it considered to be the more profitable and war-winning activity of strategic bombing. MI6, too, proved reluctant to help out, resenting and fearing that the loud crashes and bangs associated with SOE activities might upset the quieter work of its own agents who were anxious not to attract enemy attention.

During this early period SOE inherited many of the plans and personnel of Section D, MI(R) and Electra House, though their value was patchy. Very often there was scarcely anything to inherit, Italy being a case in point. With Salvadori in the United States and his friends in France scattered, SOE knew of no Italians who might be hostile to Mussolini's regime and were within easy reach. Although Britain was finally at war with Italy, there were few foundations on which to build; the problem was 'to get the horse in after the stable door has been shut', as its in-house war diary put it, 'and first of all the horse must be found'.[15]

But SOE did inherit the beginnings of one tiny anti-Italian campaign. Since September 1939, when Britain and France had gone to war with Nazi Germany, the Balkans had remained neutral, un-invaded and untouched. Based in cities as far apart as Athens, Zagreb, Bucharest and Belgrade, Section D and, to a lesser extent, MI(R) had nevertheless managed to embark on an underground war against Germany by a variety of devious means: drafting and disseminating propaganda to counter Nazi

43

influence and intentions; trying to sabotage trains en route to Austria and Germany; drawing up plans to prevent German vessels from plying the Danube; preparing coups and revolts; bribing politicians; smuggling arms and explosives across borders; and so on. A good deal of this activity was in the hands of young British agents who were absolute novices in this line of work. 'We were all very young, very inexperienced, very amateurish and very ignorant,' remembered one of them, who, as a 24-year-old journalist in 1940, had been sent out to Budapest to bribe locals and print propaganda.[16] Nevertheless, and despite the prolonged ban on anti-Italian planning, some of the more successful activities included a few tentative preparations for Italy's entry into the war.

Partly responsible for that early anti-Italian activity was a young Englishman, Alec Lawrenson, a schoolmaster's son from South Shields. When war with Germany broke out, Lawrenson, then twenty-nine, had been lecturing in English at the University of Ljubljana on behalf of the British Council, an organisation set up to promote British culture and English-teaching overseas. Not long afterwards, a man named Julius Hanau arrived from Belgrade to see him. Hanau, a South African businessman and Section D's chief agent in Yugoslavia, asked Lawrenson if he would be willing to work for him, too. Lawrenson agreed to do what he could.

The fact that Lawrenson was able to achieve anything against Italy from Yugoslavia owed almost everything to the advice and capabilities of his friends and contacts among local Slovene nationalists. Beginning in 1918 and formalised in 1920, Italian control of what became known as Venezia-Giulia, which contained a quarter of the Slovene population and over 150,000 Croats, had sought from the start to suppress any Slovene or Croat feeling through a radical policy of denationalisation, to the point of stamping out Slovene in schools, forbidding Slovene names to be given to new-born babies, and arresting, and sometimes

44

executing, Slovene patriots who tried to protest: of the nine people condemned to death by Italy's Special Tribunal prior to 1940, five were Slavs. Having endured twenty years of this, the men with whom Lawrenson was in touch burned with hatred of all things Italian and included many with long experience of anti-Italian work.[17] By 1940, with their help, which included ready contact with the oppressed and unhappy Slovene minorities inside Italy, he had started to introduce propaganda – letters, news-sheets and posters, mainly – and encourage and help his friends to tamper with goods trains crossing the border. One method of sabotage was to daub small balls of pitch filled with abrasive steel filings on to the axle-bearings of rolling stock. By February 1940, 12,000 of these 'hotbox drops,' as they were called, had reportedly been smuggled across.

For months this was about as far as Lawrenson could go. With Britain in desperate straits and fast losing footholds and friends on the Continent, he was hamstrung by the priority placed by British policy-makers on doing nothing to endanger either Italian or Yugoslav neutrality. He had also found himself distinctly out of favour with the local Foreign Office representative, T. C. Rapp, the British Consul in Zagreb. Alarmed that a member of the British Council should be moonlighting as an unpaid secret agent, Rapp went so far as to refuse to give Lawrenson the mail sent up to him from his Section D masters in Belgrade. In the end, Lawrenson's superiors intervened, Rapp was instructed not to interfere, and Lawrenson resigned from the British Council to become a full-time and paid-up member of Section D with the cover of vice-consul in Ljubljana.

After Italy entered the war and Section D was wound down, Lawrenson, who was absorbed into SOE and given charge of its work in northern Yugoslavia, broadened his efforts and helped organise the dispatch of anti-Fascist newsletters and leaflets to thousands of Italian addresses taken from telephone books. He also helped to equip the Slovenes with some unusual pieces of

45

coal. Hollowed out and filled with high explosive and a heat-operated detonating device, these were meant for secreting inside coal trucks and locomotive tenders on lines inside northern Italy. Lurid rumours of what might be afoot eventually reached the Italians. 'In an unknown house on the outskirts of Zagreb explosive material is handled, destined for terrorist action in Italy,' reads an Italian report from September 1940.

Explosives in the form of fountain pens and small pocket bombs with terrific destructive power are said to be manufactured there. The Englishmen have this material transported by certain of our younger [Slovene] nationalists to Italy, where they employ it, according to instructions, for destruction of railway carriages and stations, barracks, factories and ammunition dumps.[18]

Arrests among his co-conspirators and other enemy counter-measures would soon curb Lawrenson's work. Then, in April 1941, everything that he was trying to do was extinguished when a lightning German Blitzkrieg swept through the Balkans. Lawrenson was among the men overrun, and he saw out the war as a prisoner in Germany. But though short-lived and small-scale, his efforts would remain, for months to come, the only subversive activities inside Italy in which SOE engaged that would have much result at all. They had been dangerous, too, and not without cost.

⊙

In the early summer of 1940, a letter arrived at the British Council offices in London from Geoffrey Frodsham, director of the British Council Institute in Zagreb. In it Frodsham highlighted the growing hostility shown by the Germans towards British Council teachers working in Yugoslavia. 'In German eyes the whole British Council and all its activities are thoroughly suspect,' he had typed, 'and all its officers are looked upon as secret agents or the like. This is quite clearly shown by the attacks in the German Press on the Teaching Department here, and the personal attacks over the wireless on myself ... The Germans, making no distinction between cultural and political propaganda themselves, cannot believe that we do so.'[19] Lincolnshire-born and the son of a bishop, the 38-year-old Frodsham was an unmarried Cambridge graduate who had taught abroad since 1932 when he had taken up his first post in Prague. At noon on 8 September 1940, four months after writing that letter, he was found in bed in his Zagreb flat, dead.

His late father had been a zealous and adventurous evangelist in Southeast Asia, but 'Geoffrey Frodsham could never have championed a particular cause', considered the author of his *Times* obituary, printed a week later. 'His mind was detached and his habits bookish ... [T]emperamentally he bore less resemblance to the sturdy Frodshams than to the artistic Swinburnes, his mother's family.' In Czechoslovakia and Yugoslavia this quiet and gentle man had become, 'in spite of himself, a cultural missionary'. But 'the blows delivered by the Munich agreement and the German occupation of Prague' had been hard to bear, while that summer there had been 'a still greater blow – the capitulation of his beloved France'.[20] Now he was dead in a flat full of gas from a disconnected pipe in the kitchen.

When Frodsham's body was found, the police let some of his friends inspect the scene. One was Alec Lawrenson. 'At first sight the circumstances of his death appeared to indicate suicide,' he wrote afterwards. 'The flat was full of gas and the windows were tightly shut ... Accident was out of the question [as] ... the rubber tube through which the gas escaped into the flat had been carefully propped up after it had been disconnected from the gas-ring.'[21]

For Lawrenson, however, Frodsham's flat was the scene of a murder. His friend had been 'suffocated,' he felt, and the gas turned on 'in order to give the appearance of attempted suicide'. He noted that 'no attempt had been made to pack the window crevices with paper, etc.', and that Frodsham's flat was on the ground floor: 'he normally slept with his windows open so that it was easy for any person to enter the flat from the street. Both the front door to the flat and the main house door were fitted with spring locks; once inside the flat it would be a simple matter to open these doors from the inside and let them slam-to after leaving.' Lawrenson noted, too, that the night had been a hot one, which made it even more odd that Frodsham's windows were found closed, while little alcohol had been found in Frodsham's blood, which dispelled one idea suggested by the Zagreb police that he might have succumbed to some sort of drunken accident. As for Frodsham's mental state, Lawrenson learned that a British Council colleague in Zagreb had found him in 'an equable frame of mind' at dinner the previous evening; the pair had also agreed to meet for lunch the next day. 'It might be added that [he] was devoted to his mother, who was in part dependent on him, and that there was no message of any kind left for her.' Also, Lawrenson felt, it was inconceivable that Frodsham would have 'made away with himself' while leaving 'everything in disorder, even to the extent of leaving compromising papers and material in the flat'.[22]

By 'compromising' material, Lawrenson meant 'secret'. The objects left lying around included pieces of explosive-filled coal. Earlier that summer, while still employed by the British Council, Frodsham had started working quietly on the side for SOE. Having known him for years, Lawrenson had sought him out because he needed a good assistant. '[He] worked hand in hand with me in Slovenia and Croatia,' Lawrenson wrote of him later. 'I introduced him to all my contacts in this territory and he accompanied me twice to Belgrade.' Frodsham was 'keen, conscientious and completely reliable'; he seemed to have been 'looking forward to a long and successful period of activity for SOE'; and he had died when he was being relied upon: Lawrenson, away visiting sub-agents, had left him in charge.[23]

This seemed to provide further grounds on which to doubt that Frodsham's death was suicide. It also emerged that he had died not long after three Gestapo killers were heard to have arrived in Belgrade with orders to murder Julius Hanau, Lawrenson's boss. Lawrenson himself had been warned to watch his back after a report was received that 'the chief Gestapo agent' in Ljubljana was 'a dangerous assassin'.[24] On top of that, Frodsham had last been seen alive in a bar frequented by Germans and complaining of a headache: 'possibly due to dope', Lawrenson thought. There was a question mark too over the 'gratuitous efforts' made by Frodsham's housemaid to prove that the death had been suicide when his body was found next day.[25]

Lawrenson had no doubts as to how Frodsham had met his end. 'I was firmly convinced', he wrote, 'that D/H 36 [Frodsham's 'symbol'] had been the victim of assassination – almost certainly engineered by the Germans.'[26] His colleagues agreed. Although investigations went no further and no assassin was ever unmasked, SOE files record Frodsham's death as 'killed in action' and that his colleagues in Yugoslavia urged London to reassure his mother that his death was 'not rpt not suicide'.[27] It is possible that that reassurance never reached Frodsham's family. His name seems to be absent from official lists of Britain's wartime dead. It is missing, too, from the war memorial of Magdalene College, Cambridge, his beloved alma mater. Indeed, the loaded tone of his *Times* obituary may well indicate that the family had details of his death only from the British Council, which had been studiously kept in the dark about his clandestine activities in order to avoid an 'unfavourable' reaction. Certainly someone failed Frodsham's family. Years later, when he emerged from his German internment, Lawrenson heard that Frodsham's mother first learned of her son's death when she read about it in the paper. Unworthy, too, Lawrenson felt, was the fact she failed to receive a suitable pension in recognition, as he put it, of the 'short but valuable services' of a man 'killed in the performance of his duties'.[28]

3

'Garibaldi's curse'

Days after Italy's entry into the Second World War, police officers arrived at the door of 175 Sussex Gardens, a London boarding house in a terrace of Georgian homes close to Paddington Station. They were there to remove an Italian called Fortunato Picchi. He was five feet tall, balding, a little overweight, forty-three years old and unmarried, and had rented a room there for two decades. Once head waiter in banqueting at London's Savoy Hotel, he now worked at Fleming's Hotel on Half Moon Street, the well-to-do Mayfair street that served as fictional home to P. G. Wodehouse's Bertie Wooster.

Picchi was at home when the police reached the door. At precisely that moment, apparently, Schubert's 'Ave Maria' was playing on his gramophone. His room, someone would write of it, was 'modest, tiny, exceedingly well kept, always provided by the solicitude of a rare friend with a bunch of fresh flowers'. On its walls were pictures of blue Italian skies. Among his books were *The Life of Michelangelo Buonarroti* and G. M. Trevelyan's *Garibaldi and the Thousand*. And pinned above the bed and written in Picchi's hand were these words of Garibaldi's:

England is a great and powerful nation, foremost in human progress, enemy to despotism, the only safe refuge for the exile, friend of the oppressed. If ever England should be so circumscribed as to require the help of an ally, cursed be the Italian who would not step forward in her defence.[1]

At least 18,000 Italians were living peacefully in Britain in June 1940. Many considered it their home, had found jobs and raised families there. More than a few were Jews who had recently fled

Italy to escape Fascist oppression, but the majority had been there for years. Once Italy declared war, however, the British authorities rounded up thousands of them, regardless of their reasons for being in Britain or their opinion of Mussolini. Considered enemy aliens whose reliability and loyalty were uncertain, the majority of these, like Picchi, soon found themselves interned on the Isle of Man in requisitioned camps and drab boarding houses. They included Italians whose allegiances lay with Mussolini's regime, but a great many were anti-Fascist and pro-British. For the latter it was a miserably unjust fate, though it could have been much worse. In July, sailing from Liverpool for camps in Canada, almost 500 Italian internees lost their lives when the *Arandora Star*, a British passenger ship, was hit and sunk by torpedoes fired from a German U-boat.

In late 1940, when the British Chiefs of Staff, responsible for the higher direction of Britain's war effort, laid down that 'the elimination of Italy' was of primary strategic importance, it was among Italians interned in Britain that SOE began to search for volunteers willing to be sent into Italy as clandestine agents.[2] Precipitated by the personal and energetic intervention of Hugh Dalton, SOE's minister, this search would provide a sobering introduction to the difficulties of targeting Italy. It was also a search that turned up the first Italian volunteer to be dispatched by the British to fight Fascism on Italian soil. He would parachute into Italy, as a participant in the first operational drop in British military history, in February 1941.

Hugh Dalton prided himself on his knowledge of Italy and Italians. During the First World War, as a young lieutenant in the Royal Artillery, he had served with the British contingent sent to fight on the Italian front and earned an Italian decoration for valour, the Medaglia di Bronzo al Valor Militare, during the retreat from Caporetto. Later he wrote a memoir, *With British*

51

Guns in Italy: A Tribute to Italian Achievement. Dalton had also spent time in Italy between the wars on parliamentary and diplomatic business. On one occasion, in December 1932, he had met and spoken with Mussolini.

That encounter had taken place at the Palazzo Venezia. They had chatted in Italian of the First World War, public works and politics. It was an occasion that left Dalton more impressed than he later cared to admit. '6.15 see the Duce,' he wrote in his diary at the time.

Approach through a long series of rooms ... Many plain clothes detectives including one who sits opposite me while I am waiting.

Finally ushered into an immense room, with marble walls. At the far end the Duce, standing, with upturned eyes reading a book. He advances to meet me, when I am half-way across the room, 'with a friendly smile,' as the journalists say.

We spend half an hour together ...

He has charm and intelligence. Very small brown eyes. He turns them up and the whites show, like a clown at a circus. Less tall than I expected. But strongly built ...

Yes, charm, intelligence, energy, and no play acting. That is for the gallery.

When it was time to go, Mussolini walked Dalton to the door and told him to visit again whenever he was next in Rome. 'There is no other living man whom it would have thrilled me more to meet,' Dalton's diary entry ends. 'Ruth [Dalton's wife] thinks he has conquered my susceptibilities too much.'[3]

Tall, bald, pugnacious and prickly, Dalton was a man of 'immense energy ... genuinely kind-hearted', remembered Gladwyn Jebb, his closest adviser on SOE business. A career Foreign Office man, Jebb had been assigned to assist Dalton with his new clandestine duties. The pair had known each other for years – Jebb had once been his private secretary – and got on well. 'It must also be admitted that Dalton was often the reverse of easy,' Jebb also recalled. '[I]n moments of stress, more particularly when the war was going badly, I was often the target of his frustrated energy. The whole of Berkeley Square House [where Dalton had his office] occasionally shook with roared insults.'[4] One of those moments may have been sparked by the arrival on Dalton's desk, in late November 1940, of a report spelling out precisely how little SOE was achieving against Italy.

The drafting of that report had been precipitated by news reaching London of Italian reverses and defeats in Africa and the Mediterranean. An ill-equipped Italian offensive from Libya into British-held Egypt had been halted, while Italy's invasion of Greece, launched in October, had gone badly from the start with Greek counter-attacks forcing some Italian units to retreat beyond the Albanian bases from which the invasion began. Then, on the night of 11–12 November, biplanes of the Royal Navy's Fleet Air Arm devastated half of the Italian Navy's capital ships during a lightning raid on the Italian port of Taranto. Days later, noting that the moment seemed 'particularly favourable' for intensifying subversive work against Italy, the Foreign Office asked SOE to explain what it was doing about it.[5]

That inquiry was sent first to Gladwyn Jebb. He promptly passed it to Sir Frank Nelson, head of what was then known as SO2. Early in its existence, SOE was composed principally of two parts: one, known as SO1, was responsible for propaganda and would be hived off in the autumn of 1941 to become a separate organisation, the Political Warfare Executive; the second and larger part was SO2, whose field – the more violent forms of subversion – would be the kernel of SOE's work throughout the war. Nelson was a quiet, able and well-liked man who had blended a career in business and administration – for which he was knighted, aged forty, in 1924 – with seven years in Parliament as a Conservative MP. Latterly, under the cover of British vice-consul in Basle, he had been working for Claude Dansey's Z organisation. From when he took up his new post in August 1940, Nelson's commitment to the job was total. 'He seemed to have no family life,' one SOE colleague recalled, 'and was in the office seven days a week from about a quarter to nine until very nearly midnight.'[6]

Nelson, who had just moved with his staff into offices at 64 Baker Street, now found himself confessing to Jebb that the matter of action against Italy was 'one of our major worries down here'. No one was behind his Italian desk, Nelson said. There were no Italian recruits and not much in the way of plans. One idea was to parachute into northern Italy a few friendly Italians (though SOE had none yet on its books) but it did not impress him much: 'I must in all honesty point out to you', he told Jebb, 'that the very nebulous advantages of sending the parachutist type into Italy are almost certainly out-weighed by the disadvantages of the information they will almost certainly give away if and when they are caught.' Getting 'the desperado type' into Italy – he meant an agent trained in commando-type sabotage – was also under consideration, 'but quite frankly, beyond the advantage of being able to say that we have put people into Italy by such and such means, I am not hopeful of any results worthy of the name'. He finished his report: 'Generally, we never cease to try to get down to this problem, but I fully realise that polite generalities of this kind are of no use to you or the Minister, and all I can say at the moment is that we will re-double our efforts to find some method of penetration.'[7]

This was the report that now sat on Dalton's desk. 'We must buck up our Italian efforts,' the Minister scrawled across it in red ink.[8] And in his diary he wrote:

I feel very explosive, C.D. [Nelson] not yet having got anyone in his Italian section, and nothing serious being done by us to hammer the Italians. I therefore summon Gladwyn, C.D. and A.D. [George Taylor, Nelson's chief of staff] to a conference and blow them all up ... Why don't they ask for more assistants? I have got to take the Italian thing in my own hands ... I could not answer the P.M. if he asked me, 'What are you doing to Italy?'[9]

Three weeks later, Churchill did ask that question. 'In accordance with my instructions from the Prime Minister,' Dalton told Jebb, 'I desire that all possible effective action against Italy shall be pressed forward without delay.'[10] He carried on fuming in his diary. 'We must by all means hit hard at Italy,' he scribbled. 'I am tired of excuses and obstruction. I will, if necessary, sack all the subordinates who are failing to do their job. This is a critical moment of the war. Italy is in the market.'[11]

As to the means of taking the war to the Italians, Dalton's ruthless mind was racing. He told Churchill 'of the Slovenes with their leaflets, etc.' and mused to him on the possibility of dispatching future agents to cause trouble in Milan. 'P.M. says, "They will all be killed." I say, "No doubt, but that is all in the war. If they can add only a little to the confusion and loss of morale, they will help us to a quicker victory."' Dalton also wondered in his diary about offering, 'and quickly, a fair price to decent Italians who will get rid of Mussolini and his gang'. He even considered backing less decent Italians:

[T]here is no place, today, for stupid doctrinaire prejudices against 'Fasc*ism*' [*sic*] as such. If some Fascist toughs will murder Mussolini and a few more and then join with others, representing the Royal Family, the Army, Industry, the Italian workers and peasants, we must not reject them for the sake of some thin theory. What we want is that Italy shall stop fighting against us and, if possible, fight against Germans instead.[12]

Dalton did not expand on where Fascists like that might be found. In any case it was committed anti-Fascists that he really wanted. Already, in September, he had demanded intelligence about the penal colonies off Sicily where Mussolini was known to imprison his enemies. The first step had been to ask the Foreign Office to help identify the right island where the prisoners were held. A fortnight later, an unfortunate subordinate had to tell Dalton that a reply from the FO had still not arrived. Dalton again detonated – 'this was all much too damned slow' – and demanded to know who in the Foreign Office was responsible for 'this atrocious indolence ... A few hours steady browsing through some files is all that they are asked to do.'[13] In time it became apparent that the Foreign Office doubted the wisdom of SOE raiding the islands to spring the prisoners. One concern was that 'large-scale raids' would be hard to execute. Another was that 'the Italians would try to make capital out of the fact that we were so hard up for agitators that we had to obtain them by hole and corner methods'.[14] The idea was finally given up when General Sir Hastings Ismay, Churchill's chief of staff, advised against it. By then it had been heard anyway that all political prisoners had been moved from the islands 'months ago'.[15]

Dalton also wanted to look for suitable Italians closer to home. Surely, he thought, volunteers could be found among the frustrated and unhappy hundreds now languishing on the Isle of Man. He resolved in his diary to bring 'George Martelli up from the country to hustle about and get things going'.[16] Martelli was an Italian-speaking journalist with an RNVR commission who had covered the war in Abyssinia for the *Morning Post* and penned two books about inter-war Italy. More recently he had run the Italian, Spanish and Portuguese sections of the Foreign Office's Political Intelligence Department, preparing reports from Foreign Office and MI6 sources, and had travelled once already to the Isle of Man to recruit Italians for a clandestine broadcasting station.

The plan to scour the camps for SOE was given added urgency when Dalton spoke in early December 1940 with Admiral Sir Roger Keyes, Director of Combined Operations, a new headquarters created in July to devise and carry out raids against the enemy by naval and army forces. A seasoned old warrior now desk-bound in Whitehall, Keyes was formulating plans to assemble a special force to raid Italian targets in the Mediterranean – islands and coastal railways and the like – and wanted from Dalton 'some good, tough and reliable Italians' to accompany his men 'and after landing go off into the blue'. Keyes said he needed the Italians by the middle of December when a convoy containing his raiding force was due to set sail for Malta or Crete. Dalton dispatched Martelli to the Isle of Man to 'rake the camp for suitables'.[17]

Half a century later, Martelli's obituary recorded how in later life he became a 'prolific' yet 'trenchant, contentious and mildly xenophobic' contributor to the letters page of the *Daily Telegraph*.[18] But he had never been a man disinclined to speak his mind. 'Martelli is rather indiscreet', observed one officer who lunched with him in August 1940. 'I was very upset by the way he kept mentioning SIS [MI6] in a normal voice in a crowded club room at the Reform. On the other hand, he appears to be very intelligent.'[19] Now, prior to setting out again for the Isle of Man, he submitted to Frank Nelson a pessimistic but prophetic memorandum on the whole issue of recruiting Italians interned in Britain. The great majority, Martelli explained, were either Fascists or 'non-politically-minded people of peaceable instincts, e.g. waiters, small traders, ice-cream merchants, etc.' As for Keyes's immediate needs, Martelli considered that half a dozen volunteers might come forward, but it would be difficult, in such a short space of time, to be sure of their ability, while any reliable men would be wasted on Keyes's enterprise unless he could bring them out afterwards. As Martelli put it, 'to land them on Italian soil with a load of explosives, without any prospect of re-embarkation, would be an invitation to suicide in the most painful circumstances'.[20] Nelson and Dalton agreed that the matter required deeper thought. Keyes was told that more time was needed to produce 'the "strong-arm" men' requested.[21] He replied that he was now in 'no great hurry' for his 'toughs'.[22] Martelli left anyway for the Isle of Man and began his enquiries. A few men came forward. Interviews were held. By the time he left the island a few days later, he had found five Italians who seemed to have potential as prospective saboteurs.

Then SOE received a fresh request from Keyes's headquarters. Two Italians were wanted who were 'willing and fit to be landed by parachute'.[23] This time the call was urgent: they would need a fortnight's special training and have to be ready by the beginning of February. Pencilled notes in one SOE file state that the pair would require instruction in the use of Thompson sub-machineguns, Colt .38s, fighting knives, grenades and 'Capsules E', the latter being ampoules of ether which could be employed as a sedative.[24] Parachute training was to follow at Ringway airfield outside Manchester. To allow for casualties, Keyes's request was increased to three. SOE told Keyes that it would act 'without delay'.[25]

By this time, Martelli's five Italians – now known in SOE as 'the Quins' – were in the Scottish Highlands undergoing para-military and physical training at a commando school near the village of Lochailort. Two of them, however, were swiftly assessed to be unsuitable for any subversive purpose whatsoever. Both were aged around forty. Both had lived in Britain for about ten years. Watching them as they went through their training was a young Canadian, John Macalister, a former Rhodes Scholar at the University of Oxford, who would later be sent into occupied France as an SOE agent and die in Buchenwald concentration camp. In early 1941 Macalister's job was to help monitor new SOE recruits and consider their suitability for operations. He judged these two to be 'hard working' but 'extremely docile' and 'completely lacking in heroic qualities'. Both were returned to civilian life.[26]

Another Quin was Rinaldo Purisiol. Born near Venice, he was a 47-year-old ship's engineer who had served during the First World War in Italian cruisers and submarines. During the Spanish Civil War, so he said, he had fought with the International Brigades, taking part in the defence of Madrid, before returning to the sea to ship Republican arms from Marseilles to Alicante. In 1940, after the German invasion of Belgium, he had arrived in Britain from Antwerp aboard a British boat on which he was employed as chief mechanic; after being paid off in London, he was promptly interned. 'A revolutionary with a reasoning mind,' reads an early report on him: 'Without doubt he is prepared to go to any length to destroy fascism. Loves Italy.'[27] Another observer saw him as a 'soldier of fortune grown old and wary and somewhat careful of his skin. Socialist and republican in his ideals; has a good, perhaps too good, opinion of himself.'[28]

A fourth Quin was Emilio Salsilli. Another who had fought in Spain, Salsilli was consistently described in reports as a convinced communist, tough, brave, and ruthless. 'Average intelligence, poor education, no moral standards,' reads one assessment. 'Courageous, strong-willed if convinced, average common sense. There is in the nature of this student a latent cruelty which could make him a dangerous killer . . . Could be extremely useful.'[29]

SOE sent a man to Scotland to select the best of the Quins. He picked the two Spain veterans but found the fifth trainee to be the most impressive: 'a man of no political background who had been a waiter at the Savoy'. This man was Fortunato Picchi.

All were brave men, all three were ready to risk their lives, but it was when Picchi, white as a sheet, made his honest, moving speech of acceptance that I knew I had found the [best] man ... [He] said that he would not be fighting against his country but to free it from an odious dictatorship, that Britain, where he had found hospitality and friendship, was fighting for her life, and that if he had to die, he could do so in no finer cause.[30]

From Scotland, Purisiol, Salsilli and Picchi – now known collectively and inauspiciously as 'the Lambs' – were sent to Ringway. It was there that the decision was taken that only one of them would be required for Keyes's operation. The chosen Lamb was Fortunato Picchi.

⊙

In the province of Prato, a few miles west of Florence in hills rich in heritage and famous for their wine, there sits the little Tuscan town of Carmignano. It was here, in August 1896, that Fortunato

Picchi was born, one of the seven children of Ferdinando Picchi and Jacopina Pazzi. His father was employed in a textile works in the nearby Bisenzio valley. In 1915 Picchi joined the Italian Army, serving in the ranks of the 64th Infantry Regiment and fighting for the Allies in Macedonia where he was apparently wounded and decorated for gallantry. Demobilised in 1919, he worked in Italy as a hotel porter, waiter and chef before leaving for England in November 1921.

Settling soon into simple lodgings in London, Picchi found work at the Hyde Park Hotel in Knightsbridge and then at the Ritz on Piccadilly. For a time he worked as head waiter at London's Ambassadors Club, off Regent Street. He made a few return trips to New York as a restaurant waiter on the White Star Line's RMS *Majestic*, the world's largest ship at the time. Then in 1927 he moved to the luxury and glamour of the Savoy, on the Strand, to work as head waiter in banqueting. His boss was an explosive Italian called Zavattoni who was so pro-Fascist that he kept a black-shirt and dagger in his office. The Savoy's press officer, Jean Nicol, would remember Picchi's 'round face', 'large brown eyes' and 'earnest, searching expression', and how his 'mild manner and soft voice' were a welcome counterweight to 'the robust solidarity' of the volatile Zavattoni.[31] Picchi would remain at the Savoy for the next twelve years.

All accounts paint Picchi as a quiet, intelligent man of culture and integrity. 'He had no wish to become a waiter,' remembered his friend and landlady in Sussex Gardens, Florence Lantieri, an Englishwoman in her sixties (her husband, Carlo, was a London-born cheese merchant). 'He was by nature an artist, and his ambition was to be a sculptor; he was never happier than when he had a chisel and hammer and a piece of marble.'[32] '[Waiting] was not a trade he would have chosen,' agreed another member of London's Italian colony, the exiled anarchist Silvio Corio, 'but he grew to like it, especially, as he confessed, because it gave him free hours during the day, "when the sun is strong," so that he could ramble in parks and fields. Give him a book to read under a sturdy tree, with a faithful dog at his feet, and he was content.' The dog was an Alsatian called Billy and Picchi walked it most mornings. Another passion was watching Arsenal play on Saturday afternoons. In time Picchi became so anglicized that he liked to be called Wilfred, 'but he had not become naturalized. He had grown so English in outlook that it did not enter his head that it was necessary for him to do so; the formality seemed well-nigh meaningless.'[33] He last visited Italy in 1931. Among friends, the retiring Picchi was known for his kindness towards others. He was 'wonderful' with children, his landlady remembered: 'They seemed to see in him someone who had always kept part of his childhood with him, and though grown up, thought and saw things in the same way as they did.'[34]

As for politics, 'Picchi had been a lover of freedom from his youth, but politically he had matured rather slowly,' Corio wrote:

From the days when Fascism began to show its ugliness without a mask, Picchi had become almost intolerant of political parties: he had arrived at the settled conclusion that programmes, speeches, protest resolutions were not enough, even useless, if not dangerous, because they dissipated energy. He believed action necessary but could not find an effective opening.

Added to this, Corio said, had been Picchi's conviction that Italy would never ally with Germany against Britain, a course he was heard to describe as 'unnatural'.[35]

In September 1939, Picchi lost his job at the Savoy. The hotel needed to reduce its staff and he was one of several who had to go. The following January he found fresh work as head waiter at Fleming's. Then Italy declared war. Picchi, so Corio would write of him, was 'astonished, dumbfounded'.[36] 'I was with him then,' Florence Lantieri recalled, apparently. 'And I remember him saying to me, "It's incredible. Surely they can't be such fools? Don't they remember Garibaldi's curse?"' Thereafter 'he had been like a man in a daze. He did not believe it to be possible; and to quieten his soul he had listened to his music for hour after hour.' Days later the police came for him and he was en route to the Isle of Man. 'I know he never expected to be interned, but he felt no bitterness at being taken away. He was only too well aware that many of his countrymen were disloyal . . . But when in internment he found himself living side by side with avowed Fascists he experienced great unhappiness.'[37]

For six months Picchi was held in Douglas in what was known as Palace Camp. A collection of thirty requisitioned hotels and boarding houses, it was surrounded by double rolls of barbed wire and patrolled by British soldiers with fixed bayonets. Back in London his landlady worried about his health. 'He was a martyr to asthma, and I've known him sit for three days and nights on end, unable either to eat or drink, with hands clasped behind his head in an effort to get relief.' From Douglas he wrote home,

and we could realize the struggle that was going on in his soul . . . He wanted to do something to help free his native country of her tyrants. Anything, anything that would be of service. Never once did he write of his own future; never once did he write of what he might get out of it all when the battle was won. He was a man who had stored within himself great courage, patience, loyalty, true affection, and utter selflessness.

Then, in December, looking 'a little worn and a little sad', he was suddenly home:

He said that he had been released from internment, but that he had to go away again at once, for he had some special work to do. I remember him filling the glasses from a bottle of sherry we opened for him. I asked him what the toast should be, and he, with his lovely smile, raising his glass high, said, 'Let's drink to the King!'[38]

Days later Picchi was off again, this time into training schools to be watched by men whose job was to scrutinise him closely and assess his motivations, strengths and weaknesses. None of these early observers were professional psychologists or psychiatrists.

None had any knowledge or experience of the conditions an agent might face in wartime Italy. Many were young NCOs in the Intelligence Corps, selected principally for their language skills and knowledge of security, not all of whom were immune from the popular prejudices of the day. What is clear from assessments of Picchi, however, is that those who watched him through his training were impressed.

'An idealist, apart from politics, who is in many ways more English than the English,' reads one report. 'An excellent worker and organiser who cannot allow failure. Wants, above all things, for everyone to be treated fairly, and according to their deserts. Is prepared to share in all [of] England's trials and has no desire to be treated in any way differently from the English soldier.'[39] Another noted his 'guts' and 'excellent English (with accent)' and how he seemed 'genuinely grateful for [the] opportunity given him here, and for his treatment during and after internment'.[40] A third recorded that while interned he had tried to volunteer for mine-sweeping: Picchi was 'anxious to serve in any capacity, however dangerous'.[41] Positive reports continued when he was finally sent to Ringway and learned to parachute. 'He carried out his day and night drops with the minimum of preparation, which in view of his age was a remarkable feat,' it was noted. '[He] was quite obviously prepared to go anywhere and do anything required of him.'[42]

At Ringway Picchi was assigned to X Troop of the 11th Special Air Service Battalion, a precursor to the Parachute Regiment. This was the unit to which Sir Roger Keyes had allotted the impending operation. Issued with British battledress and identity discs, Picchi assumed the identity of a Free French soldier called Dupont, one of the party's interpreters. 'Uniform did not change him much,' remembered one of X Troop's officers, Lieutenant Tony Deane-Drummond. 'He was still the suave and polite little man, with a bald top to his head and a slight middle-aged spread, who might be expected to be in charge of banquets at the Savoy.'[43]

⊙

Deane-Drummond and the others were handpicked volunteers and in charge was Major T. A. G. Pritchard. Thirty years old, Trevor Pritchard was a regular officer and a big man, a former Army boxing champion, whom the men called 'Tag' behind his back. Their target was to be a 100-metre stretch of modern aqueduct hidden in hills in southern Italy. Thirty or so miles inland from Salerno, it spanned the Tragino, a mountain stream that tumbled through a gorge into the narrow valley of the Ofanto River, and was part of the Acquedotto Pugliese, an extensive system of pipelines feeding water from the Apennines to the important naval ports of Brindisi, Taranto and Bari. Cutting the system at that point, it was hoped, might cause significant upset to the Italian war effort. That, at least, was the aim laid down in the orders and planning papers. More than one of the commandos who took part would suspect that the primary purpose of the raid was to test Britain's fledgling airborne force and reap associated propaganda gains.

Codenamed 'Colossus', the operation called for eight twin-engined Whitley bombers to fly out from a forward base on British-controlled Malta and drop a raiding party of thirty-six men directly on to the target: the first-ever deployment of British parachute troops. Once the aqueduct had been destroyed, the party would then split into groups, march westwards to the coast, and be picked up by a submarine at a pre-arranged rendezvous. 'The Chiefs of Staff have examined the project and consider that there are reasonable chances of success,' Churchill was told when the outline plan was put before him in January 1941.[44] 'I approve,' was all that he wrote on it.[45]

At dusk on 7 February, with X Troop aboard, the eight Whitley bombers took off from the RAF airfield at Mildenhall, Suffolk, bound for Malta.[46] All eight reached the island the following morning. Next day, the crews repaired fabric holes damaged by enemy bombs dropped overnight (Malta, just sixty miles from Italy, was now under regular Italian air attack) while X Troop packed its parachute containers and Pritchard chatted with the commander of HMS *Triumph*, the Malta-based submarine that had been assigned the task of retrieving his party from the Italian coast once their job was done. On 10 February, each Whitley was serviced for the final time and loaded with the last of the containers. At four in the afternoon, the crews were briefed. By half-past four, the parachutists were ready. Tea was drunk and boiled eggs were eaten. Thirty minutes before take-off, Pritchard finally told the men exactly where they were going. Until that moment, most had thought they were bound for Italian-occupied Abyssinia. 'Maps of East Africa had been left in offices and pictures of railway bridges near Addis Ababa examined,' Deane-Drummond recalled. 'All the troops cheered when they heard that it was going to be Italy.'[47] Dressed in battledress, smocks, fur-lined helmets and gloves, X Troop clambered into the aircraft.

The first of the Whitleys left Malta at sunset. Six carried the Colossus team and their containers. Two, as a diversion, went to drop bombs on railways and Foggia airfield. Light flak and cloud were met over Sicily. Over the mainland the sky was empty and clear. Afterwards the crews reported that, apart from fog in the valleys, 'the weather was absolutely perfect and visibility was comparable with early dusk on a fine day. Detail on the ground stood out, and the snow covered peaks, rocky valleys and clustered mountain towns and villages made a beautiful scene.'[48] At half-past nine, five of the troop-carrying Whitleys arrived over the target and began twisting into the valley to drop their parties. There was little wind, the aircraft had no trouble with the tight manoeuvring required, and the ground seemed quiet and sound: 'smooth, cultivated, mostly newly sown fields'.[49] In the moonlight, as the aircraft ran in again to drop the containers, the crews could pick out parachutists beginning to move around.

Faulty container-release systems, however, prevented three Whitleys from dropping their full complement of stores, with the result that half of the party's Bren guns, Tommy guns and ammunition, plus a lot of explosives, were brought back to Malta. But of more serious consequence was the loss of one of the Whitleys assigned to bomb Foggia. When the aircraft's port engine failed, the pilot signalled back to base that he and his crew intended to bale out or crash-land. This emergency message, which was sent in a basic code liable to be intercepted and broken by the enemy, stated that the crew would attempt, after dark, to make for the mouth of the Sele River where they hoped someone might pick them up. This was the very spot from where *Triumph* was expecting to extract the Colossus party.

Among naval commanders watching events, news of this development immediately raised the possibility of the pick-up point becoming compromised. Instructions were dispatched to the submarine to proceed with care. Senior officers, however, remained very anxious. On 13 February, Sir Dudley Pound, First Sea Lord, suggested to his fellow Chiefs of Staff in London that, because 'the enemy would now probably be aware of the rendezvous', it would be unwise to 'risk the probable loss of a valuable submarine and its crew against the possibility of bringing off a few survivors'.[50] When the other Chiefs agreed, *Triumph*'s mission was cancelled. Hearing of this, a furious Sir Roger Keyes tried immediately to reverse the decision, telling the Prime Minister that 'I consider our failure to make any effort to carry out the salvage arrangements, promised to the parachutists, a clear breach of faith.'[51] But the Chiefs were unmoved, the decision stood, and the men of Colossus, oblivious to all of this since they had no radios and could not be informed, now had no means of escape. Later Keyes remarked with feeling: 'it can only be hoped that no troops arrived at the beach to meet with disappointment'.[52]

⊙

In the days that followed, reports and rumours began to reach London of Colossus' fate. On 14 February, three days after the drop, an Italian communiqué proudly announced the round-up in southern Italy of a party of British parachutists. 'They were armed with machineguns, hand grenades and dynamite for the purpose of interrupting our communications and destroying hydro works,' it read; all were captured 'before they could carry out their plans'.[53] But a concrete report of what had really happened would reach London only in 1942, after one of the raiders, Tony Deane-Drummond, having failed twice to escape from his Italian prison camp, successfully slipped out of a fourth-floor window in a Florence hospital and, five days later, made it over the border into neutral Switzerland.

On the night of 10–11 February 1941, Deane-Drummond had jumped from the first aircraft to drop and landed fifty yards from the aqueduct, spotting at once that the target was unguarded. Joined by the five men who had also dropped from his Whitley, who included Fortunato Picchi, he sent them off to clear some nearby farm buildings and seize any occupants found. They rounded up a couple of dozen, including one elderly man who, after addressing the British in English with a broad American accent, turned out to have worked as a bellhop at the Waldorf Astoria in New York City. By now more parachutists were arriving. Among them was Pritchard, who promptly issued orders. Covering parties took up their positions. The captive Italians were put under guard. Explosives were gathered. And Lieutenant George Paterson, in the absence of the demolitions expert, Captain Gerrard Daly, of whose party there was still no sight, began to prepare the target for sabotage.

Paterson, a young Canadian, was Daly's assistant and knew what he had to do.[54] But on breaking the surface of a supporting pillar with his chisel he found the aqueduct to be constructed of reinforced concrete. This was a much more formidable proposition than the masonry the party had been led to expect. With insufficient explosives to carry out a full demolition, Paterson decided to concentrate on bringing down an outer pier rather than the larger central one as originally proposed. Helping to shoulder the boxes of guncotton as he laid his charges against its base were some of the local Italians whom the British, with Picchi's assistance, had asked to act as a carrying party. These locals 'worked with a will', Deane-Drummond recalled, 'saying that it would give them something to talk about for the rest of their lives in a part of Italy where very little happened'. When finished, they were returned to the farm buildings 'where two or three were trussed up to encourage the others, warned by the interpreter that the sentry outside the door would shoot to kill, and locked in with the women and children. No sentry was posted.'[55] Half an hour after midnight, Paterson and Pritchard lit the fuses and ran for cover. The explosives detonated. The outer pier collapsed and the waterway broke in two.

Pritchard now split his party into three. Each group was placed under the command of an officer and would attempt independently to cover the fifty miles to the sea: all believed that the rendezvous with HMS *Triumph* was still set for five nights later. Weapons and equipment were reduced to a minimum: Brens and other large weapons were taken to pieces and pushed into the ploughed-up mud; each party was left with a single Thompson sub-machinegun; each soldier kept only his Colt pistol, a thirty-pound pack, and rations to last a week. Leaving behind one unfortunate parachutist who had broken his ankle in the drop, the parties bid farewell to each other and struck off in different directions.

Pritchard and his party, which included Deane-Drummond and Picchi, travelled above the snowline at first and kept going until dawn. Then, worried about being spotted in daylight, they dropped down the mountainside and hid for the day in a wood. After dark they set off again, pushing steadily west, skirting the village of Sant'Andrea di Conza, and pressing on along a road for a few more miles before heading up the mountain again. By dawn on 12 February, struggling through mud and snow and up and down steep slopes, they had covered twenty miles.

The going was difficult enough for young commandos in peak physical condition: Deane-Drummond would remember that his whole body by now was 'limp with exhaustion'.[56] But it was a terrible ordeal for a man like Picchi. At one point he approached Pritchard and asked to be left behind, for he was struggling with the pace and feared he would jeopardise the others' escape. His offer was refused but impressed his companions. Pritchard would recall that Picchi pressed on with 'renewed vigour'.[57] Deane-Drummond, too, remembered how 'Picchi kept up very well, although he appeared to be suffering from some chest disorder and coughed continuously'.[58] This was possibly his appalling asthma.

While searching for the next daytime hiding place, Pritchard's party ran into trouble. The maps they carried showed a suitable wood high on the mountain above them. They climbed over and above the snowline but to their alarm and dismay found only bare slopes and a farm. As dawn broke, men scrambled in the snow to conceal themselves behind boulders and juniper bushes, but the tracks they had left had been seen. First a farmer hove into view and stared hard at the British before shuffling off. Picchi was sent to talk to him, returning with the news that, although the man was no threat, some local women and children had also spotted the party and, worse, had gone to inform the police. Then more locals began to appear. 'First came the village dogs,' Deane-Drummond would report, 'led by three pointers; then the village children, wondering where the dogs were going; then the women, racing after the children to bring them back, followed by the men going out to protect their womenfolk.'[59] By the time a frightened peasant finally levelled a shaking shotgun at Pritchard and said he wanted the British to lay down their weapons, a sizeable crowd had gathered.

Seeing that resistance would see innocents killed, Pritchard told his men to surrender. 'There was dead silence for a moment,' Deane-Drummond recalled, and then one man asked in an incredulous voice: 'Aren't we going to make a fight for it, sir?' I had never seen such a look of anguish on anybody's face as on Tag's at that moment. He just looked at the women and then at the man who had asked the question, and said that he was sorry but that they would have to give in. Our hearts ached as we put down our pistols and told Picchi to tell the Italian that we were giving in because of the women and children.[60]

Eventually the local police arrived. Pritchard and his men were taken down to the village of Tearo where they were held in police cells and told by a Fascist officer that they would be shot the next day. In the evening they were driven by lorry to the town of Calitri where, in the foul-smelling waiting room of the railway station, they dozed on the floor and were reunited with the two British parties last seen when leaving the aqueduct: both groups had also been caught that morning. Finally a train arrived and all were taken to Naples where waiting trucks ferried them to cells in the city's military prison. A few days after that, they were joined by the injured man they had left at the aqueduct and then by Gerry Daly's party. Dropped in the wrong gorge and too far from the aqueduct to take part in its destruction, Daly and his companions had heard the detonations while pushing hard to reach the target and had resolved straight away to make at once for the coast by a series of night marches. They were still at liberty four days later, but they were also eighteen miles shy of the sea with only hours remaining, or so they thought, to rendezvous with the submarine. Pretending to be German airmen who had crashed in the mountains and hoping to negotiate the use of a vehicle, they tried their luck in a village café but were recognised as being British and arrested. With that, every member of Colossus was in enemy hands.

It was in Naples that the interrogations began. It was also in Naples that the Italians became particularly interested in Fortunato Picchi. In an attempt to prevent his true identity from being revealed, the commandos, once captured, had immediately ceased to use him as an interpreter. But when Deane-Drummond, waiting to be interrogated, saw him in the corridor outside their cells, Picchi seemed poised to abandon his cover story. 'The officers were questioned first and, just before going in, Picchi spoke a few words to me,' Deane-Drummond recorded:

He said that he would tell 'them' who he really was and that 'they' would understand, as nobody liked the Fascists. He was not fighting Italy, he said, but only the Fascists. I told him that our orders were quite definite, we should say absolutely nothing except our rank and name, and that I thought that his other course would be very dangerous for him. I was then called in to be questioned and I did not see Picchi again.[61]

The last of the parachutists to see him were his cellmates. Concerned about his agitated state after he returned from one interrogation, they tried to raise his spirits. 'I think it is all up with me,' he told one of them, Lance-Corporal Doug Jones, a young Devonian, 'They know who I am.'[62] That night Jones sat with his arm round Picchi's shoulders, gave him his blanket and tried to persuade him to sleep. In the morning Picchi was taken out again. This time he did not come back.

Tag Pritchard would remember that Picchi had shown 'no apprehension' when told in Malta that they were heading for Italy,

which was not surprising, as throughout our short acquaintance we were most impressed by his singleness of purpose in making every effort required of him to defeat Italy ... In our opinion he was an extremely courageous man, with a great urge to work for the downfall of the Fascist Party. This spirit was enough to cause him to return to Italy the way he did, fully realising the implications of failure to get away again.[63]

But perhaps Picchi had been unwilling, or felt unable, to show concern or try to pull out. Or perhaps, as Deane-Drummond's testimony suggests, he may simply have failed fully to grasp the gravity of the risks he was running. Reading the reports of his Italian interrogators, it is certainly difficult to believe that planners in London had given sufficient consideration to his cover story and fate if he was caught.

During his first interrogation, Picchi tried to stick to that story and said that he was Private Dupont, a Free French soldier. The Italians suspected immediately that this was a lie, and in his next interrogation he gave up his real name, parents, birthplace and date of birth and tried to explain what he was doing there. He told the Italians that he had moved to London in 1921 and had worked for years at the Savoy. He described himself as a bachelor who lived alone and he gave them his home address: 175 Sussex Gardens. He said that he had been interned in June 1940 before enlisting in the Pioneer Corps in December 'out of gratitude to England'. Training had followed at various locations in England, he said, though he claimed not to know exactly where, and he had learned to parachute, after which he had been attached as an interpreter to a group of paratroopers and dropped into Italy. 'He would have had the chance to withdraw since he was aware of the mission's destination,' Picchi's interrogators noted, 'but he did not do so on account of his true love for, and adopted duty to, the English.'[64]

If Picchi had hoped that a version of the truth might help him, he was to be fatally mistaken. The official machinery turned, fast, as the Italian authorities began the search for corroboration of his story. A dossier compiled in Florence by the Questura, the general police headquarters, shows that family members in Tuscany, including his brothers, sisters and ageing mother, were quickly run to ground and visited. Letters and photographs were demanded, unearthed and taken away. Investigators even traced old colleagues at the Grande Albergo Reale in the Tuscan resort in Viareggio, where, as a young man, Picchi had worked as an assistant porter. Shown a photograph, these men confirmed that, yes, this was Picchi.

Soon the Italian authorities had no doubts about his identity. Nor had they doubts about his nationality, the terrible implications of which were realised on 5 April when, having been brought to Rome, he was put before the feared Special Tribunal. As *Il Messaggero*, the city's daily newspaper, reported afterwards, Picchi was accused of having served, 'although an Italian citizen, in the armed forces of the English State which is at war with the Italian State', and of having assisted 'during wartime ... the military operations of the enemy'.[65] The proceedings of the tribunal were brief. They concluded the same day with a death sentence.

Before dawn the following morning, Picchi wrote to his mother. Hurriedly handwritten on both sides of a single small sheet of lined paper, the letter still survives. '*Mia carissima Mamma,*' it begins, '*Dopo tanti anni ricevete da me una lettera . . .*' Translated, it reads in full:

My dearest Mamma

After so many years you receive from me a letter.

I'm sorry dear Mamma for you and for all at home for this disaster, and the pain it will bring. By now it is over for me, all that remains is the world of pain or pleasure, I do not care much about dying. I repent of my actions because I have always loved my country and must now be recognised as a traitor. Yet in all conscience I do not think that that is so.

Forgive me dear Mamma and remember me to all. I ask you especially for your forgiveness and your blessing which I need so much. Kiss all my brothers and sisters and to you dear Mamma a hug, hoping with the grace of God to be reunited in heaven.

> With many kisses
> Your child
> Fortunato
> Long live Italy!!
> Sunday, 6 April 1941[66]

It was Palm Sunday. In the cool and quiet of the still-dark early hours, Picchi was removed from the prison of Regina Coeli and driven through the empty streets and into the countryside south of the city. Usually trips like this were made with the prisoner handcuffed in the back of a van, with ropes, stakes, a simple wooden chair and perhaps a priest sharing the journey. Always they ended at Forte Bravetta, a remote, squat, grey-bricked fortress, empty and obsolete, that had been built in the nineteenth century as part of a great defensive chain around Rome. Here the prisoner would be removed and led to a spot inside the fortress walls. And it was here, by a high bank of earth built as a berm to protect the entrance from enemy bombardment, that Picchi was seated and bound in the chair with his face towards the bank, leaving his back and the back of his head exposed to the rifles of the firing squad: the Fascist way of disposing with traitors. As dawn broke, he was shot.

⊙

During the planning for Colossus, the hope had been that success would have 'far reaching effects upon the course of the war' and an 'incalculable' impact upon enemy morale.[67] Afterwards it was learned that the Italians had repaired the aqueduct within days and the temporary shortage of water had caused little disruption. When the first reports reached him of the probable capture of the party, Winston Churchill expressed regret at the raid having been allowed to go ahead. 'I do not remember having been consulted in any way upon the proposal,' he told Sir Hastings Ismay. 'The use of parachute troops was a serious step to take . . . and I would rather not have opened this chapter.'[68] While gently reminding the Prime Minister that he had in fact approved the operation, Ismay acknowledged that it had failed.

In fact, although no lasting physical damage was done, there had been positive results. There were benefits for British planners, for example. Lessons learned ranged from the vital need to improve methods of dropping containers of kit, to the disadvantages of men using reflective parachutes in moonlight. Moreover, the sheer fact that a British commando party had made a successful landing disconcerted the Italians considerably. Fear of future raids led to hundreds of Italian soldiers being deployed around the country to guard and camouflage potential targets, from aqueducts to dams and bridges.

The operation also had a sizeable propaganda impact. Once the Italians had broken the story with their communiqué from Rome, British newspapers spent days presenting the raid in a wholly positive light, with front-page reports telling at last of offensive British exploits and encouraging a Blitzed and war-weary British public to recognise the courage and initiative of the men who had taken part. 'BRITISH PARACHUTISTS LAND IN ITALY' read the headline of the *Evening Standard* when Rome's broadcast was heard.[69] 'PARACHUTISTS NOT TO DIE', it declared the next day when more news from Rome reported that the captured soldiers would be treated as prisoners of war since they had been caught while wearing British uniform.[70] 'The veil is lifted this morning on an amazing British secret,' the *Sunday Pictorial* proudly announced:

Without a word leaking out we have trained parachute troops – and dropped them in Italy . . . Despite the capture of some of our men, the news that we are not only up to date in this branch of warfare, but have actually carried out the first paratroop landing ever made across sea and over a hostile coast, will gladden every Briton. When they floated across the sea, when they floated down on to enemy soil and set about their tasks, they were making a new page in our history.[71]

The same sentiment was expressed, with more reserve, in *The Times*:

The landing of parachute troops in Southern Italy is a small matter in itself. Yet it is not surprising that it should have excited world-wide interest or that it should have been embroidered with speculation. Obviously, to drop parachutists in a country which is not in the process of being invaded is an act of exceptional daring, demanding the highest qualities of determination and abnegation in the troops concerned.[72]

Even the German press commented on the raid, apparently. The *Völkischer Beobachter*, the Nazi Party's daily newspaper, was said to have declared uncharitably about the British use of parachute troops: 'This imitation of German methods was one of the worst examples of stealing ideas in war.'[73]

Press interest was revived when Rome radio announced on 6 April that a traitor, Fortunato Picchi, had been shot in connection with the raid. Picking up the broadcast, the BBC Home Service repeated it. British newspapers drafted stories. The Ministry of Information stopped almost all. By then the War Office in London knew that Picchi had been captured: the name 'Private Dupont' had appeared on a list passed by the Vatican to British diplomats in neutral Switzerland. But it also seemed possible that the Italians might not have killed him and were simply reporting his death as a means of fishing for a British reaction.

The story was not spiked for long. Listening to the Home Service when it repeated Rome's report had been Florence Lantieri, Picchi's landlady in Sussex Gardens. Afterwards she telephoned the BBC to confirm the dead man's name. Then she placed this death notice in *The Times*:

PICCHI. On Palm Sunday 1941 Fortunato Picchi sacrificed his life for the cause of freedom. A brave man of high ideals. Until the day breaks, dear. – F.[74]

The notice appeared on 15 April. Later that day she rang Frank Snow, a finance officer on SOE's London staff with whom she had had some contact, and asked 'very tearfully' if he had time to speak:

She told me how it had come as a great shock to her when she first heard the BBC broadcast that an Italian had been executed by the Italians. She went into a very pathetic description of her feelings, and how her heart had stopped and how nice the BBC people had been to her when she phoned them to ask the name of the Italian . . . The whole [of our] conversation which did not last three minutes was purely [because] the good woman wanted to talk to someone and perhaps find a little comfort in doing so.[75]

Although a brief report in the *Daily Telegraph* on 7 April had named Picchi as the man whom Rome claimed to have shot, it was the publication of the death notice that prompted the Ministry of Information to release the stories prepared previously about him. 'SAVOY'S PICCHI DIES FOR US' declared the front-page headline of the next day's *Daily Express*. '[I]t has been established that the 5-ft.-nothing Italian whose bald head, fringed with black hair, had bobbed to most European and American celebrities was the Fortunato Picchi the Duce claims to have shot as a traitor ...'[76] Under the title 'MR FORTUNATO PICCHI – LIFE SACRIFICED FOR FREEDOM', *The Times* even published a brief obituary.[77]

In later months, others were inspired to spread Picchi's story further. *Time* magazine printed an article about him entitled 'Little Fortune'.[78] *Bulletins from Britain*, a news-sheet produced by the British Information Service for circulation in the United States, included an account. So did *Free World*, a monthly magazine aimed also at an American readership. *The Remaking of Italy*, a Penguin paperback published in 1942, was dedicated to his 'glorious memory'.[79] Also in 1942 a chapter was devoted to Picchi in *Went the Day Well*, a book of pen-portraits of men and women of different nationalities who had all died fighting the Axis, ranging from British and Commonwealth servicemen to a Luxembourger, a Norwegian, a Chinese, a Greek, a pair of Yugoslavs and a Czech. Picchi was the book's only Italian.[80]

The Savoy Hotel probably played a role in seeing at least some of these accounts printed. The hotel's press officer, Jean Nicol, would later recall having done all she could to alert editors to Picchi's story after she received a sudden visit from:

a little old lady, trimly dressed and with neat tight curls, [who] came into my office and announced herself as Picchi's landlady; she had, she said, been notified of his death and she had called about some belongings of his in the hotel . . . When I heard the full story I was anxious that it should become widely known, not only as tribute to Picchi, but also it was a matter of pride to the hotel and the rest of the staff that one of their number – and, indeed, one of those very Italians whose presence [in Britain] had been questioned – should have died so heroically.[81]

4

'Desperados' and 'Thugs'

In December 1940, Frank Nelson recorded without enthusiasm that he was sending a man from London to sweep for recruits among Italian prisoners of war captured in recent fighting in North Africa. This officer would have 'a charter to collect and train a band of anything up to a hundred Italian desperados'. Nelson, who was under mounting pressure for action against Italy, not least from an increasingly impatient Hugh Dalton, did not like hurried action, which would 'undoubtedly result in some kind of half-baked scheme reflecting credit upon no-one, but I have no alternative in view of the direct instructions I have received from the Minister, which may be taken as a Cabinet Order'.[1] The officer given command of the mission was the brother of the man who would create James Bond.

In 1940, Peter Fleming was already well-known in his own right as an author. *Brazilian Adventure*, published in 1932, told of his travails in the jungles of central Brazil trying to nail down the fate of the missing Percy Fawcett, a British Army colonel who had gone there looking for the lost city of El Dorado. *One's Company* and *News from Tartary*, both published in 1936, covered Fleming's subsequent journeys in the Soviet Union and China. In 1940, after joining the Army and seeing a little action in Norway, he had been tasked with preparing and equipping stay-behind parties of local volunteers, men of the MI(R)-inspired Auxiliary Units, who would emerge from hidden dens to harass a German invasion of Kent; 'very keen on poisoned arrows' one colleague remembered of him.[2] An adventurer with little love for military convention, Fleming, by then a 33-year-old captain in the Grenadier Guards, joined SOE that December. 'What are your hobbies?' asked one of the forms that he was given to fill in. 'Filling up forms' he scribbled, adding 'Medium' when told to describe his physical appearance and 'Very few' when asked for his political views.[3]

French was the only language that Fleming said he spoke. Six months after Italy entered the war, SOE still had scarcely a man at its headquarters with detailed knowledge of Italy or able to speak to Italians in their own tongue. This is not to say that it had not tried to recruit them, but an Italian recruited from an internment camp would never have been considered sufficiently reliable for a senior staff role, while few British nationals could be found with the requisite skills. Italian studies were not widely developed in pre-war Britain, which hardly helped. On rare occasions, names came to light of serving British officers with Italian backgrounds: men who had worked or studied in Italy, for example, or had Italian parentage. But SOE, being new and unproven, found itself poorly placed to compete with the host of other organisations, from the Ministry of Information, the BBC, MI5 and MI6 to the many branches of military, naval and air intelligence, that suddenly needed to increase their own stocks of Italian-speakers.

One man whom it did manage to acquire was George Logie, who became the first head of Frank Nelson's one-man Italian desk at about the time that Fleming was brought on board. A pre-war employee of Lazard's Bank, Logie had a little Italian background, which included a stint in Rome in 1939–40 gathering intelligence for the Ministry of Economic Warfare, but was much more familiar with Germany. Born to British parents living in Dresden, he had spent the First World War interned in Germany and even served briefly in the German Army. A friend would recall that Logie, 'fired with a neophyte's enthusiasm' on joining SOE, though he was then pushing fifty, had first volunteered 'to be dropped blind with a transmitter into the Rhineland where he had many friends'.[4] Logie was not behind the Italian desk for long. The following spring, the War Office poached him for a finance post. This led to the leaderless Italian section being combined with the Greek desk under the command of Derrick Perkins, a pre-war merchant banker, who knew more about Greece than he did about Italy.

Logie was not the only Italian-speaker whose services SOE failed to retain for long. It would lose the straight-talking George Martelli when SO1 became the Political Warfare Executive in 1941. By the time he had left, Martelli's pessimistic assessments of SOE's ability to find the right sort of Italians in Britain had proved, if anything, too optimistic.[5] Hopes were briefly raised when dozens of Italians were released from internment and allowed to join the Pioneer Corps, a British unit used mostly as manpower for labouring and engineering. Then, in early 1941, Martelli visited their training centre at the seaside town of Ilfracombe, in North Devon, taking with him a list of thirty pre-selected names. He ended up interviewing about half the hundred-odd Italians there. All but nine he rejected out of hand. Of those nine, he recommended just one as 'really suitable'. His expectations had not been high, but Martelli found the result 'more disheartening' since the Pioneers represented 'the pick of the Italians in this country from the point of view of (i) fitness, (ii) political reliability [and] (iii) willingness to serve our cause'.[6] Subsequent sweeps by other recruiters were similarly unproductive.[7] Not all Italians were un-interested in fighting; some volunteered with enthusiasm. But even many of these declined to continue when told they might have to kill their own countrymen.

When attempts to recruit Italians in Britain were effectively drawn to a close in the summer of 1941, SOE also felt that the publicity given to Fortunato Picchi's capture and execution had done more harm than good. Picchi, although loaned to Sir Roger Keyes for the duration of Colossus, had been recruited by SOE and remained on its books, and staff officers at headquarters had tried to keep his name and fate out of the public eye, even managing to stop the War Office from making a film about him. Some tense correspondence with Sir Walter Monckton, Director-General of the Ministry of Information, was necessary before the reality hit home that the story was never one they were ever likely to control. 'I will of course remember how essential it is that no reference should be made to the existence of SOE,' Monckton replied when asked to tone down the reporting.

[But i]t is always rather a delicate matter to criticise the handling of a story which we have no power to stop. I think that the Editor would tell us that the story of this little Italian waiter from the Savoy, giving his life to help us against the Fascists, was, in his view, moving and inspiriting. He would, no doubt, say that it was rather like telling the story of a brave fireman killed at work in an air raid. You would not refrain from publishing such a story, lest you should discourage the other firemen.[8]

Picchi's death did cause some Italians in Britain to wonder what fate had in store for them, too, if they did what the British wanted. When he was killed, SOE had eight Italian volunteers in training. Two were the pair of Spanish Civil War veterans who had almost been selected for Colossus. The others had been found during further searches among internees and the Pioneer Corps. These eight were then reduced to six when two of them, including one of the original Quins, Rinaldo Purisiol, became too undisciplined and indiscreet to keep. Then the unsettling news about Picchi appeared in the papers. Soon afterwards, a more impressive man decided to drop out. This was Leonida Rosa, a forty-year-old former *maître d'hôtel* at the Piccadilly Grill Room who had lived in London since 1920. Then another trainee, a twenty-year-old Jew from Trieste of Polish-Turkish parentage who had come to London in 1939 to escape Italy's new racial laws, was deemed unsuitable for further training. This left four, of whom one, Emilio Salsilli, the last of the Quins, was also side-lined. He remained 'anxious to do real work', it was noted, but 'in view of the Picchi incident, [he] absolutely excludes the possibility of going to Italian territory'. Salsilli was 'convinced that the Italian

Government already have his name and photograph and that his relations in Italy have probably been arrested'.[9]

Three of the discarded trainees were sent eventually to a secret establishment hidden in the Highlands known as 'Number 6 Special Workshop School'. Also known as 'The Cooler', it was a place where ex-students and ex-agents could be held until their SOE knowledge was irrelevant to operations. All three remained there until almost the end of the war, with one, Leonida Rosa, becoming the camp cook, and another, Rinaldo Purisiol, being given the boiler to look after. Purisiol calmed down after being sent to Scotland, where, among the British staff, he also became a regular subject of affectionate, if facetious, commentary. 'From the loving care he gives to the boiler (commonly known to the staff as "Mrs Purisiol") even to the extent of getting up in the middle of the night to feed it, it might appear that he would welcome some work connected with mechanics,' one officer noted.[10] A skilled metalworker, Purisiol eventually found such an outlet by 'producing queer shapes' from a small hand-forge.[11] The nature of his creations would suggest that he remained of a warlike state of mind. Apparently they included special equipment for Norwegian raiding parties and a folding steel bow for silent killing.

In the end, SOE would turn up in Britain only three Italians, in addition to Fortunato Picchi, whom it would manage to use for more than stoking boilers and cooking. One was Giovanni Verdeu, the one 'really suitable' man whom George Martelli had found at Ilfracombe. In his early forties, technically Italian but born in Trieste to Slovene parents, Verdeu had fought in the Austrian infantry during the First World War before becoming a professional seaman, eventually fleeing Italy in 1930 when police found anti-Fascist propaganda in his house. 'He came over the Alps, without a passport, to France,' SOE noted, 'and walked 620 kilometres on foot.' After a few odd jobs in France he became a mechanic on a yacht belonging to the racing driver Montague Grahame-White. Then he moved to England, where, when Italy entered the war, he was working in a boatyard.[12] Despite condemning his 'primitive' education, SOE had no doubt about Verdeu's aptitude for action: 'all the individual qualities of an old hand . . . great cunning and determination . . . tenacious and can be guaranteed to turn up trumps on any job. A born saboteur.'[13] One training school commandant was more brisk with his verdict: 'no brains, but is prepared for anything'.[14] There was one problem: Verdeu's hatred of Italians was uncomfortably extreme. Never destined for Italy, he was eventually sent out to the Mediterranean and did useful work on motorboat, submarine and schooner operations.

Like Verdeu, the other two Italians were ex-internees recruited from the Pioneer Corps. Both were Jews who had come to Britain to escape persecution. One was Ernesto Ottolenghi, a businessman aged about fifty, who had studied in Britain, served during the First World War in the Italian Air Force, and, afterwards, become a director of textile factories in Bradford, Naples and Turin. SOE liked him but concluded that he was 'too old and unfit' for an operational role.[15] 'Convinced anti-Fascist,' it was noted as he went through paramilitary training on the banks of Loch Morar. 'First class intellectual and moral qualities, worn out body . . . Has a dislocated shoulder. His hand is so small that he cannot reach the trigger of a .38 revolver except with his middle finger.'[16] Considered 'too good a man to be wasted', he ended up in the Middle East helping with recruitment and propaganda.[17] Lastly there was a much younger man, Giacomino Sarfatti, who had been studying agriculture at the University of Reading. Other than Fortunato Picchi, Sarfatti was the only Italian found in Britain who would prove both willing and able to return to Italy before the Armistice.

⊙

The idea of recruiting from among Italian prisoners of war had occurred first to SOE's office in Cairo in the summer of 1940. More precisely, it occurred to SO1, whose officers at that time were the only ones outside the Balkans doing any kind of anti-Italian SOE work. In charge in Cairo was Lieutenant-Colonel Cudbert Thornhill, a veteran intelligence officer who had been British military attaché in Petrograd during the Russian Revolution in 1917.[18] Much of his current job involved drafting and disseminating propaganda – subversive leaflets and the like – to be scattered by the Royal Air Force over Italian-occupied African territories and circulated among prisoners of war.[19] In August 1940 Thornhill began suggesting steps to forge Italian prisoners into 'anti-Fascist instruments'. Efforts should not be limited to making these Italians 'vaguely friendly', read a proposal he co-wrote with Freya Stark, the explorer and travel writer, who was then working for the Ministry of Information in Aden. 'We should, in fact, be training a "Fifth Column".'[20]

The principal stimulus to the idea of recruiting prisoners came with the spectacular series of military victories masterminded by General Sir Archibald Wavell, British Commander-in-Chief in the Middle East. After Italian forces had invaded Egypt in September 1940, a stunning counter-attack by Wavell's combined British and Commonwealth forces, though heavily outnumbered, chased the Italians out and away, then thrust deep into Italian-held Libya. Some 20,000 Italian soldiers were captured within hours. Thousands more gave up as the advance drove on; 133,000 would be in the bag by February 1941, by when Wavell was waging another successful campaign against Italy's colonies in East Africa.

For a time, both the Foreign Office and the Prime Minister wanted to exploit Wavell's successes by raising a military force of 'free' Italians recruited from prisoners and civilian internees. Presciently, the War Office and Wavell himself were much less keen: they agreed that harnessing Italians to the Allied cause would have intelligence and propaganda worth; they were much less sure that suitable volunteers could be found with ease.[21] In the end, no free Italian force was ever formed. But Hugh Dalton, at Churchill's insistence, made sure that SOE pressed ahead with a plan of its own to sweep the Middle East for Italian candidates for its less conventional purposes. This idea soon grew into a scheme to send a mission to search for anti-Axis Spaniards, Frenchmen and Italians – especially Italians – and establish a school where they could be trained. Peter Fleming was put in charge of it.

Fleming moved fast. First, he handpicked a team to go to Egypt with him. Most he had known for some time. Captain Norman Johnstone, for instance, was a fellow Grenadier. Oliver Barstow, a second lieutenant in the Royal Horse Artillery, was the younger brother of an old friend whom Fleming had invited first but was too busy to come along. Next, he took his team to the Highlands for a crash-course in commando training. Done with Scotland and before leaving London, the party was then issued with various tools that it was felt that Fleming might need. These apparently included £40,000 in notes and sovereigns, some of which could be used as bribes, and a mini-arsenal of explosives and booby traps plus a pair of Thompson sub-machineguns. According to one source, a supply of poison was acquired too.[22] Since the plan envisaged the mission as responsible for training and raising a force suitable for raiding the Italian coast, orders were also sent out to Cairo to put a mass of additional material at Fleming's disposal 'for instructional and operational purposes'. This included 20,000 pounds of gun cotton, tens of thousands of feet of fuse, 100 pistols, ten Bren guns, thirty-five more Thompsons and two Vickers machineguns.[23] Only one of Fleming's officers could speak Italian, so the party was also issued with Italian grammars.

It was about now that Fleming's pre-war travels in Tartary gave birth to the mission's name: Yak. It was also about now that a rumour reached the sensitive ears of Hugh Dalton that some considered that what Yak Mission was about to do might infringe international law. 'From whom does this fatuous defeatist inhibition emanate?' Dalton demanded of Gladwyn Jebb, fuming at this 'new snag-hunter's triumph' and 'new spanner flung into my works':

I recall in the last war finding Czech deserters arrested by one of my sergeants in a high Alpine village for speaking neither Italian or English. I had them liberated as Allies. They played their part in the battle of Vittorio Veneto, and my guns covered their advance. I recall also that the Germans recruited, from among Irish prisoners of war, help-mates for [the Irish nationalist Roger] Casement . . . It is utterly intolerable that we should be warned off the great host of more than 100,000 Italian prisoners of war on some thin-lipped and thin-blooded pretext of pseudo-legality . . . I just won't have it!

George Martelli has been vainly combing internment camps of Italian civilians in this country. There is nothing tough there at all; all waiters and small tradesmen, and so it will be with the Italian communities of like texture in Cairo and other Levantine rabbit warrens. Do I understand that obstacles are being put in the way of recruitment among these Italian prisoners of war for service in our adventures against Italy? If so, tell me who is responsible and I will do my damndest to do him in.[24]

By now Peter Fleming was already thinking about how to accomplish his task. He expected to recruit Slovenes and some Piedmontese and was wondering about placing stool pigeons among the more 'disgruntled' prisoners. He also felt that concern for prisoners' rights, as laid down in the Hague Convention, was 'stupid and unhelpful'. 'Peter Fleming came to see me this afternoon,' Dalton recorded as Yak Mission prepared for the off. 'I liked him.'[25]

With their instructions unchanged, Fleming and his men finally left for the Middle East at the end of January 1941, sailing from the Clyde, aboard a troopship of commandos. A complicated journey lay ahead. Italy's belligerence and France's collapse had closed the most direct routes to Cairo and limited to a minimum all passage via the Mediterranean. Yak Mission disembarked at Freetown and transferred to a Dutch freighter that took them to

Takoradi on the Gold Coast. From there they eventually flew to Egypt, whereupon the central task with which the mission had embarked was almost immediately abandoned. As they began to poke about the camps around Cairo, it quickly became clear to Fleming and his men that very few prisoners were even remotely interested in being recruited.

This failure prompted a bored and restless Fleming to give up and look around for something more interesting to do. He quickly found it. Wavell, whose Middle East responsibilities included the eastern Mediterranean, was at that time anxiously watching events in the Balkans where the Italians, from their bases in southern Albania, had attacked Greece in October 1940. For a while, the Greeks had done well. By 1941, however, the fighting had reached a wintry stalemate with both sides grimly dug in. Wavell had dispatched a British force to help but his resources were terribly thin, especially since he was fighting the Italians in East Africa as well. When word reached him that Fleming's irregular services were available, he felt he knew where they could be put to good use. Fleming and his men found themselves heading for Greece, ostensibly to train and organise stay-behind parties 'on [the] lines [of the] work done by him in Kent'.[26]

Arriving at the end of March, Yak Mission was not in Greece for long. On 6 April the Germans invaded Yugoslavia and sent more forces sweeping across the Greek frontier, tipping the balance so decisively in the Balkans that, within days, they easily ejected Wavell's force: the last British troops in action on mainland Europe. After various adventures, Fleming's team was caught up in the frantic evacuation. At the dockside at Piraeus they boarded a private yacht, the *Kalanthe*, which the Royal Navy had requisitioned and placed at the disposal of the British Legation staff from Athens. Packed with British and Greeks, including women and children, and protected by Yak Mission's guns, the yacht got under way at dusk on a late April evening.

The following afternoon, while moored in the bay of a little island called Polyaigos in the Cyclades, the *Kalanthe* was spotted by three marauding Junkers 88s. 'First attack comes over the hill from the east,' Fleming wrote in his diary:

He comes on machine-gunning hard, masthead high, and we engage him, eight men standing nakedly to the tall Lewis gun mountings. You really need a grouse butt of some kind for this sort of thing. He is shooting short, and when he has gone over his tail gunner sprays the water miles beyond us.

I think my gun has jammed, but it is only the cocking-handle forward. Nobody seems to have been hit. A Marine is coming aft to look at my gun. I send Clarke forward to take his place, then the second bugger comes into the attack, not giving us more than two minutes between doses. This time he has us ... I daresay his bullets whistle round us but I don't remember noticing them.

Four bombs come out of him. Our fire has no effect. I *think* two bombs were short, one a near miss, and the fourth a direct hit just forward of amidships ...

The ship flies skywards in the middle. The air is black with smoke, steam, oil and coal. I find myself staggering, holding on to the tilted deck.[27]

The *Kalanthe* had exploded. Nine on board were killed. Two of these were Fleming's men: thirty-year-old Lance-Bombardier Philip Edgar Clarke; and 28-year-old Oliver Barstow, whose sister, Nancy Caccia, wife of the Legation's first secretary, had been on the boat with him. Fleming himself received wounds to his head, shoulder and leg. He and the other Yak Mission survivors returned eventually to Cairo, but they had lost their coherence as an organised force and soon went their separate ways. Fleming left SOE not long afterwards.

☉

When searching overseas for Italian volunteers, SOE did not confine itself to the Middle East. Hopes were high of finding more than enough in the United States alone. In February 1941, certain that plenty of Americans among the millions of Italian extraction would want to help the British rid Italy of the Fascists, SOE's Baker Street headquarters instructed its New York representative to find and recruit up to 200 volunteers suitable for being shipped across the Atlantic for special training in Britain. One in three, Baker Street said, should be suitable for long-term missions in enemy territory. The remainder should be 'thugs' suited to sabotage and commando-type raids.[28]

Since the United States was still neutral, covert Canadian help was laid on to allow any suitable men to be dispatched quickly to Britain once they were recruited. In small groups, wearing civilian clothes, and with the assistance of the Royal Canadian Mounted Police, they were to be smuggled over the border into Canada without the knowledge or permission of the American authorities. From there they would be taken to Halifax, Nova Scotia, and put aboard boats bound for British ports. SOE was well aware that it had to tread carefully in this way. 'Operations here must be conducted with utmost delicacy,' New York told London. 'Any slip on our part in the present temper and violent opposition to [the] Lease-Lend Bill [sic] might [result and] affect great issues.'[29]

Soon New York reported that they had found some good recruits and that the first batch was poised to set sail. London expected at least some of these men to be experienced and motivated veterans of the Spanish Civil War. As Hugh Dalton put it, he was eagerly awaiting the imminent arrival of 'tough Italian recruits from the U.S.A. who will want to be trained somewhere for eventual employment against Fascist Italy'.[30] Then, on 19 April, the first twelve volunteers arrived, stepping ashore at Gourock from a Canadian troopship, and it became very clear that they were not at all what Baker Street had expected. On paper they might have seemed to possess adequate potential. All were Italian-born, seven were now American citizens, and most could offer varying degrees of military experience: six had fought in the First World War; four had fought in Spain; and one had fought as a French

Army officer in France in 1940. Their occupations seemed a little lowly, ranging from cook, liftman and lamp-manufacturer to trouser-presser, bricklayer and doll-maker, though there were also two doctors among them. Ages were a worry: seven were over forty and one was probably sixty although he said he was fifty-five. But it was the attitude of the majority that caused SOE the most concern. All of the party had been under the mistaken impression that they were going to the Middle East to spread anti-Fascist propaganda and start a 'Free Italian Legion' raised from prisoners of war. It was also what they wanted to do, and some persuasion was required before they agreed to be sworn in to the Pioneer Corps and begin paramilitary training, at an SOE school at Belasis, near Dorking in Surrey, whereupon several were promptly found to be irretrievably unfit. None said that they were willing to do active operational work.[31] In the end, most were sent instead to India to work among Italian prisoners on behalf of the Political Warfare Executive.[32]

While the party was still in England, the most problematic member had been 46-year-old Andrew Ingrao, whose own fate provides an interesting glimpse of wartime British attitudes to the detention of foreign nationals without charge. A Sicilian-born doctor who had fought as an Italian infantry officer in the First World War, Ingrao had practised medicine in Naples before moving to the United States in 1929 and taking up a post in Psychology at Columbia University. In 1937 he became an American citizen. 'He is grumbler No. 1 and the main factor in stirring up discontent among the others,' read one early SOE assessment. 'He is a "know all" and will not be taught anything.' It was also felt that he was intolerably indiscreet. 'Makes himself conspicuous in public by gesticulating and talking in Italian, although he has been told many times to speak English . . . He goes out for walks by himself at any hour of the day, and again in local cafés attracts attention by drinking out of the bottle.' It was observed, too, that it seemed unlikely that he would achieve much with Italian prisoners anyway. 'His lack of self-control and manner of shouting down anyone who disagrees with him would hardly produce the effect desired.'[33]

Ingrao was earmarked for a swift return to the United States. In June 1941, however, while waiting at Euston Station for a train to take him to Fort William where he was to board a boat home, he gave his escort the slip and ran off. Eventually he turned up at the American Embassy where the staff promptly handed him to Special Branch, pointing out that because he had taken an oath to the British crown he had forfeited his claim to American protection. By now he had become so loud, irresponsible and awkward that his case was put before Herbert Morrison, the Home Secretary, who ordered that he be discharged from the army and detained, under Defence Regulations, for being in possession of information dangerous to the state. Long months followed in various prisons, including a sizeable stretch in Swansea. Neither the Home Office nor SOE was indifferent to the fact that Ingrao had come to Britain with good intentions, under a misapprehension of what was expected of him, and was now detained under no formal charge. At the same time, they could not secure an acceptable level of assurance that on returning to the United States he would not immediately disclose all he knew. 'On the evidence produced we have no option but to keep Ingrao here,' Gladwyn Jebb commented on the case. 'This is our funeral & we shall have to stand any racket when the war is over.'[34]

During his detention, Ingrao bombarded SOE with outraged letters demanding his release. Most of these served to make his liberty less likely. 'In one of his earlier letters he admitted that there were good grounds for detaining him,' SOE noted:

As time went on his letters contained a more threatening note and on the 19th November 1941 he writes: 'I can assure you that it will not take such a long time for me to consult one of the best New York lawyers . . . nor to consider how big an indemnity to demand, for it will be proportionate to my stay in gaol . . .'

On the 26th November 1941 he writes: 'Once in America I will sue Lord Halifax [the British Ambassador in Washington, DC] for a million dollars for each month of agony . . . I intend to provoke the biggest scandal of the war . . .'

On the 11th February 1942 he writes: 'A book on "How I was Kidnapped by the British Government". I have it already outlined in my mind and I will write it down as soon as I shall be back in my country. I am sure it will be a best seller in America for a number of years because it will contribute to a better knowledge of European civilisation.'[35]

Ingrao stayed in detention for twenty-three months, eventually being released when it was felt that whatever secrets he had known were out of date, whereupon, on returning to the United States, he offered, for cash, to stay silent about his experiences. In London, officers discussed the matter. There was agreement that Ingrao should be refused his 'Danegeld' and told to 'go to hell'. One suggestion was that the American police might be present at any handover of money, 'with a view to taking criminal proceedings against him for blackmail'. Harry Sporborg, assistant to SOE's chief, doubted whether this was worth it: 'I pointed out that although this would be the normal procedure in this country it would be quite hopeless in the United States where blackmail is regarded no[t] as a punishable crime but as a rather unsporting type of business procedure.'[36] No money was handed over, whereupon Ingrao, as expected, went to the press. 'HELD IN BRITISH PRISON 2 YEARS SAYS AMERICAN', began one newspaper story. 'Freed at last after 23 months of what he describes as [a] harrowing experience in prisons in England, Dr Ingrao today is living in New York. . .'[37] Assessing Ingrao's indiscretions, MI5 was not overly concerned. '[T]his sort of thing is bound to come out sooner or later,' one officer felt, adding that 'it is a thousand times better to have it out while people can still remind themselves that there is a war on.'[38]

When, in 1941, Baker Street enquired as to how on earth Ingrao and the others had been recruited, New York explained that they themselves had not interviewed or selected the men. Instead, anxious to prevent the American authorities from discovering any British involvement, they had handed those tasks to the Mazzini Society. This was a cultural association, founded in the United States in 1940 and partly funded by the British, whose members were now dedicating their efforts towards steering the country's vast Italian-American community away from Fascist orientation. Doing his best to direct that battle was Alberto Tarchiani, one of the Italian exiles who had been introduced to Section D in Paris, but the fight was not easy.[39] 'Fifteen or more years of extremely efficient and widespread Fascist propaganda have unquestionably had a very powerful effect,' SOE's New York office told London in December 1941,

and there is no doubt that a very large percentage of Italian-Americans remain convinced that the Axis is in the right ... Especially since the Ethiopian war, the main theme of Fascist propaganda has been to inculcate into them the idea that England is the one country that has prevented and is still preventing the development of their homeland.[40]

The Japanese attack on Pearl Harbor, followed by Mussolini's declaration of war on the United States four days later, began to change that mindset (although a good number of Italian-Americans would continue to resent Britain for many months to come). It also terminated SOE's ability to explore the United States for volunteers, though the search had failed to become any more fruitful since the Mazzini Society's limited efforts among its membership. In November 1941, New York had offered Baker Street 28-year-old Frank Cali. New York-born to Sicilian parents, he had spent eighteen months fighting on the Republican side in Spain. Described variously in New York's reports as 'small and slight but tough and ready for any job', 'a fanatical anti-Fascist', 'keen as mustard', 'anxious to go to Sicily on any mission you require', and 'a tough little nut and a good chap', he sailed for Britain in mid-December.[41] When he arrived, it did not take

London long to spot his obvious flaw. 'He appears to be suitable for our work but will, we are afraid, not be of much use owing to his poor knowledge of Italian,' New York was told. 'It appears that he has not spoken the language since he was a boy.'[42]

The last American found by SOE's New York office was forty-year-old Giovanni Realdini. Born in Philadelphia of Italian parents, he certainly seemed to have the language skills: New York noted that he had 'a natural gift for the Italian tongue' and 'a perfect accent'. The problem with Realdini, however, was his character. 'He entered the United States Navy in the last war and very soon got into trouble for striking a superior officer,' New York reported.

He has a rather sketchy record of arrests and some convictions over a period of the last twenty years. He has been a pugilist for a short time but his main source of income has been from confidence work and from card games, dice, cheque forging and possible counterfeiting. At the moment his fortunes seem to be at [a] low ebb but this is nothing to concern this type of man.

Perhaps some of these traits could be useful, New York wondered.

He is the type who can talk himself out of "tough spots". Physically he can take care of himself . . . and [he] can handle all sorts of lethal weapons.[43]

He also wanted an income with which to support his disabled younger brother, and seemed 'genuinely anxious' to do 'something worthwhile for Uncle Sam' and atone for his past misdemeanours.[44]

But although they recommended Realdini to London, even SOE's New York men had their doubts this time. 'The more I think about this chap,' one of them ruminated, 'the more certain I feel that London will not want to have anything to do with him.'[45] That feeling proved sound.

⊙

British backing of Italian anti-Fascists on the far side of the Atlantic also explains an odd incident that intrigued the United States Border Patrol in McAllen, Texas, in April 1941. A local man, C. G. Fink, reported that his son, Melvin, a cabdriver in the town, had allowed someone to use his name to purchase a car. The same man was also paying his son to try to drive him into Mexico. Fink junior was then questioned at the Border Patrol office 'in an effort to obtain some clue' to explain the stranger's actions, 'as well as to determine any illegal enterprise or un-American intention'.[46]

'Young Fink, age 19,' the Border Patrol wrote in a report that ended up with the FBI, said that the man had given his name as 'Emmett Williams' and 'never told him anything about his plans, other than that he wanted to go to Monterrey':

In that connection, he offered Fink $25.00 and expenses to drive him to that point, and requested that he be allowed to purchase an automobile in the youth's name because he did not have a driver's license. He also explained that he did not want to enter Mexico at Brownsville or Laredo because the roads were bad, and because he could not get the proper papers from the immigration at Brownsville. [Fink] stated that [Williams] seemed very anxious to go to Mexico, and on one occasion while he was driving him, went to the McAllen airport and priced the service of a plane to Monterrey. Fink noted that he had large denomination bills of money when he would pay for various items, but didn't find him to be noticeably free with his money. Fink related that on one occasion he drove him to Hidalgo, Texas, to the international bridge, and that he got out of the car and looked at the bridge and river, then returned to McAllen.[47]

The same day, 7 April, this strange behaviour led the Border Patrol to find and question 'Emmett Williams'. He gave his real name, admitted that he was carrying a large amount of money, 'and evidenced a number of large denomination bills to us, which he said was about $2,000,000 [sic: probably $2,000.00]. When questioned as to his source of income, he was at first reluctant to answer.' Then he explained that he was 'anti-totalitarian and anti-fascist' and was making his way to Mexico City to make arrangements for anti-Fascist Italian exiles fleeing Nazi-occupied Europe to seek refuge in Mexico. This work was urgent, he said, and because he had not yet acquired the proper entry papers he had sought to buy a car in someone else's name, 'figuring that it would be easier for a local person to obtain [an] entry permit for an automobile than attempt it himself'.[48] Although his story still sounded odd, Williams had done nothing illegal and the border authorities let him go.

Emmett Williams was Max Salvadori. Since arriving in the United States at the end of June 1940, he had returned to his teaching, resumed his old friendships with men like Alberto Tarchiani, and generally done as much as he could sensibly manage for the anti-Fascist cause. He had also remained in close and covert touch with the British. Salvadori had barely left Liverpool on the liner *Britannic* when he had been approached by a fellow passenger, a 44-year-old civil servant travelling cabin class with his wife. This was William Stephenson, H. Montgomery Hyde's 'Quiet Canadian'. A decorated fighter pilot in the First World War, Stephenson was a wealthy and well-connected Canadian financier and businessman en route to work in New York for MI6. A little later, on Churchill's personal authority, Stephenson became director in New York of British Security Coordination. This was the cover name of an umbrella organisation responsible for smoothing all British intelligence and security activities across North and South America, including those of SOE and MI6, and engaging in a host of covert activities, from collecting intelligence and recruiting prospective agents to penetrating unfriendly diplomatic missions and countering enemy propaganda. Written at the end of the war for a very limited readership, the history of British Security Coordination describes Salvadori as one of its 'most valuable agents' and 'indeed the first of BSC's recruits, for he was enlisted by WS [William Stephenson] when both were travelling in the same ship en route to America from England in June of 1940'.[49]

Salvadori's earliest work on behalf of the British in New York seems to have been a previous mission to Mexico in August 1940. His tasks were to report on local politics, uncover the activities of Italian Fascist agents, and take soundings of Mexican attitudes to the war. Returning to New York a month later, he submitted to Stephenson's office a full report on his findings. Then he returned to his wife and family and resumed his teaching duties at St Lawrence University in upstate New York. Life became a little quieter.

In November 1940, a frustrated Salvadori wrote to Claude Dansey, his old MI6 handler, saying that he wanted to do more. 'In my opinion,' he told Dansey, 'there is little I can do here for our cause. But if I find a proper covering I think that I can go to countries not friendly to yours or try to establish contacts with unfriendly groups.' He pointed out that his ongoing game of manipulating Italian officials still seemed to be working. The Italians appeared to have interpreted his departure from Britain as 'a sign of reconciliation', while he had explained away his brief trip to Mexico in August 'as an attempt at finding shelter in a neutral country in case of an extension of the conflict'. The 'quiet life' he had been leading since should also have 'allayed suspicions'.[50]

When he tried to return to Mexico the following April, Salvadori was again on a mission for the British. To judge from a typed report in English that survives among his personal papers, it also appears that his dealings with young Melvin Fink came only after he had explored and exhausted a host of other options of crossing the border illegally. Having flown into Houston on 29 March but still lacking the necessary visa, Salvadori had gone first to Galveston to sound out local fishermen on the possibilities of sailing to Tampico. None of the fishermen were willing. Next he went to Brownsville, on the Rio Grande, the river that served as the natural border between Texas and Mexico, and contacted some Mexican smugglers. But they were not prepared to play either, saying that illegal crossing had become too dangerous. Then he tried some more fishermen, these ones in Port Isabel, but they also proved unable to help.

As Salvadori explains in his report, in which he calls himself 'XX' and writes in the third person, it was time to attempt something more drastic. He would try to swim the Rio Grande.

April 3. XX goes to Boca Chica, but does not find either fishermen or owners of pleasure craft. At 9.p.m. swims through the river, a little worried by reported presence of alligators. Arrangements for keeping clothes dry fail completely. Reaches opposite bank and walks all night back and forth in a clearing, waiting for the clothes to get dry.

April 4. By 9.30.a.m. clothes, documents and money are nearly dry. Leaves hideout. Finds group of huts occupied by Mexicans. Attacked by three dogs and severely bitten on leg. Natives highly suspicious and unfriendly. Worried by presence of another river, XX talks with a native. Realizes that he finds himself on a peninsula which until 1938 was part of Mexico. The main section of the river having changed bed, the peninsula is now American soil . . .

Because of the wound and of the unfriendly attitude of the natives, XX walks back to Brownsville, which he reaches at 2.p.m. Feels a complete fool.

That afternoon Salvadori learned that papers had to be shown by anyone trying to get into Mexico by train or plane. 'Telephones to Mexico City asking if he can have the visa for which he applied on March 14th. Reply is "mañana".' The following day Salvadori went to McAllen and found 'a youngster' prepared to help him. This was Melvin Fink. Two days later, on 7 April, Salvadori bought the car for $300 in Fink's name, since 'to cross into Mexico with a car it is necessary to prove ownership'. Alterations were made to the car 'in a way as to hide a person'. Then, at three that afternoon, 'XX is stopped and questioned by Border patrol. Doubtful points to be cleared: what [is the need] for the car? Why staying at hotel under different name? Why so much money? (XX is completely searched) . . . XX's honesty convinces the border patrol.'[51]

Having abandoned the car idea, failed to bribe Mexican consular officials in McAllen, found his name freshly added to an American border 'blacklist' as a possible '*quintacolumnista*', and finally decided that it was 'useless to cross without papers', Salvadori returned to Galveston and 'ends where he should have begun. In Galveston gets in touch with a cousin he has never known before. Offers to the cousin 100 d[ollars] for papers necessary to enter and leave Mexico (tourist card and registration card). Cousin gets documents and sells them. Data are modified on registration card.'[52] On 10 April, wielding these documents, Salvadori entered Mexico by taxi at Laredo and took a train to Mexico City.

Quite why Salvadori had been so keen to get into Mexico is not adequately explained by his account to the border authorities. His real mission, according to his surviving private papers, was more hands-on: it was to sabotage a radio station. This was located in Mexico City and the British believed that the Nazis were using it 'to communicate with German submarines in the Gulf of Mexico'.[53] Once in the city, 'explaining that the organization to which he belongs should act concretely against the propaganda of its main enemies', Salvadori secured the help of an old and trusted socialist Italian friend, Domenico Sandino, who was living in the city. Sandino agreed to do what he could. A reconnaissance revealed that setting fire to the target was not an option since it was built of concrete, brick, metal and tiles. Therefore they would need to find some explosives, or 'surgical instruments' as Salvadori called them in his report.[54] By late April it was proving impossible to get their hands on these and time was running out: Salvadori would soon need to go home. He finally left Mexico on 26 April, flying back to New York the next day, but with a pledge from Sandino that he and a friend would still carry out the attack. In May Salvadori heard from Sandino that his man had indeed tried to blow up one of the station's masts. Sandino enclosed newspaper reports in *El Universal Gráfico* and *El Universal* carrying details of the damage.

Back in New York City, Salvadori, who had left his university post in January, settled down to writing articles for the Overseas News Agency, an organisation concerned with reporting worldwide news. The job was effectively a front to allow him to work more wholeheartedly for the anti-Fascist cause and to continue to liaise closely with Stephenson's office and SOE, for which he acted as a link to the Mazzini Society. During the summer of 1941 he also began to be investigated by both the FBI and the Immigration and Naturalization Service (INS). Curious about his movements and the bizarre goings-on reported by the McAllen Border Patrol, both organisations were concerned about his politics and loyalties. The INS thought he might be 'a dangerous Italian undercover agent'.[55] The FBI, as a note undersigned by its Director, J. Edgar Hoover, explains, wanted to know whether Salvadori should be considered for 'custodial detention pending investigation in the event of a national emergency'.[56] The INS carried out most of the early inquiries, probing Salvadori's background, interviewing his friends and acquaintances, even questioning him itself. The idea that he might be an Italian agent was swiftly demolished by a mass of testimony affirming his anti-Fascism, to be replaced by a growing conviction that he was an undercover agent working for the British. In one revealing interview in New York in August 1941, Salvadori confirmed that he had worked for the Ministry of Economic Warfare but was evasive when asked if he remained, indirectly, in 'British service and pay'. 'I won't answer that,' he responded; 'I help by pro-democratic propaganda among the Italian people.'[57] That October, having found no evidence of 'un-American activities or sentiment', the INS closed its file on him.[58] The FBI remained interested, however, and continued its inquiries: if Salvadori was really a foreign agent operating undercover in the United States, he needed to be watched, whatever his allegiances.

Salvadori also assisted the British when an attempt was made to trawl for recruits among Canada's 100,000-strong Italian community: in the spring of 1942, going north to do some interviewing, he sifted through a succession of potential candidates in Toronto, Hamilton, Niagara Falls, Sudbury and Montreal. In 1943, a party of half a dozen Canadian volunteers, all in their twenties, would eventually be sent to Britain for specialist training. Their escort, an Italian-speaking Intelligence Corps NCO, noted when they arrived that they possessed 'more fighting spirit than any other Italian students I have come across' and were 'all decent, good-hearted men, though some of them are very crude and rough'.[59] As he watched them through their training and came to know them better, he also began to doubt whether they were very suitable for operations: 'hardly any of them speaks Italian . . . only one can be said to have lived in Italy, and . . . they are incapable of behaving inconspicuously. They are Canadian; in other words, they shout rather than talk, sing on the least provocation, drink rather excessively, and hunt women perpetually.'[60]

None of those six would go on operations before the Italian surrender, but three of them would parachute later into German-occupied Italy to work with SOE missions attached to Italian partisans. Their names were Ralph Vetere, Peter Lizza and Frank Fusco.[61] SOE also interviewed in Canada a young man called Giovanni Di Lucia. Born in Ortona, Abruzzo, in 1913, 'John' Di Lucia had moved to Niagara Falls as a boy and later graduated in romance languages from New York's University of Rochester. It was at Niagara Falls, in April 1942, that Max Salvadori spoke to him. 'Produced good impression,' Salvadori wrote down:

Seems to be honest, upright, of good morals, hardworking, decided, sincerely convinced in the righteousness of the cause of the United Nations. He also seems to be still young for his age . . . Thinks more as [an] Italian than as [a] Canadian, is deeply anti-Fascist. Speaks Italian as a native.[62]

Dropped into northern Italy in early 1944 to work with local partisans, though not as an SOE agent, Di Lucia was captured soon afterwards. The Germans, before killing him, let him pen a last letter. 'I am giving my life for a good cause,' he wrote to his parents. 'This was expected and I am ready to face it. I die happily. May God bless and protect both of you.'[63]

⊙

In October 1941, Frank Nelson confessed 'the complete failure which we have so far made of Italy . . . We have no Italians under training . . . we have so far entirely failed to recruit any suitable type of Italian.' In defence he pointed out that,

as Martelli and others discovered themselves, the type of Italian internee in England is completely unsuited for our kind of work; and it was the experience of the Fleming Mission to the Middle East early this year that generally speaking the Italian soldiers who were taken prisoner were for the most part perfectly content to remain prisoners, and showed no desire whatever, either for money or for any other reason, to return to their country in an adventurous capacity.[64]

But at that moment there was one light on the horizon. It took the shape of a fifty-year-old Italian anti-Fascist who had contacted SOE after surfacing suddenly in neutral Lisbon among thousands of refugees seeking escape from Axis-dominated Europe. Sporting spectacles, a grey goatee and a serious expression, he carried a fake Polish passport with forged visas and stamps, was accompanied by his formidable Anglo-Italian wife, and had recently escaped from France where he had lived in exile for more than a decade. His name was Emilio Lussu.

5

'A mass of difficulties'

Among the finest Italian memoirs of the First World War is *Un anno sull'Altipiano*. An English edition, *Sardinian Brigade*, remains in print. The author, who had been an infantry officer and company commander in the Italian Army's distinguished Brigata Sassari, recalls in its pages his searing experiences on the Austro-Italian front. One noted passage is his powerful account of terror-stricken soldiers poised to go over the top on the Asiago plateau in July 1916:

Captain Bravini had his watch in his hand and was following the inexorable passing of the minutes . . .

'Ready for the assault! Officers, to your places!'

Wide and staring, the men's eyes seemed to seek ours. They met only mine, for Captain Bravini was still gazing fixedly at his watch . . .

'Ready!' shouted Bravini again.

To attack! Where was one going? Out into the open, away from the cover afforded by the trenches. Machine-guns, stuffed with ammunition, were lying in wait. Those who have not been through such moments do not know what war is . . .

The 10th was directly in front of me and I could distinguish every man. Two of them moved, and I saw them, one beside the other, place the barrels of their rifles under their chins. One leaned forward, pressed the trigger, and slipped to the ground. The other did the same.[1]

The book's author was Emilio Lussu. Born on the Italian island of Sardinia in 1890, in a village called Armungia in hills northeast of the capital, Cagliari, he had been a popular officer known for showing concern for the plight of his men. While still at the front, and in spite of his youth, he had been made president of a federation of ex-servicemen. By the end of the war he had been wounded twice and decorated four times for valour. After it he devoted his life to law, politics, writing and revolution.

In 1921, still only thirty, Lussu had been elected to Italy's parliament. He represented the Partito Sardo d'Azione, the Sardinian Action Party, which he had co-founded the previous year with a platform of social democracy and Sardinian autonomy. In 1924 he returned to Sardinia after resigning in protest at the murder of Giacomo Matteotti, the socialist deputy kidnapped and killed by Fascist thugs. Then he became a target himself. The island was not at all a Fascist stronghold and, to pacify its politicians, Rome began to sponsor quasi-military gangs in an attempt to assert its authority. In 1926, when a baying crowd of Fascists surrounded Lussu's home in Cagliari, one tried to get in through the window and Lussu shot him. It was a killing committed in self-defence but Lussu was sentenced by the Fascists to five years' *confino* and dispatched in chains to Lipari.

In 1929, Lussu was one of the two political prisoners who joined Carlo Rosselli in the daring escape from the island that made headlines worldwide. Settling in exile in Paris, he started working for Giustizia e Libertà and married Max Salvadori's redoubtable sister, Joyce, who became a professor of philology at the Sorbonne. They had first met in Geneva when Joyce delivered a secret message from anti-Fascists imprisoned with her brother on Ponza. 'Lussu had no intention of settling down with a wife and family,' she later wrote. 'To his way of thinking such things were incompatible with the life that he led as a militant rebel. I, on the other hand, was convinced that I was just the ideal companion for an active revolutionary and I missed no opportunity of telling him so.'[2] The couple lived together in borderline poverty in Paris' Latin Quarter, moving whenever OVRA agents found out their address. In exile, Lussu also wrote. *Marcia su Roma e dintorni* (1933), published in English in 1936 as *Enter Mussolini: Observations and Adventures of an Anti-Fascist*, recounted his political experiences up to his flight from Lipari.

Un anno sull'Altipiano appeared in 1938. In May 1940 he was among the Italian anti-Fascists in Paris whom his brother-in-law introduced to Section D. When the city fell a few days later, Lussu and his wife, on foot, carrying little suitcases, joined the columns of refugees fleeing south.

In May 1941 a story reached London that Lussu was in Marseilles. It seems to have come courtesy of Umberto Calosso, an anti-Fascist of Italian roots who was assisting with Allied propaganda in the Middle East, and it was the first the British had heard of Lussu since the Germans marched into Paris eleven months before. 'We would naturally like him here,' George Martelli put in. 'Lussu is one of the best known and most able of the Italian anti-Fascists.'[3] Martelli also urged speed, since the Gestapo was reportedly on Lussu's tail. Facilitating an escape from southern France, which was Vichy-controlled and not yet under German occupation, was not an impossible proposition, but plans for a rescue were still being laid when, in June, Lussu appeared in Lisbon and made contact with the British Embassy. Wielding a home-made Polish passport and accompanied by Joyce, he had managed to flee France through the Pyrenees.

Soon Lussu was talking to one of SOE's representatives in Lisbon, a businessman by the name of Laurent Mortimore. Lussu told him that Italy would soon be ripe for revolution. With that in mind, he wished to return to France and make his way to Corsica from where he would establish himself on Sardinia and organise 'total action . . . including sabotage and revolt'. If successful, he would extend that activity to the rest of Italy. He also said that, while he wanted this action to be '100% Italian and not dependent on British money', he was keen for British involvement. Lussu struck Mortimore as 'a first-rate man and undoubtedly a daring organiser', who wanted to 'prepare a revolution in Italy and also start immediately on subversive work, sabotage, etc.' He was 'full of energy and dynamic' and 'full of ideas: some of them may be good'. Jack Beevor, another of SOE's Lisbon men with whom he began to deal, took a similarly positive view. Lussu, he reported, was 'a proud and independent creature' and 'an enthusiast and an idealist of an extremely active type, and although he throws his arms about and spreads out vistas of extensive schemes, he is a fair critic of himself'.[4]

As officers in London began to learn more about Lussu, hopes for anti-Italian action grew. Here was an energetic exile with prestige, contacts, experience and ideas. Soon one of those ideas was at the centre of SOE's plans for Italy: Lussu's grand project for a Sardinian-based rebellion that would inspire revolt across the Italian mainland.

⊙

Within days of Lussu appearing on the scene, SOE went into action on his behalf. It started by helping a dozen or so of his anti-Fascist Italian friends to escape from Vichy-controlled Morocco. After the French defeat in June 1940 they had all fled to Casablanca, another hub for refugees fleeing Europe, and Lussu wanted them out so they could assist him with his plans. Getting refugees out of Casablanca was a notoriously ticklish business. (Humphrey Bogart's fictional Rick was supposedly attempting at about this time to get Victor Laszlo out of the city.) Eventually, at a cost of nearly £1,000 and with the help of a friendly Greek colonel in Rabat, SOE secured visas to let Lussu's friends leave for the United States and Mexico. Among them were Alberto Cianca and Aldo Garosci, two more Giustizia e Libertà members whom Max Salvadori had introduced to Section D in 1940, and Leo Valiani, a political journalist and ex-communist friend of the author Arthur Koestler. Valiani had recently been imprisoned with Koestler in Spain (and is 'Mario' in Koestler's 1941 memoir, *Scum of the Earth*).

When that was done, and to demonstrate the sort of support that the British might be able to offer, Lussu was flown by flying boat to Malta and briefed by SOE officers there about aircraft drops, submarine landings, coded communications and wireless links. With the Axis now dominant across Continental Europe, this tiny territory had become a crucial jumping-off point for British special operations in the Mediterranean: it was from Malta that the Colossus party had dropped into Italy in February; it was a Royal Navy submarine sailing from the island that put SOE's first team into German-occupied Yugoslavia in September. Lussu returned to Lisbon a few weeks later, apparently 'in splendid form' and 'delighted' with his discoveries on the island.[5]

Through its office in New York, SOE also acted as a channel through which Lussu exchanged news and views with Italian anti-Fascists living in exile in the United States. While this mechanism proved useful to Lussu, it also allowed SOE to open and read his correspondence. Lussu knew this and drafted his letters carefully, but they still provided an authentic sense of his passion for the cause as he saw it. 'I am striving to bring about a plan which pre-supposes co-operation with the English,' he wrote to Alberto Cianca in October after his friend had reached New York. 'In spite of so many difficulties of every sort it is clear that we must return to the struggle with all our energies.' To Aldo Garosci, who was evidently having doubts about the effectiveness of Giustizia e Libertà, Lussu wrote:

[N]ations have been trampled underfoot, states have been wiped out, military, political and secular powers have crumbled away. And it surprises you that 'G. and L.' should have failed to achieve anything of value? Who has?

... 'G. and L.' lives on and will continue ... It will live and, moreover, it will fight. Europe has entered the decisive phase of the political struggle; we must not be content with hoping for victory on the Anti-Fascist front: it is our duty to collaborate in causing it and to take an active part ...

I must speak very strongly to you ... You are making a big mistake in dissociating yourself from 'G. and L.' You owe a great deal to our movement; without it you would be a political castaway. 'G. and L.' has orientated you. You need 'G. and L.' more than 'G. and L.' needs you ...

The tone is typical of Lussu's directness and self-belief. 'I know you well,' he went on at Garosci, 'you will get nowhere alone. You might perhaps write a book or found a review, and if so, you may count me amongst your readers, but, politically, you will be at a standstill.'[6]

Also obvious from Lussu's letters is his steady belief that anti-Fascists and Italians in general had to reject and overthrow Mussolini's regime in an autonomous and independent way. 'The formation [abroad] of a Provisional Government would mean that we should only be able to re-enter Italy backed by British bayonets,' he wrote to another of his old friends now in America, Alberto Tarchiani, in another letter read by SOE. 'Even Anti-Fascists in Italy would lay in a stock of tomatoes and rotten eggs to bombard us with on our triumphal entry into Rome . . . Fascism would be overthrown, at the end of the war, by the British and not by us.' For Lussu, action was everything. 'Only the prestige of action, of success, can cause the rapid development in Italy of a political movement of revolt,' he told Cianca; 'we must work like slaves to make action possible . . . we must have the guts to involve ourselves inextricably . . . If one considers what may happen in Italy if anti-Fascism remains unexpressed before the end of the war in some decisive action, one's brain reels.'[7]

To SOE, everything seemed to be progressing rather well. Then, in November 1941, a few days after his return to Lisbon from Malta, Lussu tabled his detailed plan. At once it was realised that dealing with him was not going to be hurdle-free. Much of what he proposed was already known: his intention to travel, with his wife, to France and then to Corsica from where they would begin working into Sardinia; his wish for a free force of Sardinian volunteers to be raised, trained and armed and landed on the island when the time was right; and his desire to coordinate everything with British military aims and capabilities. What caused alarm was his new request for a formal British declaration 'that Italy will be guaranteed the metropolitan and colonial boundaries possessed by her previous to the advent of Fascism'.[8] That statement was vital, Lussu stressed. It would reassure anti-Fascist Italians ready to rise up in Sardinia or rebel elsewhere in Italy that they would not be fighting to destroy their own country. 'An Italian revolt against Fascism could only be popular if the Italians felt they had gained a constitution and regime freely chosen by themselves. Sardinians should be regarded by Italians as helping to liberate Italy and not as being "sold to England".'[9]

Gladwyn Jebb, right-hand man to Hugh Dalton, SOE's minister, spotted the implications as soon as Lussu's plan arrived on his desk, and spelt them out for his superiors:

Lussu suggests that H.M.G. should declare that Italy, if she revolted against the Germans, should be allowed to retain her metropolitan and colonial frontiers as they existed in 1922. This would, of course, mean reinstating the Italian administration in Eritrea and Italian Somaliland, which would have an unpleasant reaction in Africa generally, [and result] in debarring us from making any appeal to the Arabs in Tripolitania and Cyrenaica . . . and in infuriating the Yugoslavs in denying them the possibility of liberating the 600,000 Slovenes in Venezia Giulia. Nor could we even, I think, go so far as to promise a 'liberated' Italy any 'compensations' elsewhere, in accordance with the technique adopted during the last war. To offer them Tunis, for instance, would finally discredit us with all Frenchmen, from Marshal Pétain to de Gaulle.

Jebb felt 'pretty sure' that this would be the Foreign Office's opinion:

I therefore think it is hardly necessary to ask them for their views . . . What I should hope, therefore, would be that Lussu may be persuaded to go to Corsica and make his preparations without any political guarantee of any kind . . . It is our function in SOE to promote revolution by any means and in any place that we can, thus preparing the ground for any action by the armed forces, and if Lussu can get an organisation going in Sardinia (which I must say I rather doubt) all we can say is 'Good Luck' to him.[10]

Dalton was more impressed by the plan's potential. 'This is the most hopeful Italian idea I have had put up to me yet,' he wrote when he read it. 'Let us push it hard ... Sardinians are good fighters, much above the Italian average.' But he agreed that Lussu could not possibly be given the political assurances he wanted. 'Let Lussu be discouraged from asking for precise and awkward undertakings, and be offered harmless generalities instead,' Dalton instructed imperiously, failing completely, as events would prove, to gauge the strength of Lussu's conviction. 'Pick out suitable bits of the Atlantic Charter, including free for all to decide their own form of Government; freedom from fear and want; social security and improved labour standards, access to war materials, etc. This could be made to sound quite attractive.'[11]

Thought was duly given to exploiting the Atlantic Charter, a recent declaration by Churchill and Roosevelt that the Allies were fighting to 'ensure life, liberty, independence and religious freedom and to preserve the rights of man and justice'. Eventually, in December, an Italian translation signed personally by the Deputy Prime Minister, Clement Attlee, and addressed to the Sardinian people was dispatched to Lisbon for Lussu to read. 'The Charter is intended to ensure that the vanquished nations equally with the victors shall enjoy both independence and economic prosperity,' added a special tail piece proposed by Jebb and approved by Dalton, 'as soon as the Nazis and the whole system which they have endeavoured to fasten upon Europe have been utterly and finally destroyed.'[12] Lussu read it and was not convinced. An explicit assurance about Italy's borders, he told Mortimore in Lisbon, was 'indispensable' if Italians unhappy with Fascism were to be persuaded to take action against it.[13]

In January 1942, with the war still going badly for the British, a motion of no confidence in Britain's Prime Minister was debated in the House of Commons. Before the vote was taken, Churchill was the last to speak. 'I offer no apologies, I offer no excuses, I make no promises,' he ended his address. 'I avow my confidence, never stronger than at this moment, that we shall bring this conflict to an end in a manner agreeable to the interests of our country, and in a manner agreeable to the future of the world . . . Let every man act now in accordance with what he thinks is his duty in harmony with his heart and conscience.'[14] Churchill won the motion by 464 votes to one. Watching all of this from a seat in the public gallery, though perhaps not understanding it since he spoke no English, was Emilio Lussu. SOE had secured him a seat in the gallery in the hope that he would be suitably 'thrilled'.[15]

Days earlier, SOE had flown Lussu to Britain after hearing that the Portuguese police had discovered his real identity. He had landed at a grey and wintry airfield at Barnstaple on 23 January. Joyce Lussu followed two days later. The couple were waved through the usual security formalities and brought immediately to London, their real names being omitted from all paperwork, and then lodged in an SOE apartment at 7 Park Place, off Piccadilly. Soon Lussu was engaged in fresh talks. These began with an Englishman who had joined SOE a few weeks before. His name was Cecil Roseberry, and he was the newly appointed head of its tiny Italian desk in London. His arrival marked a watershed in SOE's approach to tackling Italy.

Colleagues would remember Roseberry as 'very intelligent', 'a real gentleman', and 'short, dark and earnest'.[16] One who saw him around the London office recalled 'a very dapper man' in 'a very neat grey suit' who 'loved what he was doing'.[17] Born at Shoeburyness on the Essex coast in December 1891, he was the second son of a Durham-born Royal Artillery quartermaster sergeant who had married the daughter of an Essex carpenter. Despite these relatively humble origins, Roseberry had gone up to St John's College, Cambridge, in 1911 to study natural sciences, though owing to troubles at home he came down without a degree and headed instead for the Continent to learn languages and business.

For much of the First World War he had been British vice-consul at Narvik. After the war he had returned to London and spent the best part of twenty years employed as a merchant for Indian firms. Latterly he had spent a year in Norway, Switzerland and Finland before returning to Britain in the summer of 1941, joining SOE, and taking on the Italian role in October. He replaced the Greek specialist Derrick Perkins, who had manned the joint Greek–Italian desk for the preceding six months.

A dedicated Italian desk (it was known in Baker Street as 'J Section') was soon up and running once again, and Roseberry was to remain at the helm in London until 1945. His duties would include preparing plans for Italian operations, seeking permission to carry out those plans, keeping senior officers abreast of what the section was doing, and coordinating London's anti-Italian efforts with those of its overseas offices in places like Lisbon, New York, Cairo, Malta and Berne. Conscientious, committed and empathetic, he was to earn the respect and friendship of even the most hard-bitten anti-Fascists, Lussu among them. They, in turn, would gradually help him to understand the scale of the difficulties standing in the way of fostering successful resistance in Italy. Most of them knew him simply as Major 'Alp'. The pseudonym had been his mother's maiden name. Impressing these Italians was no small achievement given that Roseberry had no Italian background and knew little of the language. When possible, he and the Italians conversed in French.

Roseberry used his first chats with Lussu to question him closely about what he wanted. 'I explained that I was neither competent nor authorised to discuss questions of higher politics nor to indicate the Government's attitude towards Italy,' Roseberry recorded afterwards. 'I warned him that large sections of the people of this and associated countries regarded Italy as a nation guilty of the worst treachery and deserving of no consideration, and that we should win the war whether Italy continued to fight under fascism till the end or not.' Lussu, in response, 'appeared convinced that we shall win, but is equally convinced that his plan, if it succeeds, will shorten the war'. Lussu also explained that he saw no chance of successfully restoring Italians' 'pride' and preparing them 'for the sacrifice which a revolution entails' unless, in return for their help in shortening the war, their country emerged 'with at least the position she held before fascism usurped control'.

I asked [Lussu] if this meant specific assurances regarding such geographical questions as East Africa, Cyrenaica, the Dodecanese, Trieste and Fiume. He replied that he, and thousands who thought as he, regarded all extra-metropolitan Italy as a liability and a liability which they would happily dispense with ... But for the security of peace any cession of territory should be made by Italy ... He must at all costs avoid any implication that he, before setting out on his mission, has (without any authority or mandate) 'agreed' to such cessions. It would at once be inferred that in return for British support, he had sold 'the Empire'.

Roseberry was impressed by Lussu's 'sincerity, his earnestness, his balance and apparent lack of personal ambition'. He felt, too, that Lussu's plans had great potential and that 'somebody of authority' should speak to him at a very early date. 'I am aware of the undesirability if not of the impossibility of giving any geographical undertakings,' Roseberry added when reporting their discussions, 'but it is surely within our competence to give him the measure of confidence in our goodwill towards a "free Italy" which he needs before embarking on an enterprise in which he risks the life of himself and his wife and civil war in his own country.'[18]

It was decided that Gladwyn Jebb, Dalton's right-hand man on SOE matters, should talk to Lussu over dinner at London's Travellers Club. It might have seemed a suitable venue. Housed on Pall Mall in purpose-built premises inspired, it is said, by Raphael's Palazzo Pandolfini in Florence, the Travellers had been founded as a meeting-place for gentlemen travellers, their foreign guests, and visiting diplomats. Jebb, meanwhile, had served for four years in the British Embassy in Rome. Yet his meeting with Lussu on the evening of 9 February went disastrously. When Jebb cut short the dinner to return to the office for a ten o'clock meeting with Dalton, Lussu interpreted his departure as a tactical escape and began to wonder if he should even be bothering with his plan. Next day Lussu told Roseberry that he had 'spent a delightful evening with a charming, intelligent and sympathetic gentleman' but, when they reached the stage where Lussu expected the conversation would turn to 'serious issues', Jebb had left to return to his 'duties'. Lussu had concluded that his host had been instructed to be 'nice' to him 'but not to touch on questions of political import'.[19] Jebb, for his part, disclosed afterwards to Dalton his own dim view of Lussu. 'I felt far from confident that he would make a successful revolutionary,' Jebb wrote of him. 'He is an enthusiast who regards persons and things with the eye of faith rather than with the perhaps less pleasing regard of the practical politician.' Jebb added, vaguely, that he sensed 'rather instinctively' that Lussu, if he ever made it to Sardinia, would have difficulties with his wireless set or fail to take even elementary security precautions.[20]

Roseberry was not pleased about this. '[Lussu] is an earnest, intelligent and bold man and his project offers possibilities which we would do wrong to miss.'[21] Next to see him, it had been hoped, would be the minister. But after reading Jebb's report of what transpired at the Travellers, Dalton reacted violently. 'This man is a source of increasing embarrassment,' he minuted of Lussu. 'The sooner he goes away the better. He should not see any minister. It does not even seem that he is likely to do his job well in Sardinia.'[22] Dalton's outburst so jars with his earlier praise of Lussu's ideas that it may have had more to do with other matters on his mind, not least a concern for his job. Dalton had a taut relationship with the Foreign Secretary, Anthony Eden, whom he was due to see the next day, and it is likely that Churchill moved to appease

Eden and another enemy of Dalton's, Brendan Bracken, when, a little later, a Cabinet reshuffle saw Dalton moved to the Board of Trade. Roundell Palmer, 3rd Earl of Selborne, replaced him as Minister of Economic Warfare and SOE's boss.

At SOE headquarters, however, Roseberry was not the only officer to be dismayed at the lack of enthusiasm forthcoming for Lussu and his plan. Its shrewd and dynamic Director of Operations, Brigadier Colin Gubbins, was determined, too, to get things moving. With Roseberry present, Gubbins met Lussu in a London flat on the afternoon of 12 February, three days after the disastrous Travellers Club dinner. Gubbins's opening gambit was to tell Lussu that he quite agreed that the success of his project required assurance over Italy's pre-1922 borders. Roseberry noted that this 'forthright' statement 'almost stunned' Lussu. Then Gubbins followed it up with a lie. He said that while it was 'difficult, if not impossible, for a politician or statesman to give an undertaking at this stage,' he could 'safely assure' Lussu that a suitable statement could be secured once Lussu's preparations seemed complete and his chances of success appeared reasonable.[23] Gubbins added, more honestly, that he would look into recruiting suitable Sardinian prisoners of war from camps in India for Lussu's liberation force and find some captured Italian weapons and ammunition with which to arm them; he would also arrange for Lussu to visit the United States to secure the support of his anti-Fascist friends there.

Lussu was delighted. He accepted Gubbins's assurances and agreed to go into the details of his plan. It was also agreed that Joyce Lussu should be taught to use codes and secret inks, operate a wireless set, print clandestine pamphlets and shoot. And all of this was apparently down to Colin Gubbins's brazen, and perhaps callous, bluff. 'I am all for getting [Lussu] down to work,' Gladwyn Jebb remarked when he heard about the meeting, 'but I must point out that the assurances given are completely bogus, & that, even if [Lussu]'s "preparations are complete & the prospects of success appear reasonable", they will not in fact be forthcoming, at any rate from H.M.G.' It seemed to Jebb 'quite possible' that Lussu would 'throw up [sic] the sponge' when confronted with that fact.[24] 'Of course the undertaking is quite bogus!' Dalton wrote in one of his last remarks as SOE's minister. 'Let us hope that [Lussu] will become so red hot, as the time gets ripe, that he won't ask for the guarantees.'[25]

⊙

Lussu left Liverpool for New York on 24 February. He sailed on the SS *Jamaica*, a civilian passenger ship, travelling with a forged passport in the name of Myer Grienspan and masquerading as an author, a Toulouse-born Frenchman, who would be visiting publishing firms. 'Please meet him and arrange all possible facilities,' Baker Street instructed their New York office. 'He speaks no English only French and Italian. Person contacting him should say *Je viens de la part de Monsieur le Commandant a Londres* . . . You are authorised to place one thousand repeat one thousand dollars at his disposal.'[26]

Lussu stayed in the United States for two months. Among the Italian exiles and émigrés with whom he spoke were his old friends from Paris, Alberto Cianca and Alberto Tarchiani. Another was Dino Giacobbe, a Sardinian now living in Boston, Massachusetts. A decorated First World War veteran who had commanded a Republican unit in Spain, Giacobbe was the man whom Lussu had in mind to raise and command the force of Sardinian volunteers he hoped would land on the island when the time was right. On the eve of his departure, SOE officers in New York told London that Lussu seemed 'very satisfied' with his time over there. The only alarm had been when 'he was harassed in a ridiculous Phillips Oppenheim manner at the dead of night by certain over zealous employees of a United States office who were abusing their confidential knowledge of his presence in this country'.[27] Sailing on the SS *Sarpedon*, a British cargo liner, and pretending to the necessary authorities that he had started his journey in Sydney, 'Myer Grienspan' returned to Liverpool on 27 April.

Back in London, Lussu told Roseberry that talks in the United States had only strengthened his opinion that without an assurance that Italy would emerge 'stronger, with more friends and with better prospects of recovery' than if it continued to fight under Fascism, 'any movement launched against the Italian Government would be branded as treachery and the instigators as traitors'. Once again Roseberry advanced Lussu's case to be given a chance to speak with someone 'of real political significance'.[28]

This time the plea received the backing of Sir Charles Hambro, who, in April, had taken over as SOE's chief from a now sick and over-worked Frank Nelson.[29] There was 'little doubt' that Lussu was 'a leader of considerable prestige,' Hambro told the new minister, Lord Selborne. 'He is perfectly honest and so far has never let us down. I think when you meet him you will realise that he is a big man.'[30] More meetings followed. This time Lussu saw Selborne as well as two Cabinet Ministers, Clement Attlee and Stafford Cripps, and the Leader of the Opposition, Arthur Greenwood.

Then the Foreign Office intervened. A secret Whitehall agreement had recently laid down in black and white that, whenever SOE contacted groups or individuals capable of exerting political influence, the views of the Foreign Office had to be sought and its prescribed line followed. In this instance, those views were so strongly against granting Lussu's wish for a declaration that all discussions were brought to an end. 'Any such declaration would run counter to the very definite line we have been taking with the Russians and with the Americans on the question of post-war frontiers,' SOE was told, 'and would at once bring down on our heads demands that similar statements should be made in the interests of the Allied Governments, more especially Czechoslovakia, Yugoslavia and Greece.'[31]

Lussu's project was shelved. By now he had sensed anyway that no declaration was likely any time soon and had told SOE that it was time for him and Joyce to leave for France without one. Each week of waiting, he said, meant lost opportunities before autumn storms made it difficult to get to Sardinia and Corsica by sea. 'Everything is suspended,' he wrote unhappily to his friends in America in another letter opened and read by SOE:

The War Office [he meant SOE] has supported me with all its authority and could not have done more than it has. Our political problem has been put to and discussed with the highest authorities . . . The reply was as follows: the Italian problem will be re-examined in full later . . . [But] without political agreement I should have found myself faced with a mass of difficulties.[32]

Cecil Roseberry would argue to the end that the British should and could have afforded Lussu greater assurance about Italy's future: 'although it is possible that the declaration might have been so vague as to have had no influence on his decision, it was surely wrong not to put it to the test.'[33] Yet it is hard to see how any declaration could have been acceptable to both Lussu and the Foreign Office. Lussu had rejected the Atlantic Charter, saying something more explicit was essential. The Foreign Office, however, was never likely to have supported a more expansive statement particular to Italy. As Gladwyn Jebb remarked when spotting the bogus nature of Colin Gubbins's assurances that, when the time was ripe, an acceptable statement would be forth-coming: 'the only foreseeable circumstances' in which such a declaration was likely 'would be when we were in the process of losing the war, and required the assistance of Italian insurgents more than those of Yugoslavia or even those of France, and were under no obligation to consult our American, to say nothing of our Russian, Allies'.[34]

Before the Lussus left London to return covertly to France, they agreed to keep in contact and were issued with forged identity papers and a cover story that they were 'a retired *homme de lettres* and his wife'.[35] 'He is still prepared and willing to collaborate with us to a limited but useful degree,' Roseberry wrote of Lussu,

and I am happy to say that his personal chagrin at the collapse of his hopes for closer collaboration has not affected his cordial regard for this organisation . . . I should set on record as a testimony to his strict regard for what he regards as moral rectitude that, having failed to receive the political assurance without which he considered full collaboration impossible, he has repaid every penny advanced by us in Lisbon, New York and London for his maintenance.[36]

Since Joyce Lussu was now wireless-trained, SOE also undertook to smuggle a set concealed in a suitcase to a contact in Marseilles for her future use. 'Exceptionally hard working and industrious,' one of her training reports had read. 'She is very determined, backed by a fanatical dislike of Fascism.'[37] In July 1942 the Lussus were taken by flying boat to Gibraltar. They left for the south of France a week later, covering the final miles aboard a little Polish-crewed felucca called *Seawolf*. Early on the morning of 18 July, the couple crept quietly ashore at Port Miou, a steep-sided anchorage fifteen minutes' walk from Cassis.

At the end of the war, the anonymous author of an in-house SOE history of its Italian work would state that Lussu's plan for a Sardinian revolt, had it received the required support, could have shortened the war against Italy by nine months.[38] Given that Lussu's preliminary chats in Lisbon, London, and the United States were as far as that plan ever went, this was an ambitious claim. No evidence was produced to back it up. There was no explanation for why nine months was the chosen estimate as opposed to twelve, for instance, or one (probably it had something to do with the fact that Allied fortunes in the Mediterranean began to recover in late 1942). In reality, it is highly unlikely that Lussu could ever have primed Sardinia for revolt.

There were many reasons why a rising on the island might have been hard to get off the ground. Lussu claimed that a Sardinian insurrection was the best way to inspire rebellions on the mainland: the island, he liked to point out, had been a cradle of revolt after the French Revolution and the last part of Italy to be conquered by Fascism. At least one of Lussu's trusted confidants, Dino Giacobbe, the old soldier whom Lussu wanted to command his force of Sardinian volunteers, was much less confident that the island offered such rich possibilities, at least while the Axis remained dominant. 'What will the Sardinians do?' Giacobbe wrote to Lussu in October 1941.

I will tell you at once what they will do; they will stand and watch ... I advise you to save the time and danger. So long as things go so unhappily for the cause of democracy (or rather for the cause of the gold standard) you will not find in Sardinia more than the usual fifty fanatics ready to do something serious for the sacred cause ... And anyway, how will the Sardinians welcome the English? With dignified reserve so long as things go indifferently for them.

Reading Giacobbe's letter, SOE observed that he was 'a red hot communist'.[39] It also agreed with him. The arrival in North Africa of Rommel's battle-hardened Afrikakorps had rapidly strengthened the Axis grip on the Mediterranean. Elsewhere Hitler's U-boats were causing havoc in the Atlantic, the Soviet Union was coping badly after being invaded by Germany in June 1941, and the Japanese would soon appear to have the upper hand in the Far East. Only in late 1942, after the British victory at El Alamein and Allied landings in Northwest Africa, would the war in the Mediterranean turn decisively in the Allies' favour. 'Surely no popular uprising or open dissention in Italy is possible as long as the Italians think the Germans are in the stronger position,' one officer remarked when he read Lussu's plan; 'the Italians have not the reputation of forsaking the strong side for the weaker.'[40]

Others privy to his plan wondered if Lussu was really the right sort of man to garner enough support. 'Lussu, in view of his antecedents, could obviously try to start some revolutionary movement by appealing to the "left",' Gladwyn Jebb thought. 'At the same time a great proportion of the population of Sardinia is Catholic and conservative.'[41] Jebb was not alone in questioning whether Lussu's 'sentimental Marxism' – as his old colleague Alberto Tarchiani described his politics – was really suited to winning over the Italian population.[42] 'Emilio does not think of other than the proletariat of workmen and peasants,' Tarchiani would write of him in 1944. '[T]he immense number of small bourgeois, who languish, and of the medium bourgeois, who suffer, and are becoming poor, do not interest him, although they are the centre of Italian life, and are those who will express political will, and will have the maximum influence on the so-called proletariat. Emilio wishes to proletariarise [sic] everybody.'[43]

There were other problems, too. In May 1942, before the idea was shelved, SOE concluded that getting Lussu into France and landing agents and stores on Corsica seemed feasible, while weapons for his rebels appeared to be available in Egypt. But it also knew that Allied forces in the Mediterranean were over-stretched and on the back foot and that the prospect of transporting arms and a body of men to Sardinia looked remote. As for his liberation force of Sardinian volunteers, SOE secured permission to recruit and train a party of fifty and began scouring prison stockades and internment camps as far away as India, but in the end no one suitable was found and no force was ever formed. All the old reluctance and apathy was encountered, plus a new attitude in India: 'Conditions most unfavourable,' London heard from its mission there, 'as prisoners enthusiastic at Japanese successes.'[44]

Stores, weapons and volunteers were as important to Lussu's plan as the principle of securing an Allied declaration about Italy's future borders. Perhaps his enthusiasm would have flagged had he been fully informed about these problems. As it was, they hardly featured during his talks in Lisbon and London because, to avoid discouraging him, the British chose not to mention them. 'Lussu was not told of these difficulties,' one officer recorded coolly at the end of the war, 'for it was considered that even if the rising were not successful it would still form a substantial contribution to SOE work.'[45]

Finally it should be noted that as Allied fortunes began to improve at the end of 1942, Lussu's collapsed. In October a coded letter reached Lisbon saying that he and his wife were safe in France and about to start work. In December came news that he was still in France but had made contact with sympathisers in Turin, Milan, Florence and Rome. He was in touch, too, with Sardinia. Corsica, however, was 'completely cut off'.[46] Days earlier, the Germans had occupied the southern half of France in response to Allied landings in Northwest Africa. It was a move that so tightened the Axis grip on French territory that it extinguished any chance of Lussu establishing himself in Corsica – his vital stepping-stone to Sardinia – as he had always proposed. Overtaken by events, he would not return to Sardinia before conventional Allied forces occupied the island in late 1943.

6

'More or less a suicide job'

In August 1942, a nine-man team of Britain's Special Boat Section, a uniformed specialist force of army commandos trained in coastal raiding, was flown from the Middle East to the battered and besieged island of Malta. On arrival they went immediately to an old limestone-bricked quarantine hospital on Manoel Island, in Valletta's northern harbour, where the Royal Navy had a submarine base. It was in this hospital, eighteen months earlier, that Fortunato Picchi and the rest of the Colossus party had spent their final night before dropping into Italy. And it was here, too, that the little SBS team began preparing for an urgent task. One of them was a 22-year-old officer in the Black Watch, Lieutenant Eric Newby. The opening pages of Newby's later memoir, *Love and War in the Apennines*, would recount the disastrous mission that followed.

At that moment, the Axis had a firm grip on the Mediterranean. Malta, fast being reduced to rubble by waves of enemy aircraft, remained a vital Allied outpost but was firmly on the defensive and running low on key resources, from food and fuel to medical supplies and anti-aircraft shells. Recently a plan had been approved in London to dispatch the largest possible convoy to restock Malta with supplies crucial to its survival, but the planners knew that the Axis would throw everything at the ships as they began to close on the island. One last-minute idea to distract the enemy's attention was to send a team of elite British soldiers to attack the enemy's airfields on nearby Sicily before the 'Pedestal' convoy came within range; tabled on 4 August, it was codenamed Operation 'Why Not'. By then the convoy was already steaming for the Mediterranean. Whatever was left of it was expected to reach the Sicilian Narrows – the ninety-mile strait between the island and the coast of Tunisia – around the night of 12–13 August.

The little commando team arrived in Malta in two groups on 6 and 8 August. Briefings followed. It was then, as Newby wrote later, that 'the bare, gruesome bones' of the plan were revealed. First, they would be shipped by submarine to Sicily's eastern coast. Then, having paddled ashore, they would penetrate the defences of a German airfield and plant explosives on as many as possible of the twin-engined Junkers 88 bombers that they should expect to find parked by the runway.

There would be no time for a preliminary reconnaissance. We had to land and go straight in and come out if we could. The beach was heavily defended and there was a lot of wire. It was not known if it was mined but it was thought highly probable. The whole thing sounded awful but at least it seemed important and worth doing. Irregular forces such as ours were not always employed in such ostensibly useful roles.[1]

Captain George 'Shrimp' Simpson, the commanding officer in Malta of the Royal Navy's 10th Submarine Flotilla, recorded that three airfields were considered as potential targets: two some distance inland and one, near Catania, a lot closer to the coast. The last was chosen after George Duncan, the young army captain in command of Newby's team, expressed a preference for it. 'It was suggested to him that Catania was likely to be a most efficiently guarded aerodrome,' Simpson noted, 'and its proximity to the shore and complete German control only enhanced the enemy's precautions. However his previous experience of German sentries had not impressed him whilst the importance of the aerodrome was an encouragement.'[2]

Newby makes no mention of it, and he was probably unaware of it, but SOE, in the shape of Major Atherton Hayhurst-France, helped his team prepare.[3] In charge of SOE's slim presence on Malta, Hayhurst-France issued Duncan and his men with maps and emergency lire. '[I]n spite of his preference [Duncan] was confident of success,' SOE observed once the briefings were done. 'He had about two miles to go [and] his target was on the nearest part of the aerodrome to his line of approach. None of the party spoke fluent German or Italian though [Duncan] had learned certain phrases.'[4]

On the morning of 9 August, with their weapons, explosives and 'Folbot' canoes, Duncan and his men boarded one of Simpson's submarines berthed in the waters lapping the old quarantine hospital. This was *Una*, a U-class submarine. Intended initially as an anti-submarine training aid for surface ships, U-class boats were small, fast at diving and hard to detect, and had proved well suited to Mediterranean work. In command of this one was 28-year-old Lieutenant Pat Norman. They sailed later that morning. On the evening of 11 August, just after ten, *Una* surfaced off Catania. Duncan's party climbed out and assembled on the casing. When the Folbots were launched, one was immediately swamped and three men had to be left in the submarine. They would be the lucky ones. *Una* last saw the remaining six, Duncan and Newby among them, paddling for the shore.

The plan required *Una* to return before dawn to re-embark Duncan's team, who, it was hoped, would have executed the raid, withdrawn to the beach and paddled back out to sea. Pat Norman kept to the plan and, at three o'clock, resurfaced and searched the dark for a torch-flashed 'S': the agreed signal that the men had made it and were ready to be picked up. There was no sign of anyone. Two nights later, having had to move offshore to recharge batteries, *Una* returned, resurfaced, and searched again. By then, reminded that *Triumph*, the same submarine that had been earmarked to pick up the Colossus party in 1941, had disappeared in the Aegean in January 1942 trying to rescue a party that turned out to have been captured two days before, 'Shrimp' Simpson had signalled Norman to abandon the pick-up as too hazardous. Simpson would record that, since the night was dark and calm, Norman chose to keep looking. Still there was no sign of Duncan's party. When he finally withdrew, 'Lieutenant Norman felt very sure that no person was awaiting recovery.'[5]

Norman was right. All six men had been caught. They had made it ashore, buried their canoes, cut their way through the thick barbed wire and made their way through the dunes and into the flat countryside beyond, but found the airfield impregnable. Shots were exchanged with an Italian patrol. Searchlights were switched on. Flares exploded in the night sky. On the retreat to the beach they lost one of their number when he stumbled into an Italian strongpoint in the dunes. The remaining five, aboard two canoes, one of which soon sank, paddled and swam out to sea but failed to pick out the submarine. Eric Newby spent hours treading water before a passing Sicilian fishing-boat pulled them aboard, took them into Catania and handed them over to the authorities. 'I remember lying among the freshly caught fish in the bottom of the boat,' Newby would recall,

discussing with the others the possibility of taking it over and forcing the fishermen to head for Malta . . . And if we had been in a war film made twenty years later this is what we undoubtedly would have done, but we had been in the water for nearly five hours and were very cold and could hardly stand.[6]

Newby would describe 'Why Not' as 'the worst possible kind of operation, one that had been hastily conceived by someone a long way from the target, and one which we had not had the opportunity to think out in detail for ourselves. I felt like one of those rather ludicrous, ill-briefed [German] agents who had been landed by night on Romney Marsh in the summer of 1940, all of whom had been captured and shot.'[7] He would remember, too, the strength of the coastal defences: wire entanglements twenty yards thick, stretching as far as the eye could see; blockhouses positioned every 150 yards. Even the crew of *Una* would report spotting shore patrols, 'noticed due to the enemy lighting cigarettes'.[8]

Another secret landing on Sicily took place two months later. At one o'clock in the afternoon of 12 October, with *Una* again berthed by the old hospital, two men in civilian clothes arrived and stepped aboard. An hour later, the submarine slipped its moorings and headed cautiously out to sea. It was a dangerous time to be sailing in daylight. After a few weeks of relative respite for the island, the enemy had suddenly renewed the bombing offensive with five raids on Malta the previous day, two during the night, and another three already that day. *Una*'s logbook records that by half-past three, barely ninety minutes into the journey, the submarine had been forced to dive twice to avoid two more.[9] Pat Norman's patrol report describes what happened next, when, on the evening of 14 October, *Una* arrived safely off Sicily once again:

2100. Surfaced in position 90° [from] Stazzo [and] 2.5 miles [from the shore]. Moon had set. Calm moderately dark night. Ideal conditions for a landing. Numerous lights to be seen throughout the towns and villages of the district. Very poor blackout.

2114. Having fixed position of submarine accurately, opened fore hatch, placed Folbot and landing party on casing. Closed [on] the coast at slow speed.

2128. Disembarked Folbot and party. No hitches occurred. Folbot last seen on correct course making good headway. Position of disembarkation 37 38.2N. 15 13E. approximately 2,000 yards [and] 100° from landing position.

2140. Started to withdraw to seaward slowly. Water was phosphorescent.[10]

The men paddling ashore this time were the two men dressed as civilians who had gone aboard *Una* at Malta. Later Norman added that they 'embarked and set out in a confident and orderly manner, and as *Una* slowly withdrew to seaward the shore was watched and it appeared that the landing had been undetected and entirely successful'.[11] One of the men was the first SOE-trained agent to set foot in Italy since Fortunato Picchi twenty months before. Recruited in Italian East Africa during a fresh sweep for volunteers in late 1941, he also had the distinction of having embarked on a mission just as dangerously ambitious as Operation 'Why Not'.

⊙

By the end of 1941, months had passed since Peter Fleming's dispiriting experiences among Italian prisoners in Egypt. In that time British and Commonwealth forces had captured almost all of East Africa. More prisoners had been taken. Tens of thousands of Italian civilians, too, were now in British hands, having been rounded up in the Italian colonies of Eritrea, Abyssinia and Somalia where they had gone to live and work. But with the wider conflict still going more or less disastrously for the Allies, few of these prisoners or internees seemed very pro-British. Even anti-Fascists among them found reasons to wonder about switching sides, after the occupying British authorities, finding themselves badly undermanned in Eritrea, decided to permit local Fascist administrators to remain in the saddle. This was not exactly 'a shining example of our intentions towards Fascism', as one SOE staff officer put it.[12]

Other difficulties met in the Middle East and Africa included finding the opportunity to recruit promising volunteers before the military shipped them off to camps in India and Britain. Also there was the ongoing problem posed by the fact that recruiting prisoners for warlike purposes was prohibited by international law. SOE knew that captured soldiers could be released for good conduct and subsequently recruited. It also knew that the protecting power, the neutral nation that monitored the treatment of prisoners, was legally bound to inform a soldier's government of his release, information that might seriously endanger the relatives in Italy of any ex-prisoner prepared to be an SOE agent. Eventually an unofficial but effective solution was found: when a good candidate was located, officers would make a 'clerical error' and simply 'forget' to notify the protecting power that he had been released.[13]

Despite these difficulties, men came forward, names were taken, and suitable volunteers began to be selected. The first twenty or so arrived in Cairo from East Africa in January 1942. Others, including ex-prisoners from POW camps, followed in later months. In all about seventy Italians found in the Middle East and Africa would pass through SOE's hands. In age they ranged from early twenties to mid-fifties. Some were communists. Some were socialists. Some were Jews. The majority were civilian internees, though many of these had seen recent military service. Some were soldiers who had deserted from Italian units during recent fighting. Several had experience of active anti-Fascist work in Abyssinia and Eritrea, printing underground pamphlets, for example, or assisting the liberating British and Commonwealth forces. One or two might best be described as adventurers, men driven by an appetite for excitement or self-enrichment.

Training came next at specialist SOE schools in Cairo, in Palestine, and on the shores of the Red Sea. Physical fitness was tested and improved. The men were instructed in unarmed combat and techniques of silent killing. They learned to handle various weapons and explosives and were taught to sabotage different targets, from factories to railway lines and locomotives. Some were taught to parachute. A few were trained in Morse and the use of wireless sets.

The haste with which many had been recruited told immediately, however. As they passed through the schools, most came to be seen as unsuitable for behind-the-lines work. Some were assessed as poorly suited temperamentally to the demands of what might await them. Some were motivated and mentally strong but insufficiently fit to cope with the physical training. Some turned out not to be keen at all. A few caused problems, especially as their training continued, the months began to pass, and they became bored, impatient and restless. One recruit asked one day for an interview. His name was Giuseppe Bucco. Born in Naples, he was an army doctor who had previously been in charge of a fever hospital in Addis Ababa and claimed to be a nephew of Carmine Senise, Arturo Bocchini's successor as chief of Mussolini's police. 'He told me that he had had enough of us,' recorded the SOE officer who spoke to him.

He explained: 'I cannot continue to live like this. It is doing me great harm mentally and physically. If I cannot be given work, or cannot be allowed to move freely in Egypt, then I must be given the opportunity to brutalise myself with drink and women. If I do not do this I will become neurasthenic.'

I asked: 'How much will be necessary for you to prevent such a happening?'

He replied: 'I will need Le. 100 a month, because I will wish to do it properly.'

I brought the discussion to an end by asking what would be his reaction if our roles were reversed and I was an Italian prisoner; and by informing him that I had never heard such a piece of brazen effrontery.[14]

Two recruits, who were discovered to be regular takers of cocaine and, when that was lacking, hashish, were re-interned when they were suspected of plotting to make a break for Eritrea. Others were found alternative employment. Some were loaned to MI6 or British field security units. One, a former aircraft mechanic, went to work in the garage of SOE's Cairo headquarters, while another, a First World War veteran in his fifties who had run a restaurant in Addis Ababa, cooked for the others while they trained.

Other recruits were assessed as better suited to the tasks that SOE had in mind. There was Domenici Baroncini, for example, a communist whose father had apparently been murdered by the Fascists, and his friend Luciano Tamoni. Both men were army conscripts in their early twenties. They had been serving together at Gondar in Abyssinia in 1941 when they had voluntarily gone over to the British lines, taking with them military plans and a machinegun. Then there was Guido De Benedetti. Educated, Jewish, and hailing from Turin, he was in his late twenties and had gone to work in Africa in 1938 to escape persecution at home. Six years later, in 1944, he would parachute back into German-occupied Italy to work with an SOE mission attached to local partisans.

Another was Giovanni Scudeller. Born in July 1914, he was a mechanic and firefighter from Verona who had gone out to Africa with the Italian Army in 1937. When SOE found him in 1941 he was in Addis Ababa, where he was employed as a civilian mechanic once again and involved with an anti-Fascist group. Scudeller was a big man, an ex-boxer, strong and athletic. One SOE observer assessed him as having 'a genuine loathing of the Italian political regime, but I do not think he has any very decided political views. He strikes me as loathing the war altogether ... He has a sound solid sort of character, is very good natured, smiling and amiable.'[15] Scudeller was another who would parachute into German-occupied northern Italy to work with Italian partisans. On the evening of 6 July 1944, during a nasty skirmish with German soldiers near the village of Rocca Cigliè in Cuneo, southeast of Turin, he was laying mines when one exploded prematurely and wounded him. The Germans reached him first and beat him to death with rifle butts.

Baroncini, Tamoni, De Benedetti and Scudeller were all deserters or internees. Among the POWs who volunteered and impressed was Franco Mola, an army medical officer in his early thirties. Captured at El Alamein, he would end up working in Cairo with Major Alexander Kennedy, a medical officer employed occasionally by SOE, who found him 'outstanding' and 'of the greatest assistance'. Aside from examining agents of all nation-alities due for dispatch to the field, Mola pressed hard to be allowed to 'do something positive as an anti-Fascist' and asked repeatedly to parachute into enemy territory. He did the training, Kennedy wrote of him, but never went, 'and I know that his disappointment was genuine'.[16] Another ex-prisoner was 23-year-old Leo Donati, a naval wireless operator captured at Addis Ababa in April 1941. Recruited in April 1943 from a POW camp in Kenya, he sailed through his wireless training and landed that autumn with an SOE team at Salerno, later doing good work as an instructor and interpreter at SOE training schools.

Then there was Giulio Koelman. Born in the port of Taranto in October 1908, he was a petty officer in the Italian Navy and, like Donati, a trained wireless operator. SOE found him in a POW camp in Nairobi in May 1943. That October, after the Armistice, he was infiltrated through the German lines in Italy and made his way to Rome to set up and work a wireless link between the Allies and Emilio Lussu, who had finally re-entered Italy and was living in the city covertly. In January 1944, Koelman moved north to Milan to work with senior members of the Italian resistance there. In August he was arrested in Genoa. Interned in northern Italy in the notorious Nazi concentration camp at Bolzano, a transit camp for prisoners headed for Mauthausen, Dachau, Auschwitz and similar destinations, he was sent on to Germany in January 1945. SOE never heard of him again.

In May 1943, SOE stopped searching Africa for Italians to recruit. The British authorities in the Middle East had called a halt to it, but SOE had outrun its local training facilities anyway and could not have coped with many more. Shipping them to Britain for training was an option but costly in time and resources, not least because the route went via South Africa. SOE tried it once. A party of five was sent back in early 1943 and it took two months to get them there. Their escort, an Italian-speaking corporal called Henry Boutigny, experienced another downside of the journey. On the troopship to Liverpool, one of his Italian charges, a thief by trade, stole Boutigny's money. The culprit finally confessed when he and Boutigny met again in Milan after the war. Even in Britain the group gave Boutigny problems, when they escaped their secure Surrey quarters to go dancing one night but ran into the military police.[17]

◉

Early in 1942, Baker Street directed that its Cairo office should do more than recruit Italians. Since the Middle East was the nearest point from which operations into Italy could be launched, Cairo, it was decided, should be responsible for planning operations into southern Italy and Sicily. When it hit home in Cairo that this would mean starting from scratch since London had no contacts or information to share, officers there were stunned. 'What were the British Embassy and the various British Secret Service organisations doing in Italy from 1922–1940???' wrote an 'appalled' Hugh Seton-Watson, the future historian, who was then working for SOE in Cairo. '[I]f the whole resources of the British Empire have failed to obtain any confidential information from Italy during the past 18 years, then God help us.'[18]

Orders were orders. Cairo began to do what it could to think up subversive schemes and ways of returning agents to Italian soil. But this, too, was to prove another problem-strewn affair. By 1942, SOE was sending agents into Western Europe with increasing regularity and comparative ease, dropping them by parachute, flying them in to landing strips, or putting them ashore by sea. Conditions in the Mediterranean were very different. The Royal Air Force and the Royal Navy had more pressing priorities, while Malta, identified early on as an excellent exit point for agents bound for Italy, the Balkans or North Africa, was soon being bombed so badly that the RAF temporarily withdrew its aircraft and the Navy sailed away its submarines. As a result, the schemes hammered out by Cairo were a strange and colourful lot, each fashioned and shaped by the quality of the slim resources to hand and the eternal conundrum of how to get men into the field.

One of Cairo's earliest ideas was to exploit the impending repatriation from British-conquered East Africa of tens of thousands of Italians who were being permitted to go home. In April 1942, to see what might be done, it sent a man down to Berbera, a dust-blown town in Somaliland on the southern shores of the Gulf of Aden. The man dispatched was Ernesto Ottolenghi, the ex-internee with the too-short trigger-finger whom SOE had considered 'too good a man to be wasted'. Dispatched by London to Cairo with a commission in the British Army and the new name of Ernest Ottley, he left for Berbera with instructions to search among the assembling Italians for suitable anti-Fascists who might be prepared, on going home, to engage in factory sabotage and shelter any agents sent in later. The repatriation scheme was limited to women, children, men over sixty, and sick, wounded, and non-combatant servicemen, so these orders were a little hopeful. Ottolenghi found just a couple who seemed to have any potential.

One of these was Ulisse La Terza. Thirty-four years old, with a toothbrush moustache and one eye fixed and staring, he was not a repatriate at all but a medical officer on the *Vulcania*, one of the liners sent out from Italy to bring the colonists back. Normally, he said, he lived in Rome and practised as a doctor in Perugia, specialising in radiology and physical therapy. He also claimed to be an ardent and well-connected anti-Fascist whose acquaintances included Mussolini's mistress (he did not specify which one) and that he might be able to rig up a clandestine wireless set in his surgery and find someone local to work it. 'Ambitious, daring, full of enthusiasm and venom', SOE wrote of him. 'Fond of the pleasures of life, particularly women ... Prepared to die.' He claimed to hate Fascism: the Fascists had sequestered his family's mines and property and he wanted 'a Free Italy'.[19] By the time the *Vulcania* sailed for Italy in late May, La Terza had promised to do what he could for the British. He left with a set of passwords to use if he ever made contact again. He also took with him half a torn lira note to produce later as a tally. SOE held on to the other half.

Six months later, another Italian repatriation ship, the *Duilio*, docked at Massawa, on the coast of Eritrea, to pick up another load of Italians bound for home. It had set sail from Italy and La Terza was on board. Amid the confusion of people getting on and off, Laurence Norris, an Intelligence Corps sergeant working undercover as a policeman, managed to get himself on to the ship by pretending to accompany a draft of repatriates. Norris spoke Italian by virtue of the fact that from 1936, after studying at the Royal College of Art, he had spent two years painting in Italy on a scholarship at the British School at Rome. Now, in a cabin that he had checked was free of hidden microphones, and after exchanging passwords and being shown half a torn lira note, he and La Terza managed to talk. Next day Norris prefaced his report of their conversation by remarking that the doctor's story 'sounds astounding and smacks of the melodrama of spy fiction . . . He has either betrayed us or is astonishingly clever – not to say lucky.'[20]

La Terza had explained that after arriving back in Italy aboard the *Vulcania* he had become a member of the OVRA, Mussolini's secret police, and was now on board the *Duilio* not as a doctor – his Red Cross position as the ship's radiologist was just a cover – but as an OVRA agent with various clandestine missions. One of these was to murder Sergeant Edmund Gross, another of the field security NCOs whom SOE was using to sift through potential recruits. A Hungarian-born Jew and former opera singer who had studied in Italy before the war, Gross had met, quizzed and briefed La Terza when he had arrived in East Africa the first time. La Terza now revealed that he had returned from Italy with a special poison with which to kill Gross if he saw him, together with instructions to bring back proof in the form of a poisoned wineglass bearing Gross's fingerprints. The poison was arsenic-based, Norris noted, which had 'a delayed action of about a week

... This he was supposed to administer to Sgt. Gross if he came on board.' La Terza also had instructions to obtain specimens of the latest British military identity cards and AB 64, the Soldier's Service and Pay Book. But the doctor's 'chief mission', Norris reported, was to get details of British minefields around Gibraltar, where the *Duilio* was due to stop after circling the African coast on its return journey before re-entering the Mediterranean, together with the departure dates and routes of British convoys. La Terza had then proposed to Norris that this particular mission could now be exploited in the Allies' favour. If the British could furnish him with some misleading information, he said, then Axis submarines could be 'lured into a trap'. To plant that information in a convincing manner, La Terza suggested that 'a bogus British traitor' should meet with him and an OVRA representative in Spain, in front of the largest church in La Línea, a town close to Gibraltar's border, at seven in the evening of 30 January 1943.[21]

SOE was not quite sure what to make of this. Was La Terza an unwilling enemy agent genuinely wishing to play a bizarre double game? Could it be an OVRA plot? 'The whole set up smells,' thought officers in London.[22] Cairo, however, felt that although La Terza's story sounded 'rather fantastic ... we are inclined to believe the man is genuine'.[23] They were encouraged in this belief when it was learned through naval channels that, when the *Duilio* left for Italy and stopped en route at Port Elizabeth, La Terza had alerted the shore authorities to the presence of eight escaped Italian prisoners who had been hidden aboard in East Africa. Although still suspicious, SOE invited its Gibraltar office to contact La Terza when the *Duilio* docked and set up the January rendezvous. La Terza was duly contacted and informed that the meeting at La Línea would be kept. It was the last that SOE would see of him. When the moment arrived, the British had a man waiting outside the church. Nobody else turned up and that was the end of that.

Another area that struck Cairo as worth exploring was the potential of one or two members of Giustizia e Libertà found among Egypt's Italian community. The most able seemed to be Paolo Vittorelli. A Jew born in Alexandria in 1915, he had been brought up and schooled in Egypt and had studied at the Sorbonne. He had met Carlo Rosselli in Paris and joined Giustizia e Libertà, which had sent him back to Egypt to raise funds among the Italians living there. Stranded in Egypt by Italy's entry into the war, he had immediately contacted the British and been put to work reading Italian newspapers, monitoring Italian radio broadcasts and penning anti-Italian propaganda. Vittorelli impressed Cairo. He was keen and he seemed to have contacts. Among the pre-war Giustizia e Libertà members whom he said he might be able to contact in Italy was Carlo Levi, whose recollections of *confino* in the mid-1930s would be published as *Christ Stopped at Eboli*. Others were Levi's mistress, Paola Olivetti, and a lawyer in Rome, Achille Corona, who would become a leading member of Italy's post-war Socialist Party. Cairo also liked the sound of Giustizia e Libertà, describing it to London as a movement 'with wide anti-Fascist ramifications before the war' and potentially 'of enormous value'.[24]

Reading Cairo's incoming messages, SOE officers in London were less positive. Experience and the testimonies of men like Emilio Lussu had suggested that Giustizia e Libertà was now 'completely broken up' in Italy and 'a movement which really no longer existed', Cairo was told.[25] 'We know several who belonged to it in the days when it was active and who share our view,' Cecil Roseberry added. 'There is no central direction and organisation for maintaining contact with people inside Italy . . . [W]e see no evidence that this group is re-organising itself either in Italy or anywhere outside.'[26] As for Vittorelli, Roseberry passed along Lussu's view that he was 'well meaning and intelligent but inexperienced . . . [Lussu's] opinion may be summed up in his own words "I would employ him to write an article but not to edit a newspaper".'[27]

Cairo made one attempt to see if any Giustizia e Libertà groups were still active in Italy. In the summer of 1942 and in the guise of a newspaper correspondent, Vittorelli's brother was dispatched to neutral Istanbul to gather intelligence and establish links with Italy. His mission did not last long as he was quickly expelled by the Turks ostensibly for being Jewish, though it seems that he may not have been the right choice for Turkey for other reasons as well. 'You ask for our recommendations concerning the type of man for the job,' SOE's Istanbul office, evidently irritated, told Cairo after fielding the young man's visit:

He should be: not too young, not a Jew, able to speak French and possibly English, have the necessary knowledge and experience to live up to the cover story he adopts, have some experience or instruction in underground work, be completely under the control of our organisation, be a good mixer and a good listener, and have the right ideas about punctuality. He should in addition be given a 'sound' passport which the Turks will respect.[28]

Cairo also tried to get a man into Italy via Istanbul. The key protagonist of this idea was an Italian businessman whom the war had stranded in Persia where he had gone to buy cotton. His name was Lauro Laurenti, he said, and he came to SOE's attention in February 1942 after approaching British officials in Tehran and offering his services as a committed anti-Fascist. A plan developed for SOE to help set him up in Istanbul from where, under his businessman's cover, he would make commercial trips to Italy. Everything seemed to start off well. Laurenti arrived in Istanbul in June and settled down to establishing his cover. In the autumn he left on his first trip to Italy. In November he returned with news that he had contacted Gioacchino Malavasi, an anti-Fascist Milanese lawyer with good Catholic and socialist contacts. Malavasi, Laurenti said, was keen on organising sabotage and subversion and might even be able to win the support of monarchists and the army, though he could do with some money to print clandestine newspapers and pamphlets and would welcome some explosives and other devices. Laurenti also claimed to be in touch with Italian Intelligence, who, he said, had mentioned the possibility of putting him in contact with one of their clandestine radio operators in Syria. Unable to corroborate any of this and always dubious about Laurenti's motives, SOE began to wonder if it should persevere with him. The problem solved itself. In December Laurenti left Istanbul for another visit to Italy, but his contact with SOE soon fell away and that was the end of that scheme, too.

Another plan, which involved one of SOE's recruits from East Africa, sought to take advantage of an official exchange of captured sick and wounded. The recruit that Cairo had in mind was Giovanni Capra, an Italian in his early thirties who had spent most of his life in France and much of his youth engaged in serious work for the French Communist Party, helping form cells in Alsace, Belgium and Luxembourg. Expelled from France in 1935 for communist activities, he had returned to Italy and promptly been conscripted into the Italian Army and sent to Abyssinia. Demobilised in 1937, he stayed in Addis Ababa, working as a hospital orderly and opening three small shops selling shoes, before being mobilised again in 1940 and put to work in a military hospital. Now, having been found in Abyssinia by SOE, he suggested that he might be able to get sent back to Italy as a nurse accompanying repatriated Italian wounded.

Cairo liked this idea. It liked the look of Capra too. 'This man is a Communist and an enthusiastic talker who would probably carry conviction among the skilled labourer type,' reads a study of him by Alexander Kennedy, Cairo's medical officer. 'He feels a little too intellectual for sabotage and that he would be most useful as a Fifth Columnist, for which I too consider he would be quite suitable . . . He is by nature an intriguer and, if he found employment in Italy, might work quite well for his employer, if sustained by the knowledge that he had a secondary purpose.' In the end, however, that scheme was abandoned when the prospects of an exchange receded and Capra declined to go home by riskier means. 'In spite of his experience of mental diseases,' Kennedy observed, 'he is not prepared to feign insanity himself.'[29] A year later he was released by SOE and settled down to a quiet life in Cairo, where he worked as a nurse, married, and set himself up as a chiropodist.

Another plan that Cairo considered was for a man to be sent to Switzerland to work into Italy from there. Again it was an idea tailored to the qualities of one of its East African recruits. This man was 29-year-old Edouard Tridondani. Born and brought up on the shores of Lake Geneva, he was 'really more Swiss than Italian', SOE felt.[30] He had also been orphaned from the age of five: his Italian father, a surveyor, had died in the First World War and his mother, who was Swiss, in 1918. After school in Montreux, Tridondani had studied architecture at the University of Lausanne before taking a job as an engineer in Montreux's Ford garage. Then his Italian nationality saw him conscripted into the Italian Army in 1934 and, the following year, sent out to Africa. He had been there ever since. Leaving the army in 1937, Tridondani had lived and worked in Khartoum and Alexandria before being put back into uniform in 1940 and attached to an anti-aircraft battery with which he fought against the British at Keren. SOE came across him when, after the Italian defeat in East Africa, he had left the army again and was working in Eritrea as a clerk in the new Asmara office of the British Overseas Airways Corporation. Noting Tridondani's 'unhappy childhood' and that he 'seemed to have become embittered with a life which has taken a different course from what he had planned', SOE came to see him as quietly impressive, secure and sound. 'Instead of settling down to the comfortable existence of architect in Switzerland, [he] was obliged to fight for a cause which is repugnant to his nature,' one officer wrote of him. 'I have the feeling that [he] is sincere when he states that his sole ambition is to do his share in the Allied cause.'[31]

Cairo's idea was to provide Tridondani with a real or faked Swiss passport that he could use to return to Switzerland. If a passport could not be secured, he would parachute into France and try to smuggle himself over the border. Then, once in Switzerland, he would 'go into the mountains' near the Italian frontier where he would set up a clandestine wireless link and attempt to get in touch with friendly contacts inside Italy.[32] Tridondani had said that he had good connections, including a friend in the wireless business and a wine-selling uncle who travelled between Switzerland and Italy, while he himself knew the frontier from mountaineering and skiing in the area before the war. Ultimately, however, this scheme, too, came to nothing. Cairo found it impossible to get him a real Swiss passport – it seems they even tried to buy one on the local black market – while the plan to drop him into France was quashed by SOE in London. 'One is always reluctant to decide not to use a willing and capable recruit,' Cecil Roseberry informed Cairo. 'A well disposed Swiss whose papers enabled him to live openly is always a welcome addition. But we do not believe that anybody can enter Switzerland and remain above ground with faked papers.'[33]

This was not the end of Tridondani's SOE career. Anxious not to waste him, Roseberry offered him to SOE's DF Section, which helped organise safe houses and escape lines. A job with DF, Roseberry thought, might make better use of his language skills, since French was his native tongue and his Italian was indifferent. Flown to Lagos and then shipped to England for further training, Tridondani lost his luggage en route and arrived 'very browned off with so much waiting about and only the few clothes he had bought in Freetown and very little money'. By now more than a year had passed since he had volunteered for SOE. In London he was asked if he was still willing to do clandestine work. 'I suggested he might have changed his mind after all these months,' recorded the man who asked the question. 'To which he replied he had waited fifteen months already and he wasn't changing his mind now.'[34]

After being commissioned as a British Army officer and receiving the *nom de guerre* of Pierre Dareme, Tridondani parachuted twice into southern France on missions for DF. His first mission saw him successfully test a new escape line to the Pyrenees and return, safe and sound, to Britain. On his second mission he was caught. SOE heard later that he had been arrested at a bus stop in Perpignan in April 1944 when his self-forged identity card failed to pass muster. It never learned what happened to him after that. His date of arrest came to be recorded as his date of death and his *nom de guerre* – not his real name – is carved into a panel on Surrey's Brookwood Memorial, which commemorates missing British personnel from the Second World War. But in 2012, research for this book found that Tridondani appears to have been put aboard a prison-train leaving the French deportation camp at Compiègne for Germany in May 1944. German documents were then located, showing that he had ended up in a concentration camp east of Hannover. This was Watenstedt, a satellite of a larger camp at Neuengamme. These documents also led to a grave. For close to seventy years, Edouard Tridondani has been buried in a marked but misnamed plot in the cemetery of Jammertal in Salzgitter-Lebenstedt. He had died in Watenstedt of 'heart weakness' – surely the result of conditions in the camp – on 4 March 1945.[35]

Yet another idea with which Cairo toyed in 1942 was the preparation of two- and three-man teams for inserting into Italian territory by submarine. These teams would be made up of the pick of its East African recruits. Cairo was keen and had reached the point of pencilling in names when, from London, Cecil Roseberry intervened. He was worried that there was a danger of Cairo launching 'single-handed operations' simply 'in the hope of building up something' due to a belief that 'a start has to be made'.[36]

'The field of recruitment for Italy is narrower than ever and we must regard the material in hand as possibly irreplaceable,'

Roseberry told Cairo, warning them off the idea. 'Not only must we therefore not risk it on forlorn hopes, but it must be made available wherever it can be put to the greatest use.' He also doubted the wisdom of moving young men in teams around Italy. 'This is workable in occupied countries with a friendly population and a good deal of unemployment; but it is difficult to fit a team into the daily life of a country at war where every man is – or should be – fully employed or enlisted and where every man's hand is against the possible agent.'[37] In the SOE office in Cairo, this counsel hit home. The idea of teams faded away and none was ever dispatched. Officers confessed afterwards that they had felt 'certain risks had to be taken in order to get the wheel turning. In other words we were looking at the position as was the case in London in June 1940.'[38]

Unfortunately, there were other men hatching plots in Cairo who were less inclined to be cautious. In the summer of 1942, MI6 officers in the city asked SOE for the loan of an Italian wireless operator. They had an agent of their own who was ready to go into Sicily, they explained, but he lacked the skills necessary to work a wireless set. When word of the proposal was telegraphed to Baker Street, it was received with alarm. Learning that MI6 intended for the men to go ashore with no local contacts and no pre-arranged safe house, Roseberry recorded that it seemed 'more or less a suicide job'.[39] Then the MI6 plan 'was put forward as being one of high importance' and SOE 'reluctantly agreed' to help out. After that, MI6 in Cairo took charge of planning and mounting the operation and SOE 'was neither advised nor consulted as to the details'.[40] Available British documents do not reveal the purpose of the operation or why it was deemed so important at that moment. (If they survive, all MI6 documents relating to it – it was codenamed 'Washleather' – remain classified.) Possibly it was conceived as a way of gathering better intelligence about Sicily's airfields at a time when the 'Pedestal' convoy was poised to come within range of the island.

The SOE wireless operator who found himself suddenly earmarked for Sicily was 31-year-old Antonio Gallo. Born in the village of Sant'Elena, in Veneto, about thirty miles southwest of Venice, he had worked for a time in Vercelli, in a cotton mill, before being called up into the Italian Army in 1935 and sent out to East Africa. Demobilised as a sergeant in 1936 once the campaign was over, he had stayed on in Abyssinia and worked for a time for the National Bank before opening a garage and petrol station in Moggio, outside Addis Ababa, which he settled down to running with his brother, another de-mobbed ex-serviceman. In 1940, Gallo married a woman living in Verona: he was still in Africa at the time and the marriage took place by proxy. SOE found him in Addis Ababa at the end of 1941. Training followed, including instruction in demolitions, parachuting, and the use of a wireless set. By July 1942 he was earmarked to be the wireless operator in a three-man team with Domenico Baroncini and Luciano Tamoni, the two young communists who had deserted to the British while serving with the Italian Army at Gondar.

A letter handwritten that summer by Gallo survives among SOE's files, addressed to the British officer who he thought was in charge of him. Writing in Italian, Gallo says that he has some knowledge of Sicily and Sardinia but prefers the idea of working much further north: 'Ferrara, Rovigo, Padova, Treviso, Verona or the province of Vercelli in the Biellese'. He adds that a suitable profession for his future cover story might be that of storekeeper or accounting clerk. He also writes that he would prefer to work in a pair with Giovanni Scudeller, the ex-boxer from Verona, 'who seems to be an excellent element and has a similar personality to mine ... [H]e can contribute a lot if he is properly guided and understood, as he doesn't lack intelligence or courage. In addition to this, he is from my region, which makes us understand each other better.'[41]

For SOE and MI6 officers in Cairo, however, Gallo's preferences were less important than the simple fact that he was the only trained Italian-speaking wireless operator available for operations. Soon he was under the wing of the MI6 office in Cairo. He was also now teamed with the MI6 agent whom he was to accompany into Sicily. This man's name was Emilio Zappalà. A Sicilian born in Catania in June 1906, Zappalà had worked for MI6 in East Africa where, after the fall of Abyssinia, he had helped to identify Italians who might be suitable for British recruitment. One of these, a man who had known Zappalà in Addis Ababa since the late 1930s, would remember his friend as 'violently anti-Fascist'.[42]

Whatever the urgency may have been for Zappalà's mission that summer, he and Gallo would only begin their journey to Sicily at the beginning of October when they were flown from Cairo to Malta. They had also been issued with kit: a 9-millimetre Beretta pistol each and spare ammunition; a wireless set together with a novel, Umberto Fracchia's *Il perduto amore*, the pages of which were to be used for encoding and decoding wireless messages; two hand grenades; a range of fake identity cards; a 1:500,000 map of Sicily; two 'L' tablets, which were tiny capsules of lethal poison to be bitten and broken if they felt the need to kill themselves; a small number of diamonds; a large amount of Italian lire; dozens of gold coins; and a variety of other gold items suitable for exchanging or melting down, including a gold compass, two gold watches, a gold bracelet, a gold-plated pen, and two gold rings, one of them set with a sapphire. On the evening of 14 October, with most of these items crammed into a pair of suitcases, Gallo and Zappalà were the two men in civilian clothes who went ashore on eastern Sicily from Pat Norman's submarine, *Una*, two months after its earlier trip to land the 'Why Not' party. According to SOE files, the landing was made close to the home of Zappalà's sister.

⊙

The precise spot where Zappalà and Gallo landed lies between Stazzo and Pozzillo, a pair of little fishing villages north of

Catania, on the way to Taormina. As they closed on the coast, the two men spotted lights moving on the shore and Gallo apparently panicked, wanting to shout and give himself up. Zappalà calmed him. They pressed on. Once through the surf and on to the beach they hid the dinghy. Then they began to walk inland, heading directly west, aiming for Zappalà's old village of Santa Venerina. Below the eastern slopes of Mount Etna, midway between Catania and Taormina, Santa Venerina lies just to the west of today's main coastal road. The terrain between the sea and the village is mostly coastal plain.

With heavy suitcases to carry, the two agents made slow progress. A journey that they had expected to take two hours took more than four. '[O]nce in a while we saw workers who were going to work; they didn't pay attention to us and neither did we to them,' Gallo recalled:

Finally we arrived at the edge of Santa Venerina. As it was already broad daylight Zappalà talked to a woman who was coming from the village and told her in Sicilian dialect that we were smugglers. He asked if she knew of someone in the area with whom we could leave our suitcases for a few hours. The woman indicated a farmhouse not too far away . . . Zappalà followed her. He entered the house while I was waiting with the suitcases on the side of the road. The hospitality he asked for was turned down so he told me he was going to go to the village on his own to see his family and that he would be back in half an hour. Before he left he hid the two hand grenades in a hole close to me. I stayed in the area that he indicated and waited for him to return. He came back, in fact, and invited me to follow him in the direction of the village without saying anything else.

These were the pair's last seconds of freedom. 'After a few steps, the Marshal of the police, with three policemen and an officer in plain clothes, stopped us and put us under arrest.'[43]

The policemen, who apparently belonged to the Santa Venerina station, then gave the suitcases a cursory search, and, retracing the agents' steps, discovered the two buried hand grenades. Soon

Zappalà and Gallo found themselves in prison in Palermo and under the scrutiny of the Servizio Informazioni Militare (SIM). Set up in the 1920s, SIM was the Italian military intelligence service, a modern organisation whose activities ranged from running agents behind enemy lines to counter-espionage work. For some time its efficiency at the latter task had been greatly increased by the attachment of personnel from the Carabinieri Reali, the senior arm of the regular Italian Army that commonly acted as a military police force. Gallo's recollections, quoted above, come from his interrogation at the hands of SIM.

The SIM officer in charge of counter-espionage in Sicily in 1942 was Major Candeloro De Leo, a 46-year-old career officer in the Carabinieri who hailed from Reggio Calabria. Posted to SIM in 1935, De Leo had been working in Palermo since 1938 after three years of counter-espionage work in Genoa. British records from 1943 describe him as 'very active . . . evidently invested with considerable authority . . . a disciplinarian.'[44] According to one of his superiors, Colonel Mario Bertacchi, De Leo was 'particularly good at investigations and the compilation of irreproachable denunciations'.[45] De Leo took charge of the interrogation of Zappalà and Gallo and questioned both men closely, exploring their lives, their dealings with the British, their reasons for returning to Italy and the purpose of their mission.

Emilio Zappalà was already known to SIM, recorded in its files as having worked for British and French Intelligence in Africa. SIM had known since 1940 that Zappalà, 'after being in service for the [French] Deuxième Bureau in Djibouti, passed over to the [British] I.S. [Intelligence Service] in Aden, keeping the French passport that he obtained from the Deuxième Bureau under the fake name of Nerces Kenapian'. Since the summer of 1941 SIM had also known that he had been engaged in East Africa in 'open and permanent anti-national and anti-fascist activity at the service of the English'.[46]

While it is possible that De Leo confronted Zappalà with his past activities, it is certain that Zappalà admitted that the

British had sent him to Sicily to gather and report intelligence. His instructions, he said, were to set up a clandestine radio north of Catania, preferably in Messina, and an intelligence-gathering network across the rest of the island, extending it, if possible, to the mainland. The British had given him guidelines on what intelligence should be sought in Sicily. Detailed information was wanted about coastal defences, for example, down to the location of machineguns and mines; they wanted to know about airfields and supply dumps, local politics and morale, the identities of local commanders, German units on the island, and so on. The British had also told him that money and other material could be dropped by parachute if he requested it, and that he should expect to be put in touch with British agents in Milan and emissaries sent from Switzerland.

Zappalà gave De Leo a good deal of information. He admitted that he had assisted the British in recruiting anti-Fascists and gathering information in East Africa. He admitted, too, to working earlier for the French Deuxième Bureau in Djibouti. But he also insisted that he had done this work reluctantly – even engaging in various pro-Italian activities while employed by the British in Addis Ababa, like helping fellow Italians to escape from imprisonment – and that he had volunteered to go to Sicily with the simple aim of surrendering at the first opportunity. Indeed, he said, he had been imprisoned in East Africa for striking a British officer over a matter of honour, and had been offered his release on the condition that he agreed to participate in this mission to Sicily. 'He accepted this proposal in order to seek vengeance,' De Leo recorded of Zappalà's account; 'he thought that once Sicily was reached, he could have presented himself immediately to the Italian authorities in order to start working against English interests.'[47]

As for Antonio Gallo, he, too, disclosed the mission's instructions and tried to make out that he had volunteered to work for the British merely in the hope of getting back to Italy: 'The mirage

149

of returning home and joining my family induced me to say yes.'
As the days passed and the pressure mounted, he, too, began
to claim that he had always intended to give himself up at the
earliest possible moment. But in addition, he said, he had wanted
to deliver Zappalà to the Italians, as 'a dangerous spy' who had
been 'an acrimonious persecutor' of his compatriots in Africa.
Zappalà, Gallo added, had never said anything about wanting to
give himself up and reveal everything to the Italian authorities:

Instead, he told me in front of an English lieutenant that only if we
were arrested in Italy would we have to play ambiguously, making them
believe we had agreed to spy for the English but without any intention of
doing so . . . He added that if by chance we ran into one of the military
guards on the coast we would have to disobey their injunctions and, if
necessary, we would have to kill them.[48]

For De Leo, neither man was innocent. Zappalà's statement
that he had agreed to go to Sicily 'for the sole reason of presenting
himself to the Italian authorities and being at their disposition'
was 'simply ridiculous'. De Leo listed the reasons:

1) – he never informed Gallo [about that intention], not even after
having disembarked in Sicily . . .

2) – he prevented Gallo, when he was on the rubber dinghy close to the
coast, from calling the attention of the coastal defence . . .

3) – he sank the dinghy as soon as they had reached the coast for the
evident purpose of concealing the landing;

4) – he walked for many hours across an area in which there were many
military defence detachments without feeling the need to engage with
any of them;

5) – he hid the bombs;

6) – he talked about the supposed pretext only when he was caught by
the police in possession of the compromising material – he could not
logically have given any other version to justify his actions.

As for Gallo, De Leo considered that his actions 'from the moment of his enrollment to the moment of the arrest' were 'no different' from Zappalà's, even if, as both men had claimed, Gallo had wanted to attract the attention of troops ashore as they neared the coast.[49]

By late November 1942, Gallo and Zappalà were in prison in Rome and De Leo had submitted a long report, accompanied by evidence, to the Special Tribunal. De Leo's report recommended that the pair 'be charged with military espionage in wartime'.[50] Their case came up on 27 November. Guilty verdicts and death sentences were immediately handed down, and at dawn the following morning a firing squad of Fascist militia shot the two men in the back. The executions took place at the same spare and lonely spot within the walls of Forte Bravetta where, eighteen months earlier, Fortunato Picchi had died.

⊙

After Zappalà and Gallo had left for Sicily, all that SOE heard of them was when Rome announced six weeks later that they had been captured, tried and shot. The news was picked up and reported far and wide. 'TWO SPIES EXECUTED', declared *The Washington Post* the following day. 'Nov. 28 (AP) – The Rome radio tonight announced the execution at dawn of two men who were said to have landed from a British submarine on Sicily a month ago to commit sabotage and spy for the British.'[51] Other papers printed the names.[52] When he learned that the pair had been caught and killed, Sir Charles Hambro, SOE's chief, was not pleased. SOE's war diary – an ongoing document compiled at headquarters from incoming and outgoing messages, memos and reports – recorded that Hambro was 'very upset at what had occurred'. He had expressed concern at 'the quickness with which the SOE man had been sent off' and directed that, in future, 'no SOE personnel were to be loaned to an outside department for an operation unless SOE had previously approved the plans'.[53]

Summarising the known details of the mission's demise, the war diary's anonymous compiler added that 'of course C could not be accused of having been careless'.[54] 'C' stood for MI6. Available records fail to indicate whether that comment was meant ironically, but SOE had a history of friction with MI6 and its unhappiness about the handling of Antonio Gallo is clear. Later Cecil Roseberry would remark that while liaison with MI6 was made easier by the fact that he had worked for it in the field before joining SOE, he had a poor opinion of the heads of the relevant MI6 sections with whom he had dealt and of the quality of support that MI6 had provided. 'It was sheer murder to put agents into a hostile country without knowing the conditions they must fulfil in order to satisfy at least the unavoidable controls,' he wrote at one point, but MI6, 'on whom SOE was expected to depend for intelligence, produced nothing helpful and, on being reproached, replied that what they got out of Italy was intelligence required by the fighting services' and that 'nothing came their way' in the nature of 'the hundred and one things which, if unheeded, would at once lead to the exposure of an infiltree'.[55]

In its own efforts at penetrating Fascist Italy, MI6 was never very successful, experiencing similar frustrations to SOE when searching for contacts and recruits and attempting to gather an accurate picture of what was happening there. By December 1941, Naval Intelligence officers at the Admiralty were still recording that the value of information on Italy coming from MI6 was 'very poor indeed'.[56] Throughout 1942, as the authorised history of MI6 puts it, Italy continued to prove 'a very hard nut to crack'.[57] To judge from SOE files and Italian sources, two of MI6's agents were Amaury and Egon Zaccaria, brothers in their twenties, who were captured on 9 October 1942, hours after landing from a British submarine at a point just north of Naples. Caught in possession of money, forged documents and parts of a wireless set, they, too, tried to protest to their interrogators that they had had ulterior motives for volunteering to help the British: in their case, they claimed that they had wished to avoid internment. This statement was not believed, particularly after evidence came to light that they came from a family of known anti-Fascists. Tried in Rome by the Special Tribunal on 9 November, they were shot the following day at Forte Bravetta.[58]

MI6 does not emerge well from Italian reporting on the inter-rogations of men like Zappalà, Gallo, and the Zaccaria brothers. At best, its officers in Cairo seem to have been grossly overconfident in the ability of these agents to stay at liberty once on Italian soil. It is an image reinforced by the fate of another MI6 agent who had gone into Sicily prior to Zappalà and Gallo's arrival on the island.

Rossi, as both British and Italian sources refer to him, appears to have been a French-speaking Italian Jew from Syria whose family lived in Tunisia, and he had gone ashore on the Sicilian coast on 7 October 1941 and been captured immediately. For months afterwards, SIM officers in Sicily made him work his wireless set to give the British the impression that he remained free and active. MI6 fell for it, to the point where Rossi was sent fresh supplies of money and instructions by submarine and two new wireless sets dropped by parachute. Only in February 1943, when Rossi seems to have succeeded in saying in one of his messages that he was working under duress, did MI6 realise what was happening.[59]

Not long afterwards, according to the later testimony of an Italian employed in the deception, Rossi made a bid to escape. Apparently he was being moved by car when it stopped for a break and he bolted for a wood, whereupon the escorting Carabinieri shouted at him to stop, fired a warning volley, and shot him through the head. (Since SIM had discovered by then his attempt to warn the British, it may be wondered if his death was entirely accidental.) That Italian testimony, provided by a man recorded in British files only as 'Dr V.', also indicates the trouble that SIM had taken until that point to ensure that the double-cross went undetected. Hundreds of messages, Dr V. claimed, had been exchanged over the wireless set. Every British request for information was telegraphed to Rome, he said, so that the main office of SIM's counter-espionage section could draft suitable answers, while the two wireless sets dropped by parachute were used to set up in Sicily two fictional wireless stations supposedly run by Rossi. At the same time the Italians took care not to over-play their hand: '[T]he sending of material and money by [British] submarine was discouraged,' Dr V. recalled, 'so as not to expose how relatively easy it would be to land in this way on the Sicilian coast.' He also believed that the Italians had profited handsomely from funds sent in by the British: 'I remember one sum of a million lire.'[60] Other SIM sources would estimate the final figure at 'about 2,000,000 lire' and state that Candeloro De Leo, who had run the Rossi double-cross, eventually turned over that cash to the Servizio Informazione Difesa. Created by die-hard Fascists, the Servizio Informazione Difesa was a post-Armistice and pro-Mussolini equivalent of SIM. De Leo became its chief.[61]

Future research among SIM records may yet confirm that the Italians gained more from controlling Rossi than money and wireless sets. Although no available British records reveal a concrete link between Rossi and MI6's decision to dispatch Zappalà and Gallo, it is not impossible that the Italian authorities were alert to their imminent arrival. Dr V. recalled from the exchange of messages that the British had been wondering about sending in another wireless operator. Indeed, one German document that survives among released British files does seem to suggest that the Italians may have caught the pair as a consequence of the Rossi double-cross.

That document is a copy of a notebook discovered by British officers in an abandoned apartment in Naples after Allied forces liberated the city in October 1943. The apartment, on Via Manzoni, had recently been home to an officer of the Abwehr, Germany's military intelligence service, and the notebook found inside had belonged to a certain Hauptmann Wilhelm Meyer, a young Abwehr counter-intelligence officer stationed in Sicily from June 1942 until July 1943. One early set of entries in Meyer's notebook, all in German, relates to the interrogation of each member of George Duncan's 'Why Not' party. '*NEWPY* [sic], *George Eric, Leutnant, N.153984,*' reads one of them; '*ca. 8 Uhr festgenommen, schwimmend, 4½ Stund in Wasser. Verweigert zäh unter Ausfragen . . .*' ('Detained about 8 o'clock, swimming, after 4½ [hours] in water. Stubbornly refuses [to speak] under interrogation . . .') A few pages on there is an entry in Italian, signed by a senior Italian NCO, dated 2 November 1942:

For several days the radio that Dr De Leo mentioned has been working in Catania. This has allowed the capture near Messina of two agents of the [British] I.S. [Intelligence Service] with a radio, half a million [lire] and precious objects, landed from a submarine in the usual dinghy on the night of 14 [October] from Malta.[62]

7

'Rather a scatterbrained project'

At dawn on the morning of 23 January 1943, as Montgomery's Eighth Army pursued Rommel's mauled forces across North Africa in the wake of the Battle of El Alamein, frontline British troops reached Tripoli, the administrative hub of Italian North Africa. Riding in from the desert on the backs of tanks and trucks, the first soldiers to enter were a battalion of the Gordon Highlanders and a company of Seaforth Highlanders. There was no resistance. The enemy had abandoned the city and gone. In subsequent days, Tripoli was searched. Piles of Italian papers were recovered. Among these was a bag of correspondence between the Ministero dell'Africa Italiana, the Ministry of Italian Africa, and the Polizia dell'Africa Italiana, the Police of Italian Africa. Inside that bag was a report on the Italian interrogation of Emilio Zappalà, the MI6 agent captured in Sicily with SOE's Antonio Gallo.

More precisely, the report described an extraordinary story that Zappalà had told his interrogators that had nothing to do with his Sicily mission. Zappalà was recorded as having said that in Cairo in 1942 he had met an Italian whom he had first encountered a year earlier, in Addis Ababa. When they met again in Cairo, so Zappalà had apparently claimed, the man had been difficult to recognise owing to surgery he had had to his face. He had also told Zappalà that he was planning, with British backing, to return to Italy to kill Mussolini.

Loud allegations that the British plotted to assassinate Mussolini have been made in Italy for years. There are various versions of this claim. At the heart of all of them is the idea of British involvement in Mussolini's killing after Italian partisans captured him on the shores of Lake Como in April 1945. Days later, his bullet-riddled corpse was brought to Milan, together with the bodies of other Fascists and that of his mistress, Clara Petacci, and hung by its ankles upside down from the roof of the Esso petrol station in Piazzale Loreto. According to the conspiracy theories, British agents in northern Italy had persuaded the partisans to kill him.

Why might the British have wanted him dead? Because, according to those who propagate these claims, a living Mussolini would have been able to embarrass the British by telling of clandestine contacts he had had with them before and/or after Italy's entry into the war. Some have claimed these contacts occurred in 1940 when Churchill, they say, wished to persuade Italy to stay out of the conflict.[1] Others have claimed the contacts took place later, in 1944–5, after Fascism had fallen and when Mussolini, sprung from prison by German paratroops, remained at liberty in German-occupied northern Italy as leader of the Salò Republic, the Fascist and collaborationist Repubblica Sociale Italiana.[2] During that later period, so the theorising goes, the British wished to persuade Mussolini to encourage Hitler to end the war in the west and join the Western Allies in a struggle against the spread of Soviet communism. These dealings are alleged to have included British attempts to accord a conditional peace and offer bribes, if Mussolini agreed to play, in the form of territorial concessions.

Mussolini is also said to have had in his possession copies of secret correspondence with Churchill that confirmed these overtures. The British, the theorists claim, wanted to get their hands on this paperwork, too, lest publication destroy Churchill's reputation as an uncompromising war leader committed to the unconditional defeat of the Axis. It has even been claimed that Churchill was so anxious about it all that he later holidayed in the Italian Lakes in the hope of turning up the correspondence for himself.[3] SOE, meanwhile, has been claimed as responsible for encouraging the partisans to silence Mussolini permanently and for seeking to retrieve the incriminating papers.[4] One story has it that an SOE operative gunned down Clara Petacci so that any shared secrets would go to her grave, too.[5]

Awkwardly for those who advance these theories, no evidence has been produced to prove that the British took steps to kill Mussolini in 1945. Nor has anything come to light to prove that the clandestine communications between Churchill and Mussolini took place. Nor has any item of their alleged correspondence been produced. Nor is there any evidence for Churchill wishing to harness the support of Mussolini and Hitler for any upcoming struggle against communism. Nor are any of these stories supported by any serious study of the Second World War, of wartime British strategy, diplomacy and tactics, or of Churchill's career, leadership and decision-making. Indeed, the image of a fretting Churchill caring enough to go scratching around lakeside shores in northern Italy seems a fantastic misconception of the man's character. 'I am sure I never had any communication with Mussolini other than that already published in my book,' he wrote privately to his advisors when, after the war, Italian claims of his wartime correspondence with the *Duce* were brought to his attention, 'and I do not remember ever having written any letter to him in my life. I have seen this old story in the Italian Press. I really do not think it is worth while paying any attention to it. Surely we should fall back on the Duke of Wellington's answer – "Publish and be damned".'[6]

As for SOE's involvement in Mussolini's death in 1945, nothing in its files suggests that it planned, considered or performed such a role. Nor do there appear to be intriguing gaps in the documentary record to suggest that incriminating paperwork has been removed or redacted. Nor does any SOE operative fit the description of the British officer, tall, slim, fluent in Italian, born in Palermo and running a network of agents in Lombardy, who allegedly oversaw Mussolini's killing and shot dead Clara Petacci.

This is not to say that the British had no interest in seeing Mussolini dead in 1945. Nor is it impossible that documents may be unearthed one day to confirm that the British had clandestine contact with representatives of Mussolini's Repubblica Sociale Italiana in the months before the end of the war. Although hardly unbiased as sources, a number of his officials and lackeys claimed later that various secret meetings had taken place with British emissaries.[7] If contacts like these had really occurred, however, it would be surprising indeed to find that any promises, deals or offers made by the British were seriously meant and, for that matter, incapable of being easily, plausibly and publicly ignored, denied or belittled in the event of them coming to light.

SOE's real plan to assassinate Mussolini has remained virtually unknown until now. This is not the alleged plot from 1945. Rather, it is a documented, *bona fide*, plan conceived in Cairo in 1942. From the paperwork it is immediately apparent that the time, thought, and resources put into it were a fraction of those put into Operation Foxley, SOE's plan to assassinate Adolf Hitler, which was finally revealed to worldwide press interest in 1998. Yet this fact makes the Mussolini plan perhaps all the more remarkable, because, unlike Foxley, it actually received the green light. Indeed, a trained agent was even dispatched with instructions to carry out the killing, albeit with a fresh target in mind: Mussolini's odious henchman, Roberto Farinacci. What follows records the SOE scheme in as much detail as seems to survive.

'The bullets pass,' Mussolini once declared, 'Mussolini remains . . . I'm convinced I shall die in my bed when my work for the Greater Italy is done.' The fact that the bullets kept missing was not for any want of attempts to kill him. Mussolini survived duels in 1919 and 1920. In November 1925, in a hotel room at Rome's Albergo Dragoni, police arrested Tito Zaniboni, a First World War hero and former Socialist deputy, who, armed with a sniper's rifle, was waiting for Mussolini to address a crowd from the balcony of the Palazzo Chigi a hundred yards away. In September 1926, while Mussolini was being driven through Rome, an anarchist marble-cutter, Gino Lucetti, threw a bomb at him. Eight bystanders were injured; Mussolini was left unscathed. The following month in Bologna a shot was fired as he was leaving a ceremony to commemorate the fourth anniversary of the March on Rome. Enraged, the crowd rounded on fifteen-year-old Anteo Zamboni, who, likely as not, was innocent, and lynched him on the spot. 'Be calm!' Mussolini called out; 'Nothing can hurt me!' On that occasion it seems that the bullet actually hit him and might well have hurt him had he not been wearing a 'corselet' of bulletproof steel.[8]

Probably Mussolini's closest shave came in April 1926. He had just delivered a speech at Rome's Palazzo dei Conservatori, on the Capitoline Hill, to the Seventh International Congress of Surgeons. Standing in the crowd outside was a thin, grey, fifty-year-old woman called Violet Gibson. The daughter of an Anglo-Irish lord, the late Edward Gibson, 1st Baron Ashbourne, she had a history of mental illness and associated acts of violence. Three years earlier, to quote from case records of the Holloway Sanatorium, she had been 'sitting on the floor of the padded room, calling for people to kill. She said she had already nearly killed one [she had recently assaulted a fellow patient], and must have some more.'[9] After being discharged a little later she went to live in Rome, where she shot but failed to kill herself before resolving to shoot Mussolini. As he emerged from the Palazzo, she stepped forward, raised a revolver, and, from a distance of eight inches, fired. 'Fancy!' he was alleged to have said after the bullet nicked his nose. 'Fancy! A woman!'[10]

Zaniboni and Lucetti were sentenced to thirty years in prison. The Hon. Violet Gibson was removed to Britain and incarcerated for the rest of her life. The 1930s saw more plots and less consideration for the lives of would-be assassins. In 1931 and 1932, for example, two alleged anarchists, Michele Schirru and Angelo Sbardelotto, were caught separately in Rome with apparent designs on killing Mussolini. Brought before the Special Tribunal and sentenced to death, they were shot by firing squad: two of Forte Bravetta's early victims.

Rome claimed afterwards that Italian anti-Fascists living in London had had a hand in sponsoring both men. Although it took a war for the British Government to demonstrate any interest in killing Mussolini, it is likely that earlier scheming among Italian exiles and émigrés had indeed occurred on British soil. One probable plotter was Emidio Recchioni, a Soho businessman by then in his sixties. Recchioni had come to London in 1899 after three years in penal colonies for publishing an anarchist newspaper in Ancona; he had also been accused of plotting to kill one of Italy's Prime Ministers, Francesco Crispi. During the First World War he came to the attention of Special Branch for subscribing to anarchist newspapers and funds and trying to dissuade young Italians in London from returning home to fight: it was noted that he had hurled 'abominable language' at a pro-Allied march of Italians living in London, calling it 'a Brothel Keepers' Circus' among other choice epithets.[11] By the late 1920s he was running a successful delicatessen, King Bomba, at 37 Old Compton Street, and seemed to the Home Office to have calmed down enough to be granted naturalisation. Special Branch, however, was still warning that 'he is an intriguer of the first order . . . always willing to subsidise any movement which is out to create anarchy'.[12] In 1931 the police suspected him of supplying funds to Michele Schirru. The following year, Angelo Sbardelotto, after being apprehended in Rome, named Recchioni as the man who had given him the bombs, the loaded revolver, and the money that he had on him when he was caught. British police surveillance records of Recchioni's movements match exactly the timing of the alleged handover, outside a Paris hotel, of the bombs, gun and cash. (Sbardelotto was also said to have told his Italian interrogators that, prior to abandoning an earlier attempt on Mussolini, he had received in Paris two bombs and a revolver from Alberto Tarchiani, the mild-mannered ex-editor of the *Corriere della Sera* with whom SOE would later work.)

Living for a time in pre-war Britain was another exile suspected by the police of wanting Mussolini dead. This was Max Salvadori. In 1934 he was described by the Metropolitan Police as 'representative in this country of a secret Italian anti-Fascist organization known as "Giustizia e Libertà" (Justice and Liberty)' and as 'the person primarily responsible' for the 'surreptitious distribution in England' of an Italian leaflet 'containing an incitement to assassinate Signor Mussolini'.[13] Although Italian Fascist officials in London spread stories about Salvadori and did brief the British police, it is certainly the case that Giustizia e Libertà plotted to kill Mussolini.[14] Salvadori himself would write of various schemes considered during his days as an anti-Fascist activist in Rome:

Various people suggested that we should make our way through the sewers to the Palazzo Venezia, to lay a charge of high explosives. It was absurd to imagine that we could get enough explosives to do any serious damage to the building; however, we decided to look into this plan, and found that it had been anticipated. Twice daily, police patrolled the malodorous sewers under the centre of the city, and there were iron gates in them in the vicinity of Palazzo Venezia and all the main government buildings. Other optimists proposed driving round the city in an armoured car, until there was an opportunity to fire at the dictator – as if there were the faintest chance of penetrating the swarm of police cars and motor-cycles perpetually on guard whenever the *Padrone* (Master) was in the streets.

Another idea was a variation on the exploits of Lauro De Bosis, a gallant young activist who, in 1931, flew from Corsica to scatter anti-Fascist leaflets over Rome and perished on the way back. Salvadori remembered that one colleague in Italy 'suggested that some of us should buy tickets for an air flight, overpower the pilot, and take over the aircraft; we would then proceed to a prearranged spot where bombs would be loaded, and, on the return journey over Rome, these would be dropped on Palazzo Venezia'. Other friends had ideas of succeeding 'where Zaniboni had failed' and wanted to 'lie in wait with rifle or machinegun' at Gola del Furlo, a gorge in the Marche often visited by Mussolini, or on the road to Castel Porziano, a coastal estate near Ostia where he liked to spend his summers.[15]

For Salvadori, actions like these had their place in 'the cause of freedom' but their 'unpractical romanticism' had little appeal.[16] Indeed, experience of the difficulty of getting at Mussolini may explain why there is no trace anywhere in any SOE file of any recommendation by any of the grizzled anti-Fascists with which it was in touch, like Salvadori, Emilio Lussu or Alberto Tarchiani, that SOE should try to bump him off. Nor did any of these men have any involvement in the scheme that was eventually tabled. Responsible for coming up with that plan was one of the Italians whom SOE had recruited in East Africa in 1941. His name was Giovanni Di Giunta.

Giovanni Di Giunta told SOE that he had been born in Troina, a hilltop town in eastern Sicily, on 26 November 1908. He had been called up into the Italian artillery in 1935, he said, and been de-mobbed in October the following year with the rank of *sottotenente*, the equivalent of a British second lieutenant. He came to SOE's attention in East Africa in late 1941 through Luigi Mazzotta, a civilian tailor in Addis Ababa who also joined at that time. What Di Giunta had been doing since 1936 and why he was still in East Africa six years later are not recorded. SOE noted that he was an intelligent man who knew a little French. It considered that he might be suitable as a 'thug', or commando-type saboteur, for raids on enemy coasts. His character was described as 'mercenary'.[17]

In January 1942, not long after he had arrived in Egypt with the other recruits from East Africa, Di Giunta was loaned by SOE to the MI6 office in Cairo. Whatever it was that MI6 wished him to do, if anything, is not recorded either. What is apparent is that it was then, with the help of an Intelligence Corps sergeant attached to MI6's Middle East staff, that he hammered out the bones of a plan to kill Mussolini. That plan was dispatched to MI6 headquarters in London at the end of the month. Presumably because assassinations were not its line of work, MI6 then passed the plan to Baker Street, with Foreign Office approval, for SOE to consider. Baker Street passed it back to Cairo, telling its men there to speak to the local MI6 office and move the plan forward if they considered it feasible. Cairo replied that it would proceed with the project 'unless further study disclosed major difficulties'.[18] Not long afterwards, with the war going badly in the Western Desert and Rommel's Afrikakorps so close to Egypt that staff officers across Cairo were burning reams of paperwork, the MI6 men who were dealing with the scheme were pulled out and sent to Khartoum. From then on, the plan was in the hands of SOE.

A few details of the plan survive among SOE's papers. The proposed assassin was Di Giunta himself. As the first step towards getting back to Italy he would assume the guise of a captured Italian soldier and be installed in a camp of Italian prisoners somewhere in the Middle East. From there he would fake an escape. To add a layer of apparent authenticity, he would seek to flee in the company of an Italian officer who was genuinely pro-Fascist. Alone or with this officer, Di Giunta would then make for neutral Turkey where he would contact Italian officials who would arrange for his repatriation. Once back in Italy he would plan and mount the assassination alone. Poisoning, or a more violent form of death, probably on an occasion when Mussolini was speaking in public, seem to have been the methods suggested.

In London, Cecil Roseberry was left unconvinced by the plan's potential. Telling Colin Gubbins, the officer in charge of

Operations, that he considered it 'rather a scatterbrained project' that 'revealed a poverty of operational conception', Roseberry observed that 'Mussolini's food was not to be got at and certainly not through the activities of an unknown individual from outside. The *Duce* would certainly not be alive today if it were as simple as all that. Moreover he seldom spoke from a specially prepared rostrum and his appearances were not heralded in advance.'[19]

Officers in Baker Street also wondered whether Mussolini should even be assassinated at all. One with such doubts was Major Jimmy Pearson, head of London's Middle East and Mediterranean desk.[20] A down-to-earth officer respected by his seniors, Pearson, ruminating on Di Giunta's plan, warned that Mussolini, although 'discredited in the eyes of a portion of the population', was still 'idolised by large sections' and 'his removal would make him a martyr'. But Pearson did not recommend that the plan be abandoned entirely. Perhaps there was a better target: Roberto Farinacci, 'the sponsor of collaboration with Germany and the mainstay behind Mussolini'.[21]

While Farinacci's name may be unfamiliar to most people today, it was well known in the early 1940s. 'Swarthy, vituperative Roberto Farinacci' was 'Fascismo's hellion', read a contemporary article in *Time* magazine. Here was a man who 'ranted against the democracies, baited Israel and the Church [and] flayed Fascist weaklings'.[22] Born in 1892 in Isernia, a small town in the central Italian province of Molise, Farinacci had started his working life as an assistant telegraph operator on the Italian state railways. Drawn to politics during the First World War, in which he served first at the front and then as a propagandist, he was soon dedicating himself to a career of corruption and shameless self-advancement. In the Lombard city of Cremona he built a formidable power-base, styled himself '*ras*', an Abyssinian term for leader, and intimidated the population with gangs of thuggish followers. His rise towards the top was rapid. In 1921 he was one of the first Fascists elected to parliament. Four years later he became the party's general secretary. Only Mussolini had greater power.

It is debatable whether Farinacci was 'the mainstay behind Mussolini', as SOE believed, in 1942. His appointment as party secretary was the peak of his political career and it lasted barely a year. Aggressive, undisciplined, increasingly unpopular, Farinacci came to be seen as a liability more than an asset and was no driven ideologue, unless untrammelled self-interest counts as an ideology. 'The *ras* of Cremona', as one historian has written, 'was a man better understood as a rough and tumble boss than as a true believing fanatic. Farinacci did not so much strive to bring "mythical thought to power" as to enjoy the fleshpots available to those in authority and to win and retain them for himself, his family, friends and clients by whatever means necessary.' Compelled to resign as party secretary in 1926, he withdrew to his Cremona fiefdom and to the running of his private newspaper. Yet he remained 'the boss of his town and a fascist who mattered'.[23] And Mussolini, aware that Farinacci still had influence, ambition and value, kept him close, eyeing him warily and employing him carefully. In 1929, portraying him accurately as an odious thug in charge of other odious thugs, *Time* described Farinacci as 'the Castor Oil Man' of Fascism. 'Politicians who rashly opposed *Il Duce* were ambushed and forced to swallow a pint, a quart, even a sickening gallon of what Farinacci called his "golden nectar of nausea".'[24] In 1936, arriving in Abyssinia to associate himself with the new imperial spirit, he went fishing with grenades in a lake near Dessie and blew off one of his hands. Hailed on his return as a gallant and wounded hero and fitted with a new metal hand, he was reappointed to the Fascist Grand Council and soon proved an enthusiastic enforcer of Italy's new racial laws.

Regardless of whether he was ever 'Mussolini's spur', as SOE also called him,[25] it is a fact that Farinacci was one of the most outspoken and constant advocates of Italy's alliance with Germany. For good measure he accompanied this stance by pouring invective on the Jews. As the Nazis took power, he railed in his newspaper, *Il Regime Fascista*, about the 'Jewish international conspiracy', the 'Jewish Bolshevik leadership' and the 'Jewish financial octopus'. By 1934 he was writing: 'Anyone who declares himself in favour of Zionism has no right to hold public posts or lucrative employment in our country.' In 1936 his newspaper announced Fascist Italy's inflexible opposition to 'international Judaism'. By 1938 his paper was attacking Jews almost daily. Farinacci's opinions on such topics were not lost on the Germans.[26] 'He is exceptionally pleasant,' Goebbels wrote in his diary when Farinacci visited Berlin in October 1940, 'a real old fascist whom one cannot help but like.' He was 'a true supporter of the Axis' and a 'chip off the old block'.[27]

SOE liked the sound of killing Farinacci: 'his removal would be popular with all classes', while 'to remove Mussolini before Italy had suffered further defeat and while Farinacci was still powerful might easily result in the rallying of the Fascist Party and an increased German control'. It was felt, too, that Farinacci was 'more easily accessible . . . frequently to be found taking his aperitif at public bars'.[28] A decision was made: Cairo should ask Di Giunta if he would kill Farinacci. Cairo asked him. Di Giunta agreed to switch targets.

It was about now that Di Giunta was preparing to have surgery to his face. The available records do not state the reasons for this. Nor do they reveal what surgery was proposed or who suggested it. It is possible, however, that the procedure was recommended in order to disguise his features in preparation for his return to Italy. Although altering an agent's looks might sound the stuff of Hollywood films, several agents during the course of the war did receive 'permanent make-up', as SOE called it.[29] What is certain is that, in May 1942, Giovanni Di Giunta's face did go under the knife. 'Cairo cabled on the 16th,' London recorded; 'the individual was now undergoing a facial operation and would be ready for action in the middle of June.'[30]

By the middle of June the operation had indeed been done and officers in Cairo were beginning to worry that Di Giunta would become 'restless' if he were not unleashed soon. Almost six months had passed since he had come up with his plan, and Cairo told London that it felt it 'essential to start him on his journey as soon as possible'. It also advised Baker Street to 'definitely decide' whether the mission should proceed and added a final word of warning. Di Giunta had said that he would kill himself if caught, but 'if he were arrested and subjected to third degree methods' his silence could not be guaranteed. Therefore London 'must understand that there must be a risk of the agent confessing his British support'. Next day, on 18 June, London telegraphed Cairo its decision: 'go ahead'.[31]

Now the wheels began to turn. More steps were taken in Cairo to prepare Di Giunta for his mission. These included 'all pre-cautions concerning documents, etc.'[32] SOE also issued him with diamonds. Readily portable and easily hidden, precious stones were far less cumbersome than coins or wads of notes and SOE was not inexperienced in shifting wealth by this means. ('They would send me a little tin full of diamonds, cut diamonds,' recalled one officer who had been tasked with channelling funds from neutral Stockholm to the Danish resistance. 'I used to look at them occasionally, admire them.')[33]

By the beginning of August, now masquerading as an Italian prisoner-of-war and operating under the codename of 'Kit', Di Giunta was in Palestine and behind the wire of No. 321 POW Camp, somewhere off the main Jerusalem–Tel Aviv road. Few records of the camp survive. One document that does exist is its war diary and this shows that escape attempts were fairly common. In November 1942 alone there were five attempted breakouts involving a total of thirteen Italians, six of whom made it through the wire, while the following February a snap search uncovered a well-dug tunnel. 'This tunnel', wrote the camp's commander, an ageing infantry colonel called Eric 'Bingy' Bingham, 'started in an unused deep trench latrine, was approximately 3 to 4 yards below earth surface, approximately 21 yards long, [and] high and wide enough to allow any man to crawl through with ease.'[34] Whether the camp had been chosen for its leakiness is not recorded. What is apparent is that the Italians who broke out of it did not include Giovanni Di Giunta.

Not long after Di Giunta entered the camp, SOE learned from MI6 that on the eve of his faked incarceration he had met and spoken in Cairo with an Italian he had known in East Africa. During the course of that conversation Di Giunta had revealed the whole of his plan. The man to whom he told it, a fellow Sicilian, was Emilio Zappalà, the MI6 agent who would be sent into Sicily with Antonio Gallo a few weeks later. Zappalà had immediately reported Di Giunta's indiscretion to the MI6 office, adding his impression that Di Giunta was by no means settled on what action he would take when he eventually reached Italy. In fact, Zappalà reported, there was a definite implication that Di Giunta might try to double-cross the British. When this news was passed to SOE, the risks of unleashing him 'and the uncertainty of his good faith' were seen at once to be intolerable and Cairo decided to scrap the entire project.[35] On 3 October 1942, Di Giunta was discharged from No. 321 POW camp and returned to British care. A single clue remains as to what happened to him after that: SOE recorded that MI6 took charge of him.

⊙

When SOE's Cairo office had asked London to decide if Di Giunta should be dispatched to kill Roberto Farinacci, the green light had been given so quickly that it seems unlikely that much final discussion occurred over the plot's pros and cons. Perhaps, if anyone more senior had ever been invited to express a view, they had simply shared Roseberry's relaxed opinion that 'if Cairo were satisfied that the man had possibilities of perfecting such a job we ought to allow him to pursue it'.[36] Added to this may have been the consideration that SOE had little else in the pipeline in terms of anti-Italian plans. Certainly officers had accepted that they could do no more than embark him on his journey to Italy and provide some funds to pay his way. Everything else rested on Di Giunta's word that he was willing to have a go.

Leafing through the surviving records of Operation Foxley, SOE's plan to kill Adolf Hitler, it is hard not to be struck by the greater time and effort expended in considering alternative methods by which he might be killed, as well as the possible consequences. Initiated in London in the summer of 1944 by Colin Gubbins, who, by then, was SOE's chief, the planning for Foxley had continued until the following spring. It boiled down to two main ideas. One was to poison Hitler on his personal train, if poison could somehow be got into the train's supply of drinking and cooking water; the second was to kill him at a spot in or around the Berghof, his alpine retreat near Berchtesgaden in southern Bavaria. The Berghof idea became the favoured one.

A good deal of intelligence appears to have been collected about the Berghof. It ranged from Hitler's daily routines to the variety of passes used by his security detachments, the location of pickets, patrols, anti-aircraft guns and air-raid shelters and the thickness and height of surrounding fences. Some of this intelligence was very detailed. SOE's account of his personal habits, for instance, recorded that Hitler was a late riser, surfacing at about nine o'clock. After being shaved and groomed by a barber he walked to a teahouse for breakfast (milk and toast) from which he returned to the Berghof by motorcade. He might then consult with his personal doctor and in the afternoon meet carefully vetted visitors. If he did not have afternoon appointments elsewhere, he remained in the Berghof, where he had a late lunch (vegetables only, about four o'clock). Sometimes he invited the Goebbels and Bormann families to eat with him. After that he worked until ten in the evening, generally aided by a clerk or by Eva Braun. He ate supper very late, between one and half past one in the morning, and eventually went to bed at three but sometimes even later.

As thinking about the Berghof developed, SOE gave consideration to three methods of assassination. One was to send in snipers in German uniforms to pick him off with explosive bullets on his morning walk to the teahouse for breakfast; if that failed a back-up team would attack the teahouse using a bazooka or similar weapon. A second idea was to ambush Hitler's motorcade. The third was to drop an SAS battalion to overrun the place.

In the end, Operation Foxley was never approved. From the outset there had been debate among senior SOE staff officers in London as to the fundamental value of assassinating Hitler. Some felt that killing him would have a positive impact on the Allied war effort. Others argued more forcefully that keeping him alive would be wiser, since Hitler was making such a mess of German strategy and because removing him, or, more precisely, the revelation that the Allies had been responsible for killing him, might make him a martyr, with the effect of rallying the German people behind the surviving Nazi leadership, by creating a fresh 'stab in the back' myth, and making post-war reconstruction more difficult. There were also grave and realistic doubts in London about the chances of success. There were fundamental problems of logistics and secrecy, for example. Even the sniper operation would have needed to clear the formidable hurdle of infiltrating and moving a sizeable team around Bavaria undetected. Today it may also be noted that Foxley had been academic in any case, since the meeting in London at which Colin Gubbins instigated the planning took place on 28 June 1944. Hitler never returned to the Berghof after he left it for the final time, a fortnight later, on 14 July.

In the autumn of 1942, when Giovanni Di Giunta was recalled from his prison camp and his plan came to its ignominious end, Italy's Fascist regime had nearly ten months left to run and Mussolini and Farinacci over two and a half years to live: like Mussolini, Farinacci was destined to be killed in 1945 after his capture by Italian partisans. It is impossible of course to know what would have occurred had one or the other been assassinated while Italy was still at Nazi Germany's side. Perhaps Fascism would have fallen sooner. Perhaps, if Mussolini had been the victim, Farinacci would have replaced him. The backfiring of a failed assassination attempt might also be considered, given that the discovery of assassination plots in the twenties and thirties had allowed Fascism greatly to strengthen its grip on the country. All of this may be intriguing to think about: counter-factual history is a game of infinite permutations.

Equally it is impossible to know what Giovanni Di Giunta might have done and what could have resulted had his plan been left to run. It seems certain that mounting an assassination along the lines proposed would have faced enormous obstacles, ranging from the formidable problem of returning to Italy, to the difficulty of keeping his real identity secure, to the challenge of preparing an assassination attempt armed only with some forged paperwork and a few hidden diamonds. It is interesting, though, that SOE's chosen killer had declared himself willing to die in the attempt. Hitler himself had once said that 'not a soul could cope with an assassin who, for idealistic reasons, was prepared quite ruthlessly to hazard his own life in the execution of his object'.[37] Whether Di Giunta had been sincere when saying he was prepared to kill and be killed is quite another matter.

The remote hill town of Troina, in the Sicilian province of Enna, sits above rolling slopes in the island's eastern uplands. Its origins date back to Greek colonists more than 2,000 years ago. In the eleventh century Norman invaders made it their capital. It is Sicily's highest town and, when Allied forces invaded in the summer of 1943, it proved an ideal rearguard position for the German 15th Panzergrenadier Division. After several days' fierce fighting, Troina finally fell to American troops on 6 August.

Robert Capa, the war photographer, accompanied one of the first patrols to pick their way into its narrow, twisting streets. A series of famous images in *Life* magazine recorded the fighting and the damage. Today, documents in Troina that survived that fate add a little more detail to the picture of Giovanni Di Giunta found in British records.

Ledgers and index cards in the town archives confirm his date and place of birth. Born in Troina on 26 November 1908, Giovanni Michelino Di Giunta, to give him his full name, was the second son of Alfonso Di Giunta and Teresina Marianna Bartolo. In all, he had three brothers, Francesco, Alfredo and Armando, and a sister, Giuseppina.[38] In Troina the Di Giuntas are remembered as an established family of noble roots. At one time they had owned land and property. By the 1930s, it seems, that wealth was shrinking; but they remained among the four or five most prominent families in the town and still had a good-sized home on Via Napoli Bracconeri.

In 1929, so the town documents record, Giovanni Di Giunta was married to Maria Grazia Scorciapino. She had been born in Troina, too, though they were married in Turin.[39] She was also sixteen years older than him. In those days, marriages in Sicilian hill-towns of couples with sizeable age differences were not uncommon. Often such newlyweds were related: the inter-marrying of close relatives was an accepted method of keeping property and wealth within a family, although limited choice might mean that sprightly nieces and nephews could be paired with ageing uncles and aunts. It is unclear whether this was the case with Giovanni Di Giunta's marriage. Nor do documents shed light on why Di Giunta and his bride were married in Turin. They do reveal a son, born in 1932. They show, too, that Di Giunta was registered again as living in the town in 1936.[40]

In 2012, one man who had known the family in the 1930s remembered the young Giovanni Di Giunta as 'an adventurous type, very athletic, very keen on fitness'. He recalled Di Giunta competing among the town's young men to see who could lift and carry around the wrought-iron benches in the square. He also remembered him as a man who was not noticeably anti-Fascist and who 'liked to navigate by fantasy ... He wasn't somebody whose stories you necessarily believed.'[41] Records and local memories in Troina reveal, too, that, after leaving Sicily and his family in the late 1930s, Di Giunta never came back. The town documents list his fate as '*disperso in Africa*': 'missing in Africa'.[42]

8

'An ideal subversive organisation'

In March 1941, Jack Beevor, manning the SOE office in neutral Lisbon, had been instructed by London to contact Thomas McEnelly, the United States consul in Palermo, Sicily's capital, who was expected to be passing through on his way home. Beevor was to see if McEnelly might be persuaded to provide names and addresses of anti-Fascist Sicilians and information about Sicily's coastline. There is no record in SOE's files of Beevor having had any success. What is clear is that its interest in causing trouble on the island lasted. Also clear is that progress in that direction was painfully slow. Nine months later, ruminating on the possibility of fomenting dissent that might detach Sardinia and Sicily from Rome's control, a senior officer at SOE headquarters in London remarked that for Sicily 'we have not got even a Lussu, and our first object must be to find out if any person or organisation exists which could raise the necessary movement'.[1]

Writing in February 1942, Hugh Seton-Watson of SOE's Cairo office agreed. Careful groundwork, he argued, was vital. Sending into Sicily Italian ex-prisoners with wireless sets but without contacts seemed 'pointless'.[2] Not everyone was so cautious, as MI6 demonstrated later that year when it put Emilio Zappalà and Antonio Gallo ashore. For SOE, the pair's demise was a serious setback. MI6 had spoken of sharing the benefits once the agents were safely established; one hope had been that they might act as a suitable reception committee for further teams. As it was, their capture left SOE mourning the loss of its only trained and available Italian wireless operator and fearing it would take months to train another. Also the arrests did little to discourage the Italians and Germans from further strengthening Sicily's defences.

Nevertheless, SOE maintained its interest in Sicily and remained optimistic about what the island might offer. It was clearly a potential stepping-stone to any future invasion of Italy, while the possibilities of its physical and human terrain seemed encouraging. 'The whole of the island is mountainous or hilly, except for a few coastal plains and a hilly plateau in the North-West,' reads an assessment drawn up by the Cairo office in late 1942. 'Owing to its nature and small density of population the island could be suitable for guerrilla warfare.' The Sicilian people, the report went on, had a history of 'spasmodic struggles for independence' and seemed little interested in Fascism:

The Sicilian is by instinct Sicilian before anything else, and he likes to blame Italy for all his troubles and miseries. They like to believe that their land is extremely rich but that they cannot exploit it because the North fears their competition. They also believe that the heavy taxes they have to pay are for the benefit of other Italian regions. These grudges are quite common in other countries too (South and North of France for instance) but they take on a stronger aspect of reality in this case owing to the nature of the Sicilian . . .

The average Sicilian [still] thinks of himself as an Italian. He would like his island to enjoy a privileged position in Italy and not to be dictated [to] by Rome but he does not think in terms of an independent Sicily . . .

[However, t]here is no doubt that within Italy itself . . . the Sicilians have been the less loyal section of the population . . . [E]ven within Europe [there are] very few examples of a particular region being so consistently troublesome within its state . . . [T]here is a strong possibility that if this tendency is carefully and tactfully exploited it may prove very useful to our purposes.

What SOE felt less able to identify was a means of exploiting that tendency. Obstacles ranged from Fascist propaganda, 'which tries to make the Sicilians believe that we intend making of their island a British possession of the same type as Malta,' to 'the peculiarities of the language and customs, the physical characteristics of the race and the parochial life of the population [which] make it difficult for anyone but a Sicilian to settle on the island under an assumed identity.' But one possible way ahead did exist, SOE thought. 'The [Sicilian] Maffia [*sic*], if and when we contact them, and provided they are ready to collaborate, would be an ideal subversive organisation for the island.'[3]

⊙

This was the not the first time that the British had considered contacting the Mafia, or *Cosa Nostra* – literally, 'Our Thing' – as it prefers to call itself. As early as February 1941, Military Intelligence officers in London had appealed to the Foreign Office for information about the 'Maffia organisation in Sicily' ('Maffia' was a common form of spelling at the time). The Foreign Office replied that it had no recent information but believed the organisation had been 'practically stamped out ... though elements of it may merely have been driven underground'.[4] This was a reference to the supposed and much-publicised outcome of a campaign waged by Cesare Mori, the 'Iron Prefect' as Fascist propaganda liked to call him, to crush the Sicilian Mafia on Rome's behalf in the late 1920s.

SOE's turn to be interested in the Mafia began in November 1941. 'We have some evidence as to [a] separatist tendency in Sicily started by former members of disbanded Mafia,' read a telegram that reached London that month from its office in Cairo, adding: 'Military events might quickly emphasise such tendencies.'[5] In January 1942 and on Cairo's behalf, Baker Street then asked its New York office to find out if the American Mafia still had contacts with Sicily and would be willing to work with SOE to 'promote subversive activities' there.[6] This British interest predated by months the fabled efforts of the United States' own authorities to harness the American Mafia to the Allied war effort.

Today, a good deal has been written about the form and value of wartime co-operation between the Mafia and American intelligence officers. Many of the claims made can be dismissed outright as myth: above all, the story that the Mafia played a key role in smoothing the Allied conquest of Sicily.[7] It remains a fact that the US Office of Naval Intelligence contacted the Mafia mobster 'Lucky' Luciano and sought his support in guarding the New York docks against enemy sabotage.[8] It is also the case that this was more progress than SOE managed to make in the city. After receiving Baker Street's appeal for help, the New York office replied that it was in touch with someone in the Mafia – whom it did not name – 'but so far without results'.[9] A few weeks later it added that the Mafia was 'not a cohesive association and had no representative abroad'.[10]

London had also asked for 'all possible information on the Unione Siciliana ... reported to be a secret society powerful in the U.S.A.' New York told London that this *was* the Mafia.[11] Actually New York was wrong. The Unione Siciliana was *not* the Mafia. That said, at points in its past it might not have been too dissimilar. Founded by Sicilian-Americans in the 1890s, it was Chicago-based and began as a charitable organisation to help settle new Sicilian immigrants. According to some accounts, it then became progressively more involved in organised crime – bootlegging, extortion, murder and the like – and rather less benevolent. One of its supposed presidents, the Chicago mobster Ignazio Lupo, known as 'The Wolf', is said to have installed hooks in his office on which to hang his victims, and burned six political rivals alive in his basement furnace.[12]

Although British understanding of America's underworld may have been somewhat sketchy, it improved a little when Max Salvadori, then in New York, was asked for his assistance. Salvadori did his best, though he had no personal links to the Mafia in either the United States or Sicily. 'Sicilians in the United States talk considerably about the Maffia [*sic*], its power and about their contacts with leading Maffiosi in Sicily,' he reported in July 1942 after asking around among Sicilian immigrants. But whenever

178

he had tried to find out more, he said, he had always found that those who claimed to be in contact with the Mafia were in touch 'through some intermediary whom it was practically impossible to discover and who probably did not exist'. He added:

To evaluate the Sicilian Maffia, one can compare it to American rackets, which flourish when the authorities are easy-going and which usually collapse as soon as greater severity on the part of the authorities increases the risks. There is little doubt that there are still many Maffiosi in Sicily. On the other hand it seems very probable that their activities as such are practically nil and that they are nearly as much disorganized as the Italian freemasonry. Every Sicilian here seems to be of the opinion that the Maffia is stronger in the United States than in Sicily and even in the United States it does not seem able to achieve very much.

'As far as I know,' Salvadori went on, 'Sicilians have a good deal of sympathy for the Maffia, chiefly since it does not seriously interfere with their activities. The Maffia satisfies their need for romanticism, adventure and mystery. Probably the less is the real strength of the Maffia, the greater is the admiration which Sicilians feel for it.'[13]

What SOE did appreciate was that it was contemplating an alliance with 'an illegal and secret society' famed for its criminality and violence. At the end of 1942, SOE's Cairo office drew up the following report:

For years the [Sicilian] Maffia – the secret society for crime and murder – held sway on the island. Murders were committed and the terrible code of '[O]merta' prevented the police from ever finding the culprit. Feuds flourished between families for generations and murder after murder was committed. No onlooker, whether implicated in the feud or not, would turn informer, even if a murder were committed in his presence. This was 'Omerta' and non-observance was punished by death . . .

Since its foundation the Maffia claims to defend the weak against the strong, to fight tyranny, and generally to redress any injustice. The Sicilians say that it has been libelled in Italy and abroad as an association of bandits, when in reality it is only an attempt to establish a state within the State on Freemason lines . . .

This is the theoretical programme. In practice the Maffia has always been trying to control justice and politics somewhat on similar lines as the Tammany Hall in America. The means employed, however, were much more ruthless . . .

This organisation has its own tribunals, the sentences of which are without appeal and generally ruthlessly carried out sooner or later. There have been cases of Maffiosi going to America to execute a sentence.

Aware that efficient Fascist policing had reduced its influence in recent years, the same report identified a possible lever that could perhaps be used to persuade the Mafia to work with the British. Might the Mafia collaborate if co-operation offered the opportunity to recover its earlier influence?

[A] weakening of the Fascist organization would help the Maffia to become reorganised and powerful. All the more so if a certain amount of help is forthcoming from the outside . . . [T]he Maffia remain a potential danger to Fascism if not [at present] a fully organised one . . . [I]f they want 'to play' with us they would be an ideal organisation for Sicily.[14]

'Sporadic attempts seem to have been made in the past to contact the Maffia,' the same report added. 'We do not feel, however, that up to now the problem has been tackled thoroughly. In our opinion it is definitely worth while going full out and trying to find what possibilities exist.' The report also mentioned, briefly, what SOE might do if and when contact with the Mafia was successfully made. Three SOE teams, each of three agents, comprising a leader, a wireless operator and a saboteur, would paddle ashore or drop by parachute. One team would be assigned to Palermo; another would go to Messina; and the third would establish itself in Sicily's second city, Catania. Each team would open a wireless link between Sicily and the Allies, co-operate with the Mafia, organise and instruct cells of local sympathisers, and prepare attacks on agreed objectives, then begin propaganda, call in supplies, and open an active sabotage campaign. Targets would include shipping, petrol dumps, ordnance and aircraft factories, roads, railways, telephone lines, aerodromes, 'high officials' and the ferry connecting Messina to the mainland.[15]

It is possible that SOE tried subsequently to seek out the Sicilian Mafia with this plan in mind. Its surviving files, however, contain nothing to suggest that anything more than a few indirect and unconfirmed links were ever established. Nor are there any indications that SOE received any assistance from the American Office of Naval Intelligence with its Mafia-befriending efforts. Nor are there any suggestions that SOE received any help from the Office of Strategic Services (broadly speaking, the United States' combined equivalent of SOE and MI6). In fact, OSS seems to have taken a deliberate decision to avoid even talking to the Mafia.[16]

A useful gauge of Cairo's knowledge of *Cosa Nostra* is provided by a document surviving among the private papers of Julian Dobrski, the SOE staff officer who was manning Cairo's Italian desk in 1942.[17] This document is a typewritten list of a dozen or so alleged Mafia members whom SOE had hoped to contact. Drawn up in August, it became an appendix to a formal report on Sicily that Cairo produced at the end of the year. Today it also sheds equally interesting light on some of those who had provided the names.

Most of the names came apparently from Giovanni Di Giunta, the same Sicilian recruit from East Africa who had volunteered to kill Mussolini but whose loose chatter saw the mission terminated instead. Di Giunta is the only Italian recorded in SOE's books as having claimed outright Mafia membership. Whether he had been genuine when claiming to be a Mafioso is very much open to doubt, however. The same family friend from Troina who remembered him in 2012, warning that Di Giunta was a man whose stories should not necessarily be believed, dismissed the Mafia-membership claim as 'fantasy' and may well have a point.[18]

Of the names that Di Giunta seemingly disclosed to SOE, most jar badly with modern understanding of the Mafia's social make-up in Sicily and its influence across the island. Though the spelling is a little awry, one name appears to be that of the Marchese Giovanni Romeo delle Torrazze. Possibly one of the least likely Sicilians to be a Mafioso, the Marchese was eighty-odd years old in 1942 and had been a high-ranking officer in the Italian Army in the First World War, an aide-to-camp to the King of Italy, a president of the military court in Palermo, and a senator; the King, indeed, had even holidayed at the Marchese's Sicilian home. A second name on the list seems to be that of another Sicilian noble, the Marchese di Bonfonello, described as 'Chief for the Palermo region'. Given the fact that these two men seem such unlikely candidates for Mafia membership – Romeo delle Torrazze is described as 'Chief for the Catania region' – it may be wondered if Di Giunta had mentioned them simply as notable Sicilians of influence, whereupon SOE made the mistake of assuming he meant Mafiosi.[19]

More intriguing are the names that Di Giunta gave of several individuals in Catania. There were two sets of brothers: their surnames were 'San Filippo' and 'Paternostro' and both were described as 'representatives' for Catania. There was also an individual called 'Ciccio Cavaduzzo' who was described as 'Chief of the gunmen'. All could apparently be found at the Café Quattrocchi on Catania's Via Etnea. 'One of the [San Filippo] brothers, Domenico, is indicated to us as a person very likely to be anti-Fascist,' SOE noted against the names. 'Domenico is a big trader in "agrumi" [citrus fruits] and used to come monthly to Rome. It is suggested that he could travel to Switzerland on business.'[20] To judge from that description, it is not impossible that this was Domenico Sanfilippo [sic], a successful *agrumi* businessman who, post-war, became owner of *La Sicilia*, the most prominent newspaper in eastern Sicily; today, a major publishing house is named after him. Cavadduzzo [*sic*], meanwhile, was the gangland name of the Ferrara family, which was, and may remain, heavily involved in Catania in organised crime. It is possible that 'Ciccio Cavaduzzo' was a member of the Mafia in 1942, although *Cosa Nostra*, which historically is associated much more with western Sicily, had minimal presence in Catania until after the war.[21]

Di Giunta was not the only SOE recruit to help compile that list. A man known as Pietro Floris also contributed. Floris, who worked for a time in Jerusalem on propaganda, was described as possibly linked to the Mafia in Tunis where many Mafiosi had fled to escape Cesare Mori's attentions. He supplied the surnames of three alleged members of the Tunisian-based Mafia: Capizzi, Corso – 'both last heard of in Addis Ababa' – and Lasala. The third and final contributor to the list was Albino Scamporrino, a lawyer from Siracusa who had lived in Palermo and went under the SOE pseudonym of Luigi Marino. He gave the names of four men in Palermo: Valerio Candela, of 464 Corso Vittorio Emanuele; a man called Castagnaro who owned the Hotel Regina on Corso Vittorio Emanuele; Giuseppe Fiore, an *olivezza* (olive-grower); and finally an *uditore* (public official) named Francesco Torretta. 'Anti-Fascist,' SOE noted of the last. 'He is, however, 65 years old but could probably put us in touch with relatives and friends. Was a big landowner, now has been ruined by Fascism.'[22] It is not impossible that this ageing 'Anti-Fascist' was the same Francesco Torretta whom the Palermo police had recorded years earlier as a young member of a Mafia *cosca* (family).[23]

Scamporrino, the man who provided the Palermo names, had lived in Somaliland since 1938 and was one of a pair of Sicilian lawyers found in East Africa by SOE who claimed to have once worked for the Mafia, as opposed to having been members themselves. The other lawyer's name was Francesco Sollima. Both men were over forty. Neither was judged to be very suitable for anything more active than drafting propaganda. Sollima, who worked well in the Middle East on producing material to be broadcast to Sicily, was considered for a time for a mission to Tunisia 'to try and fix up Sicilian contacts'.[24] But he was a sick man who required regular hospital treatment and the plan came to nothing. Scamporrino's weakness was drugs. In July 1942, just a few months after joining SOE, he was caught peddling in Palestine. He was sacked and received fourteen days in prison. On his release he was sent to Kenya and re-interned.

9

'Things seem to be going according to plan . . .'

On a November night in 1942, a small wooden fishing boat closed on the coast of southern France. Crewed by Poles and with French colours on its hull, it was the same clandestine felucca that five months earlier had landed Emilio Lussu and his wife near Cassis. This time it was poised to land six agents at the same spot. Five were to operate in France for SOE's French Section. Two of these were Englishmen: George Starr, who was destined to run one of SOE's most successful French networks; and Marcus Bloom, a radio operator, who would be arrested and imprisoned in Mauthausen concentration camp where he was eventually executed. The other three were women going in to work as underground couriers. One of them, Odette Sansom, was a young Frenchwoman who would survive capture, torture and imprisonment in Ravensbrück concentration camp, and receive the George Cross for gallantry. Her story was later told in the 1950 film *Odette*.

In published accounts of SOE activities on the Continent, next to no mention has been made until now of the sixth agent who went ashore that night. Jewish, twenty-two years old, short, dark and slight, he was the only Italian ex-internee recruited in Britain who would go into enemy territory on a mission exclusively for SOE. His orders were to make for neutral Switzerland, get across the Swiss–Italian frontier, and secure SOE's first firm link with anti-Fascists inside Italy.

This was a mission defined partly by a growing acceptance that no other means of penetrating mainland Italy seemed likely to have any success whatsoever. Experience in the Middle East of exploring other methods, like getting a man on to a repatriation ship or to masquerade as an escaping prisoner, had not been encouraging. But the immediate origins of SOE's first attempt to get a trained agent of its own into Italy lay in the fact that reports were at last reaching London of groups of anti-Fascists in northern Italy who seemed active, very aggressive, and willing to have help from the British. These reports were coming from SOE's man in neutral Switzerland who was already trying to help them by smuggling over the border suitcases of money, explosives and sabotage devices. It was to these groups that SOE's young Italian agent was being sent.

⊙

SOE's man in Switzerland was Jock McCaffery, a confident and combative Scot. Born in Glasgow to Irish parents settled in Scotland, he had lived for a decade in Italy where he had gone to train for the Catholic priesthood but ended up teaching English, working for the British Council, and penning freelance articles for the *Daily Mail*. He was thirty-five when he joined SOE in the summer of 1940, apparently on the recommendation of Douglas Woodruff, editor of *The Tablet*. McCaffery's interviewer was Lieutenant-Colonel Montagu Chidson, whose various claims to fame included being the first British pilot to engage a German aircraft in aerial combat (he had shot at it from his cockpit, with a rifle, in 1914) and snatching a haul of Dutch industrial diamonds from under the noses of the invading Germans in May 1940.

Once on board, McCaffery worked for a while at SOE's London headquarters and toured internment camps and Pioneer Corps bases to help search for Italian volunteers. In January 1941 he would be the man sent up to Scotland to choose the best of the Quins for the Colossus operation; it was McCaffery who would remember hearing Fortunato Picchi, 'white as a sheet', make his plea for selection. He also attended a few short courses to learn the rudiments of security and sabotage work, and at one point, according to his memoirs,[1] proposed that he lead a sabotage team into Italy to bring down a viaduct carrying the main road and railway line between Genoa and Rome.

First tabled in November 1940, the original idea for sending McCaffery to Switzerland was a revival of Cuthbert Hamilton Ellis's abortive mission earlier that year. By the autumn, experts in London had estimated that about a third of Italy's coal requirements were arriving from the Reich via Switzerland. Interrupting that traffic, it was assessed, would 'certainly prevent imports into Italy from being kept at the level essential for the Italian war effort'.[2] The best way to do this was to sabotage small-scale targets like turntables, sheds, marshalling yards, and pipelines feeding the Swiss hydroelectric system. Even the Prime Minister was interested. 'It is obviously most important that this should be impeded in every way,' he wrote to Hugh Dalton in January 1941. 'In view of the mountainous nature of the country through which the railways run, this should be feasible.'[3]

By then, several weeks had been spent trying to address the awkward problem of getting a man into a country that now shared its borders with the Greater Reich, Fascist Italy and Nazi-occupied and -dominated France. Frank Nelson's suggestion of seeking Swiss permission for a direct flight with diplomatic status did not play well with the Foreign Office, which was sensitive to the fact that the Swiss had not been pleased in recent weeks when RAF aircraft overflew their territory and mistakenly bombed it. There was also the delicate task of convincing the British Minister in Berne to allow SOE to have a man on his staff. As Gladwyn Jebb warned Dalton, if anything went wrong it could lead to the Swiss expelling the whole legation. Finally SOE resigned itself to sending McCaffery by the long route, via Lisbon and through Spain and Vichy France, which remained open to officials with diplomatic status. He arrived in Berne in March. By then his instructions went far beyond railway sabotage. As SOE's principal representative in Switzerland, he was to settle in for the long term and attempt to run clandestine lines into every state surrounding it.

Switzerland was not an easy place to engage unseen in secret wartime work. It was crawling with Swiss, Italian and German intelligence officers intent on identifying anyone British who was there on clandestine duty. Weeks after arriving, McCaffery wrote to London that he was being 'watched and listened to still with considerable thoroughness . . . Only last night I had a German agent planted on me.'[4] 'The country is small,' he added five months later; 'no Swiss is without a friend in the Swiss Intelligence Service; and the latter is everywhere and interested in everything: they are extremely jealous of their neutrality . . . [A]nd of course the entire country is riddled with German and Italian agents for whom nothing is too small.'[5] But his cover, he felt, was 'first rate'.[6] McCaffery had been appointed assistant press attaché at the British Legation in Berne, ostensibly responsible for reporting to London on Italian matters for the Ministry of Information, the BBC, and the War Office's Press Department. For some time he devoted his efforts to building up that cover, 'creating the impression of being a very energetic Press man by day', he told London, while 'at the expense of sleep and digestion' spending a lot of evenings out. 'I even managed to figure in several foolish incidents in night clubs which duly went the round of the town. At the end of six weeks both reputations were soundly established and it then seemed that the Swiss and our German and Italian friends might have let up a bit on their supervision.'[7]

So far as McCaffery's original mission was concerned, progress was slow. From the Legation, where he started out sharing an office but eventually took over the top floor, he busily planned and plotted. Months would pass before his efforts to target Axis rolling stock began to bear much fruit. Eventually, with the aid of an anti-Nazi Swiss named René Bertholet, local teams were recruited in Basle and various frontier posts and run by a socialist associate of Bertholet's, a German ex-policeman, Paul Schlotter. Independently, a fifty-year-old Swiss railwayman, whom SOE described as 'non-political but an ardent hater of the Nazis', was also found in Basle and ran another team in the Muttenz goods yard.[8] The chief methods of sabotage were drilling holes in tankers and tampering with brakes and axle-boxes. The assistance provided by McCaffery included consignments of finely ground carborundum for inserting as an abrasive into lubricating oil. Occasionally he was able to pass along oilcans filled with plastic explosive and little bombs disguised as coal, as well as black propaganda for pasting onto passing rolling stock. The work of these teams, which was limited only by McCaffery's ability to keep them supplied, continued until the end of the war. During 1942, according to McCaffery's reports to London, the monthly rate of sabotage sometimes exceeded 600 axle-boxes and the brake systems of up to forty trains.

Night-time tinkering in Swiss marshalling yards was all well and good. Where McCaffery hoped to make a much greater impact was in encouraging subversive activity over the border in Italy. To do this, he had to find men to help him. To do that, he found his press cover invaluable, by providing him with a believable excuse for travelling about and talking to people. While wielding that cover, on an early trip to speak to the local press in Ticino, Switzerland's southernmost canton, in late March 1941, McCaffery met 38-year-old Piero Pellegrini. Though born in Turin, Pellegrini was a stolid Swiss journalist and socialist who now edited *Libera Stampa*, a Ticino-based socialist daily. It was from him that McCaffery first heard that underground socialist groups were still active in northern Italy. Pellegrini also said that he was in touch with these groups. McCaffery liked the sound of that.

Soon McCaffery was paying Pellegrini a monthly salary, subsidising his newspaper and offering to finance his Italian friends if they proved themselves worth backing. By the summer, Pellegrini was reporting that the groups were arranging themselves into districts and cells, from Trieste across to Como, Genoa and Milan, and hoped to hasten an Italian defeat through sabotage and spreading dissent. 'Take it from me, I know my 32-landers [Italians] and speak their language (figuratively as well as literally),' McCaffery told London. Pellegrini was 'able, zealous, and honest' and 'painstaking in giving a picture containing only what could be absolutely guaranteed . . . If you do not get satisfactory results from 32-land [Italy] (though I am convinced we shall) then be quite certain that the fault will not be [his].'[9]

By the autumn of 1941, Pellegrini was informing McCaffery that these groups now had a militant arm known as the Tigrotti, made up mostly of army officers and professional men. The Tigrotti had recently damaged some factories and power stations in Genoa, he said. In December came news of more sabotage in Genoa, including the firing of 18,000 petrol drums and the bursting of a ship's boiler. Encouraged by London, McCaffery, through Pellegrini, began passing guidance to the Tigrotti on the sorts of target preferred by the British, like railways, shipping, road transport, rubber, silk and hemp. He offered Pellegrini all help and asked if the Tigrotti would be willing and able to receive and look after British wireless operators, instructors and stores.

Aside from his dealings with Pellegrini, McCaffery dealt regularly for a time in Switzerland with another committed anti-Fascist, the writer Ignazio Silone. Born in 1900, Silone had spent much of his youth as a militant socialist and in 1921 helped found the Italian Communist Party. By the early 1930s, however, his growing disgust and disillusionment with Moscow had seen him expelled from the party. His years of activism seemed over, and he was living the isolated life of an exile in Switzerland where he devoted himself to his writing. It was there that he wrote two of the great anti-Fascist novels, *Fontamara* (1933) and *Pane e Vino* (1936), stories of the struggles of Abruzzo villagers oppressed by landlords and officialdom. By 1941, it seems, he had been tempted back to political work and started working in Switzerland for the Italian Socialist Party.

Silone was 'a <u>born</u> revolutionary and subterranean organiser' with whom he was extremely keen to work, McCaffery told London after he met him in March 1941.[10] At the same time, their dealings threatened to prove 'extremely difficult. He is shot through with tuberculosis, has a strain of egotism, is disillusioned about old beliefs of his, is sceptical in general, and thinks that a British victory would have a merely negative value. Still, I shall persevere with him.'[11] In one attempt to win him over, McCaffery offered to send Silone's next novel to the London publishers Jonathan Cape, by diplomatic bag. Eventually, after 'several meals and long walks together,' McCaffery felt that he had convinced Silone 'that anyone of his ideas ought to be working wholeheartedly for a British victory if only so that they might be able to continue their own particular fight whether it conflicted with British aims or not'. Silone gave McCaffery the names of possible collaborators and promised to 'sound out the ground' with others.[12] Later, Silone would tell McCaffery that he was prepared to work with Pellegrini in trying to contact in Italy suitable socialists and communists capable of 'stirring up discontent and strife' in a common front against the Fascists.[13]

Over time, McCaffery would work more closely with Pellegrini than Silone. Eventually he would drop Silone altogether. This would appear to have been partly due to McCaffery's preference for the apparently superior energy and potential of Pellegrini's groups for delivering sabotage in Italy, as opposed to Silone's more cautious line of subtler and less violent action. It may also have had something to do with a clash of personalities and politics. At a distance of seventy years and with none of the offended and offending cast still around, it is hard to unpick precisely why McCaffery and Silone hated each other. After the Swiss police arrested him in late 1942 on suspicion of illegal activity, Silone appears to have claimed that McCaffery had shopped him to the authorities out of revenge after he had criticized McCaffery for becoming too focused on encouraging the Tigrotti.[14] According to a scribbled note among American files in Washington, DC, Silone's besotted young lover, Darina Laracy, a Dubliner in her mid-twenties, later told American agents in Switzerland that the '½ Scotch ½ Irish' McCaffery was 'dangerous, although Catholic, & VERY reactionary' and 'loathes' Silone 'and his like'.[15] By 'reactionary' Laracy probably meant 'anti-communist' and McCaffery was certainly that: he was 'very Catholic and very anti-communist' remembered one wartime colleague who worked with him in Berne.[16] For his part, McCaffery recorded that Silone's arrest had been precipitated by a recent BBC broadcast to Germany that had described the Italian Socialist Party as having headquarters in Switzerland. The Swiss had had no alternative but to respond, McCaffery explained to London, and had hauled in Silone because he had been so stupidly indiscreet about his anti-Fascist activities. Whatever the reasons behind their falling out, McCaffery certainly came to loathe Silone. He was glad to be rid of him, he told London after Silone's arrest, and wanted a story spread far and wide that Silone was discredited and that his socialist friends were tired of him.

As well as throwing much of his energy into backing Pellegrini's groups, McCaffery sought to find ways of channelling explosives and other material to them, too. Smuggling anything in either direction across the Swiss–Italian frontier could be tricky. Often both sides were tightly controlled and patrolled. The Italians were as keen to prevent the sort of cross-border smuggling that McCaffery was planning as the Swiss were eager to avoid compromising their neutrality by allowing that activity to go on. As McCaffery told London not long after arriving in Berne, 'the Italian frontier now is a devil of a job and it is a triumph to be able to get a <u>person</u> over. The carrying of stuff complicates the business infinitely.'[17] But in early 1942, while sitting one evening in a Ticino bar, he seemed to have found a solution.

Drinking next to him was a drunken Englishman who boasted that he could get anything from Italy that McCaffery cared to mention. This Englishman was Edmund Schwerdt. The Oxford-educated son of a German-born button-manufacturer who had settled in London in the 1880s, Schwerdt was thirty-nine and had been living near Lake Como when the war broke out, whereupon he had moved to Switzerland, settled in Ticino, and dabbled in a bit of covert cross-border work. After eliciting promises that Schwerdt would sober up and behave, McCaffery gave him the job of helping him pierce the frontier. Soon enough Schwerdt had acquired the services of a young Swiss friend, a radio technician called Elio Andreoli from the Ticino town of Lugano, who agreed to act as a courier between Switzerland and Italy. In February 1942, having heard from the Tigrotti that they were willing and able to receive supplies, McCaffery laid on the first delivery. A suitcase of explosives and sabotage devices was packed and delivered to Schwerdt, who gave it to Andreoli, who then disappeared over the border bound for a rendezvous with a man in Milan.

In subsequent months, more money and stores were dispatched into Italy and more reports of successful sabotage came back. Early news included the derailing of a goods train near Trieste, the destruction of water and gas mains in Genoa, and a fire in a rubber factory at Chiavari causing damage of half a million lire. In June word arrived that the Tigrotti had destroyed petrol dumps at San Quirico in Tuscany and wrecked a train carrying thirty tanks on a line to Bracciano, northwest of Rome. In September the Tigrotti reported the wrecking of the engine-room of a corvette under construction at Genoa. After that came word of the sinking en route to Sardinia of a merchant ship, the *Paolina*, after explosives were hidden in its boilers, and claims from a little Tigrotti offshoot in northeast Italy to have blown up a length of railway near Aurisina and two transformer stations in Trieste; this little group had also expressed interest in killing 'Benny', their name for Mussolini. In December McCaffery reported to London the Tigrotti's 'biggest achievement so far, a fire in the port of Genoa which had kept the [fire-]brigade, soldiers, sailors, police and two fire ships busy for the entire day . . . [It has] been described in the press as an inferno and the damage had been declared as enormous."[18]

⊙

The Tigrotti were not the only group in Italy whose successes McCaffery reported to London and to whom he would send British funds and supplies. In April 1942, not long after Schwerdt's Swiss courier had left with the first suitcase of devices for the Tigrotti, McCaffery was introduced in Berne to a youngish Italian Jew who earlier that day had been to see Air Commodore Freddie West, VC, a one-legged former fighter pilot who was working in the Berne Legation as British air attaché. Their Italian visitor presented himself as Eligio Almerigotti, an ex-army officer from Trieste. He was, he said, a prominent figure in an anti-Fascist organisation called the Comitato d'Azione, and a nephew of Fiorello La Guardia, the mayor of New York City.

The Comitato d'Azione, Almerigotti explained, covered much of northern Italy. Its members numbered about 1,500 and ranged from army officers to factory and shipyard workers and were organised in small cells. Until the United States' recent entry into the war, he said, he had been supplying intelligence to the US Embassy in Rome. Now he wanted to work with the British. To prove his story, Almerigotti showed the calling card from Rome of the Embassy's former assistant naval attaché. Almerigotti did not know it, but his visit had already been heralded by a message of introduction sent by the Americans to the British in Berne. Impressed, McCaffery gave him 30,000 lire and three weeks to produce results. Almerigotti returned to Italy.

A fortnight later, Almerigotti sent news to McCaffery of two acts of sabotage: the destruction of a factory producing magnesium powder and the burning of a dump of grain and fodder for the Italian Army. More attacks were planned, he added, and he wanted guidance, money and sabotage devices. 'My own opinion is that he is first class and worth backing all out,' McCaffery told

London. 'I should honestly give him all the cash he wants. I do not think we have any abler man on our books.'[19]

In subsequent months and with London's approval, Almerigotti was sent a lot more money, together with regular suitcases of explosives and other supplies, as McCaffery sought to respond to a steady flow of reports from him detailing further acts of sabotage, the steady spread of the Comitato d'Azione, and the organisation's growing appetite for direction and supplies. In May came news of two train-derailments on the Brenner Pass and an explosion in an airfield depot. In June Almerigotti reported a fire in a storehouse at the Monfalcone shipyard. In August he sent word of further derailments, the burning of a paper factory, the burning of corn and hay supplies, and an explosion in a munitions factory that had killed several workmen. In September there were claims of further destructive fires, including one in a ship's hold at Venice and another on the dockside at Monfalcone, and of more lethal explosions, this time at a military chemical institute near Florence and in a cartridge factory in Frosinone. In October Almerigotti sent reports of a fire in a factory making military clothing: machinery had been damaged and large quantities of wool destroyed. The following month he told Berne of another train-derailment, 600,000 lire's worth of fire-damage to a hemp factory, and even greater destruction, estimated at four million lire, caused to a paper factory in Milan. December saw three more derailments and the further destruction by fire of thousands of kilos of military clothing, the loss being estimated at another four million lire. In early 1943, Almerigotti reported even more deliberate fires, including one in a Marelli machinery factory that had caused damage worth fifteen million lire, and further railway sabotage, including a collision of two goods trains caused by jamming points outside Taranto station. By then, Almerigotti's achievements, like those of the Tigrotti, were featuring in reports of SOE successes being regularly put before Churchill.

⊙

Word of the exploits of the Tigrotti and Almerigotti's men led
SOE to send into Italy the young Italian radio operator who,
in November 1942, would step ashore at Cassis. His name was
Giacomino Sarfatti. Born in July 1920, the son of a psychologist
who had served as a liaison officer to British soldiers fighting
in Italy in the First World War, he had been brought up and
schooled in Florence. Having gone to live in England in 1938 when
the Fascists began persecuting Jews, he was a year into a degree
in agriculture at the University of Reading when war between
Britain and Italy broke out. Interned in June 1940, he volunteered
for the Pioneer Corps as soon as he was able and was serving as a
private soldier in an army camp at Ilfracombe when, in January
1941, SOE found him.

'Quiet, reserved,' Sarfatti's recruiter noted. 'Apparently dependable for a job entailing danger.'[20] Soon other observers viewed him
as one of the best of their Italian finds. 'First class intellectual and
moral qualities,' reads an early training report from April 1941,
when he was being put through his paces during paramilitary
training at Meoble Lodge near Lochailort in Scotland. 'Has a
tendency to be shy, otherwise a perfect specimen of what a young
man should be . . . Has plenty of courage, a strong will, common
sense and self control.'[21]

Not every report was so positive. There was a feeling among
some officers that he might not be suited to SOE work. 'His disposition is too gentle and he has not sufficient ruthlessness of
mind for work of this kind,' remarked the chief instructor at the
finishing school at Beaulieu. 'As a Jew he is anti-fascist and not
averse to attacking any fascist or military objective, but he has
considerable qualms about the possibility of causing the deaths
of any other Italians. He would, therefore, probably be liable to be
in two minds about any job he is given to do and could, therefore,
not be relied on to do it.'[22] But the good reports outweighed the
cautious and before long Sarfatti had been earmarked for his first
mission. In October 1941, fully trained as a radio operator and

carrying papers in the name of a Maltese called Galea, he joined a ship leaving Swansea for the Mediterranean where SOE planned to dispatch him, from Malta, into enemy-occupied Tunisia.

The voyage, which went round the Cape, took three months. Accompanying him were two SOE officers who, by spending more time with him than most, gained a little more knowledge of his qualities and character. One of these officers was Lieutenant Peter Cooper, an Englishman en route to Malta to help set up a training school. 'Whilst on the boat, both Captain [Dobrski] and myself were much impressed by the mental toughness of Galea,' Cooper wrote later:

I remember that Captain [Dobrski] pointed out to me that it was only by living with people that one really got to know them. He applied this to the fact that the report with which Galea was handed over to us stated that he was young and immature and without a great deal of experience, and might, therefore, be easily led. In fact, we formed the impression that Galea, although very quiet, was extremely obstinate, and had some very strong convictions . . .

He was well educated, and took a keen interest in politics. He spoke excellent English, and was very familiar with English political problems, as well as Italian. In political views, he was fairly well to the Left, although by no means Communist. He was rarely to be seen without a copy of the 'New Statesman and Nation' . . .

Temperamentally, I should describe Galea as extremely taciturn, reserved and strongly security minded. He very seldom spoke in the company of strangers, and even with the people he knew well he was strongly inclined to limit his conversation to 'Yes', 'No', and 'Perhaps'.

[H]e is very English in mannerisms, never gesticulating, and speaking very quietly and slowly. He is very dark and swarthy . . . has very dark black eyes . . . is sturdily built in spite of being small. He has very regular white teeth, which he shows when he laughs, which is not very often.[23]

Sarfatti's Tunisian mission never came off. Malta, which they reached in January 1942 after a final leg from Alexandria when they were bombed from the air almost all the way, was now under heavy and persistent enemy attack. By then the island was fast earning its unhappy reputation as the most heavily bombed spot of the war, and soon it was perfectly obvious that the siege made it impossible to send agents from there to North Africa or anywhere else. Instead, Sarfatti was put to work for six months in one of Malta's wireless stations, handling secret signals from missions in the Balkans. It was the worst period to be on the island. 'Blitzed, bombed but not bewildered,' read a telegram to London in April after the office shared by MI5, MI6 and SOE received a direct hit. 'No casualties except female black eye and three cars written off. Salvaging office today. Business as usual tomorrow.'[24] Sarfatti was 'greatly commended' for his 'calmness, patience and cheerfulness in a very difficult period', when the house in which he was operating was nearly hit on several occasions.[25]

In the summer of 1942, thoughts turned to ways of making better use of Sarfatti: he was SOE's outstanding Italian recruit, but he was currently doing a job any good wireless operator could do. First, the SOE office in Cairo, at a time when they were still trying to conjure something from nothing, suddenly wondered about sending him on a mission to Sicily or Sardinia. Alarmed already by Cairo's eagerness at getting men into the field without adequately considering their chances of survival, Cecil Roseberry, in London, reacted immediately. 'Have you ascertained whether a young highly educated Florentine Jew would be suitable for the locality?' he snapped when Cairo's idea reached his desk.[26] 'Galea [is] far too good to be risked on anything but [a] reasonably secure plan.'[27] But Cairo's dangerous musings also stung Roseberry into action. In signals exchanged with Berne, he and Jock McCaffery hammered out a scheme to send Sarfatti to work as a radio operator with the groups now heard to be active in northern Italy. 'Your main function will be to communicate to us their requirements in material, money, etc., to notify departure, date and rendezvous of couriers and to report progress,' reads the brief that Sarfatti was given to read in October after he was flown back to London to prepare. 'In addition to wireless work, you should give the groups the advantage of your experience in the matter of security, use of our demolition materials, etc.'[28]

Final arrangements were made. One of these required Sarfatti to write specimen letters and provide samples of his signature. This was so that SOE, in his absence, could send typewritten letters apparently written by Sarfatti to his uncle, a lecturer in law who lived in London, his only relative in Britain, letting him know that his young nephew was safe and serving some-where warm. Sarfatti also made a will, wrote some letters to be opened in the event of his death, and handed over a gold watch and a Post Office savings book for safekeeping. He was also commissioned as a second lieutenant. Then, after a few false starts, it was time to go.

Towards the end of October 1942, Sarfatti sailed for the Medi-terranean in the company of the three women couriers who would land with him in France. When they reached Gibraltar he had time to poke his nose into the shops and scribble a last letter to the Italian desk in London. 'Things seem to be going according to plan,' he wrote. 'Silk stockings are extremely expensive and not of very good quality and I didn't think of sending you any . . . Well, goodbye until sometime next year!' After that came the five-day voyage by felucca with the five French Section agents.[29]

Once ashore in southern France, Sarfatti stayed a final night with the others before setting off for a safe house in Nice. Here he was to have been collected by a contact of McCaffery's and conducted into Switzerland. That arrangement went awry and he was collected instead a couple of days later by a Frenchwoman who delivered him to an SOE agent in Perpignan. Confusion followed, since this agent thought he was supposed to be arranging Sarfatti's escape to Spain, but eventually Sarfatti managed to get himself escorted to Annecy and from there to the border town of Saint Julien-en-Genevois. Then, at night, and with the help of two women schoolteachers who waved their handkerchiefs at the appropriate moment to show him that the coast was clear, he finally crept into Switzerland.

Still Sarfatti's troubles were not over. In the dark he lost his way to Geneva and was picked up by a pair of Swiss frontier guards, then interned and interrogated. His cover story – that he was an escaping British commando of Maltese origin who had been stranded in France after the major Allied raid on Dieppe – was not believed, but he managed to send a letter to the British consul in Geneva. This saw the British military attaché intervene and successfully arrange his release, albeit to the annoyance of the Swiss. At last, more than a month after he had landed in France, Sarfatti was able to present himself to Jock McCaffery who now prepared him for the final trip into Italy. It was not the first time that the two men had met. In his early role as an SOE talent-spotter, McCaffery had recruited Sarfatti at Ilfracombe two years before.

On the morning of 17 December 1942, Sarfatti boarded a train leaving Geneva for Lugano, close to the Italian border. He was wearing good boots and his own Italian clothes, which it had been agreed he could bring out from England and wear, and he carried 3,000 lire, a fake Italian identity card in the name of Giacomo Rossi, and, hidden in a hollowed-out shoe brush, a faked medical certificate stating that he was exempt from Italian military service because he suffered from epilepsy. The only other document in his possession was a British passport to get him past the Swiss controls on the Gotthard Pass. Once beyond those, but before the train reached Lugano, he hid this in the lavatory from where it was immediately retrieved by the next man to use it. This was a young Englishman, Peter Jellinek, a former employee in Switzerland of the Bally shoe company and now one of McCaffery's assistants. Jellinek had been given the job of escorting Sarfatti, at a discreet distance, as far as Lugano. It was there, on the platform, that Jellinek had to leave him, his last sight of Sarfatti being of the latter 'holding up a surreptitious thumb'.[30]

From Lugano, with the prearranged assistance of a couple of local smugglers and a frontier guard, Sarfatti was guided to the border where he climbed a fence and crossed over, bound for Milan and a rendezvous with McCaffery's Italian contacts. 'Galea left yesterday,' McCaffery telegraphed London. 'He was absolutely content and in excellent spirits.'[31] What no one in SOE knew was that this young and gallant Italian was heading straight into one of the most intricate traps laid by Italian counter-espionage officers at any point during the war.

Six months after arriving in Berne, Jock McCaffery felt that Swiss Intelligence probably thought he was engaged in press work, 'picking up all the Italian information I can find,' while the local Germans and Italians 'probably think I am a fishy individual to be watched closely . . . But I should be extremely surprised if either of them had any inkling of the real nature of my work. The Italians probably think I am bent on subsidising newspapers, etc.'[32] Today, judging from wartime Italian records, McCaffery may have been right to suppose that he was escaping excessive suspicion. In August 1943, the counter-espionage section of SIM, which had agents all over Switzerland, was still recording in its files that he was 'assistant press attaché at the English Legation at Berne, where he lives at No. 46 Luisenstrasse'.[33] A British colleague who worked with him in Berne would remember that 'Jock kept Italy not only engraved on his heart, but altogether very close to his chest.'[34] Where McCaffery was less successful was in recruiting men to help him whose own secret lives were as guarded as his own.

There are several reasons for this. For one thing, the Second World War was not the heyday of British secret service vetting. Modern procedures of gauging a man's integrity and potential for clandestine work lay far in the future. Had such processes been in place and accessible from Switzerland in 1941, it is hard to believe that a man like Edmund Schwerdt, the drunk and indiscreet Englishman whom Jock McCaffery found propping up a Ticino bar, would have been assessed as acceptable material. An alarm bell might have rung, for instance, had someone cast an eye at the testimony of Schwerdt's first wife when she petitioned for divorce in 1934. After marrying under age while still at university, Schwerdt, according to his wife, started sleeping with other women within a year and was soon leading 'a most erratic life': spending too much money; drinking heavily; frightening and neglecting his children; and staying out night after night in London bars and night-clubs from which he would return, drunk, to his little maisonette in Lower Sloane Street, where he would submit his spouse 'to exceedingly unpleasant and disgusting forms of sexual intercourse'.[35]

When he arrived in Berne in 1941 with orders to build something from nothing, McCaffery was also a man more or less fresh to secret work. He was no more experienced in the recruitment and running of clandestine agents than he was in the capabilities of Italian counter-intelligence organisations. Within a few months he was a man under mounting pressure, too. His workload was enormous – he was responsible for SOE's lines from Switzerland into the Greater Reich and France as well as Italy – yet London was hinting darkly by the autumn that he was taking too long to deliver results. 'I know and understand how impatient you are,' McCaffery tried to explain in October. 'There are certain things that it is very dangerous to try and force.'[36] Later that month, Cecil Roseberry, who had recently taken over London's Italian desk, told McCaffery directly that his results on Italy compared poorly 'with those from other fields' and 'something concrete once a week would be encouraging'.[37] Italy was regarded in London as 'a weak spot vulnerable to subversive activity', Roseberry added, and 'ripe for subversive action'.[38] At that moment Roseberry had been in the job a matter of days; if he really believed that Italy was 'ripe for subversive action', it was not an opinion he held for long.

The fact remains that in October 1941 Roseberry wanted more from McCaffery, and was not yet as cautious as he would be nine months later when warning officers in Cairo not to do too much too quickly.[39]

McCaffery and Roseberry may have been naïve and over-confident, but the decision to gamble on a man like Schwerdt neatly illustrates how desperate SOE was to find a method of piercing the Swiss–Italian frontier and how slim were the available options. It may also say something about MI6. Headed locally by Frederick ('Fanny') Vanden Heuvel, a cosmopolitan count of Italian origin, its representatives in Switzerland were supposed to be the experts in recruiting and running agents and matters of counter-espionage; they knew what McCaffery was doing; and Schwerdt, to judge from McCaffery's memoirs, had even been one of their men at one time. Finally, Schwerdt's recruitment underlines the risks of gambling on men like him: from the point of view of what SOE was trying to achieve from Switzerland, its effects were catastrophic.

By the end of 1941, when McCaffery offered him a job, Italian intelligence had been watching Edmund Schwerdt for months. He had not been hard to shadow. Several SIM reports call him 'the well known Englishman' and record how he was frequently to be found in restaurants and bars.[40] The Italians knew that he had lived in Italy, in the Valsolda, near Como, 'where he owned a villa and led a very extravagant life'.[41] They knew that he still had contacts over the border, that he had two passports in different names and was known by at least four pseudonyms, that the Swiss military police suspected him of 'dubious activities' along the frontier, and that he had even 'stated confidentially that he is a member of the [British] I.S. [Intelligence Service]'.[42] They knew, too, that he was a drinker, somewhat eccentric, and living an unhappy and cash-strapped life. 'He is in great misery,' reads one Italian report from October 1941. 'He often has only one meal a day and he is very much preoccupied with his lot, both present and future . . . He is affected by mastoiditis and is a little deaf . . . He hopes that the war will end soon and that he will be able to return to the Valsolda.'[43] But what ultimately caused the suspicious and conspicuous Schwerdt to come unstuck was when he sought out his young friend in Lugano, the radio technician Elio Andreoli, and explained that he was looking for someone to smuggle material into Italy. Schwerdt had known Andreoli for years. What he did not know was that Andreoli, though Swiss, was working for SIM.

Described in its files as 'a correct and honest person but not in good financial circumstances', Andreoli was known to SIM by the codename 'Elda' and run by the SIM counter-espionage officer who was in charge of Schwerdt's surveillance. This officer was Eugenio Piccardo, a Carabinieri captain working in Lugano under the cover of Italian vice-consul. Piccardo had long suspected that Schwerdt was working clandestinely for the British, and, when he learned from Andreoli that Schwerdt was looking for a clandestine courier to transport 'a suitcase containing material for acts of sabotage', he saw an opportunity and acted. A contemporary report by Piccardo explains all:

Towards the end of January, I established that Schwerdt was concerned about the choice of who to entrust with the task of introducing the material into [Italy] . . . In fact, he was trying to decide between:

    1. 'Elda' my agent . . .

    2. Selmoni, Arnaldo . . . an anti-Italian, subversive element, involved in every kind of unsavoury activity such as contraband, espionage, illicit trafficking, an abuser of women, including his widowed sister . . .

In early February, at the moment when Schwerdt was in this maximum state of uncertainty – a real psychological crisis – I persuaded 'Elda' to tie up the operation but with the greatest care and above all without giving the impression that he had any personal interest in being chosen himself . . . I have persuaded him to say to Schwerdt, keeping always to generalities and not to reveal or stress specific circumstances, that he has many trustworthy friends, some of whom are favourable to the English cause; that among his most trustworthy friends are various drivers who own vehicles for hire with authorisations to circulate in

[Italy] and to make journeys into Switzerland; that he knows a driver who works with smugglers and is able to conceal packages of about 10–15 decilitres in volume in a hiding place constructed in the chassis of his vehicle . . . finally, that he, 'Elda', is willing to offer his services through his dislike of the Italians.[44]

Schwerdt fell for it, Andreoli got the job, and, from that point onwards, SIM was entirely in control of the principal route by which SOE, for months to come, was to send into Italy its supplies of money, explosives and devices.

'Punctually on the evening of 19 [February] Schwerdt passed the material locked in a suitcase over to Elda,' recorded Piccardo of the first time it happened. This consisted 'of nine carefully sealed packets and an envelope containing a pair of pliers' and a day later all of it was in Piccardo's hands.[45] As with each subsequent delivery, Piccardo sent it down to Italy as diplomatic baggage for delivery to SIM headquarters in Milan. On this occasion SIM snapped photographs of what was inside. The various items included time pencil fuses, sticks of plastic explosive, and 'fog signal' devices for initiating detonations beneath passing trains. The British had boldly wrapped the fog signals in pages of the *Daily Telegraph*.

⊙

At that moment the British were not the only ones being deceived. When he received that first suitcase for Milan, Andreoli also received instructions from the British about what he should do at the rendezvous. First, he was to be at the Arco della Pace, the great neoclassical arch at one end of Milan's Parco Sempione, for ten o'clock on the morning of 21 February. Next, he was to look for 'a man of normal stature with a brown suit and a grey coat':

He will have a copy of the weekly review 'Tempo' in his hand . . . [A]pproach him and ask if the tram No. 12 goes from there to Piazza del Duomo. The person should reply that the 12 does not pass by the Arco della Pace, but to go to Del Duomo one must take tram No. 1. After this reply . . . invite the unknown man to have a coffee [and there] . . . hand over the material.[46]

Keen of course to make further gains by smashing the Tigrotti, hopefully by arresting and unmasking the man whom the British wished Andreoli to meet, SIM made Andreoli keep that appointment. Once over the border he had the original suitcase returned and was shadowed to Milan, where, under SIM surveillance, he proceeded to meet his contact at the Arco della Pace and, as planned, adjourned to a nearby café. It was at that moment that SIM learned that Elio Andreoli, their double agent, was not alone in being more than he appeared.

To their astonishment, the watching SIM officers recognized several men sitting in the same café who were watching the meeting just as intently. These men belonged to the Milanese branch of the OVRA, the Italian secret police. As Eugenio Piccardo explained afterwards: 'It immediately became clear that the man who came to [meet Andreoli at] the Arco della Pace was an agent of the OVRA.' Andreoli and his contact were allowed to leave unmolested; then the men from SIM and the men from the OVRA spoke, whereupon both learned for the first time that they were engaged independently in similarly secret schemes aimed at deceiving the British in Switzerland. Just as the OVRA now discovered that Andreoli was under SIM's control, SIM now learned that the Tigrotti were an intricate OVRA invention designed to misdirect British energies and intentions. 'Initially Comm. Peruzzi [head of the Milanese OVRA] showed himself most surprised by the involvement of SIM,' Piccardo recorded, 'but then naturally he understood that between two operational services, each unaware of the other's involvement and working in different fields, a natural point of convergence had developed ending in the meeting of the two agents.'[47]

The chief OVRA architect of the Tigrotti deception was a man named Luca Osteria. '[S]leek black hair, brushed sharply back off face; protuberant black eyes, wide set; high cheek bones; sunken cheeks,' reads a description, much later, in British files; 'quick, precise, rather careful way of speaking'.[48] In his late thirties, Osteria was a highly experienced *agent provocateur* who had been engaged in OVRA work since the twenties, when, masquerading as a communist, he had infiltrated communist and socialist groups in Marseilles with considerable success. Similar missions followed in the thirties, to Berlin, Prague, Paris, and as far as away as Australia, until in 1940 he received instructions to prepare a counter-espionage campaign for the coming war with Britain.

'As usual, I was given full opportunity to organise this service,' Osteria recalled in 1945. At the outset this organisational work took the form of identifying Switzerland as a probable neutral base for the enemy's intelligence services, and then, 'still using the system of fictitious political party activity', seeking out Filippo Amedeo, a genuine Italian socialist living in exile in Marseilles who was known to be in touch with Switzerland. That path led Osteria to Piero Pellegrini, the Lugano newspaper editor with whom McCaffery was to deal, and other socialists. These men 'suggested to me the organising of activities of a Socialist nature' and 'asked me if I knew of people suitable for carrying on certain activities of a terrorist nature in Italy'. Osteria said he could help. 'I pointed out that I was in touch with a political organisation known as [the] Tigrotti, a group of people who had devoted themselves voluntarily to sabotage. In connection with this, I sent off a first report to Pellegrini about this organisation, which was a figment of my imagination. Pellegrini, who as far as I could make out was a person with few scruples and whose one desire was to speculate, leapt at the bait.' Correspondence began between the two men, and Osteria 'worked out on paper the whole fictitious organisation which purported to be devoting itself to terrorist and sabotage activity as well as military espionage'.[49]

After the first suitcase of explosive material and devices was sent to Milan, and SIM and the OVRA at last became aware of each other's activities, the two secret services quickly agreed that SIM should continue to run Andreoli but pass to the OVRA the deliveries from the British that were meant for the OVRA-invented Tigrotti. 'Here naturally arises a logical question,' Osteria continued in his confession in 1945; 'that is to say, how did we manage to justify [to the British] the [ongoing delivery and] use of the material?' The answer was simple. Genuine accidents, he explained, like fires, factory explosions, train derailments and so on, were carefully presented to the British via an unsuspecting Pellegrini as deliberate acts of 'foul play'.[50]

Osteria would recount, too, how he had gone on to encourage Pellegrini and the British to believe that the Tigrotti were well placed to receive material landed by submarine on the coast of mainland Italy; 'I also asked for the dispatch of a wireless transmitter.'[51] As its records confirm, this alternative to sending stores over the Swiss border was exactly what SOE wished to hear. It was not easy for SOE to keep McCaffery stocked with supplies secreted in diplomatic bags sent from Lisbon, a route that anyway became impossible after the German occupation of southern France. Nor could the bags carry very much. By December 1941, SOE had sent to Lisbon for onward passage to Berne just 26½ pounds of plastic explosive, together with 550 delayed-action relay switches, 152 fake fog signals, 496 detonators, 36 magnets, one tin of abrasive tablets and paste, and one tin of itching powder (for covert sprinkling in enemy laundries, for example). Nor was it very secure or straightforward for McCaffery to hide and move these sorts of supplies in and around a neutral country.

Various methods of improving the means of supply were considered. One idea that never left London's drawing board was a proposal of McCaffery's for the RAF to drop stores by parachute directly into Switzerland. He had suggested Lake Bienne, where he could offer a safe house on an island where signal fires could be lit. Another idea was for pro-Allied sailors on neutral ships to ferry, directly from Lisbon to Italy, small consignments of explosives disguised in sardine tins. This came to little, but it was anyway blown from the start because McCaffery had broached the topic with the Tigrotti. This allowed Luca Osteria to get as far as insinuating himself in Genoa among various crewmembers. Comparing British reports from Lisbon and Berne, and with the comfortable benefit of hindsight, it seems that on that occasion the OVRA showed more of their hand than was wise. In August 1942, a pro-Allied Dutchman put in at Genoa with instructions from SOE to contact one of the Tigrotti. The Dutchman's name was Heeres, he was the captain of the steamer *Abdul*, and he intended to hand over a tin of sardines as a simple test of the route's potential for smuggling into Italy more warlike stores. Afterwards McCaffery heard from Pellegrini that the Tigrotti's man had approached Heeres but received no response to requests for the agreed password and found that he had no supplies to hand over. Heeres, however, would report on his return to Lisbon that he had never been approached by anyone and, moreover, had been alarmed to find himself watched. SOE appears not to have thought that discrepancy worth investigating, if it noticed it at all.[52]

Eventually, in May 1943, after SOE heard from Italy that the Tigrotti were ready and able to receive stores at a secluded spot on the coast, a British submarine landed and buried a wireless set and eight containers packed with 200 pounds of explosives and fifty incendiary bombs in a bay near the Adriatic town of Vieste, on the Gargano Peninsula, in Apulia. Osteria claimed later that he had suggested the spot and, when Pellegrini warned him that the delivery was imminent, set off personally to retrieve the set and supplies: 'I had to hire some mules and pass myself off [to locals] as an engineer of the military engineers on a special mission.'[53] He failed to get there in time, however, and heard afterwards that some fisherman had discovered the containers and alerted the local police.

More stores were sent in late August, when the British submarine *Sybil* sailed into the Gulf of Genoa to land five tons of explosives in seventy-two watertight containers in the vicinity of Gallinara, an island off the Ligurian coast between Alassio and Albenga. Osteria had apparently recommended that location after liaising with the Italian Admiralty and passed along the coordinates to Pellegrini with an equally convincing request for the top layers of the containers to be made up of contraband commodities like coffee and tea. *Sybil*'s crew, who were new to this work but had practised hard with the containers before leaving port, were alarmed to find the sea off the island being swept by searchlights, while 'the entire coastline was covered with fishing rowing boats working on the shallow banks'.[54] Nevertheless, they succeeded in getting all seventy-two containers into the water, sliding them down a special wooden chute hooked to the fore-hatch to stop them banging noisily against the saddle tanks, and leaving them submerged like lobster pots. On this occasion, it seems, Pellegrini's warning of the landing arrived late, and Osteria first learned of it when he was summoned to the offices of the Italian Admiralty to be told 'that a considerable quantity of containers full of explosive material and devices had been found off the shore of the Ligurian Riviera . . . on the sea-bed and linked together by means of a chain of floats'.[55] After soothing the navy's concerns that the discovery might indicate enemy intentions to invade, Osteria proceeded to the spot and, with the assistance of some Italian soldiers on coastal defence duty, recovered more than fifty containers.

By 1943, McCaffery had been convinced of the authenticity of yet another anti-Fascist group that deserved British support. Known to SOE as the Wolves and seemingly active in and around Milan, their leader was heard to be a young Swiss called Cavadini who worked in Ticino but had a house across the border in Como. By May, McCaffery was describing Cavadini as 'going very strong'. His organisation was reported as 'spreading' and claimed to have recently 'eliminated' a 'fair number' of German soldiers 'and offered us uniforms if we had any use of them'. One of the Wolves served with the Milanese anti-aircraft defences and was 'working his way steadily round the batteries doctoring guns', while others were slashing vehicle tyres and detonating small charges to bring down telegraph poles.[56] Italian records identify Cavadini as Enrico Cavadini, born in July 1910, who worked as a teacher of art and drawing at a school in Arogno, in Ticino, 'but when necessary [as] a clerk as well'. They also reveal him to be a man who seemingly started out as 'a genuine agent on the English payroll' before being rumbled by the OVRA, which 'managed to get him hooked' and 'play for both sides but in Italy's favour'.[57]

The duping of the British in Switzerland was not limited to the OVRA's Tigrotti ruse and SIM's control of McCaffery's courier. The most successful Italian plant of the lot was a man whom McCaffery met and recruited in person, to whom he explained in detail what SOE wished to do in Italy, and to whom he subsequently sent significant quantities of supplies and cash. This was the Italian who had introduced himself to the British in Berne as Eligio Almerigotti, the ex-army officer from Trieste who claimed to be in touch with another set of anti-Fascists in Italy and whom McCaffery considered 'first class and worth backing all out'. In reality, Almerigotti's real name was Eligio Klein and he was another agent run by SIM.

Klein was thirty-five years old when McCaffery met him. 'Full, flabby face,' recorded an interrogator when the British caught up with him again in 1945. 'Gesticulates a great deal. Has a very noticeable habit of pulling at his coat collar. Speaks with [a] Triestino accent, and has a slight impediment in his speech which makes him unable to pronounce his Rs properly.'[58]

Born in Trieste when the city was still Austrian, Klein had worked there before the war as a journalist on a small newspaper called *Piccolo*. His real army career was more modest than he made it sound when he and McCaffery met: it seems to have consisted in fact of a few months' conscripted service in the ranks. While it is possible that he was, as he insisted to his interrogators, a nephew of Fiorello La Guardia, whose first wife, Thea Almerigotti, shared Klein's mother's surname, it is interesting that Klein seems to have been unaware that Thea had been dead since 1921. Certainly his claim to have passed naval intelligence to the American Embassy in Rome was accurate, albeit intelligence that came from SIM and was designed to impress and exploit the Americans without disclosing anything significant.

It was SIM that then sent Klein to Berne, in February 1942, to contact the British and find out what they were planning. Within days it had heard back from him about McCaffery's eagerness to set up 'a centre of information and sabotage', possibly in Milan, and supply it with a wireless set and other material. Klein even sent a detailed pen portrait of the man he had met: 'lived 11 years in Italy . . . was correspondent of the Daily Mail and professor of English . . . has a wife and a child of three in London . . . average height . . . robust constitution . . . youthful (36–37 years) . . . face slightly pitted . . . grey-brown eyes . . . trimmed, reddish-blond hair.' Almost the only important thing that SIM did not learn about McCaffery, whom Klein described as the 'head of the [British] I.S. [Intelligence Service] in Berne', was his name.[59]

Much later, when the war was over and Allied interrogators got their hands on him, there was general agreement that Klein was best understood as an unscrupulous and opportunistic mercenary who had fallen into the world of secret work more by accident than by design. '[He] does not give an impression of having a great deal of physical or moral courage,' reads one British report:

He is undoubtedly endowed with a certain amount of cunning, and possibly even intelligence. He is a plausible individual of doubtful ethical outlook, who has almost certainly no higher motives than his own personal safety and interests . . . The most likely explanation [for his actions] is that [he] drifted into intelligence out of greed and fondly imagined that it would be a very simple way of earning easy money.[60]

An American interrogator made much the same assessment. Although 'fundamentally cowardly' and 'not a man of outstanding intelligence or education', Klein was 'a convincing liar' and 'a person of extraordinary cunning and self assurance'. Aware by then of the tricks pulled by SIM on the Americans in Rome and the British in Switzerland, his British interrogator observed ruefully of Klein's doubtful character: 'The Italians, however, seem to have had the advantage of realising this at an early date, and used him as a mere cut-out.'[61]

That observation was accurate. SIM was never convinced of Klein's reliability and integrity and always sought to keep him under very strict control. Its ability to do so was helped inordinately by McCaffery's unwavering faith in Elio Andreoli, SOE's courier to the Tigrotti, whom he decided to use as his go-between for all dealings with Klein too. Since Andreoli was one of its agents, SIM was thus able to receive every consignment of money and stores from Switzerland that McCaffery believed he was sending to Klein's organisation. It also allowed SIM to intercept and read every incoming message that McCaffery penned to Klein before it reached him, as well as compose all of Klein's replies and reports to the British, since these, too, were channelled through Andreoli. That correspondence was often written in secret ink but this posed no problems for SIM, who learned early on that the ink came from water in which tablets of pyramidon, a painkilling drug, had been dissolved, and that it could be read by employing the appropriate developing salts taken from the stores sent in by the British. An unexpected benefit of being able to monitor everything so closely was that it also enabled SIM to reinforce its low opinion of Klein. On one occasion it allowed them to catch him trying to siphon off, for his personal use, some of the incoming British money.

Mirroring the OVRA's handling of the imaginary Tigrotti, SIM also used Klein to cement the trust of the British by reporting, as if from him, genuine factory and railway accidents and similar incidents that they dressed up as convincing acts of anti-Fascist sabotage carried out by his men. This was delicate work and great care was taken to get it right. A marshalling yard accident, for example, would be reported to a SIM representative working in the directorate of the Italian railways; then it would be carefully considered to see if it seemed suitably persuasive to be represented to the British as a deliberate misdeed. By having Klein's fictional anti-Fascists appeal to Switzerland for directives and guidance, SIM was also able to fish successfully for details of targets that interested the British and thus ensure that these reports of apparent sabotage underlined his organisation's worth. Although SIM officers in Milan were the ones who ran Klein and drafted his letters to McCaffery, the main SIM headquarters in Rome was responsible for coordinating much of the effort and for studying and responding to British requests and questionnaires. They were assisted in this by the Italian General Staff, which drafted and approved the intelligence that SIM sent back to the British.

SIM, like the OVRA, was also able to coax the British into sending material into Italy directly. In early 1943, McCaffery heard from Klein that he was able to receive a parachute drop of supplies into Lake Viverone in northern Italy. If given a few days' notice, Klein said, he could provide a safe house nearby. 'Here we have really got something,' McCaffery told London, stressing that he had the 'greatest confidence' in Klein's abilities.[62] SOE went to work. Six containers were specially prepared at Aston House in Bedfordshire, a secret research and development facility known as Station XII. Each one was designed to float with three to six inches protruding above the surface and to remain waterproof for a week. Then, at nine in the evening of 13 April, a four-engined RAF Halifax bomber took off from Tempsford airfield, not far from Aston House, bound for northern Italy. Five hours later, in spite of terrible visibility, the aircraft made it successfully to the spot and parachuted the containers into the lake. Afterwards McCaffery heard from Klein that two of his men had rowed out and searched the lake, but they had recovered only one container before 'a bunch of young recruits on a day's outing in hired boats' had suddenly appeared; these recruits had discovered another container and had raised the alarm, 'and soon the place had been swarming with police and sightseers'.[63] In reality, five containers were hauled out of the water. All ended up in SIM's hands.

Drawn up afterwards by appropriate technical specialists, a long inventory of what SIM found inside reveals the range of colourful items that SOE and the Royal Air Force had taken so much trouble to send. The attention to detail is typical of the care taken by the Italians over every aspect of the deception. There were 'packets of plastic explosive in oiled paper, each package weighing approximately 2 kg and in the shape of small sticks', plus dozens of 'small, black, round incendiary bombs'. There was a plethora of primers and detonators and various types of fuse:

metal boxes containing incendiary devices in celluloid for delayed detonation . . . metal boxes containing time-pencil detonators . . . black-painted metal tubes containing a series of small yellow truncated cones for initiation purposes . . . rolls of instantly igniting quick burning fuse coloured orange-red . . . rolls of detonating fuse coloured grey . . . rolls of slow-burning Bickford fuse coloured black . . . containers of tarred cardboard, capacity ¼ litre, with added fuses and caps . . .

There were penknives and pliers and boxes of Vaseline. There were bobbins of copper wire and rolls of insulation tape. There were objects that the Italians failed to identify: 'special metallic pencils of unknown purpose (very delicate tools protected in cotton wool)' and 'plastic phials of approx. 50 cubic cm containing an unidentified liquid'. Lastly 'there was a small booklet of instructions with a red cover written in French entitled: "La technique du sabotage". There were 15 of these.'[64]

215

More stores were sent in subsequent weeks. On the night of 16/17 June, thirty-five floating containers were dropped by parachute into Lake Varano, the largest lake in southern Italy, a long, thin, salt-water lagoon on the Gargano Peninsula. This time McCaffery heard from Klein that his men had found the stores. Two months later, on the night of 17/18 August, nine more containers were dropped at the same spot. August also saw more supplies landed from the sea, when a three-man landing party paddled ashore at night from the submarine *Seraph* and buried four wireless sets on the rocky Portofino peninsula. One of these men was a pre-war Arctic explorer, Captain Andrew Croft. A fire-eating SOE officer who would later parachute into France and win a DSO, Croft would recall in his memoirs that the sets had been dug in beneath 'some luxuriant maquis bushes' and their exact location communicated to 'the Italian Resistance' who were due to pick them up.[65] 'The secreting of the stores was carried out very quietly, and all traces of our work carefully removed,' adds the report of the British officer in charge of the party, Captain McClair of the Special Boat Section; 'I have every reason to believe the enemy will not suspect a landing.'[66] Today, with access to both British and Italian records, it is clear that McClair and his companions were particularly exposed. Quite apart from having landed stores at a spot suggested by SIM, they had been briefed beforehand to make for a certain barber's shop in Genoa if they found themselves stranded ashore. The address for this safe house had also been passed to the British by Italian intelligence.

SIM secured more from SOE than material and money. Once McCaffery and the British were taken in by Klein and his contacts, the Italians found themselves able to watch and destroy communications between the British and genuine anti-Fascists. One such was Eugenio Paladino, an Italian engineer in his forties to whom McCaffery was introduced by an American banker in Zurich in the autumn of 1941. Paladino, who lived in Rome, had a sideline in the tobacco business that took him frequently through Switzerland on business trips to Germany. He told McCaffery that he was happy to report back about those trips and to explore the possibilities in Italy of arranging safe houses and the receipt of agents and stores. In May 1942, with the intention of providing Paladino with a secure means of maintaining contact, McCaffery put him in touch with Klein in Milan. Not long after that, Paladino was arrested in Rome, found guilty by the Special Tribunal of passing intelligence to the Allies, and sentenced to thirty years in prison.

Another line into Italy that fell victim in this way and at about this time was what McCaffery had described to London as 'a very good thing in Milan . . . in the shape of two first-class Yugoslavs'.[67] These were a pair of university students who appeared to have good contacts, and McCaffery was confident that, among other things, they could help agents to cross Italy's border with Slovenia. In April 1942, McCaffery delegated the task of contacting them to Edmund Schwerdt. Schwerdt gave Elio Andreoli, his Swiss friend, appropriate instructions. SIM did the rest. 'I have taken all possible precautions to act safely and to exploit these contacts to the full,' reported the SIM officer overseeing proceedings. 'I consider it necessary, however, to follow and control the Yugoslav students' activities to the furthest degree possible before suppressing their work.'[68] In June, after a delivery was made to their Milan apartment of explosives, instructions, 35,000 lire, and 'a "Leica" camera 1x3.5 (already loaded) plus an additional lens and 7 rolls of film', those arrested included a man from Trieste who had come to visit the pair and a Bulgarian student in whose room they had scheduled their next meeting with Andreoli.[69]

And then there was the fate of SOE's young wireless operator, Giacomino Sarfatti. When he turned up in Milan in December 1942, stepping off the train from Como just hours after crossing the border, SIM had been expecting him for months. McCaffery had always been open with Eligio Klein about his wish to send him a wireless operator, and in recent months had warned often of his impending arrival. This was a time when the trials and executions in Italy of suspected British agents were reaching a peak: the Zaccaria brothers, shot on 10 November; Emilio Zappalà and SOE's Antonio Gallo, shot on 28 November; Ettore Vacca and Giuseppe Giacomazzi, both shot in December; and Laura D'Oriano, the only woman to die at Forte Bravetta, who would be shot there in January 1943. But SIM did not plan to arrest Sarfatti immediately.

Instead, SIM decided to keep him tightly under Klein's wing, to make him feel protected, undetected, and freely in contact with the outside world. This, it was hoped, would neutralise Sarfatti's ability to engage in any kind of anti-Italian activity, while allowing SIM to keep deceiving the British in Berne by maintaining an illusion that all was well and that he was safe among friends. So, when Sarfatti sought out Klein in Milan, SIM made sure that he received every impression that Klein was doing all he could for him: he fixed up Sarfatti with a rented room in an apartment on Via Marcona; he bought him suitable clothes and supplied him with a ration card; to provide some local cover, Klein gave him an attaché case of medicines so that he could pretend to be a pharmaceutical salesman. Klein also handed him a suitcase sent over the frontier by McCaffery in readiness for Sarfatti's arrival. It contained, among other items, an automatic pistol. Later he delivered a wireless set that had also been smuggled across. Meanwhile, through its ongoing control of Elio Andreoli, McCaffery's Swiss courier to Milan, SIM was also able to open, read and reseal every item of correspondence that Sarfatti and McCaffery exchanged.

SIM's delicate handling of Sarfatti was helped by his absolute faith in Klein, his only contact in Milan, whom he had been told by McCaffery to trust completely. '[The British] agent Giacomo Rossi [Sarfatti's cover name] has to date been inactive,' reads one early SIM report about him, evidently because, according to instructions received from the English service, he should try for a certain period only to orientate himself and to get to know 'Giusto' [SIM's codename for Klein]. He conducts a normal life: goes out of the house in the morning and afternoon in order to become accepted by the inhabitants of Via Marcona 81 as a commercial agent for pharmaceutical products; he eats his lunch in a trattoria in the neighbourhood of Via Marcona 81 and passes his evenings in a cinema or theatre. He often likes to walk around the city and for preference dines in the Restaurant 'Brenta' with 'Giusto'.[70]

From his chats with Klein, SIM soon learned that Sarfatti was an Italian citizen and 'that he has his parents and a brother in Italy, who, however, he has no intention of visiting (he has so far given no information about them)'.[71] It knew that he had joined the Pioneer Corps after being interned in 1940 and had later received training in 'techniques of sabotage and espionage'. It knew that he had reached Italy after landing in France 'by a motor fishing boat' and been arrested in Switzerland where he had rolled out a cover story of being a British commando who had been at Dieppe.[72]

SIM gathered, too, that Sarfatti had received his final instructions in Switzerland from a man called 'Mac'. 'This was probably the chief I met in Berne,' Klein pointed out in one report.[73] It knew, too, that Sarfatti's orders included the task of sending back 'documents of every type, including official ones, such as passes, military discharge papers, identity cards, etc'.[74] It even knew that he carried a pill of quick-acting poison, to be swallowed in case of arrest, and that he somehow managed to lose it. When he wrote to Berne to say that he wanted a new one, SIM read the request and resolved to swap the new pill, when it arrived, for a harmless replacement, so that the real one could be sent 'for chemical analysis' and the production, if possible, of an antidote, 'which could be administered in case of need . . . [It has been] learnt in recent correspondence with the leadership of the Gestapo that various different spies in the pay

219

of the enemy had swallowed poison pills in order to escape the interrogators.'[75]

Sarfatti's untroubled time in Milan lasted until the eve of the Armistice. It was prolonged by the fact that, as SIM knew well, he was there mainly to play a waiting game, since his orders were to stay in place and do little until SOE really needed him. One SIM memorandum in February 1943 noted that Sarfatti, 'in chatting with [Klein], revealed that, to date, he did not know the use he was supposed to make of the radio transmitter [he had received], but that he was keeping it in accordance with the instructions of his superiors that it would be useful at some [later] stage for communicating directly with London matters of particular importance.'[76] Confident that it was controlling him so effectively that he knew nothing of particular importance, SIM was happy to allow him to use the set and remained hands-off even when SOE began to request information about enemy troop movements. Since Sarfatti asked Klein for the answers, SIM ensured that suitably ineffectual responses were sent. At one point, after learning that Sarfatti needed more room for his aerial, SIM even arranged for Klein to move him from his pokey room at 81 Via Marcona to a spacious apartment at 8 Via Spartaco. Feeding the wire out of the attic, into the courtyard, and back in through the bathroom window, Sarfatti was soon getting a better reception.

⊙

From an Italian point of view, the total control of SOE's lines from Switzerland was an outstanding success. For a good two years, the Italians consistently misdirected British energies and intentions and routinely soaked up British money, explosives and devices. As the head of SIM's counter-espionage section, Colonel Mario Bertacchi, later wrote, they had also gained a 'pretty comprehensive picture' of British methods. Careful monitoring of correspondence from Switzerland had provided unique insight into 'how agents were treated, how they were paid, how they communicated with them (invisible writing), etc.' The Italians had learned, too, about British procedures for infiltrating material: 'across the borders in suitcases . . . dropped by plane in lake areas . . . disembarked by submarine . . . placed in the seas near the coast . . . Very important too was the examination of the technical means used in the drops and in written reports and in particular the knowledge of the various sabotage materials, which were studied [and] tried out.'[77] Other gains were details of genuine anti-Fascists and of British objectives and projected plans, the latter deduced from lists of desired targets sent to McCaffery's contacts in northern Italy, as well as the ability to deceive the British by planting misleading information coming purportedly from anti-Fascists. In Bertacchi's opinion, SIM's hoodwinking of the British was its greatest counter-espionage achievement of the war and might have lasted years if the Armistice had not interrupted it. Another man who acknowledged what the Italians had done was Raymond Rocca, post-war deputy head of the CIA's counter-intelligence staff. In 1945, when the Allies finally caught up with Eligio Klein, Rocca was his American interrogator. What the Italians had achieved, Rocca recorded after learning the details, 'must be regarded as a classic example of a deception operation'.[78]

10

'As much alarm as possible'

On a cold and very dark night in January 1943, three weeks after Giacomino Sarfatti had crossed the Swiss–Italian border on his mission to Milan, a British submarine surfaced half a mile off the southeast coast of Sardinia. A hatch opened. Figures appeared on the gun platform. A rubber dinghy was hauled out, inflated and lowered over the side. Then four men climbed in with weapons and kit and began paddling for the shore, aiming for a secluded spot on a wide flat beach flanked by a watchtower and two little houses. It was ten to three in the morning. At four o'clock they reached the beach.

Two of the party were young Cornish sailors trained to land agents and stores on enemy coasts. The other two were SOE agents with orders to stay ashore. One of the Cornishmen, Seaman Webb, now stayed with the dinghy while the other, Leading Seaman Taylor, helped the agents carry their kit through the dunes and a mile and a half inland and bury it. When that job was done, Taylor returned, alone, to the beach. He and Webb re-launched the dinghy and began paddling back out to sea, peering hard into the darkness for the submarine.

There was no sign of it. With a brisk wind behind them, Taylor and Webb kept paddling. Still there was no submarine. By now it was broad daylight and they were miles out to sea. Frightened and desperate, they turned again for the shore. 'We get to about a mile within the land when a sailing ship comes bearing down on us,' Taylor wrote afterwards in a little scribbled note, 'so we decided to get rid of our guns maps and everything [and then] . . . layed [sic] down in the boat and waited and he passed.' At midday the two sailors were still at sea, 'just about knocked up and trying to get to shore and hide', when they suddenly spotted a periscope poking out of the water about five hundred yards astern, 'so we turn round to meet the S/M [submarine] and just as we get there he surface [*sic*] and only about three hundred yards from the shore'.[1]

Taylor and Webb scrambled aboard. A knife was put into the dinghy to make it easier to pull inside, while the submarine's first lieutenant leapt into the sea to rescue the paddles as they began to float away: it was vital to leave no clues that men had gone ashore that night. Four minutes after surfacing and with everyone safely on board, the submarine dived. Its commander, an experienced officer who had landed his first agents on Guernsey in 1940, was Lieutenant Ian McGeoch, a 28-year-old Scot. '1223 [hours],' reads his report of his role in the landing; 'Embarked boat and its occupants who were understandably relieved to find that we were not an enemy U-boat, the periscope having looked at them, they said, in a hostile way.'[2]

The two SOE agents whom McGeoch had put ashore were, after Giacomino Sarfatti, the next to set foot on Italian soil; they were also the first and last to be sent to Sardinia while Italy was hostile. Their orders were to reconnoitre sabotage targets, gather intelligence, transmit reports, and recruit locals willing to put up resistance to the island's Axis occupiers. It was a mission that had little to do with Emilio Lussu's earlier plan for a Sardinian rebellion. Rather, its immediate origins lay in the fast-changing course of the Mediterranean war where the balance of power was shifting firmly in the Allies' favour: with Allied control of North Africa seemingly imminent, British and American planners were eager to maintain the offensive and had instructed SOE to explore, with some urgency, the ways and means of causing trouble in southern France, southern Italy and the Italian islands. It was also a mission whose ultimate outcome would prove of value to one of the major Allied deception schemes put into practice in the Mediterranean. Yet it began so disastrously that, if anything had been learned from MI6's recent efforts to put agents into Sicily and Italy, few lessons seem to have been heeded when SOE came to land these two on Sardinia.

⊙

One of the agents who went ashore that night was Salvatore Serra. He was a native Sardinian, tall and swarthy. 'Black hair; black eyes,' reads a physical description in his SOE personal file; 'full mouth with firm square teeth, but definitely too many'.[3] 'Heavy shaving mark,' records another pen-portrait; 'Chest covered with thick black hair. Legs also hairy.'[4] According to the file he had been born in February 1909 in Solarussa, a little town in the west of Sardinia, and was the son of a farmer. After some local schooling he had joined the Carabinieri with which he served for ten years before deserting in Abyssinia in 1938 and fleeing to British Somaliland. There he had been allowed to live at liberty until detained in 1940 when Italy entered the war. Then, destined for an internment camp, he was shipped to India.

Serra had come to SOE's attention in December 1941 while languishing at Dehra Dun, the same camp from which Heinrich Harrer, the Austrian author of *Seven Years in Tibet*, would famously escape. More precisely, Serra had come to the attention of Colin Mackenzie, a highly capable Scot who had been sent out from London to establish an SOE presence in India. One of Mackenzie's early instructions was to search the camps for prospective Italian recruits; he himself had learned Italian while a young businessman in Milan in the twenties. 'We were careful to paint the job we were offering him in pretty dark colours,' Mackenzie told London as he dispatched to Britain for specialist training 'this first volunteer to be shipped'.

We pointed out to him that it was extremely dangerous, that, in the moments of extreme danger, he would be entirely alone, that there could be no glory attaching to the work during the war, and that, once he was in a thing of this kind, he was in for the duration whether he liked it or not.[5]

Arriving in London in March 1942, Serra's first stop was the Royal Victoria Patriotic School, close to Wandsworth prison. Known also as the London Reception Centre, it was a screening centre for incoming aliens of intelligence interest. 'This is a somewhat unusual and difficult case,' wrote Serra's investigating MI5 officer. 'The man himself is an unusual Italian, unemotional and quiet, not very talkative. We have no means of checking up his background, and his statements as regards his political tendencies we must either take or leave.' Doubt was cast on aspects of Serra's account of fleeing Abyssinia to escape arrest for making anti-Fascist propaganda. Possibly, the MI5 officer mused, Serra had fled for some other reason. Perhaps he was even 'an escaped criminal'.[6] SOE decided to take him anyway. Soon enough he was enlisted as a private in the Pioneer Corps and had started his training.

Observations by escorts and instructors while Serra passed from course to course paint a picture of a quiet, simple and likeable man of modest ability. 'This man seems to be of a sincere type,' reads one early report. 'Does not appear pleasure seeking and usually turned down my offers to take him to the cinema. During the six days I was with him he showed no interest in women whatever.'[7] One man who came to know Serra better than most was an Intelligence Corps NCO, Ernest Saunders. In April, Saunders reported from Water Eaton Manor, a training school outside Oxford:

[Serra] only speaks Italian, and ... is [further] handicapped by the limited nature of his boyhood education. He cannot do the simplest calculation without laborious resort to pencil and paper. His character is one of extreme simplicity. He does not seem to have any interest in games or pursuits of any description. Slow in his mental processes, I cannot imagine him as an organiser or leader, but he is of the type who will follow a respected leader until the end. He is an ardent Royalist ...

He has a great respect for the British people and I do not think this is affected in order to gain our good graces. His anti-fascism is not bitter, not the result of persecution, but has rather been handed down to him from his father.

His morale is high, although he is rather stupefied at the number of the subjects he has to study . . . Repeatedly he expresses a desire to accompany British Commandos on French coast raids, and he imagines that when he has finished his training he will be sent to join some such special corps.[8]

'My early good impressions of this student's reliability are strengthened with further acquaintance,' Saunders added a few days later. 'All persons with whom he comes into contact seem to take a liking to him . . . He looks forward to the time when he will be able to go into action and feels confident that he will give a good account of himself.'[9] Three weeks after that, having accompanied Serra to SOE's training school at Arisaig, Saunders continued: 'He is still as eager in his work and as anxious to please as ever . . . His complete unpretentiousness has made him popular all round.'[10]

By the end of May, with his training complete, Serra was back in London, billeted in the Victoria Hotel on Northumberland Avenue off Trafalgar Square. Also, Saunders noted, he was unhappy. 'His shy nature, combined with his lack of knowledge of English, lead him to avoid crowds and public places, and he prefers to sit in the hotel bedroom all day and feel very bored . . . London has a definitely upsetting effect . . . and I suggest that he should be kept in the country as far as possible.'[11] This was also the time when Emilio Lussu's scheme for Sardinia was in the process of imploding. SOE had hoped that Serra might be fashioned into a wireless operator of use to Lussu; when he had been found to lack the aptitude for radio work, a hope had remained that he could be used in some constructive way and Lussu was even brought to the Victoria Hotel to meet him. Even as Lussu's plan fell apart, it was still thought that Serra's knowledge of Sardinia might prove useful. With no immediate prospect of any operational role, however, and in view of his evident discomfort in London, it was decided that he should kill time in the Cooler, SOE's holding school in Scotland for trainees and agents too sensitive to release. Serra arrived at the Cooler in early June.

'A good man and a keen worker, he is settling down nicely,' the staff reported after he had been in the Cooler a fortnight.[12] 'Spends most of his time cutting the grass ... helping [Rinaldo Purisiol] in the forge, and chewing gum,' read another report a few weeks later. 'It is amazing how this man and [Purisiol] have formed this habit; they are never without a piece of gum, even on parade.'[13] More weeks passed. 'This man works away quietly and causes no trouble,' it was reported in August; 'The other day he asked if there was any news for him from London ...'[14] In September he was 'still wondering how much longer it will be before he can leave here'.[15] Finally, in October, Serra was escorted back to London and returned to the arms of Cecil Roseberry. Shortly after that, he found himself teaching Sardinian dialect to an Italian-speaking SOE wireless operator. His name was Gabor Adler and he was the man who would land with Serra on Sardinia.

Gabor Adler was neither Sardinian nor even Italian. He was a Hungarian Jew. According to SOE records, he had been born in September 1919 in Satu Mare, a city today in northwest Romania, and had lived in Budapest until 1922 when he left with his parents to live in the northern Italian town of Merano in the Tyrol. From 1930 until 1934 he went to school at Esslingen in Germany. Then he returned to Italy, where he worked in Milan in an advertising office, then for a Russian engineer, then for a Russian fur merchant, before leaving to live in Morocco in 1939 after the introduction of Italy's new racial laws.

Settling in Tangiers, Adler had worked as a waiter, cook and housepainter before approaching the British Consulate – where he had been doing some decorating – to ask if he might volunteer for the British Army. In November 1941, with the consul's help, he sailed in a small boat for Gibraltar. After that he was brought to Britain under the auspices of de Gaulle's Free French Forces, reaching Gourock in January 1942. When Adler's arrival and Italian background became known, SOE, in its desperate search for reliable Italian-speaking recruits, persuaded the Free French to release their claim on him. He began his SOE training in February.

Adler emerges from the files as independent and highly intelligent. He spoke multiple languages. He was extremely fit. Overall he was a man very different to Serra and much more typical of the sort that SOE was keen to recruit, even if his motives for wishing to fight seemed to be somewhat mercenary. 'This man is very intelligent and quick-witted and keeps abreast of the course of study without much effort,' recorded one observer, Sergeant Paul Garvin, who had been assigned to escorting and watching Adler at Chicheley Hall, an SOE school near Newport Pagnall, where he began his paramilitary training.

He takes everything in his stride, without, however, displaying any marked degree of enthusiasm. He is an all-round man and displays an equal aptitude for both the mental and physical side of the course.

He is inclined at times to display a rather superior and critical attitude . . . In the last few days he has settled down much better and reacts with docility to the various regulations of the school. He has a very redeeming sense of humour even if it is at times markedly cynical, is an agreeable companion and, once you have got to know him, very easy to get on with. He does not appear to have any marked anti-fascist or anti-German feelings, and I would say he is in the game to get as much as he can out of it . . . I think his main object in volunteering for the British forces is to enable himself to get a British Passport after the war (he is a Jew of the International type, without any particular national root) . . . and he is continually asking me how much one gets paid for this and that.

I have gathered that one of his professions was that of interior decorator. He can draw very artistic maps . . . He is quite well educated and seems to have led a fairly athletic life. He denies he has had any previous military training, but the way he handles the various weapons would lead one to suspect that he has had some previous acquaintance with them.[16]

'He has no personal quarrel with Germans or Italians,' Garvin also observed while still at Chicheley Hall; 'he and his family have suffered no active persecution from them, they have never invaded his own country, and he has only a vague sympathy for his fellow Jews in the sufferings they have undergone.'[17] Garvin recorded, too, that Adler 'finds the continual confinement to barracks very irksome, and frequently talks about the good times he is going to have when he is let out … When he learned that a soldier gets a free railway warrant when he goes on leave, he at once pulled out a map of England and started planning all the towns he hoped to visit.'[18]

From Chicheley Hall, Adler went to other secret schools. They included Thame Park in Oxfordshire where he learned to use a wireless set. Not untypical of prospective agents as their training progressed and the realities hit home, he also began to display some anxiety about what could lie round the corner.

He states that he is perfectly willing to carry out any task which is assigned to him to the best of his ability, but he does not view with any enthusiasm the prospect of being turned loose on his own in an enemy country. He doubts if he has the qualities necessary for such a mission; for example he says he could never bring himself to kill another man in cold blood, even if his own safety or life depended on it. He maintains that he has never been under fire or experienced actual fighting, and that until he does so he would not have the necessary presence of mind or ruthlessness to carry out a solo mission successfully.[19]

SOE does not seem to have been particularly worried by Adler's concerns. Probably it helped that he had been self-aware and honest enough to highlight them himself. 'Adler was quite frank with me on the point of being unable to say whether he could take a life,' wrote Cecil Roseberry in November 1942, 'and in fact asked to be put under fire for a time to test his reactions.'[20]

In the event, even if Roseberry had been inclined to arrange for an expensively trained agent to be shot at, there was no time for that request to be met. Adler's training was complete, he was freshly commissioned as a second lieutenant in the British Army, and plans were in place to send him and Salvatore Serra into Sardinia.

⊙

The Second Battle of El Alamein, fought in Egypt in October and November 1942, was the turning point in the North African campaign and one of the most critical engagements of the entire conflict. The greatest offensive victory by the Western Allies since the outbreak of the war, it removed the threat to Egypt and the Suez Canal and was the catalyst for an advance by Montgomery's Eighth Army that would ultimately prove unstoppable. Then, on 8 November, the Anglo-American invasion of Northwest Africa began with landings at Oran, Casablanca and Algiers, burdening the Axis with another front to their rear. Months of hard fighting lay ahead before all of North Africa was in Allied hands, but the interest of Allied commanders in spreading offensive action to Europe's southern shores grew quickly. One early outcome was a meeting in London in November 1942 at which senior SOE officers discussed plans for Corsica and Sardinia.

Both islands were occupied by Italian troops. Both islands were potential stepping-stones for any major Allied invasion of southern Europe. For Corsica it was agreed that a small team of French agents should be infiltrated with orders to build and prepare a guerrilla organisation whose principal task, timed to assist an Allied landing in Sardinia, would be to neutralise local aerodromes. For Sardinia it was decided that a second team would go in to help prepare the way for that landing by recruiting friendly locals to receive and guide parties of airborne troops and commandos, and by locating suitable reception points and identifying sabotage targets. SOE's Italian Section had the job of

Benito Mussolini, the Italian Fascist leader, on the balcony of Rome's Palazzo Venezia in 1938.

Anti-British propaganda produced in Italy in 1940 implying, somewhat unsubtly, British intolerance of fledgling nations.

Fortunato Picchi photographed after his capture in 1941. A former waiter at the Savoy, he was the first SOE recruit to be sent into Italy.

A young Fortunato Picchi in a photograph seized by Italian investigators in 1941.

The spot inside Forte Bravetta, Rome, where Picchi and other captured agents were executed. Victims would be sat astride a chair and shot in the back.

Emilio Lussu, politician, patriot and revolutionary, who sought SOE's help with raising an anti-Fascist revolt in Sardinia.

Mazzini Society membership card for Andrew Ingrao, a troublesome Italian volunteer dispatched to Britain from the United States.

SOE's half of the 1-lire note used for contacts with Ulisse La Terza who used the other half to identify himself. An Italian doctor who proposed to establish a wireless set in Rome, he also claimed to be an agent of the OVRA.

HMS *Una*, the Royal Navy submarine that landed Antonio Gallo and Emilio Zappalà on the Sicilian coast in October 1942. Weeks earlier, *Una* had put ashore Eric Newby's 'Why Not' party.

The Arco della Pace in Milan. In February 1942, SOE sent its first suitcase of explosives and devices to a secret rendezvous here from neutral Switzerland.

The first suitcase and its carefully wrapped contents, including a box containing fake fog signals wrapped in a copy of the *Daily Telegraph*, photographed after their interception by Italian counter-intelligence officers.

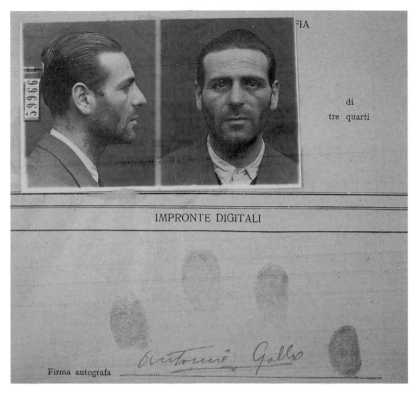

IMPRONTE DIGITALI

Firma autografa

SOE agent Antonio Gallo photographed and fingerprinted by his Italian captors. He was executed shortly afterwards at Forte Bravetta.

Gabor Adler (*left*) and Salvatore Serra (*right*) who went into Sardinia in January 1943.

SOE radio operator Branko Nekić, caught and killed in Sicily in August 1943.

SOE radio operator Giacomino Sarfatti, unwitting pawn in an Italian deception plan.

Max Salvadori in a photograph pasted onto a false Italian identity card that he carried in Sicily in August 1943. His fair hair has been dyed brown.

'This is the approx. scene of my drop on Lake Como.' A post-war photograph annotated by Dick Mallaby.

Mallaby after his extraordinary exploits in Italy in 1943. Sewn on his shirt is the ribbon of his Military Cross.

In a tent in Sicily on 8 September 1943, Major General Walter Bedell Smith countersigns the Italian Armistice. Italian General Giuseppe Castellano, wearing a black civilian suit, looks on, with Franco Montanari, his interpreter, to his left. Bedell Smith's interpreter, SOE's Teddy de Haan, stands in the centre.

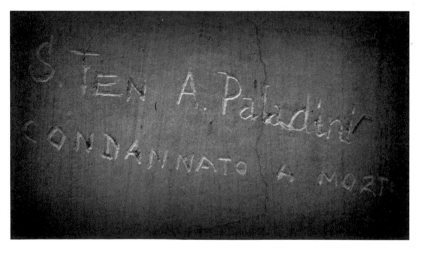

Inscription on a cell wall of the Gestapo prison in Via Tasso, Rome. The writer, Arrigo Paladini, escaped execution and was liberated from the prison on the same morning in June 1944 that Gabor Adler was shot.

selecting the Sardinian team. The two men selected were Gabor Adler and Salvatore Serra.

In December, the pair flew to Algiers where they settled down to wait for an available submarine to take them to Sardinia. By now, in line with a general seeping away from Cairo of planning and control in the Mediterranean, SOE had established in Algeria a fresh base close to Dwight Eisenhower's new Allied Forces Headquarters, the body now commanding most operations across the Mediterranean theatre. This new SOE base, codenamed 'Massingham', was housed in a former luxury beach resort just outside Algiers: 'a big village of splendid villas', one Italian agent would recall, 'now devastated by sand, because no one cleans them . . . on a beach which seems to me one of the most beautiful in the Mediterranean'.[21] Responsible at 'Massingham' for Italian affairs was an RAF squadron leader, Harold Crawshaw. Born in Brittany, Crawshaw was forty and had worked before the war as a chartered accountant, a job that had included a seven-year stint in Italy. Poached by SOE from the Air Ministry, he had worked in London as Roseberry's assistant until heading to North Africa in November. Now he arranged for the two new arrivals to be housed in conditions of strict secrecy in an isolated farmhouse outside the city.

'I am pretty well tied to them as they can't be allowed out alone very much,' Crawshaw wrote to London in mid-December; 'we all mess together and they are fairly happy cooking and looking after the place. Their other physical needs' – Crawshaw did not enlarge on these – 'I have attended to but things aren't as easy here as in London.' He added that he hoped it would not be long before they were off,

as the security angle is very difficult. Soldiers in British uniform who look a bit queer and who cannot speak a word of English are rather too noticeable here with the result that the boys are confined to the house more than is good for them. However, they are a good couple and they are bearing up pretty well.[22]

By early January, a Royal Navy 'S' class submarine, Ian McGeoch's *P.228*, had been assigned to the landing role. More than forty years later, McGeoch recalled that the night before sailing for Sardinia he was taken to a farmhouse 'where the two agents had prepared a magnificent supper of chicken and pasta and all sorts of things and we had a splendid and fairly bibulous evening. And then the next day we all set off.'[23]

P.228 got under way from Algiers on the afternoon of 5 January 1943. The Sardinian coast was reached early on the morning of 8 January. Carefully the submarine closed on the pinpoint where the agents were to go ashore. The chosen spot, forty or so miles up the coast from Cagliari, Sardinia's capital, and below the wooded lower slopes of Mount Ferro, was an isolated beach immediately north of a rocky promontory bearing the Torri di San Giovanni di Sarrala, an imposing conical watchtower built in the 1760s. All seemed quiet. Then McGeoch took the submarine back out to sea where his crew and the agents made their final preparations. Later he recorded that Adler in particular 'inspired great confidence'. At a minute past midnight on the morning of 9 January, *P.228* proceeded landwards a second time. Soon the rubber dinghy was out of the hull and McGeoch was watching it 'heading slowly but surely for the shore'.[24]

The following day, when the two Cornishmen were safely back in the submarine, one of them, Frank Taylor, reported that progress had been a little difficult due to a strengthening off-shore breeze, while 'at the last moment [Serra] got cold feet and was very frightened all the way in the dinghy'.[25] Serra had also refused to paddle, so that 'the efforts of the other agent (Adler) were largely wasted because the boat turned round'.[26] But the landing was successful, Serra seemed 'alright' when the beach was reached, and Taylor was sure that no alarm had been raised.[27]

At 'Massingham', staff and signals officers waited to hear from Adler that the mission was safely established ashore. On 15 January, an SOE receiving station seems to have picked up a message preceded by Adler's callsign enquiring about the strength of his set's signal. Then a month passed without another sound. This silence was not unexpected. Before leaving for Sardinia, Adler had been told not to hurry when opening up wireless contact. Then, on 19 February, a second signal was received. More followed in subsequent days and soon there was a regular flow. These early messages explained that the two agents had found the coast heavily guarded so had decided to bury their equipment, move inland and hide in towns. They had since recovered their kit and were now quite safe in a house belonging to one of Serra's friends, though finding food was difficult. Serra was reported as about to set off to gather news and find more friends. Urging the pair to be careful and send minimal signals traffic, SOE congratulated them on their progress.[28]

⊙

Today, Italian documents and testimonies reveal that Gabor Adler and Salvatore Serra had been captured within twenty-four hours of going ashore. On 12 January 1943 the Carabinieri in Cagliari reported that 'an Englishman' and 'an Italian subject who was a deserter' had been arrested on the coast two days before. 'These men were provided with a wireless transmitting device, and had been landed by an enemy submarine in the neighbourhood of S. Giovanni di Sarala [sic] (Commune of Tertia, province of Nuoro).'[29] The two prisoners were promptly passed to SIM, remembered Colonel Mario Bertacchi, who had been chief of its counter-espionage section at the time, and eventually revealed 'their mission, their signal plan, etc.' Then SIM's Controspionaggio section decided to attempt 'a double-cross': 'W/T [wireless telegraphy] communication with the enemy secret service was established and numerous signals exchanged'.[30]

Much later, in 1945, SOE ran to ground two Italians who had worked for the SIM counter-espionage section in Sardinia in 1943. One of these men was Major Cesare Faccio, a man warmly regarded by his SOE questioner as 'bluff, hearty, straight-forward, cheerful, and not too well educated'. Faccio was aged about fifty and a career Carabiniere who had been posted to SIM after convalescing from wounds suffered at El Alamein. He had run the SIM Cagliari office from March until September 1943 after being sent there to replace a Sardinian SIM officer, a major called Sanna, who had been in charge when Adler and Serra were caught. 'Maj Sanna had not dealt with the case very intelligently and there had been some delay in his reports reaching Rome,' Faccio recalled. 'When the reports did arrive, SIM at once realised the great importance of the case, and sent Lt-Col Faga to Cagliari to take the case in hand.' Faga was 'a very experienced professional SIM officer', explained Faccio, and immediately and thoroughly re-interrogated Adler and Serra 'and at once began doubling the set back to the British'. By the time that Faccio arrived, Colonel Faga had 'started the doubling off on the right foot' and felt that Faccio could 'keep it going nicely'.[31]

Faccio, who impressed SOE as 'very obviously not a proper SIM officer', went on to describe how, on discovering on his arrival in Sardinia that Adler was languishing in Cagliari prison, he had thought this 'very hard' on the young man. Faccio had therefore decided to let him live instead in his officers' mess. By the time that orders arrived from Rome in May to send Adler to the main-land, the two men had become 'quite good friends'. Adler had even accompanied Faccio on car drives around the island. But this had not meant that Adler had co-operated, Faccio stressed. Adler's attitude had struck him as 'one of complete indifference'. He had given away 'nothing of what he had seen or heard in England' or, indeed, any other information of importance. The 'double-cross' had been conducted without Adler's 'consent or collaboration' and he had never worked the wireless set himself, 'the transmitting being done by an Italian lieutenant.'[32]

The second Italian whom SOE interviewed was a sergeant-major named Antonio Silvestri. In 1945 he was working for the

Allies in the SIM office in Rome, having, like Faccio, switched sides after the Armistice. The SOE officer who spoke to Silvestri considered him 'an excellent type, serious and intelligent. He was careful and precise in his statements and showed every sign of doing his best to tell everything he knew which was of importance, and to stress the difference between what he knew first-hand and what he knew from other people. His statements can probably be considered as very reliable.'[33] According to a captured American officer who met him in Cagliari in the summer of 1943, Silvestri was the son of an Italian father and Japanese mother and before the war had lived in Shanghai and worked for American Express. In Cagliari, remembered the American, Silvestri had been Faccio's 'secretary interpreter' and knew, 'according to him, 4,000 Chinese ideograms'.[34]

Silvestri, who spoke excellent English, explained to SOE in 1945 that he had been sent from Rome to Sardinia in May 1943 to replace a junior SIM officer in Cagliari's counter-espionage office. Neither Serra nor Adler was still on the island when Silvestri arrived. From his new colleagues, however, he had managed to gather something of the background to the case. Once ashore, 'these two individuals found themselves more or less lost,' he recalled, 'and committed the imprudence of asking a shepherd (or some such individual) for directions'. This man, or someone else who had noticed their 'manner and obvious ignorance', promptly alerted the authorities with the result that the two agents were arrested the same day. Silvestri believed that they had been treated well and that Adler 'certainly lived with the commander of the SIM C/S [the Controspionaggio section] and ate at the same table'.[35]

In Cagliari, Silvestri had had the role of providing English translations for the signals being sent over Adler's wireless set. He explained in 1945 that 'all incoming messages from the British were repeated back immediately to Rome, which then signalled back the message which was to go to the British in reply'. These outgoing messages, which he translated into English, were then enciphered and transmitted. 'On one or two fairly rare occasions Cagliari drafted the reply on its own initiative, but all texts in and out were submitted to Rome.' Listening to him speak in 1945, SOE observed that Silvestri

considered that the whole operation of doubling had been very successful [and was] quite sure that the British were taken in by it. To demonstrate his point he explained that on one occasion the Italians had asked for certain supplies of stores to be dropped and the stores had in fact arrived. On another occasion the British asked for most important details on the fortifications and military dispositions on Sardinia, and, by co-operating with the local Sardinian Military HQ, the necessary information was 'planted'. The military authorities were particularly pleased over this matter.[36]

Mario Bertacchi, the SIM counter-espionage chief, would remember that Adler and Serra were taken from Sardinia and imprisoned in Rome 'as soon as their presence on the island was no longer necessary for playing the double game'. Bertacchi also recalled that SIM was particularly anxious to avoid repeating the same mistakes 'as in the Rossi case'.[37] This was a reference to the MI6 agent in Sicily who had tried to indicate to the British in one of his messages that he was sending them under duress. Bertacchi evidently believed that SIM had got things right with the Sardinian deception. He was mistaken. Almost from the start, SOE had rumbled that Adler and Serra were blown.

As the first few messages began to arrive from Adler's set, fears had quickly grown in Algiers that something was seriously wrong. SOE wireless operators receiving Adler's coded signals spotted that his messages referred to Serra by his real name and not as Pisano, his agreed *nom de guerre*. More worryingly, Adler's security checks were missing. Security checks were a series of letters that an agent would insert in his outgoing messages as a means of indicating to those receiving them that he was operating freely. If checks were absent or corrupt, it might indicate that an agent was working under duress or someone else was working his set.

SOE knew that the security check system was primitive and unreliable: sometimes agents made mistakes or simply forgot to include them. For this reason a team of Adler's old instructors who had trained him at Thame Park were put to work at an SOE signals station in Buckinghamshire to listen to his messages and record what they thought. On the night of 26 February, all four were manning receivers when the Morse of the next message was heard from faraway Sardinia. It was brief. The signal merely mentioned again the mission's food problems and claimed that recent Allied bombing had caused a 'great number [of] victims [and] damage and revenge feelings' on the island.[38] But it was enough for each of the listeners. All expressed 'grave doubt' about the identity of the operator: the quality of the Morse seemed well above Adler's standard.[39]

There were other disturbing signs. In March an Italian prisoner being interrogated in Algiers was reported to have claimed that in Cagliari in January he had heard a rumour – 'everyone was talking about it' – that four [sic] agents carrying a wireless set 'and lots of money' had been captured after landing by submarine 'somewhere near Cagliari'. One captive, he said, had been 'a Sardinian deserter from the Carabinieri'.[40] Then the same spy story began to be discussed by captive Italian submariners whose vessels had recently been sunk off Algeria and whose conversations were bugged as they shared cells between interrogations. 'He wanted to know whether there was a curfew in Cagliari when we left,' remarked one prisoner, a chief boatswain from the Italian submarine *Tritone*, about his interrogator's line of questioning; 'I told him I never went out [at night]'. 'There can't be a curfew there,' said his cellmate, a torpedo officer from the submarine *Avorio*; 'Why do they imagine there might be curfew?' 'There was something of the sort,' the *Tritone* boatswain replied;

'There was a curfew about the 16th or 17th January. People said they had captured some men who landed from a submarine near there.'[41] In another cell the boatswain from the *Avorio* also wondered aloud about the point of the curfew: 'Shore leave [at Cagliari] for petty officers was from two to six ... because there were supposed to have been some parachutists or submarines about. The English landed some men.' To which his cellmate, the *Tritone*'s chief engine-room petty officer, responded: 'They soon caught that "carabiniere". They captured a "carabiniere" who was a Sardinian.'[42]

SOE then set about trying to confirm whether Adler and Serra were really in enemy hands. Since it was felt that if Serra had been captured he 'would probably have been dealt with already as not being any use', a message was transmitted to Sardinia asking innocently for the names by which Serra had known a fellow trainee, plus the latter's age and the name of a mutual friend in India, with the explanation that the trainee was in London and wished to have proof that Serra was working for the British.[43] A few days later, a reply came back. It contained the correct responses and the name of another authentic friend. Serra, SOE grimly deduced, was 'obviously still above ground'.[44]

A second attempt, based on the persistent use of Serra's real name in all signals coming from Sardinia, proved more conclusive. At the end of April SOE transmitted a message telling the pair to expect the arrival of a new agent by the name of Pisano. 'Pisano will shortly be ready to join you,' the message read. 'Can you receive him and how do you recommend [us] sending him?'[45] Since Adler would know that Pisano was Serra's *nom de guerre*, SOE felt that this message would surely provoke surprise and a request for clarity if Adler were really in control of his set. Two days passed. Then a reply was received. 'Very glad Pisano is ready to join us,' it began. 'We can receive him and give him convenient hospitality.'[46] Days later, a second message arrived: 'Pisano can easily be sent by submarine and landed on deserted beach south

[of] Cape Palmeri . . . Let us know landing date and time. Serra will be on the spot with two friends who will receive Pisano, give him proper hospitality and accompany him where required. Cheerio.'[47]

⊙

So far as the British were concerned, discovering that the Italians were operating Adler's wireless set was only the beginning of this affair. In early May, SOE's Harold Crawshaw alerted the Algiers office of A Force, Dudley Clarke's famous deception organisation, to what was going on. 'S/Ldr Crawshaw has absolutely no doubt whatsoever that [Adler] is being run by the Italians,' A Force recorded; 'it is even possible that he has been killed'.[48] In charge of A Force's Algiers office, which was a sub-headquarters to Clarke's main office in Cairo, was Lieutenant-Colonel Michael Crichton. Keeping in close touch with Eisenhower's planning staff, Crichton and his little team were responsible for doing all they could to assist with imaginative schemes aimed at deceiving and discomfiting the enemy. They were also well briefed on tactical and strategic requirements. When he heard about what was happening in Sardinia, Crichton, to quote from SOE's files, attached 'the utmost importance' to the matter.[49] Soon A Force was considering how to exploit it in support of what was known in secret circles as Plan 'Barclay'.

Plan 'Barclay' had been born out of the Casablanca Conference in January 1943 when Churchill and Franklin Roosevelt, with their senior aides and military chiefs, had mapped out afresh their strategic aims. One outcome of these discussions had been the decision to prepare for an invasion of Sicily, and 'Barclay' had been devised as a deception operation aimed at diverting enemy attention from Sicily's defence by deceiving the Axis about Allied intentions in the Mediterranean. It involved an extraordinary range of imaginative measures. Intricate but entirely artificial threats to Greece, Sardinia, Corsica and southern France were developed, including, for example, a fictitious 'Twelfth Army' in the Eastern Mediterranean, poised to invade the Balkans, complete with vast numbers of dummy landing craft constructed in Cyrenaica and Egypt to suggest to enemy spies and reconnaissance aircraft the presence of an invasion fleet. The most famous ruse, though never formally integrated into 'Barclay', was Operation 'Mincemeat', the scheme wherein a dead body in the uniform of a Royal Marines officer was slipped from a submarine into the waters off Spain in the hope that the corpse would wash ashore as if from a plane crash at sea. Attached to the corpse was a briefcase of papers and plans suggesting that the Allies intended to invade Sardinia and Greece. The hope was that the Germans would see and believe the documents.

With the Italians apparently thinking that they were successfully controlling Adler's set, A Force saw a useful opportunity to spread misinformation in Sardinia itself. It also hoped to draw and identify what it termed 'enemy smoke'. This meant misinformation that the enemy wished to plant on the Allies. If spotted and accurately interpreted, 'smoke' could help to establish the enemy's real intentions and any secrets he was trying to hide. Vital to achieving any of this was the need to prolong the illusion that the British were unaware of what the Italians were doing, so regular meetings began to be held in Algiers at which A Force, MI6 and SOE officers discussed the progress of the case, ruminated over the latest signals received, and prepared all outgoing messages.

In the hope of reaping the greatest benefit, it was understood by all in Algiers that nothing should be rushed. To begin with, they decided to carry on sending 'the sort of messages SOE would send' and refrain from attempting anything too ambitious or unsubtle.[50] Soon, though, A Force began to feed in to the traffic indications that the Allies might wish the mission to provide support for an imminent landing. 'Proceed urgently with organising local elements,' read one message sent to Sardinia in early June. 'How do you think your friends could help by sabotage, civil disobedience, etcetera, in event [of] military operations?'[51] 'What arms and money do you want?' read another a few days later. 'If we supply arms and money what action could you hope [to] organise among local sympathisers in near future?'[52]

Meanwhile, as A Force had hoped, messages were coming back from Sardinia to suggest that the Italians were hooked: requests for stores, directions and information. 'We have consulted Serra's friends who are very reliable and ready to work with us,' read one awkwardly phrased message received in Algiers in May. 'Before trying to organise favourable elements they wish to know which are your aims and how long would it be at their disposal and with how many means and specialised men would you be able to supply us. Cheerio.'[53] 'We are working with all our might,' read another received in early June. 'However [a] substantial increase in organisation depends chiefly on [the] possibility of sending us men, arms and money.'[54] To help Serra's 'friends' to organise 'local sympathisers', Sardinia repeated at the end of the month, 'you should send us Italian money, automatic guns and sabotage material.'[55]

By then, A Force had decided that a tangible display of trust was required to show that the Allies believed that their agents in Sardinia were free. More than words were needed: already Algiers had had to explain away the non-arrival of the imaginary 'Pisano' by saying that he had lost his nerve and was no longer coming. It was with this need in mind that Cecil Roseberry made a proposal of particular ruthlessness. To perpetuate the idea that the British were still being hoodwinked, perhaps SOE might 'sacrifice' a real agent by sending him in to act as Adler's 'assistant'? Possibly, Roseberry thought, 'one of our doubtful Wops'?[56] He meant one of the ex-prisoners and internees who had volunteered for SOE service but proved unreliable, un-trainable, or otherwise unsuitable. ('Wop', a common but derogatory British term for an Italian, was frequently used as formal SOE shorthand [like 'Huns'

241

for Germans and 'Japs' for Japanese] in order to keep the length of telegrams to a minimum.)

Roseberry was not alone in being so cold-hearted. Both A Force and other SOE officers seem to have liked his idea and an unsuspecting Italian was considered for the job. The identity of this man is never stated explicitly in SOE's surviving records, but an otherwise inexplicable reference to a 'cover' being proposed for this one-way ticket suggests that it was probably Luigi Mazzotta, whose *nom de guerre* was 'Cover'. A tall, athletic man with thick black hair and a thick black moustache, the 31-year-old Mazzotta was the son of a bricklayer from Lecce and a tailor by trade who had been in Africa since 1935 after being called up into the Italian artillery. Demobilised in 1936, he had lived in Mogadishu, where he opened a shop as a tailor and outfitter, started a dry-cleaning business, and bought three haulage trucks, before moving in 1939 to Addis Ababa. Emilio Zappalà had recommended Mazzotta to the British in Abyssinia in 1941.

SOE had never been sure about Mazzotta, even though he claimed that his parents were socialists whom the Fascists had persecuted. 'In spite of his well-built appearance, I am satisfied that this man is too full of fear to do anything very active of an operational kind,' was the view of Cairo's medical officer, Alexander Kennedy, in October 1942:

He is by trade and by nature an industrious tailor who has joined anything that would offer temporary economic security. He has no interest in getting on with the job and is quite satisfied with his present life if he gets enough money for clothes and girls. It is true that he has lost everything and has the Fascists to thank for it, but this will not make him undertake any dangerous operation. If captured, he would at once tell all he knew . . .

This is a man of weak character, who will always take the easier course and who will take no risks.[57]

'I cannot find any signs in Mazzotta's make-up of definite anti-Fascist bias,' recorded another officer in April 1943, after Mazzotta arrived in Britain as one of the five Italians whom Cairo had shipped back by sea for special training. 'He might possibly prove unsuitable for such dangerous work owing to the shallowness of his motives.' Particularly odd had been his frank admission to suddenly liquidating his businesses in 1939 to fund 'a life of ease and pleasure' in Addis Ababa and then, until the British arrived, doing 'absolutely nothing except spend his money': evidence, the officer thought, of 'a highly temperamental and highly eccentric character'.[58]

Despite agreement in London that the 'sacrifice' of one Italian 'might save lots of our own troops', it was eventually decided that sending a live agent to be captured might not be very wise.[59] This was not because of any sudden concern or consideration for the man's life. It simply reflected a degree of worry that, as Cecil Roseberry put it, 'dropping a victim' who might 'break down under treatment' could endanger the wider operation.[60] But to give the Italians something, steps were taken with RAF consent to parachute supplies instead. After a failed attempt in June, a drop of four containers of money, weapons and sabotage devices was finally and successfully made at precisely one o'clock on the morning of 17 July on to the slopes of Monte Cardiga. A Halifax flying from Algeria carried out the sortie. At the controls as it came in to drop was Flight Lieutenant John Austin, an experienced 'special duties' pilot for whom the day was his twenty-sixth birthday. The report made afterwards by Austin and his crew reveals that SIM was well aware of the agreed ground procedures. 'Nothing seen at first,' reads the report, 'but on aircraft flashing "B," three bonfires were lit up and ground answered with "A". Cargo was dropped at 0100 from 3–400 ft., heading 110° mag at 140mph . . . [Rear gunner] saw "chutes" open normally.'[61]

Six days before that drop, Allied forces had landed in Sicily. But the landings did not see A Force terminate the channel provided by Gabor Adler's wireless set. On 20 July, after considering different projects to invade Sardinia, capture Rhodes, and land in southern Italy, Allied commanders decided to put American and British forces ashore at Salerno, south of Naples, and across the Straits of Messina. This decision led to the execution of a new deception plan, codenamed 'Boardman', which sought to protect those landings by weakening Axis forces in southern Italy. One strand of the plan, to quote from A Force's records, was to heighten the threat of an Allied invasion of Sardinia. This, it was hoped, would help 'anchor' enemy forces there and draw reinforcements from the mainland.[62] To help with this, A Force sent a series of fresh messages to Adler's set requesting intelligence and urging readiness.[63] It also introduced another theme: the spectre of Emilio Lussu.

The idea of telling the Italians that Lussu was on Sardinia had been suggested by Cecil Roseberry: as well as 'hinting broadly at an invasion', he felt, the ruse might persuade the Italians to go looking for Lussu and divert attention from wherever he really was in France or Italy.[64] A message was sent to Sardinia stating that a 'well known' Sardinian anti-Fascist, with his own communications and organisation, was now on the island making preparations for immediate action in the event of large-scale Allied operations. 'You will recognise him by small grey beard.'[65]

By September, with Allied landings on mainland Italy imminent, A Force was trying to cause 'as much alarm as possible' over Adler's wireless set.[66] 'Is your group now ready for action?' read one message sent to Sardinia. 'Most important have all arrangements completed within ten days.'[67] 'Inform Serra and his friends to use password DOGFOX repeat DOGFOX to any Allied Army Field Security Police or Intelligence officers,' read another.[68] A final message included an assurance that Allied troops would arrive 'as liberators and not conquerors'.[69] Two days after that, Italy surrendered and the Sardinian end of the wireless link went dead.

⊙

For months after their capture, SOE heard nothing about the subsequent fate of Gabor Adler and Salvatore Serra. In October 1943 a report was received that the pair had been in prison in Rome when Italy surrendered. That claim was heard again in the summer of 1944 when advancing Allied forces overran the city. 'If my memory is right, they should have been found to have been imprisoned in the Regina Coeli prison [in September 1943],' Mario Bertacchi, the former SIM counter-espionage chief, told SOE; 'I do not know where they are now.'[70] Both men were listed officially as missing.

Once the war had moved on and the dust had settled, 'Barclay' was assessed to have helped fan Axis fears that an Allied attack on Sardinia had been a genuine possibility during the run-up to the Sicily invasion. 'Boardman', too, was judged to have worked well. But though A Force assessed that the channel provided by Adler's set on Sardinia had been 'used to good advantage' and paid 'a good dividend', care should be taken not to exaggerate its contribution.[71] Like Operation 'Mincemeat', it was merely one of a host of efforts aimed at manipulating the enemy's assessment of Allied intentions in the Mediterranean in 1943.

In fact, it was not even the only radio game played on Sardinia with a captured Allied wireless set. Shortly after midnight on 1 July 1943, paddling ashore from three US Navy PT-boats, a five-man Secret Intelligence team of the American OSS landed, soaking wet, at the bottom of a cliff on the island's northwest coast. OSS was a latecomer to Mediterranean operations and had embarked upon its anti-Italian planning with a degree of over-confidence and misplaced ambition well illustrated by the fate of those five men. After scaling the cliff and starting inland, this little party – all dressed in US uniforms – ran straight into an Italian observation post and were captured. Under pressure and threats from Cesare Faccio, the same SIM counter-espionage officer who was at that moment doubling Gabor Adler's wireless set, the team's wireless operator, Lieutenant Charles Taquey, gave up his signal plan. This allowed the Italians to double his set, too, but Taquey's plan included a secret sign to indicate capture and OSS spotted it. Enemy signals intercepted later by Bletchley Park strongly suggest that Taquey's set, too, was used as a channel for Allied misinformation. In August, one message sent to Berlin by the Rome office of the German Abwehr reported that, according to Italian intelligence officers, 'the American I.S. [Intelligence Service]' had recently instructed its agents in Sardinia to gather information about German and Italian troops and coastal and air defences, organise reception committees, explore local attitudes to the Allies and bribe officials.[72] An 'American attack on Sardinia' was expected soon, Berlin was told.[73]

Despite being one ruse among many, the 'tripling' of Gabor Adler's wireless set worked. Later testimonies of SIM personnel confirm Italian confidence in having controlled it and the belief that the stores dropped by parachute had been genuinely intended for him and Serra. It is evident too that the messages received over the set caused the Italians considerable alarm. Still in Sardinia when the Armistice was announced, the five OSS men captured in July were delivered safely into Allied hands on 16 September and were soon recounting their tale. 'During our captivity,' Lieutenant Taquey wrote in an account apparently never shared with the British, 'the Italians proved to be afraid of a Separatist Movement that would have been helped by the Allies. From their radio contact with the British they got the impression that Lussu, the pre-fascism champion of Sardinian Autonomy, was to be smuggled into Sardinia.' One result of this news, Taquey reported, was a raid 'conducted by Faccio' that saw the arrest of 'minor people'. Another result was that SIM began to wonder whether the luckless OSS team, too, was in on the Lussu plan. 'Faccio was persuaded that [Antonio] Camboni [the team's Sardinian-born leader] knew everything about it and he tried to make him speak,' Taquey recalled. 'Camboni maintained that he did not know anything definite but that chances were that Lussu who is rather old and unable to stand physical hardships would not be found in Sardinia.'[74]

⊙

'We get the final laugh out of this,' Cecil Roseberry remarked in 1945 when learning of Sergeant-Major Silvestri's belief that SIM had deceived the British. 'Far from <u>our</u> being deceived by the doubled wireless set, we pinned our ears back right from the first message received and limited our traffic to innocuous stuff until – very soon – we were completely satisfied that the set was being worked by the Italians.' Roseberry noted that Adler himself had provided the first clue 'by referring to Serra by that name instead of Pisano, the name by which he was known to us. We like to think he did this deliberately.'[75] Later, an A Force summary of the case recorded that Silvestri's interrogator, 'with a nice sense of delicacy towards one who had proved a worthy opponent . . . allowed the Sergeant-Major to go his way with no further inkling as to the true history'.[76]

It seems clear from Italian sources that Adler had deceived the Italians about his identity. Mario Bertacchi recalled that one of the agents was an ex-Carabiniere 'of unsavoury antecedents' called Serra, while '[t]he other claimed to be a British soldier named Armstrong, but he contradicted himself, appeared unwilling to talk and it was never possible to clear up the question of his position and nationality'.[77] Cesare Faccio told the British that 'Armstrong' had claimed to be an Englishman whose father, a British-naturalised Italian, had died when Adler was young, whereupon Adler's English mother had married a man called Armstrong who worked for the Home Office. Her son had then taken his name.[78] Silvestri, too, knew of Adler only as 'Armstrong'. It was 'perfectly evident' that he was not English, Silvestri added; 'even in writing English it was noticed that he made the most obvious grammatical mistakes. Equally it was known that he could not have been an Italian, as his Italian was very far from perfect.' Only later, Silvestri said, had SIM 'discovered' that Adler 'was a Spaniard, or at least of Spanish origin, although he may genuinely have possessed British nationality'.[79]

To date, no records have surfaced to suggest that the Italians knew Adler by any other name than John or Giovanni Armstrong. Nor have any documents come to light that suggest anyone ever discovered that he was Jewish. As for Adler attempting to alert SOE to his capture and fate, confirmation seems to come from comparing British records against Antonio Silvestri's testimony. At precisely the moment when the British were receiving signals from Sardinia that omitted their security checks and referred to Serra by his real name, Adler had apparently had the opportunity to manipulate their content. Silvestri recalled that when the doubling-back began and the first signals were exchanged, 'the original messages back to Base were drafted by Armstrong personally and submitted to Cagliari for approval. After a short while things seemed to be going so well that Armstrong and Serra were sent to Rome and the Cagliari office took over the whole thing.'[80]

Adler's conduct deserves recognition. It should not alter the fact that he and Serra had been dispatched to Sardinia on a mission as dangerously hopeful as that on which Emilio Zappalà and Antonio Gallo had been sent to Sicily a few weeks before. It had not been long since Cecil Roseberry had described MI6's mooted Sicily mission as 'more or less a suicide job' and expressed alarm at the idea of agents going ashore with no contacts or pre-arranged safe house. Roseberry had also warned SOE's Cairo office about the difficulties of fitting young male agents 'into the daily life of a country at war'. But British and Italian sources appear to agree that Adler and Serra had fallen foul of the very fact that they were so out of place. 'A prisoner of war informed us that "British agents" in Sardinia were caught because they approached a shepherd whilst he was guarding his flock,' reads one British report, tallying with Italian accounts. 'No native would ever do this.'[81]

The extent to which the two agents had stepped into the dark is brutally underlined by the fact that they seemingly went ashore with no one expecting their arrival: all they appear to have had were the names of a few contacts who would have to be approached cold and might not even help. Chief among those contacts were a local lawyer, Salvatore Mannironi, and a veterinary surgeon by the name of Ennio Delogu. SOE apparently knew of these two simply because Dino Giacobbe, Emilio Lussu's 'red hot' communist friend in Boston, had mentioned them to Lussu in 1941 as possible sympathisers. 'Dr Ennio [Delogu],' Giacobbe had told Lussu in an intercepted letter opened and read by the British, 'is a great admirer of yours and one of the best men in Sardinia, an idealist who is ready for anything.' As for Mannironi, Giacobbe described him as 'a sound young fellow if ever there was one; he is head of the Catholic Action Party in Sardinia and cousin of my wife'.[82] Both men lived in the same valley near the town of Nuoro in eastern Sardinia. It is no coincidence that Adler and Serra went ashore at a point on the coast not far from there. In his letter, Giacobbe had suggested that landing spot and detailed the route inland to the valley. Two early messages sent to Algiers from Adler's set reported that he and Serra had been unable to contact 'Mannizoni [*sic*]'.[83] Algiers' reply, sent before SOE decided that the set was under Italian control, advised the pair against making contact 'unless carefully explored in advance. If made you can say Giacobbe is well, living in Boston and working for Giustizia e Liberta.'[84] In the aftermath of the two agents' capture, Mannironi and Delogu were arrested and imprisoned along with Mannironi's brother and several other suspects. Possibly these were the 'minor people' whom OSS's Lieutenant Taquey would hear had been rounded up by SIM. Indeed, Mario Bertacchi would later reflect that SIM's exploitation of Adler and Serra had failed to produce 'very satisfactory results' from the point of view of counter-espionage:

Serra's and Armstrong's principal brief was to busy themselves in the political field in order to set up communications between Sardinian anti-Fascist elements and allied troops and thence procure arms and other means for them. But those Sardinians whom they were supposed to contact proved unprepared and unwilling to collaborate with the enemy or for some reason mistrustful.[85]

That explanation may be qualified by the fact that those Sardinians had known nothing about SOE or its plans and had no expectation of any sudden visitors from the sea.

A balanced picture of the Allies' success in exploiting Gabor Adler's capture must also acknowledge the terrible consequences of SIM's success in exploiting Salvatore Serra. The British began to learn of this only when Mario Bertacchi was interrogated in 1944. Serra, he said, had admitted to his captors that the submarine that had landed him and Adler in Sardinia had also landed agents in Corsica. 'It was therefore decided to transfer Serra to Corsica and escort him round the island in the hope of a chance meeting with one of those men. This did in fact lead to the capture of one of these agents and from this first step there followed a whole chain of highly successful operations.'[86] Antonio Silvestri would tell his interrogators, too, of hearing in the SIM counter-espionage office in Cagliari 'that Serra had been used on an expedition to Corsica, where he had been of great assistance in identifying and capturing other Allied agents.'[87]

Those Italian accounts were not quite accurate: the only agents aboard Ian McGeoch's *P.228* when it sailed from Algiers in January 1943 had been Salvatore Serra and Gabor Adler. But it had been the case that a couple of months later the Italians on Corsica had embarked on a wave of arrests and rounded up two Allied agents, both Frenchmen, who, weeks earlier, had been in Algiers and under SOE's wing at the same time as Serra and Adler. Their names were Godefroy ('Fred') Scamaroni and Jean-Baptiste Hellier. Both belonged to SOE's RF Section, which worked to support and supply Charles de Gaulle's Free French

Forces. The 28-year-old Scamaroni was a Corsican civil servant who had joined de Gaulle in 1940 and attempted once already to encourage resistance on the island. Hellier was Scamaroni's wireless operator. He was thirty-six, came from Limoges, had worked before the war as a heating engineer and stove-fitter, and had fought in the French infantry against the Germans in 1940. Together with a third agent, a man named Jickell who was to work as Scamaroni's assistant, the pair had left Algiers on 30 December 1942 aboard HM Submarine *Tribune* and gone ashore on the Corsican coast, twenty miles south of Ajaccio, Corsica's capital, during the early hours of 7 January.

Scamaroni and his team had then spent two months seeking to establish themselves in Corsica and organise a resistance movement. Possible dropping zones and landing beaches were located. Sympathisers were recruited. Then, while drinking in an Ajaccio bar, Hellier was arrested. It was said afterwards that three Italians had been seen to approach him, hustle him into a car, and drive off; and that night, apparently dragging a beaten and bleeding Hellier, Italian soldiers burst into the house in the capital where Scamaroni was sleeping and arrested him, too. In time, dozens of their local helpers were rounded up. Imprisoned in the citadel at Ajaccio, Scamaroni refused to give up his secrets and suffered appalling tortures. His body was burned with hot irons. His fingernails were ripped out. Then, according to one account, he managed, while unobserved in his cell, to work a piece of wire into his neck, pass it behind his windpipe, and tear out his throat. When his body was discovered, Scamaroni had apparently written on the wall in his own blood: *'Je n'ai pas parlé. Vive de Gaulle! Vive la France!'*[88] Hellier was shot in Bastia in July.

Some suspected Hellier of betraying his friends. Even a recent study of the French Resistance describes him as 'unreliable,' drinking too much, and 'proclaiming he was going to give himself up'.[89] This is not the character that emerges from SOE records. Before he went into Corsica, Hellier had been considered 'a very capable and dependable man, of whose genuine loyalty and sincerity there can be little doubt'.[90] After his arrest, SOE thought it 'inconceivable that he would go over to the enemy' unless he thought he could outwit them.[91] Today, the memoirs of a SIM officer called Virginio Sias confirm that Hellier did not go over willingly. They also suggest that there be truth in a local tale that Hellier had said to a prison-mate in Ajaccio that a team of agents who had been with him in Algiers had 'sold' him to the enemy.[92] At the beginning of 1943, Sias was working for SIM in Trieste; dispatched to Ajaccio in March to strengthen the SIM counter-intelligence office, he did not arrive alone: with him, under escort, was Salvatore Serra. After being moved from Sardinia to Rome's Regina Coeli prison, Serra, fearing execution, had accepted a proposal to collaborate actively. Sias recounts how Serra identified Hellier by the eczema on his earlobe. [93]

11

'The Explosive Topo Lads'

In August 1943, beneath a bridge in Sicily outside the coastal town of Barcellona Pozzo Di Gotto, a British Army officer was made to dig his own grave. Caught in enemy territory dressed as a farmer and carrying explosives, he had been interrogated by German officers and earmarked for execution at the hands of a firing squad of Italian Carabinieri. According to an eyewitness, he dug with mock deliberation, refused to be hurried, and, in a final show of defiance that astonished the men preparing to kill him, said the hole must be comfortable and lay down in it to check. Finding it too narrow at the shoulders, he dug a little more and declared he was ready. Then he stood at the foot of the pit, bid farewell to his mother, cursed the Germans, and was shot.

The dead man had been a member of a small SOE team accompanying regular British forces taking part in Operation Husky – the invasion of Sicily – launched four weeks before: the first major thrust by the Allies into southern Europe and the first serious attempt to occupy any part of Italian or German soil. Until the Allied invasion of Normandy, Husky was also the largest operation of its type ever attempted. Under the overall command of Dwight Eisenhower, the assault forces alone numbered more than 150,000 troops, comprising George S. Patton's US Seventh Army, Bernard Montgomery's British Eighth Army, and two airborne divisions, with thousands of aircraft and naval vessels in support. SOE's contribution was a handful of men with a couple of trucks and jeeps, some rucksacks of explosives, a few wireless sets and the dangerous job of doing whatever they could to assist with the battle while searching the island for sympathetic Sicilians.

⊙

The decision to proceed with the Sicily landings was taken by Churchill and Roosevelt at Casablanca in January 1943. The hope was that a successful invasion would help knock Italy out of the war, divert Axis forces away from the Eastern Front, and provide the Allies with valuable experience of amphibious landings prior to invading Northwest Europe. In February, with planning for Sicily well under way, SOE was directed by Eisenhower's headquarters in Algiers to make cautious but 'immediate' preparations for 'the establishment of communications and the formation of an organisation' to assist the coming invasion.[1] The importance of this task was underlined in March when SOE received its yearly directive from the British Chiefs of Staff. 'One of the first objects of our offensive strategy in 1943 is the elimination of Italy,' the Chiefs declared. 'You should encourage revolt against the fascist government and the Germans. Sabotage in Italy itself should be mainly conducted against communications, and electric power stations, preparations being made for attacking specially vital points in the enemy's communications when the right moment to strike comes.'[2]

Ultimately SOE proved powerless to establish in Sicily any agents or contacts of any sort before the landings on the island began. In fact for a long time it seemed likely that SOE would contribute nothing to the invasion at all. What SOE wanted was permission to send in with the invading troops 'a small SOE staff party' to make and handle local contacts, search for suitable sea and air bases, and generally 'seize any opportunities which may arise'.[3] The planners took some persuading. The concept of 'a small SOE staff party' was based on the model of a similar unit, codenamed 'Brandon', that had participated in the Allied landings in Northwest Africa in November 1942 but contributed little.

While trying to secure a berth in the invasion fleet bound for Sicily, SOE was not alone in feeling stymied. Max Corvo, a young and precocious Sicilian-American who was head at the time of the overseas Italian desk of OSS's Secret Intelligence section, would later record that OSS hopes of operating in Sicily had also been frustrated. OSS would achieve very little in the way of operations into Italy before the Italian surrender, and, though it had been agreed that the Mediterranean would be a British sphere of influence, Corvo wondered if this exclusion from Sicily was another example of excessive British obstruction.[4] It is true that the British were often worried by the growing presence in the Mediterranean of energetic Americans whose ideas, plans and policies might conflict damagingly with their own. But it is also the case that contemporary files do not suggest that obstacles were put deliberately in the way of OSS's desire to work in Sicily. The reality seems to have been that senior planners were wary of any clandestine organisation, British or American, taking part.

Only in May 1943, after Cecil Roseberry flew out to Algiers to argue its case, did the Husky planners concede that SOE could feature in the landings. And only in June, with less than a month to go, did they finally agree that a uniformed SOE team of two officers, three wireless operators and a driver could land in Sicily seven days after the invasion with a jeep and a fifteen-cwt truck, followed, a few days later, by a second small party permitted to work in civilian clothes. These two tiny teams would be attached to General Miles Dempsey's XIII Corps, part of Montgomery's Eighth Army, and operate with the cover-name of 'G (Topographical) Liaison Unit'. A fortnight before the landings, XIII Corps required a gentle reminder when it was found to have 'completely forgotten' that SOE was taking part.[5]

In overall command of 'G Topo', as he christened it, was Malcolm Munthe, a 33-year-old British Army major. He was also earmarked to lead the first team to go ashore. The son of Axel Munthe, the Swedish-born physician who had written *The Story of San Michele*, Malcolm Grane Ludovic Martin de Munthe had been born in London and brought up there and in Italy. Fluent in French and Italian, he was fluent, too, in Norwegian and Swedish and had already seen secret service in Scandinavia. In late 1939, freshly commissioned in the Gordon Highlanders, he had been sent to Norway to organise clandestine shipments of arms to Finland, which the Soviet Union had suddenly attacked. The following spring, during Germany's conquest of Norway, he received shrapnel wounds in the head and leg and was captured. Escaping from hospital, he tried several times to flee to the safety of neutral Sweden and finally succeeded after a gruelling journey, on foot and through snow, when he was reduced to stealing clothes from washing lines and eating scraps of the newspapers he was using for insulation. In Stockholm he helped out at the British Legation with the secret formation of guerrilla groups in Norway and the dispatch of agents and supplies, before returning home in August 1941 and working for a while at the London end of SOE's Norwegian planning. He transferred to Mediterranean duties in 1943 and was hurriedly earmarked for the command role in Sicily. One wireless operator who was to work with him on the island would remember Munthe as 'a cool customer, dead cool; as crafty as a bag of monkeys'.[6]

Munthe arrived in North Africa from London only on 20 June. On the eve of the landings he gathered his spearhead team in a busy assembly camp close to the bomb-shattered port of Sousse, in Tunisia, where Dempsey's XIII Corps was preparing to embark. The last-minute nature of the team's preparations meant that all were British servicemen. Some joined it only days before the invasion. His three wireless operators were Sergeant Denis MacDonell, Corporal Bill Beggs and Signalman Harry Hargreaves. Corporal Charles Borg, a former policeman in the Royal Maltese Constabulary, had the role of driver and general assistant. Borg spoke some Italian; MacDonell, Beggs and Hargreaves did not.

Munthe's second-in-command was Captain Gilbert Randall, the Salonika-born son of an Italian mother and a British father.

In 1941, as a new lieutenant in the Duke of Cornwall's Light Infantry, Randall had been the one man among Peter Fleming's Yak mission who could actually speak Italian. Blown into the water when the *Kalanthe* was attacked on its short-lived voyage from Greece, he had made it eventually to Cairo. Unlike the rest of Yak Mission, he was still there six months later when SOE's office in the city had to find a man to comb for volunteers among Italy's colonies in East Africa. Promoted captain in June 1942, he had then spent ten months in Palestine as adjutant of SOE's main Middle East training school on the slopes of Mount Carmel. 'Capt. Randall I liked very much,' Denis MacDonell remembered. 'Steady, easy-going – a typical Englishman type. Many a yarn we had lying under the night skies in Sicily.'[7]

Equipment, too, was organised. Munthe detailed the kit list down to the last shirt, pistol and mess tin:

Each man had with him in pack and blanket roll – one blanket, 3 pairs socks, black gym shoes, 1 spare shirt, 1 spare khaki shorts, 1 ground sheet, 1 gas cape used as mackintosh, housewife [toiletry kit], double mess tin, feeding irons, 2 pullovers, pistol . . . [and] each man carried a hip flask of whisky . . . Over and above the personal weapons carried by each man we had one rifle and 2 Sten guns . . .

Fearing we might not be able to get stores sent to us from base HQ at an early date, and thinking also that we might need to send personnel through the enemy lines during the first days, we took with us a couple of unobtrusive rucksacks containing the following: 40 lbs 808 [explosive], 40 lbs plastic [explosive], 50 time pencils (half hour to 2 hours), pressure switches, etc, detonators . . . 12 gammon grenades, 10 Italian pistols, 6 wire cutters . . . 4 bottles best whisky (for presentation purposes only and when operating with American Army these are of the greatest value), 12 torches with spare batteries and coloured filters, foreign paper and cardboard with which to make passes, also inks, fine pens, rubber gum, etc (essential for making documents to resemble passes used in enemy territory) [and] thinnest Japanese silk for writing messages which are subsequently sewn in the lining of the garments worn by the personnel.[8]

Less success was had in securing and issuing guidebooks and proper maps. Munthe managed to steal from a Tunis library 'an excellent book with town-plans'.[9]

◉

Operation Husky was launched with an assault by parachute and glider-borne troops on the night of 9/10 July 1943, preceded by intensive bombing and followed in the early morning by amphibious landings along Sicily's southern coast. These opening hours of the invasion did not go smoothly. Strong winds, poor visibility, and anti-aircraft fire caused more than sixty gliders of the British 1st Airlanding Brigade to crash at sea, killing and drowning 250 men. Impatient and uneasy Allied naval gunners shot down two dozen American C-47s. Winds and offshore sandbars, meanwhile, caused serious problems for the seaborne troops as they homed in on the shore.

In one landing craft was Malcolm Munthe. Some hours before, he had left his team under Randall's command, made his way down to the docks in Sousse, and boarded a landing craft bound for Sicily with a frontline battalion of the Queen's Own Cameron Highlanders. 'As I had no experience of landings I thought I had better observe the beaches myself before arriving with my party, vehicles, etc.', he explained later; 'G Topo was intended to land on D plus 6 but we understood we might have difficulty.' It was good that he went. 'Cape Passero, near where the Camerons landed, looked a very unsuitable place for us to land. I was glad I had not taken my party there. Gliders lay washing about in the shallow water on the rocks.'[10]

Returning to Sousse the next night, Munthe collected Randall and the rest of his men, boarded another landing craft and sailed once more for Sicily. They arrived off the coast a day later, going ashore in the dark among a mass of British soldiers, munitions and equipment at a point just south of Siracusa: the ancient port of Syracuse. The town was now in British hands and Munthe intended to make his first base there. 'Unloading was very rapid in the clear moonlight,' he remembered, 'especially as a fire had been started by a local saboteur on the end of a pier, and an air raid for which no doubt it was the signal was expected at any moment. When our two vehicles were ashore the raid started and the place was ablaze with our Ack-Ack fire.'[11]

Orders had been issued that no vehicles should move on the roads, but Munthe instructed his party to 'drive straight through the MP [Military Police] point' and make immediately for the town, a move that 'caused some slight confusion but was lucky as a shell fell a moment or two later exactly on the former site of our 15 cwt. truck'.[12] 'I drove the jeep with Capt. Randall beside me on a hair-raising dash through the shell-pocked streets,' Denis MacDonell recalled. 'Bombs were falling uncomfortably near but we made it . . . In the 15 cwt. driven by Major Munthe was enough H.E. to blow us all off the face of the earth.'[13] In a bomb-damaged house Munthe found 'an exhausted Town Major asleep under a writing desk' but could not trace XIII Corps headquarters, so an uncomfortable night was spent in a gutter, under mosquito nets, and in noisy proximity to a battery of British anti-aircraft guns.[14] Harry Hargreaves would remember the imaginative Munthe wanting to secure a nighttime car-alarm to protect the truck. The alarm took the form of an organ grinder's monkey. 'We want to get one of those monkeys,' Hargreaves recalled Munthe saying, 'because if we put the monkey inside the lorry, and anybody comes and tries to pinch anything out of the lorry, it would wake us up.'[15] The owner of the gutter became G Topo's first Italian contact.

Before the landings, Munthe had had a reasonable idea of what he would try to do in Sicily. 'The objective of my unit was immediately to get in touch with any anti-Fascist elements with valuable connections behind the fighting line,' he wrote later, 'with a view to encouraging revolt against Fascist forces, and form guerrilla bands which we would arm by parachute.'[16]

Within four days of coming ashore, he and his men had found five Italians who appeared to have encouraging credentials and potential. They included Antoni Graffeo, a communist with an 'embryo organisation' in Palermo, and his friend Guerrino Totis, 'an ex-communist who had fought in Spain'; an ardent Waldensian Christian by the name of Marchesi 'who looked upon us as soldiers of the protestant faith militant'; and 'a wizened journalist of about fifty' called Giansiracusa who claimed to be friendly with an anti-Fascist professor at Catania University by the name of Canepa. This seemed like a promising start. But as Munthe would also recall, 'it quickly became apparent that though they could all talk, few of them were prepared to risk their skins or to go in for parachute training with a view to crossing the enemy lines'.[17]

If contacts had existed prior to the landings and targeted approaches been possible, Munthe and his men might have achieved more in the weeks they spent in Sicily. As it was, while hunting for contacts in Siracusa and other liberated towns, they were reduced to seeking the help of British Field Security police, 'who proved invariably helpful and often in possession of valuable black-lists of potential enemies,' and picking up leads from locals in the street, 'by chance conversations, by offering cigarettes, etc.' They also worked with MI6 personnel, who were doing the same thing,

though more in theory than in practice since they on the whole proved jealous and empty handed behind a façade of omniscience. Under these circumstances it became evident that if one was to be in the running for procuring from Italian police, post, or local government offices, such precious things as blank fascists' membership passes, rubber stamps, fascists' black list records, &c, one had to be there before S.I.S. [MI6] and Amgot [Allied Military Government] authorities, or else wait until later on when their material had been collected and sent to their base HQ and then finally redistributed on request to ourselves. This was a roundabout and useless way of working.[18]

Lack of local knowledge was one thing. Their work was made little easier by local temperaments and the promise of imminent liberation. Indeed, efforts to find helpers became scarcely more productive even when SOE finally thrust into the frontline the one man among its numbers with hard-won experience of the anti-Fascist struggle: a man whom a passing SOE security officer would remember seeing at Munthe's headquarters 'stripped to the waist in the very hot weather, and wearing from chin to waist what appeared to be a thick curly black wig. He stared at me with his very blue, unblinking eyes, expressionless but watchful.'[19]

⊙

After two-and-a-half years of anti-Fascist work in North America and Mexico, Max Salvadori had been summoned suddenly to London in early 1943. The call reached him via the British Consulate in Mexico City. Salvadori had been living in Mexico with his family since the spring of 1942, having gone there ostensibly as a representative of Alexander Korda, the Hungarian-born film producer, to report back on how Korda's films were doing. Unsurprisingly there had been more to Salvadori's presence in Mexico than that. Korda had connections to Claude Dansey and British Security Coordination in New York, and the job that he had given Salvadori was a cover for more clandestine activities. Among these was contact work with anti-Fascist Italian refugees arrived from Europe who might wish to work for the British.[20] SOE records have Salvadori on a salary of $120 a month with an additional monthly family allowance of $250. His SOE symbol was 'G.408'.[21] On hearing that London wanted him, Salvadori immediately settled his affairs and departed for New York. En route he stopped in Los Angeles and thanked Korda for his help.

Sailing from Halifax in mid-February aboard the *Oregon Express*, a Norwegian cargo ship, Salvadori was in London by 1 March. '[H]e has been of very great value to this organisation,' read a preceding letter of praise from SOE's New York office:

He is very intelligent, conscientious and energetic and has ... good experience in political underground work. He is violently anti-fascist and is prepared to undertake any work which takes the form of aggressive opposition to fascism ...

[Salvadori] is most anxious to become a member of the British fighting forces, and is quite determined to get into the British Army: he wants to be in the ranks and in the front line. We have always told him that he can be of greater service by fighting with his brains. If he is militarised for the purpose of his new work we hope that he will find a reasonable compromise.[22]

In London Salvadori received a warm welcome. Though they had not met before, Roseberry, having heard that Salvadori was keen on more active work, had been anxious to get him, hoping that this enthusiastic and experienced Italian-speaker would prove especially valuable now that the war seemed poised to spread finally to Italian soil.

A three-month circuit of SOE training schools followed. To Salvadori's delight, a swift commission in the British Army was also arranged. It was something he had wanted for years. 'If one is convinced that the war is right and necessary, one should take part in it as a combatant, not as an arm-chair critic or radio orator,' he wrote. 'There can be no victory without military discipline: better to obey some wrong orders than to evade orders.'[23] Finally, in July, in uniform and with the rank of captain, Salvadori flew out to North Africa to lead the party about to follow Munthe's into Sicily. At Sousse, before departing for the island, he went to see the grave of a Royal Artillery officer killed ten days before the end of the North African campaign. The dead man, Major Arthur Galletti, was his cousin. It had been Arthur's British passport that Salvadori had used to get into Switzerland when fleeing Italy ten years before.[24]

Before leaving London, Salvadori had discussed the matter of who should be in SOE's follow-up party for Sicily. Salvadori had wanted Italians. He had particularly requested the services of

Alberto Tarchiani and Alberto Cianca. Having agreed to work more closely with SOE, these two had been brought to Britain from the United States, sailing on the *Queen Mary*, at the end of June. At first it had been proposed that they should form the nucleus of an Italian political and propaganda organisation in North Africa and make broadcasts from there to Italy in the name of Giustizia e Libertà. When that scheme foundered, Salvadori took on the pair for Sicily instead. Their role, as SOE assured the Foreign Office to put diplomats' minds at rest, would not be a political one. They would be assisting on the island in enabling trained agents 'to acquire the necessary atmosphere and cover' before going into enemy territory, while 'their prestige and reputation as anti-fascists and their possibility of finding local sympathisers would make them valuable helpers'.[25]

Others whom Salvadori wanted included an exile he had found in Mexico, Renato Pierleoni, who had been one of Emilio Lussu's friends whom SOE had helped to flee from Casablanca. He also wanted two of SOE's most impressive finds from East Africa, Guido De Benedetti and Giovanni Scudeller, whom he had recently trained alongside in England. He wanted Henry Boutigny, too, the British NCO who had been in charge of that pair since their early days in Cairo and whose money had been stolen during their voyage back to Britain. But as it turned out, apart from Salvadori only two members of his team made it to Sicily in time to participate in operations before the fighting on the island was over.

Neither of these men was Italian. One, a radio operator, was actually a Yugoslav. This was Branko Nekić. According to SOE files, Nekić was twenty-eight years old and had been born at Crikvenica, on the coast of Croatia. After three years at the Dalmatian naval school at Bakar, he had spent most of his working life at sea: he joined SOE in January 1942 after escaping to Britain from the port of Oran, in Algeria, where the Vichy French had interned the steamer on which he had been sailing as second mate. Sturdy and swarthy, Nekić impressed SOE as worldly, strong-minded and temperamental. He was capable, too, and experienced. 'Is taking all this in the most natural way,' it was noted during his training, when it also became apparent that he was not an innocent in SOE's line of work. 'Is very reliable on security matters,' reads another comment; 'has been in guerrilla schools in C[entral] Europe where he was taught security and . . . on his wanderings all over the world, found by experience that he could not be careful enough.'[26] The nature and location of those schools and his reasons for attending them are not recorded and remain an intriguing mystery. With his training complete, Nekić was commissioned in the British Army as Second Lieutenant Bernard Newton and promptly sent out to Cairo.

Sicily was to be Nekić's first taste of action with SOE, but it was not the first mission for which he had been considered. Originally he had been assigned as a wireless operator to a team due to parachute into Yugoslavia to work with royalist 'Chetnik' guerrillas. That plan was sidelined when the officer he was due to accompany decided not to take him. Nekić's personality may have been to blame for that. In Cairo, officers of SOE's Yugoslav Section considered him 'a most difficult person to get on with . . . temperamental, egocentric and opinionated'.[27] It was decided to reassign him to Italian operations but his character remained a concern. When, in May 1943, a new plan took shape to send him into Slovenia, SOE officers reported him 'in a very bad state of mind and of doubtful use to anyone at the moment'. Of note was his 'overbearing and quite impossible' attitude towards 'all people whom he considered as Other Ranks or working class'.[28] Nekić was switched instead to the party being sent to Sicily, although there were those who felt he would still be better used 'in his own part of the world' as he was 'definitely anti-Italian' and 'could not pass as an Italian'.[29] But if he caused any problems in Sicily, none of Munthe's men left any record of it. Munthe would write that Nekić was 'placid but keen to serve' and 'skilful with our miniature long-distance wireless transmitter'.[30] Salvadori would remember him talking about his mother.

The other member of Salvadori's team who reached Sicily in time to do something useful was Captain Dick Cooper, a rough and ready soldier with a remarkable past. He had been born in Baghdad in February 1899 to an English father and Italian mother and brought up in Asia Minor. In later life he claimed that by the age of ten he had already been rescued from wolves, kidnapped by wandering tribesmen, and wounded by a bullet during the Young Turk revolution. At Gallipoli in 1915 he had apparently won a Croix de Guerre fighting, underage, with the French Foreign Legion. Between the wars he had spent another decade in the Legion, then, in Britain, worked as a night telephonist at the International Telephone Exchange, penned some memoirs – *The Man Who Liked Hell: Twelve Years in the French Foreign Legion* – and served eighteen months' hard labour for 'robbery with violence' and another six for stealing; he had also been bound over for assault and, when sentenced for the final time in 1933, asked for ten more crimes to be taken into account. Bringing him on board in 1941 and noting that he had 'gone straight' and wished 'to continue to run straight', SOE was tempted to see his criminal record almost as a plus. One officer remarked: 'The fact that he appears to have got away with ten other offences, for which he was not caught, may suggest that he was fairly resourceful.'[31]

Sicily was not Cooper's first SOE mission. After finishing his training he had volunteered for work in French North Africa, which led to him being put ashore with a wireless set on the Algerian coast in the summer of 1942. Quickly arrested as a suspect enemy agent, he had been imprisoned in the desert before being transferred to an internment camp in Vichy France from which he eventually escaped to Spain. Returning to England in early 1943, he joined SOE's Italian Section and was sent out to the Mediterranean; fluent in Italian, he had served briefly in Italy during the First World War and lived afterwards for two years in

Messina, in northeast Sicily, where his sister still lived and their father was buried. Harry Hargreaves would remember meeting Cooper in North Africa before embarking for Sicily and how he 'took us to a place, it was one of the French forts,' and into the dungeons, 'and there lo and behold was his name scratched up on the wall'.[32]

Flying out from Tunis on 25 July, Salvadori and Cooper were the first of SOE's follow-up team to arrive on the island. It was a hazardous trip. Their pilot landed first near Palermo, Sicily's capital, on a mined airfield still being vacated by the Germans. Then he tried another strip in the south where, Cooper would recall, an enemy fighter strafed them as they sprinted for the cover of a few olive trees. They finally reached Siracusa the following day and found Munthe installed on the top floor of a building in the old part of town. They were still not out of danger. 'German aircraft were passing overhead, machine-gunning,' Salvadori recorded. 'Two women were hit as we were crossing the marketplace.'[33]

Returning to Italian soil for the first time in a decade, Salvadori found apathy and anti-British feeling more widespread and much stronger than he had expected. After a week based in Siracusa and finding no one worth recruiting, he decided to try his luck in Palermo, which was now in American hands. To get there was not straightforward: Munthe would write admiringly that Salvadori, dressed as a civilian and behind the wheel of a civilian car, sped 'across the most atrocious roads of central Sicily infested with remnants of the escaping Italian Army in 14 hours non-stop'.[34] But even in Palermo Salvadori made little progress. Irish-Americans and Italian-Americans among the invading US troops were particularly obstructive. Some locals, he observed, 'seem to have been coached by those who believe that Britain is the real enemy. Fascism, Germany . . . these are side issues. The arch-enemy is British imperialism, from which the United States will protect all good Sicilians.'[35]

Later Salvadori reflected that most Sicilians simply did not want to fight. 'From Syracuse/Catania to Palermo I met many people,' he wrote of his time on the island:

Not one could be recruited for SOE activities on the Continent [*sic*] or could give useful and reliable information on the situation. For Sicilians the war was over and this only mattered . . . For most, to fight alongside Britons (inclusive of Commonwealth and Empire troops) was treason [while] to fight for a free and democratic Italy was laughable . . . [To fight] against Germany was understandable, but why risk one's life to do the Allies' job?[36]

While Salvadori was hunting for helpers in Palermo, Munthe was sticking to the heels of the frontline British infantry and coming under pressure from Eighth Army to employ his little force in a tactical role that would help reap more immediate rewards. Eighth Army's task was to push northwards from its footholds on Sicily's southern coast, capturing in succession Augusta, Catania and the airfield at Gerbini, before a final thrust for Messina in the northeast. Augusta had been in British hands since 13 July and Munthe was being called upon by Eighth Army headquarters to 'get something going' in the busy industrial port of Catania.[37] Overlooked by the imposing mass of Mount Etna, Catania was Sicily's second largest city and still in German hands. The British had halted a few miles short of it along the line of the Simeto River, the muddy watercourse that curled across the Catania plain. Vicious fighting was taking place along its banks and in the malarial marshes, canals, ditches, fields and orchards all around.

Munthe set up camp near a spot called Lentini on an escarpment above the plain, among olive trees and the stench of rotting bodies, and put his mind to doing what he could to help. His first effort took the form of sending two friendly Sicilians, in local clothes and carrying forged passes, over the Simeto, through the enemy lines and into the city. Their task was to look for Professor Canepa, the university man rumoured to be a staunch anti-Fascist; they also had instructions to encourage Canepa's organisation, if he was found to have one, to cut German telephone lines and otherwise 'harass the enemy in every way possible without causing instant reprisals'. Both messengers apparently made it to Catania. Both came back with news. The first returned saying he had failed to find Canepa. The second came back saying that the professor had left for Florence and, without him there to lead it, 'local patriot action' seemed unlikely.[38]

Next, Munthe decided to send one of his own men over the river and into the city. The chosen agent was Branko Nekić, the wireless operator of Max Salvadori's team. He had arrived from Algiers a few days before. The instructions that Munthe gave him were to interfere with the railways between Catania and Messina, disrupt the local telephone system, kidnap or otherwise dispose of certain Fascists known to be assisting the Germans, report enemy dispositions, and deliver a letter urging surrender to two Italian generals still fighting in northeast Sicily. To help him he was assigned a fresh pair of volunteers, two more local youths, to whom Gilbert Randall had given some rudimentary training in explosives and fieldcraft.

On the eve of their attempt to get through to Catania, Munthe carefully disguised Nekić and the two young Sicilians as farmers, with 'baskets and a sack containing food, melons, wine and clothes in the approved local style'. He also took pains to secrete various items and devices among their belongings:

I had worked on the melons for hours and when we at last packed them into the jeep they showed no signs of containing 30lbs of explosives, nor were the time pencils detectable in the wine bottle. The wireless set was hidden in the old clothes. Each man had sewn in his trousers' lining a note written on silk in a special code of my own to enable him to pass back into our lines at the end of his mission.[39]

When the time came to leave, Munthe and Randall drove the party in turns to a point twenty miles west of Catania where soldiers of the 5th Battalion of the Northamptonshire Regiment were preparing an attack for the night of 2/3 August. Slow progress and severe casualties in the fighting on the Catania plain had prompted Montgomery to launch a flanking offensive through more rugged terrain. An experienced unit that had fought in North Africa, the 5th Northamptons had arrived in Sicily a week before. Now occupying positions north and east of the town of Catenanuova, they had lost more than forty men killed and wounded from mortars and machineguns when trying, on 1 August, to push up the road towards nearby Centuripe and engage the Germans on the ridges around. The plan for 2 August was to attack again into the hills. At the last moment, the battalion's adjutant asked Munthe if he would assist through the lines an Italian youth sent up by the intelligence staff at headquarters. Munthe was 'entirely opposed to this idea in principle' but reluctantly agreed for the boy to follow in the wake of Nekić's party. Then, under cover of darkness and 'in the confusion of bangs and flashes as the retreating Germans blew up their ammunition and bomb stores on [Gerbini] aerodrome, we got our men through the line and safely into enemy territory unobserved at a quiet point on the north bank of the Simeto'.[40]

Nekić's little wireless set had a range of less than fifteen miles. In order to ensure that any messages from it could be heard, Munthe borrowed a mobile army signals van plus its driver and a pair of operators. Then he added young Harry Hargreaves to transmit and receive Nekić's messages and pushed the van as far as possible in the direction of Catania. 'We moved it up to "Dead Horse Corner", the furthest point we dared move it in daylight,' Munthe wrote later, 'then waited for the dark to fall and rushed it over a low pontoon bridge while our guns were just opening up a considerable barrage and holding the enemy's entire attention. Once over the river we dug it down amid bamboo reeds on the edge of a vine field littered with German corpses.' Under mortar fire, in hundred-degree heat, surrounded by swamps, mosquitoes and heat-bloated bodies, Hargreaves sat in the van and listened hard in his headphones for any incoming signal from Nekić. Nothing was heard. Eventually, and 'with a feeling of great depression', Munthe had to withdraw the listening van to 'more healthy regions' and out of range of Nekić's set.[41]

For a day or two, Munthe, in his olive grove at Lentini, continued to think of ways of getting men into Catania. One idea was for Dick Cooper to try to get through in civilian clothes. This was abandoned after he and Munthe conducted a sobering reconnaissance. The Germans, they discovered, were turning back all refugees trying to flee the fighting line. A similar idea, but even more ambitious, was for Munthe himself to get through disguised as an elderly peasant woman riding a donkey and accompanied by Corporal Beggs, whose job, if they made it, would be to operate the miniature wireless set hidden under the old woman's skirts. Beggs, though he came from Blackpool, seemed sufficiently dark to look like a local. Before that plan could be attempted, however, Catania fell. British troops entered the city on the morning of 5 August. At once Munthe and his men moved up from Lentini. 'There wasn't a living soul to be seen between the river and the city, only corpses along the road,' Salvadori recorded. 'The city itself seemed to have been abandoned.'[42] There was no sign of Branko Nekić.

⊙

Settling into a fresh headquarters in Catania's Piazza Cavour, Munthe drew up fresh plans to meet a new request for intelligence about enemy equipment in Messina, the last enemy stronghold in Sicily. On the night of 9/10 August, near the bombed-out town of Bronte, Gilbert Randall managed to put through the lines a man from Messina who was willing to contact friends and deliver letters. It was a nasty moment for Randall. Approaching a ravine full of snipers, he was nearly shot. It was also the last of SOE's attempts to do something in support of the campaign in Sicily; and, once again, little came of it. By the evening of 17 August, the entire island was in Allied hands.

'We were all glad when this campaign ended,' Denis MacDonell reflected years later. 'Many memories of Sicily remain – the oppressive heat of the Catania plain, the freshness of Mount Etna's slopes, the stench of Dead Horse Corner, not to mention the numerous air raids, panic stricken civilians, etc.'[43] Dick Cooper had one particularly horrible experience once the fighting was over. After a successful search for his sister, Hetty, whom he found alive and well in a village outside Messina, Cooper joined her on a pilgrimage to their father's grave. The cemetery, not far away, had suffered months of bombing. Blown out of the soil, shattered coffins and their contents lay scattered everywhere and their father's coffin was among several that had slid into the bottom of a crater. 'All had burst open and as we reached the edge of the hole we could see my father's feet protruding.'[44]

With the enemy gone, Munthe and his men stayed in Sicily for some days. Max Salvadori made a few more contacts that it was hoped could prove useful on the mainland. Their quality remained very mixed. One or two of local interest were passed along to regular British forces. One result was that a German-inspired stay-behind group of snipers and telephone wire-cutters was run to ground in hills near Floridia, a town west of Siracusa. Another contact that Salvadori apparently made was Guido Jung, a Sicilian Jew who had once been Mussolini's Finance Minister.

Munthe's team also managed to get its hands on a large stock of German and Italian weaponry, which he and his men quickly loaded into trucks and hid under a requisitioned villa near Siracusa. SOE had told Munthe to try to get his hands on weapons like these, which were urgently required for guerrilla groups with whom it was working in the Balkans. Getting the arms off the island, however, was not straightforward. In the way was a complex web of military bureaucracy and officers demanding the correct paperwork. That the task was achieved at all, Munthe recalled, owed much to 'bluff, home-made seals and rubber stamps' and 'the frantic efforts and tact' of SOE's Adrian Gallegos, an Italian-speaking naval officer who, aboard a requisitioned schooner, finally sailed the arms out of Siracusa harbour and into SOE's arsenal.[45]

Later, Munthe would describe that last escapade as 'only one example of many instances where the lack of proper recognition and understanding of [SOE]'s legitimate means obliged us to have recourse to time wasting and apparently privateering devices'. His mission's directives in Sicily had been approved at the highest levels, but the problem was that, in the field, 'an advance party like ours comes up against men much lower in the Army hierarchy but who are nevertheless all powerful on the spot and who require to be convinced by more than a mere major's word'. Some 'useful things we lacked' included:

(a) Sufficient and convincing looking documents, movement orders, passes and 'authorities' permitting one to operate with the various units of the Regular Forces one is apt to mix with. Thus when [one is] finally obliged to approach a high placed officer at Army HQ or Army Group HQ he is not able to veto an immediate operation by saying, 'Your documents authorising you to be attached to us makes no mention of using MTBs, parachute aircraft, fishing vessels, etc.'

(b) Unit rubber stamps for use on movement orders, and other instructions issued by the CO to cover the activities of members of his force, are absolutely essential. To carve one out of an old piece of India rubber and use blood for an ink pad takes time and is dirty and what is worse often will not stand close examination . . .

(c) A convenient name like 'Special Forces' was not in use in North Africa and the name 'G. Topo. Liaison Group' proved a rather heavy strain on efforts to keep the group's security story intact. All explanations broke down when without any maps at all we were recommended by a well meaning officer of Movements at Sousse to the Colonel in whose camp we lived, to draw him a rather special map. We made excuses lasting three days and on the fourth he arrived at 0800 hrs. Our only course was hastily to leave the camp. On another occasion we were referred to in a crowded mess as the 'Explosive Topo Lads'.

It is arguable that SOE should never have been used for such a dangerous tactical activity as trying to run agents and operations in the middle of a battlefield. Doing the same job at Anzio in January 1944, Munthe's fighting war would come to a premature end when he was seriously wounded by a mortar bomb that killed another SOE officer, Captain Michael Gubbins, the 22-year-old son of Colin Gubbins, SOE's chief. Most of Munthe's recollections quoted in this chapter come from a report that he wrote in hospital.

Nevertheless, lessons learned in Sicily did prove useful when the Allies began to land on the Italian mainland: SOE teams that went ashore at Salerno and Anzio were, as a consequence, better prepared in terms of kit and authority. But that benefit aside, Munthe and his men had achieved little more in Sicily than recruiting a handful of volunteers of limited and short-term worth, securing a few enemy weapons and playing an indirect role in uncovering some enemy stay-behind parties. Munthe wrote later with regret that when Catania, Eighth Army's most costly objective, finally fell, 'apart from getting intelligence we had been able to do virtually nothing to assist in its capture'.[46] It was not much of a record for the risks run. It also came at the cost of Branko Nekić.

⊙

In October 1943, the two young Sicilians with whom Nekić had crossed the Simeto suddenly regained contact with SOE. The pair explained that they had never reached Catania. After getting across the river that night together with the local boy whom Munthe had also put through the lines, the little group had bedded down together in an abandoned hayloft. Next morning, they said, the boy had betrayed them: 'after eating breakfast off our iron rations,' Munthe recorded, the boy 'had gone straight to the nearest German HQ . . . and led the way back to their hiding place'.[47] All were caught. The two Sicilians said that they had been separated from Nekić and eventually removed to a mainland prison near Reggio. There, during an air raid, they had managed to escape. The last they had seen of Nekić, they said, was in Sicily, and they knew nothing more about him.

Word of Nekić's ultimate fate reached SOE a few weeks later. The source was unexpected. At that moment Munthe was in Naples, having gone ashore with the recent Allied landings at Salerno, and was engaged once again in searching for Italian volunteers who might wish to fight for the British. One man who came forward was a Carabiniere called Attilio Moro. 'He had no idea who I was,' Munthe wrote after talking to him, 'and was merely recounting how the loathsome pressure of the Germans made his squad of Carabiniere [sic] in Sicily kill one of the bravest men he had ever seen. His chance allusion to the "Good idea of hiding explosives in melons" made me realise he was relating Newton's [Nekić's] death.'[48]

Moro had also explained that Nekić had given away nothing during three days of interrogation by the Germans. Everyone present was convinced that he was a Pole. Moro recalled, too, how impressed the Carabinieri had been as Nekić dug his own grave. He also remembered Nekić's final words. 'Before they shot him he had cried in Italian, "God bless you Mother. I shall not see you again. Damn the vile Germans."'[49] In his memoirs Munthe would add that the Carabinieri had refused to kill him and that the overseeing officer had had to take out his pistol and do it. Branko Nekić's name can be found today on a panel on the Cassino Memorial in Italy, which commemorates 4,000 servicemen with no known graves.

Moro himself did not have long to live. On 14 November 1943, ten days after giving Munthe his account of Nekić's death, he was attached at the last moment to a four-man team of SOE saboteurs, all Italians, due to embark on a raiding mission to sabotage enemy vehicles behind the German lines. 'I will lead,' he was reported to have told the others while lying in a bamboo thicket before crossing no-man's land, 'and if I am not shot, you follow.' He apparently added: 'I have seen a brave man give his life for the Allies, so I know dying is not difficult.'[50] Moro set off and was killed 'almost instantaneously', taking the full force of a burst of fire from a concealed German machinegun.[51]

Very little about Moro is recorded in SOE's files. 'My impression was that [he] clearly felt it his duty to do whatever he could to combat the Germans and Fascists,' recalled Ernest Saunders, one of SOE's Italian-speaking field security NCOs, who had been responsible in Naples for looking after its Italian volunteers prior to them going into action. 'He was a supporter of the Monarchy and I remember him saying that as a Reale Carabinieri [*sic*] he must follow the lead given him by his king.' Saunders felt 'fairly sure' that Moro was unmarried and came from the northern Italian town of Alessandria, in Piedmont, where he lived with his family.[52] When the time came to search for next of kin, however, SOE knew so little about him that none could be found. His name appears on no British memorial.

12

'Big and serious stuff'

On a series of summer nights in 1943, days before the Allied landings in Sicily, a British submarine, HMS *Sportsman*, surfaced off the coast of northwest Italy near the resort town of Bordighera. Two secret agents were aboard. Their names, according to British files, were Alberto Rossi and Alessandro Floro. Each night the crew tried to persuade them to leave the submarine and go ashore. '3 attempts made in all,' SOE reported afterwards; 'Rossi refused every night.' The first night, Floro, 'naturally unwilling to go alone', also refused. The second night he agreed to go but upset his canoe 'apparently deliberately'.[1] On the third night, equipped with money, papers and a wireless set, but on his own, Floro was finally and safely deposited on the shore.

Sportsman's 27-year-old captain, Lieutenant Richard Gatehouse, was not impressed. '[His] submarine was endangered [on] three consecutive nights,' SOE recorded after receiving his angry feedback on the two agents' antics. 'He refuses to carry again "so-and-sos who do not intend to land".'[2] Decades later, in an interview with London's Imperial War Museum, Gatehouse still remembered these 'two Italian so-called agents' and how he had found their refusal to leave his submarine 'somewhat aggravating'. Gatehouse would also recall his dim view of imperilling valuable assets to place agents behind enemy lines. 'I used to call it "Boy Scouting in the moonlight",' he told his interviewer, 'and I personally to this day think that this business of landing agents to blow up railway lines or railway tunnels or the like was a complete misuse of a submarine.'[3]

Gatehouse has not been alone in doubting whether the wartime work of irregular units like SOE justified the resources employed

– and put at risk – to support them. Senior Royal Air Force officers, for example, claimed at the time that strategic bombing could achieve much more than sabotage and resistance on the ground, and that RAF aircraft assigned to assisting SOE could be better used elsewhere. Some historians, too, have doubted whether behind-the-lines efforts were really worth the trouble, arguing that the scale and significance of some SOE successes have been grossly exaggerated since the war, and noting that Axis-dominated Western Europe proved incapable of rebelling on the scale that many Allied onlookers had originally hoped.[4]

A rounded picture of SOE's wartime record must take account of its failures and the obstacles that had stood in the way of success. Trying to get to grips with Italy, for example, its officers, inexperienced and under-resourced, had learned only slowly that Italian opponents of the Fascist regime, when found, were rarely able to do very much. Early progress, wrote Cecil Roseberry, was badly hampered by 'a total disregard for the fundamental difference between working into enemy territory and working into occupied, friendly, territory'.[5] It took time and casualties for the British to learn the hard way that Italy was no easy target.

But SOE's activities – Churchill called them its 'naughty deeds' – were not limited to encouraging and fostering resistance and waging subversive warfare.[6] 'Bombs, sabotage, parachutes, etc, are of course only the shop window,' as Lord Selborne, its minister, put it.[7] Given the need-to-know nature of its operations at the time and the inaccessibility of its archives for over half a century, it is perhaps not surprising that Richard Gatehouse, for instance, seems never to have discovered that the two Italian agents he tried to land that summer had in fact belonged to the Soviet NKVD, forerunner of the KGB. That the British, through the auspices of SOE and the Royal Navy, had the task of putting them ashore derived from an agreement signed in Moscow in 1941 whereby SOE and the NKVD had pledged to 'give all possible assistance in introducing each other's agents into occupied territory'.[8] What

Rossi and Floro's precise mission was, SOE never knew; but it was unlikely to have been something very active like blowing up bridges or tunnels. Both men were trained wireless operators. Rossi was sick with tuberculosis. Floro had a disabled arm and went ashore with no explosives. Probably their mission was to contact Italian communists.

There are plenty of examples of SOE activities that were a world away from violent sabotage: from blockade-breaking in Scandinavia, where it secured shipments of Swedish ball bearings vital to British industry, to procuring on black markets and in neutral cities vast amounts of foreign currency (funds that proved as valuable to Treasury coffers and those of MI6, the War Office and the Air Ministry as they did to its own operations).[9] As Roseberry would write at the end of the war, SOE, by virtue of its versatility and contacts, had been able to act as a medium 'for handling and developing many issues for which no department or unit has been specifically formed', and make important war-shortening contributions 'which could [not] have been foreseen in any charter which might have been given'.[10]

Another example was its handling of a secret proposal, aimed squarely at shortening the war between Italy and the Allies, that a trusted emissary put before SOE in Berne in the winter of 1942–3 on behalf of Marshal Pietro Badoglio, one of the most senior army officers associated with the Fascist regime. The son of a Piedmontese mayor, Badoglio had resigned as Chief of the Italian General Staff in 1940 but remained one of the regime's military heroes, with his reputation as a victorious commander linked inextricably to Fascism's success in pacifying Libya and conquering Abyssinia. Honour after honour had come his way; Roberto Farinacci once remarked that all that was left for Badoglio was to be made a cardinal or canonised.[11] He was also, as one historian has described him, 'a very political man' who had 'successfully ducked and weaved with the Fascist dictatorship for two decades'.[12] Badoglio was no dedicated Fascist. He openly ridiculed Fascist colleagues. He took pains to ensure that the army officer corps remained free from party interference. And eventually, through the secret emissary sent to Berne, he made this proposal to the British: a military coup, led by Italian Army officers and properly coordinated with Allied plans, to overthrow Mussolini.

⊙

That contact between the British and Badoglio began in May 1942, when Jock McCaffery in Berne received a visit from Luigi Rusca, a co-director of Mondadori, the Italian publishing house. Over talks that summer and autumn, Rusca explained to McCaffery that Badoglio, whom he knew, was convinced that the Allies would win the war and, moreover, was prepared to attempt a coup at the right moment and establish a military government. Badoglio and his friends, Rusca added, also wanted the formation of a pro-Allied Italian military force outside the country. As commander, they recommended Annibale Bergonzoli, an Italian general who was currently a prisoner in British hands in India.

Signalling these details to London, McCaffery added his own opinion that this could be 'really big and serious stuff'.[13] Baker Street agreed. Badoglio, SOE noted, 'invariably crops up whenever there is talk of a movement inside Italy. Such information as we get from time to time indicates that, despite his retirement from active life, he receives an ovation whenever he appears in public and that he does not hide his opposition to Mussolini.' In London, Cecil Roseberry thought it especially significant that Badoglio reportedly claimed to consider himself no longer loyal to Italy's royal house, which was publicly associated with backing Mussolini's regime. As for the captured Bergonzoli, 'he was always a picturesque and popular figure'.[14] A quick enquiry to the War Office about Bergonzoli's recent 'attitude and conduct' confirmed that 'as a prisoner he is a delightful person to deal with and causes no trouble'.[15]

A gnarled old general whose impressive beard had earned him the nickname '*barba elettrica*' ('electric whiskers'), Bergonzoli had commanded Italian divisions in Spain and, before his capture in Libya in early 1941, a corps of the Italian Tenth Army in Africa. The War Office also knew that he loathed Mussolini's regime. By March 1941, Wavell was reporting that the imprisoned Bergonzoli 'talks freely':

States that he sent back three Divisional Generals from Bardia and that even in Spain his men were "snivelling wretches" who funked and prayed to the saints when they should have been fighting. [He says that] Mussolini will not listen to or believe unpleasant truth. Bergonzoli affirms his dearest ambition is to live so that he can rebel against [the] rottenness of [the] present Italian regime.[16]

This seemed encouraging.

'[I]t may well be that he genuinely does desire to throw out Mussolini and put an end to the Fascist regime,' wrote Victor Cavendish-Bentinck, chairman of the Joint Intelligence Committee, 'in which case it seems to me that he would be a more useful [Free Italian] leader than third rate émigrés of doubtful reputation . . . or antiquated and out of date politicians such as Sforza.'[17] This was a reference to Count Carlo Sforza, an ageing Italian diplomat who had fled from exile in France to the United States in the summer of 1940. Well into 1943, Sforza would be periodically discussed and suggested by various exiles and émigrés as a possible leader of a free Italian movement or government-in-exile. Unconvinced that he was sufficiently popular, and wishing anyway to keep its hands free, the Foreign Office refused to touch him.

There were doubts in London as to whether Bergonzoli, too, was cut out to be the right type of free Italian leader. Wavell had reported that Bergonzoli, while evidently anti-Fascist, felt that 'military dictatorship' was 'the only possible form of revolution in Italy': a report that led Cavendish-Bentinck to wonder if

Bergonzoli was 'sufficiently socialist or democratic to qualify for the privilege of working with us'.[18] The War Office chipped in with its own observation that Bergonzoli had 'an excitable and somewhat unstable temperament' and that the elite Italian Bersaglieri had considered him 'rather a mountebank. Rushes about paying surprise visits to units and can rarely be found in his office. Rides horses, motor cycles and ordinary bicycles . . . apt to interfere in the administration of minor units.' Reading this, one Foreign Office official concluded: 'This means, in effect, that we must write "Electric Whiskers" off.'[19] From SOE's standpoint, though, Bergonzoli's eccentricities would not have mattered much. The real value of a free Italian force, as Roseberry put it, lay in 'the moral effect inside Italy of the knowledge that Italians outside the country were actively supporting the anti-fascist powers,' and that there existed 'a combatant unit armed against the Axis'.[20]

Still bruised by its experience of Foreign Office priorities during the Emilio Lussu affair, SOE decided to keep quiet about its contact with Rusca until Badoglio made a definite move. By the end of 1942, such a move seemed under way. In further discussions in Berne, Rusca told McCaffery that Badoglio and another senior military man in Italy, Marshal Enrico Caviglia, hero of the Battle of Vittorio Veneto in 1918, were united in wishing to treat with the Allies. They had also selected a personal emissary whom they wished to send out as their representative, on the condition that he would be allowed to form a free Italian army. This was General Gustavo Pesenti, a former governor of Italian Somaliland, whom McCaffery reported was poised to fly out for an Allied airfield. 'Pesenti is unmarried and all arrangements have been taken to look after his only dependents, who are his two sisters,' McCaffery reported in January 1943. 'An aeroplane and pilot [in Italy] are now in readiness to take off with [him]. All they require from us is the word Go.'[21]

Sir Charles Hambro, SOE's chief, now revealed the full story to the Chiefs of Staff and the Foreign Office. Deliberations followed. Papers were requested and read. In readiness for a positive decision and instructions to push forward, arrangements were even made to prepare for the dangerous and delicate task of ensuring the safe arrival at an Allied airfield of an enemy aircraft flying from enemy territory. Pesenti's plane should aim for Benina airfield in Libya, it was decided. To ensure that it could be identified correctly and not shot down, it would need to make landfall between Tokra and Apollonia at a speed of 150 miles an hour and at a height of 3,500 feet, and either cross the coast with its undercarriage down, or fire green flares every four minutes or when approached by Allied aircraft. Once the plane was on the ground, everyone on board would have to disembark unarmed. Pesenti should present himself as 'General Rosino' or 'Count Rosino' and be ready to share details of Badoglio's aims, plans, ideas and support.[22]

On the morning of 18 January, the War Cabinet met in London and discussed Badoglio's approach – and decided to ignore it. 'The Cabinet considered that the advantages likely to be derived from this proposal were not sufficient to outweigh the disadvantages and the risks involved,' the Foreign Office's Sir Orme Sargent told Hambro afterwards. The 'main disadvantage', Sargent explained, was that, if Pesenti managed to come out to Libya, 'negotiations with him could not continue without some undertakings being entered into on our side. The Cabinet's final decision was therefore that without further instructions from them no response should be made to Marshals Badoglio and Caviglia.'[23] The bad news was dispatched to Berne. McCaffery passed it to Rusca.

An 'off the record' explanation for the War Cabinet's decision, Roseberry would remark scurrilously, 'was that the left-wing members [of the War Cabinet] could not agree to negotiations with effete Italian aristocrats'.[24] In fact, the official reasoning in the records chimes closely with the long-held views of the Foreign Secretary, Anthony Eden. As Eden told Churchill a little later, he was 'quite certain' that if discussions began with Pesenti or any serious emissary sent from Italy, the question would crop up of what 'hope' the British were prepared to hold out for its future.

'Our present line is to make no promise whatsoever, but merely to offer Italians (through our propaganda) the alternatives of sinking or surviving. We do not promise them a suit of clothes or food. We hope that this tough line, supplemented by heavy [bombing] raids and the threat of invasion, will suffice to frighten the Italians out of the war.'[25]

The War Cabinet's decision to dismiss the Pesenti proposal was not the end of the matter. Busy in Casablanca at the latest inter-Allied conference, Churchill had been absent when the proposal had been discussed. At Casablanca he and Roosevelt announced a joint agreement that no armistice would be offered to Germany, Italy, Japan or their satellites until the unconditional surrender of their armed forces. But in February, after returning to London and giving Badoglio's approach some thought, Churchill instructed the War Cabinet to reconsider the proposal. 'There can be no harm in hearing what they have to say, as long as we do not make any commitments,' he explained to Eden. 'I am not going to take the responsibility of carrying on this war a day longer than is necessary to achieve full victory.'[26]

With Churchill laid low by a bout of pneumonia, another month passed before the War Cabinet discussed the matter afresh at a meeting in mid-March. Two days later, Sargent gave Hambro better news: SOE could 'proceed' with getting Pesenti out to Libya, 'provided it is understood that he will come out unconditionally and that no commitments will be entered into without the prior authority of Ministers'.[27] SOE informed McCaffery at once. He was also sent new landing and recognition arrangements to pass along, which remained the same as before except that Pesenti's pilot should aim for Tokra and circle twice two miles north of the airfield. McCaffery moved quickly, sending a courier into Italy with a message for a friend of Rusca's, a lawyer in Milan named Antonio Cettuzzi, urging Rusca to make contact. A reply came back that news could be expected from Rusca in April. But in fact no news would ever arrive. McCaffery's line to him was dead.[28]

Rusca had not gone quiet voluntarily. News eventually reached McCaffery in Berne that he had been arrested in Italy 'for expressing anti-Fascist views'.[29] As SIM records now reveal, this was a charge that disguised another success for Italian counter-espionage officers at SOE's expense. McCaffery's misplaced faith in his couriers and contacts had ensured that SIM had been monitoring his communications with Rusca since December 1942. 'I await your news with impatience,' reads one of McCaffery's intercepted letters, penned when SOE was holding out for a definite move by Badoglio: 'Matters have now taken on an accelerated pace. If our friend wants to act, he has to hurry.'[30] Surviving today among SIM's wartime paperwork, that letter had been sent to Rusca through the hands of Elio Andreoli, McCaffery's Swiss courier, who happened also to be a SIM agent.

By April 1943, on the eve of his arrest, SIM was supposing that British interest in Rusca indicated the existence of 'an Italian political movement of seditious character'.[31] It was also aware that McCaffery was trying urgently to get hold of him. This knowledge came from McCaffery's latest letter to Eligio Klein, the next link in his chain of contacts into Italy. McCaffery had decided on Klein as his way of contacting Antonio Cettuzzi, the Milanese lawyer in touch with Rusca. 'Cettuzzi is linked to "Dr Vulp" (the pseudonym, as is known, given by the enemy service to Dr Rusca),' SIM officers recorded after Klein spoke with Cettuzzi at his legal practice in Milan. 'Cettuzzi himself is waiting to move to Switzerland with the help of Dr Rusca, who ought to be in Rome requesting that a visa be granted to each of them.'[32] Rusca was arrested in Rome soon after that. Condemned publicly as an *anti-fascista mormoratore*, or 'muttering anti-Fascist', but really because of his suspect contacts in Switzerland, he spent the last months of Mussolini's regime languishing in *confino* in Avigliano, a remote hill-town in southern Italy.[33]

⊙

Much later, once Mussolini had gone and Italy was on the Allied side, Cecil Roseberry would hear Badoglio and other senior Italian officials criticise Britain's reaction after contact, through Luigi Rusca, had been made with Berne. 'It is a great pity your government did not agree to this proposal,' Roseberry was told; 'it would have ensured proper collaboration and have enabled us to act much earlier.'[34] As it was, they said, the British response 'had postponed the overthrow of Fascism by many months'.[35] Roseberry, a man rarely given to flights of fancy, highlighted that claim as suggesting an intriguing might-have-been.[36] He himself had spent months in London pleading for ammunition with which to encourage SOE's Italian contacts to knock Italy out of the war sooner.

'If leaders are to come out into the open,' Roseberry had written in December 1941, 'they must be shielded from the accusation of merely being our hirelings and must themselves be convinced and be able in turn to convince others that opposition to the Germans and a withdrawal from the war will benefit Italy, or, at least, save her from utter ruin.' To achieve that, 'some form of political reassurance' was necessary.[37] A year later, Sir Charles Hambro was still requesting Foreign Office help 'to enable us to show our Italian friends that England is willing to give them leadership and hope ... to make it possible for us to persuade them to do really effective work in support of our Armed Forces'.[38] SOE still wanted what Emilio Lussu had wanted: a declaration that encouraged Italians to equate their patriotic feelings with the overthrow of their government, by assuring them that they would thereby serve the best interests of their country. If that could be achieved, 'The feeling that such an action was treacherous – in fact the main obstacle – would be gone.' A suitable declaration, 'announced by the Allied Governments, that we are not aiming at the dissolution of Italy but only of the Fascist Government and the evils it has perpetrated, will provide the motives for rallying Italian dissidence at home and abroad and giving it a patriotic focus'.[39] As it was, British policy-makers would never permit SOE, or British propaganda, to do much more than take the line that Italy's defeat was inevitable, and stress that it was within Italians' power – and in their country's interests – to get out of the war.

Allied insistence on Italy's unconditional surrender, declared publicly at Casablanca in January 1943, has been heavily criticised since. Italians anxious to see Fascism fall were unreasonably deprived, it is argued, of vital direction and drive.[40] That debate is beyond the focus of this book. It is worth noting, however, that none of SOE's Italian contacts felt confident enough to attempt a coup even as the war approached the mainland, seemingly preoccupied by a fear of finding themselves playing a lonely, dangerous game for which few might thank them even if they won.

⊙

SOE actually received its next Italian feeler before word arrived that it had lost contact with Rusca. In April 1943, 'with the utmost secrecy,' a forty-year-old diplomat on the Italian consular staff at Lugano contacted the British Legation in Berne. This official was Filippo Caracciolo, Duke of Melito. 'Tall, slender, rather sickly looking,' reads a later British report on him, 'but friendly and courteous . . . Seems to know a great deal about Italian political life and gives the impression he enjoys talking . . . Married to an American. Speaks good English.'[41] Accompanied by his wife, he spoke with Jock McCaffery for the first time on 16 April. Caracciolo told him that he represented the Partito d'Azione, the Action Party, an anti-Fascist movement – it was in fact backed particularly by Giustizia e Libertà supporters still in Italy – that, he said, had helped organise recent strikes in northern Italy and was ready to do more 'at an opportune moment'.[42]

'The Duke made an excellent impression,' McCaffery told London the following day. He belonged to 'the sphere of Italian anglophile aristocracy' but was clearly keen on future action 'along serious democratic lines', while his movement, he said, was 'growing steadily' and in touch with other groups and wanted 'more publicity and especially on the British radio'. Caracciolo told McCaffery that he would contact the party's heads in Italy 'and bring back what their possibilities are in various fields: army, navy, industry, transport, etc.' McCaffery's opinion was that the Partito d'Azione 'has great possibilities . . . I believe we can get serious action from [these] people and that we should envisage and work towards the biggest scale possible. I mean a national revolt or, better still, a switch over.'[43]

As talks developed, that optimism seeped away. 'Disappointing,' McCaffery telegraphed London after one meeting at the end of April; 'much blah'. The 'moment for a full revolt' had not arrived, Caracciolo had told him. The situation was 'confused and premature'. Older army commanders were still loyal to the King. Younger ones were unwilling to assist with a revolt that could end up a fiasco or, if successful, saddle them with blame for Italy's military defeat. At one point Caracciolo 'let slip [a] most important remark which I think is key to the whole position': in the event of a successful revolt 'and they took over the country, then peace terms would have to be signed by them. Terms may well be harsh and they would then stand before [the] country and history as [the] people who had accepted such terms.' McCaffery's view was that the party 'want to play a waiting game . . . creating opposition and confusion . . . but not staging or leading anything on their initiative, so that (a) if people are stirred up to spontaneous combustion and [the] regime is defied or overthrown, or (b) if we land or otherwise knock Italy out of the war, they will be able to step in and take over but without bearing any responsibility.'[44]

At a meeting at the Foreign Office on 1 June, Baker Street described the Partito d'Azione as 'newly formed' and 'generally pro-British in outlook' but lacking 'heavyweights' and 'probably not capable of achieving very much'.[45] Until the Armistice, not a great deal occurred to change that opinion. Through Caracciolo, the Partito d'Azione requested forms of assistance that the

Allies could not possibly provide. It asked for information about planned Allied landings so that it could prepare for them. It wanted to know about possible peace terms. It wanted, too, a political committee of exiles to be formed outside Italy through which emissaries could be sent and received, ideally with Carlo Sforza as head. London refused all of these requests, to ensure that diplomats' hands remained free and that Allied plans stayed secret.

Little changed when one of the party's leaders, Ugo La Malfa, joined Caracciolo in Switzerland at the end of June. A forty-year-old lawyer and economist, La Malfa, McCaffery reported, was 'energetic' and 'au courant with [the] whole internal situation'. He wanted to go immediately to London to speak to the Foreign Office, 'render any assistance' and 'make open propaganda'. Caracciolo would go with him and declare himself the 'first official to openly break away'.[46] Baker Street knew that La Malfa was a good type. A pre-war member of Giustizia e Libertà, he was well known to Max Salvadori, McCaffery was informed, 'and you can trust him ... He has always worked quietly and concentrated on steady long-term preparation.'[47] Baker Street also knew that a 'sympathetic reaction' could not be guaranteed if they ever managed to make it to London and turned up at the Foreign Office: La Malfa and Caracciolo may be 'sincere patriots', McCaffery was warned, 'but a patriot can achieve nothing without being a realist and practical'.[48] In the end, no one went to London[49] and the Partito d'Azione played no role in spearheading any coup. Caracciolo, however, whose contacts included Badoglio's son, Mario, would continue to send reports to Berne shedding useful light on the general mood in Rome, while acting also as a channel by which SOE urged his contacts to get Italy out of the war.

⊙

Another approach came in June 1943. It arrived in Berne in the short and portly shape of 42-year-old Adriano Olivetti, an Italian entrepreneur and engineer who would later transform his father's typewriter business into the world-famous Olivetti computer company. McCaffery met him on the evening of 14 June in the Berne home of Allen Dulles, representative in Switzerland of the American OSS, whom Olivetti had recently contacted. Later the longest-serving director of the CIA, Dulles had been in Berne since the previous November. He also felt poorly served by the State Department in terms of guidance and directives. When it became clear that Olivetti was of interest, he let McCaffery take the lead.

Olivetti was not unknown to the British in Berne. For two years he had had occasional dealings with Frank McGill, a Scotsman working in Switzerland for General Motors. McGill had been quietly using his Swiss factory to manufacture for McCaffery various lethal devices that he tested out secretly in the woods around his house, but his contact with Olivetti had been on a business basis only. It was only when Dulles and McCaffery met him that Olivetti revealed his single-handed efforts at bringing about Italy's removal from the war.

'According to himself he has always been anti-Fascist,' McCaffery told London afterwards. 'He has wide Jewish contacts and appears to be part or wholly Jewish.' Olivetti had also stated that he was 'with Giustizia e Libertà' and had helped Carlo Rosselli to arrange the escape from Italy of the Italian socialist Filippo Turati in 1926. Olivetti had a wide circle of powerful contacts, McCaffery went on, and, some weeks ago, thinking that the time was 'long over-ripe for action', he had set out to speak to representatives of all potential opposition elements inside Italy, 'intending then to come and see whether we would treat with him'. Those with whom he had spoken ranged from the royal house and Badoglio to the Partito d'Azione and the Communist Party, and he had now arrived in Berne 'certain' that he could organise sufficient Italian opposition to overthrow the Fascist regime. Olivetti also had a plan. First, a measure of coordination would need to be achieved between the various individuals and groups opposed to Mussolini. Next, the Fascists would be overthrown and replaced by an outwardly neutral but inwardly pro-Allied government, under, say, Badoglio. Next, Allied forces would land on Italian soil and Italy would switch sides. Olivetti also proposed that a committee of prominent anti-Fascists be formed abroad that would be recognised by the Allies at a suitable moment as Italy's real government. He suggested it include not only exiles and émigrés but also men currently inside Italy who would be willing to be smuggled out, like Ugo La Malfa and Carlo Levi.[50]

McCaffery was impressed. '[Olivetti] strikes me as an energetic and gifted person who has shown great talents for organisation in industry,' he told London. 'If he is all right, as I think he is, it is [the] best bet so far.'[51] Reading McCaffery's telegrams, Cecil Roseberry wondered about Olivetti's motivations. As a Jew and someone once 'mixed up' in Liberal activities, Olivetti, Roseberry wrote, 'must be a shrewd, self-protecting individual to have remained head of a manufacturing firm which has almost a monopoly of the typewriting business in Italy. His business under "autarki" [sic] would be one which prospered as the result of fascist economic policy and would have suffered from the entry of Italy into the war but for the suitability of his plant for switching over to munitions work.' Nevertheless, Roseberry added, 'whether such people as Olivetti are inspired by pure anti-fascist motives or from self-interest, we should give them every encouragement'.[52] And he agreed, as he told McCaffery, that Olivetti revealed 'acumen and ability' and that his plan seemed promising.[53]

Since Allied forces were already poised to land in Sicily, there was concern in Baker Street that Olivetti's plan would take time to develop and was based on the assumption that no invasion would be launched very soon. There was certainty, too, that time would be needed for the Foreign Office to be sounded out – 'most probably without success' – on the ever-awkward topic of an outside Italian committee.[54] McCaffery was told to impress on Olivetti the need to move fast so that his contacts would be better placed to act when the landings came. McCaffery did so. When told that a committee could prove problematic, Olivetti immediately abandoned that plank of his plan. It had not figured in his original ideas anyway, he said. Talks over, Olivetti left Switzerland to hold discussions 'with Badoglio and others' in Rome.[55]

Then, at the beginning of July, Olivetti suggested something else: the involvement of the Vatican. In a letter sent from Italy, Olivetti explained to McCaffery that he had received 'complete assurance' from his contacts in Rome that, if approached officially by the Italian royal house or the British government, Pope Pius XII would permit 'conversations and negotiations' between Italy and the Allies to take place discreetly in the Vatican, a tiny island of neutral territory in the middle of Fascist Rome, where the British had a resident minister. There might even be possibilities, Olivetti added, for negotiations with a view to the 'simultaneous breaking away from the Axis' of Italy, Hungary, Romania and Finland. He therefore suggested that the British help him speak to the Pope.[56] On the face of it, Olivetti's offer seemed to hold enormous promise. Contemplating it in London, however, SOE decided that it was still far too nebulous to put before the Foreign Office. These were just words; much firmer evidence would be needed before the highly sensitive matter of covert discussions in the Vatican could even be considered. A letter from McCaffery was couriered into Italy explaining to Olivetti that any proposal to use the Vatican 'must be accompanied by proof of serious backing'.[57]

To SOE's shock, Olivetti then jumped the gun: he sent a friend to contact D'Arcy Osborne, Britain's Minister to the Vatican, anyway. Olivetti did warn McCaffery that his friend, when he turned up, would identify himself as 'Edward Cartin' and hand over a letter signed 'Ruben'.[58] But when SOE alerted the Foreign Office, which tried to warn Osborne to expect a mysterious visitor, it was too late. As the Foreign Office learned when Osborne replied, not only had 'Edward Cartin' already visited the Vatican but he had also delivered a message that Osborne found 'far from explicit' and 'made no sense ... And I destroyed the text, so I could not now transmit it [to you] even if I wanted to.'[59] Not that much of this mattered. On the last day of July, the Foreign Office told SOE to pull the plug on Olivetti.[60]

By then, Olivetti was out of play anyway, having been arrested in Rome on 30 July. Precisely what had happened remains a little unclear. What is certain is that SIM had once again been monitoring events, courtesy of McCaffery's courier lines from Switzerland. Within days of first meeting Olivetti, McCaffery had entrusted Eligio Klein with the task of acting as a go-between once Olivetti returned to Italy. The first exchange of correspondence took place on 28 June at a rendezvous at a garage in Ivrea, the home town in Piedmont of the Olivetti family firm. 'Much as he strove to appear calm, Olivetti was, to the contrary, consumed by ill-concealed fluster,' SIM recorded after he was handed a packet sent down by McCaffery. 'As soon as he held the bundle in his hands, he quickly inspected its seals and then quickly put it in his pocket.' Then Olivetti handed over his own letter for McCaffery, which SIM was soon opening and reading:

Olivetti's reply was enclosed in a white envelope without an address, bearing two wax seals of a golden hue with the initials "G.S." ...

Internally, the missive was made up of a single page written on a machine and wrapped in light green tissue paper ...

One can learn from the letter's content that ... having [obtained] the Pope's consent, Adriano Olivetti will be able to begin discussions in the Vatican City with an as yet undesignated representative of the American and British governments for an examination of the situation in Italy and of the talks that could be begun immediately in Rome for the simultaneous separation of Italy, Hungary, Romania and Finland from the Axis ...

The letter in question has been restored with great care to its original state [and] ... I have successfully taken note of the stamp of the seals used by Olivetti so as to have an identical one produced immediately (as

I did a long time ago in the case of the seals used by the English service) in order to be used were it necessary to check subsequent missives . . .[61]

Italian documents may yet confirm that Olivetti had been arrested on SIM's orders rather than those of the OVRA or the regular police. For what it is worth, SOE would be told after the Armistice that, upon discovering what Olivetti was up to and the identities of the very senior Italian personalities involved, SIM, with an eye on the future, had decided not to interfere.

⊙

In July 1943, three days after Allied forces began landing in Sicily, Sir Charles Portal, Britain's Chief of the Air Staff, proposed to the Prime Minister a plan to kill Mussolini in a lightning attack by RAF bombers on the *Duce*'s office and home. The idea had been suggested once before, a year earlier. At that time there had been a ban on dropping bombs on Rome and the proposal was quickly turned down. Now, in the light of the Allied landings on Italian soil, the head of Bomber Command, Air Chief Marshal Arthur Harris, wanted fresh permission to have a go. Portal, agreeing with him, put the idea before Churchill. 'I suggest that if Mussolini were killed or even badly shaken at the present time this might greatly increase the chance of our knocking Italy out at an early date . . . I therefore ask your permission to lay the operation on.'

Two years earlier, Portal had expressed squeamishness at the ethics of an SOE plan to parachute into France a party of agents in civilian clothes with orders to ambush a busload of enemy aircrew.[62] Now he was advocating a plan to pick off the head of an enemy state by using high explosive bombs dropped from heavy bombers roaring in low over its heavily populated capital city. 'Harris would use the Squadron of Lancasters (No. 617) which made the attacks on the dams,' Portal explained, outlining the plan for the Prime Minister; he was referring to Guy Gibson's famous 'Dambusters' force of four-engined bombers that had attacked Germany's Möhne and Eder dams a few weeks before. 'The attack would be made just above the roof tops,' he went on, 'and would give the only chance of destroying the two buildings without much other damage.' The buildings Portal meant were the Palazzo Venezia, the grand fifteenth-century palace just north of the Capitoline which housed Mussolini's office, and the Villa Torlonia, a nineteenth-century villa in the outskirts which was home to his official residence. Both were 'unmistakable', Portal added, 'and neither is within 1,500 yards of the Vatican City or the Vatican churches. Strict orders would be given against taking any action against anything in Rome except the two specified targets.'[63]

Permission to bomb Mussolini was never granted. Possibly this was due to the calming voice of the Foreign Secretary, Anthony Eden. When the Harris/Portal plan was finally made public in Foreign Office documents released in 2010, British press coverage claimed incorrectly that Eden had proposed the project to Churchill.[64] In fact an accurate reading of the declassified paperwork shows not only that Portal had authored the memo but also that Eden had argued against him. 'I do not like this,' Eden told the Prime Minister after reading Portal's proposal. 'The chances of killing Mussolini are surely very slight, and those of "shaking" him not much greater. If we fail to kill him, we shall certainly not do his reputation any harm, we may even raise his stock of waning popularity.' Pointing to the 'odium' that would undoubtedly result from 'knocking the older part of the City about and causing civilian casualties', Eden concluded: 'My advice is to lay off the present proposal because the target is a too difficult one to warrant the attempt on military grounds, and because on psychological grounds it would be exploited to our disadvantage unless 100 per cent successful.'[65]

Eden's observation about Mussolini's 'waning popularity' was sound. Throughout Italy, tolerance of the Fascist regime had been in terminal decline for months. Old radicals were beginning to stir. New groups, like the Partito d'Azione, had started to organise. Clandestine leaflets and newspapers circulated in ever-growing numbers: *L'Unità*, the official communist journal, had reappeared; the Partito d'Azione began to publish *Italia Libera*. Even the Church was becoming active. This growing dissent did not represent an immediate threat to the regime. Nor, it should be noted, had SOE played any role in fomenting it, despite all the reports of successful underground work that were still being regularly sent to Churchill and the Chiefs of Staff and everyone still believed were genuine. ('Urgent requests for large quantities of explosives and incendiaries have been received,' SOE confidently told the Chiefs in May. 'A group in Venice claim to have set fire to dock warehouses which destroyed timber, cotton and other raw materials . . .')[66] Yet the shifting mood in Italy was real enough. In the spring of 1943, heavy Allied bombing of northern Italy was the principal reason for a famous series of local strikes, the first serious labour trouble in eighteen years.

For growing numbers of Italians, the war was increasingly real and brutal, defeat and invasion seemed likely, and Fascism was obviously responsible. '[E]vents in Russia, the occupation of Tunisia and the complete expulsion of Italy from Africa, [plus] the continuous air raids on the various districts and the consequent deadly and destructive effects, have further increased doubt as to the final success of the war,' read an official Italian assessment of public opinion in Sicily's capital, Palermo. 'The population is terrorized by the results of the last air raids and by the certainty that nothing can be done to prevent them and much less neutralize them . . . [E]verybody asks on what facts the heads of the Axis powers base their certainty of victory.'[67]

That assessment was among a stack of official memoranda from Italy's principal regions, all dating from May 1943, all drawing similar conclusions, recovered later from Mussolini's office in the Palazzo Venezia. 'Public morale is very depressed,' read a report received from Genoa:

The population foresees other military defeats, and as the air and sea forces of the enemy are known to be formidable, the certainty that our armed forces will not be able to stop the expected enemy operations is spreading everywhere.

The faith in victory, that for so many months has nourished such rosy hopes, has now changed into troubled pessimism, and no propaganda is capable of mitigating it because after so many delusions the public does not believe any longer either what the papers or the wireless say . . .

[A]lso these other reasons help to keep people depressed:

The increasing food difficulties . . .

The more violent bombardments on the Italian cities that cause more and more material and moral damage . . .

The fear that the Anglo-Saxons may land in Italy, and precisely in this part of it so as to be able to get to the heart of Germany more quickly . . .

The more and more disquieting news that the soldiers returning from the various fronts in the Balkans bring back . . .

The depressing efficacy of the propaganda of the enemy's wireless broadcasts: because, despite the prohibitions, many people listen in to them and spread them as news heard in Italy.

News from Naples was little different:

On the whole, there is a deep desire [here] for peace, and the speech made by the Duce on the 5th of May did not succeed in reassuring the minds of the people. Therefore a kind of indifference is reported for everything that has to do with the manifestations and the propaganda of the Party, which more or less openly is considered responsible for having in the past under-valued the enemy and drawn the nation into war . . .

The economic situation is precarious because of the always increasing costs of living. Everybody complains of the cost of living.

'Public opinion is consistently growing worse,' echoed a report from Rome. 'Faith in victory seems to be almost totally lost.'[68]

On Sunday, 25 July 1943, less than a fortnight after Eden had advised against trying to kill him, Mussolini's twenty years in charge of Italy came to a more natural end. At two o'clock that morning, after a nine-hour session in Rome of the Fascist Grand Council, a majority of war-weary Fascists approved what was essentially a motion of no confidence. Mussolini, who was present, seemed not to take the outcome seriously. That afternoon he turned up for an audience with King Vittorio Emanuele III as if nothing had happened. It was then that both his premiership and Fascism really came to a close. Emboldened by the backing of senior military officers who had also had enough, the King told Mussolini that Fascism was finished and a new government would be formed with Badoglio at its head.

Arrested before he left the palace grounds, Mussolini was whisked away in a windowless ambulance and locked up in Rome in a Carabinieri barracks. Later he was shifted to Ponza, the same penal island where Max Salvadori had spent six months' *confino*. News of Mussolini's fall reached the world the same evening. Salvadori himself heard it over a radio in Sicily hours after he had flown in to join Malcolm Munthe and 'G Topo'. 'So it is ended,' Salvadori recorded. 'I didn't close my eyes all night except for a few minutes when I had nightmares, seeing flames everywhere . . . Those who said they had no use for liberty will see now whether dictatorship is so wonderful. Ruins and blood will end twenty years of drunken dreaming.'[69]

News of Mussolini's removal was followed immediately by public assurances from Badoglio that Italy would remain at Germany's side. '*La guerra continua*,' he famously declared: 'The war continues.' The Allies expected this, since the Italians were clearly cautious of German reaction; but they also expected attempts by the Italians to sue for peace. Badoglio, it was noted in an intelligence assessment put before the War Cabinet in London,

has always been anti-Fascist and anti-German. He is therefore not the man who would be chosen to lead the last defence of Fascist Italy as an ally of Nazi Germany . . . The only reasonable conclusion [to draw] is that the change of government is intended as a first step towards Italy's withdrawal from the war . . . We may, therefore, in the very near future, receive serious peace overtures from the Italian Government.[70]

It is unlikely that the British had ever had in their hands a channel for knocking Italy out of the war earlier. The prevailing Allied demand for Italy's unconditional surrender had reflected a realistic assumption of what was needed to bring its leaders to the negotiating table: a costly thrashing on conventional battle-fields; plenty of morale-sapping high explosive dropped on Italy's population from the air; and blasts of propaganda holding Mussolini responsible for all of Italy's woes, while implying that fortunes would improve once he was gone. Even then, it still required the presence of powerful Allied forces poised to land on the Italian mainland, plus a palace coup backed by senior military men. Indeed, though Badoglio and the King had finally done away with Mussolini, a continuing fear of precipitating a German occupation and counter-coup would see them hesitate to go much further. 'The Italians wanted frantically to surrender,' as the Allied commander in the Mediterranean, Dwight Eisenhower, wrote later. 'However, they wanted to do so only with the assurance that such a powerful Allied force would land on the mainland simultaneously with their surrender that the government itself and their cities would enjoy complete protection from the German forces.'[71] In fact, the key surrender talks would only begin when a fresh Italian peace emissary went far further in his dealings with the Allies than his masters in Rome had authorised.

13

'The man who fell from the sky'

Until 1943, the only British candidate considered for SOE work inside Italy had been Captain Charles Piercy, the descendant of a wealthy Welsh engineer who had gone to Sardinia in the 1860s to build railways and stayed. Known to friends and family as 'Chappy', Piercy was in his late forties, had served in the Royal Field Artillery and Royal Flying Corps in the First World War, and was married to Maria della Neve Massimo, the daughter of an Italian nobleman and a Bourbon princess with family ties to the Habsburgs. 'Captain Piercy has an Italian as well as a British passport and is a big land owner in Sardinia,' SOE observed in 1941. 'He had a plan for landing in Sardinia and raising the island in revolt. He seems to be slightly mad.' It was noted that MI6 felt that 'as well as being mad he was also bad' and that a question mark hung over his loyalties.[1] According to Claude Dansey, 'the gentleman in question is utterly unreliable, and probably dangerous,' while his relatives by marriage were 'undesirable'.[2] Apparently there was even cause for thinking that before leaving Italy he was 'a double agent'.[3]

Not much in SOE's files expands on those statements but they would seem to have been damning enough. There is no indication in any surviving file that much time or effort was expended in exploring what Piercy, whether mad, bad or not, had to offer, even in regard to Emilio Lussu's plans for Sardinia. In the end, the first Briton to be dispatched to Italy as an SOE agent was Dick Mallaby. He was also the last SOE agent to be sent into Italy before the Armistice.

It has been claimed by one British historian of wartime Italy that the Foreign Office had sent Mallaby to speed the efforts of

Badoglio's government at negotiating Italy's surrender.[4] That claim is incorrect. Mallaby's mission had been planned for months, had nothing to do with the Foreign Office, and had not been conceived as a way of assisting anyone to surrender. The real idea behind dropping him into Lake Como was based on a much earlier plan to send in a wireless operator to help the anti-Fascist 'groups' in Italy with which Jock McCaffery in Switzerland was believed to be in touch.

That earlier plan had been tabled in August 1942 when the prospect arose of parachuting an Italian wireless operator into northwest Yugoslavia. From there, SOE hoped, he could be helped into northern Italy and begin working with McCaffery's various contacts, acting in the same way that Giacomino Sarfatti would do in Milan. By October a suitable man was available. This was Bruno Luzzi, a Tuscan in his early thirties who had been one of Cairo's first recruits from East Africa. SOE had found him the previous winter working as a clerk in Addis Ababa. 'This man is physically fit and psychologically well within normal limits,' Cairo's medical officer, Major Alexander Kennedy, wrote of Luzzi:

He is somewhat of an idealist and is evidently willing and able to do something practical about it . . . He is a man who can, I think, be trusted to work alone and who will face dangers with a full knowledge of their seriousness . . . There is every reason for his loyalty as he comes from a moderate socialist family and has had his efforts to succeed in Abyssinia frustrated by the Fascist Party . . . [He] is fond of women and will always find them but I doubt if he gives much information away in this manner.

Months went by while SOE tried to get Luzzi into Yugoslavia, everything hanging on the ability of its Yugoslav Section to arrange the necessary parachute drop and reception. The idea was to drop him to a spot from where he would be guided to the coast and put aboard a Trieste-bound steamer in the guise of a seaman seeking work. But postponement followed postponement. 'He is still keen in spite of his months of waiting,' Kennedy noted in October, 'but has become rather stagnant through having nothing to do.'[5] As more weeks passed, Luzzi's mood worsened. By the end of the year he seemed 'troubled with nerves'. A 'to-be-expected reaction when a man is kept too long', Cecil Roseberry observed from London. 'Still, better to develop nerves before [rather] than after being embarked on an operation.'[6] It was at that point that the British sergeant who was instructing Luzzi in the use of a wireless set, a young Italian-speaking Englishman, offered to take his place. This was Dick Mallaby.

⊙

Cecil Richard Dallimore-Mallaby was born on 26 April 1919 in Nuwara Eliya, a colonial hill station in Ceylon, where his father, Cecil, was a tea planter. After Mallaby's mother, Mary, died when he was one, his father moved to Tuscany where he inherited an estate called Villa Poggio Pinci, near Asciano, a small hill town about fifteen miles from Siena, remarried and started to farm. Young Dick was schooled first in Asciano, then for two years by Franciscan friars in Lincolnshire, before returning to Asciano and finally studying at Siena's *istituto tecnico* and a *liceo scientifico* in Modena. In the summer of 1939, abandoning hopes of university studies to become a wireless engineer, and seen off by his father on the platform at Milan, he travelled back to Britain to join up, reaching Dover on the day that war broke out.

Mallaby's military career began in the infantry. In October, after applying for all three services, he was called up into the Devonshire Regiment and, as a private, assigned to signals duties. But a year after that, still in Britain and keen to be more active, he volunteered for 2 Commando, with which Fortunato Picchi would drop into Italy. Three months later, he ended up being posted instead to 8 (Guards) Commando, another new unit. He sailed for the Middle East in February 1941. That summer he was part of a small detachment from 8 Commando sent to the besieged North African port of Tobruk. There he saw action for the first time, patrolling into the surrounding enemy-held hills.

After Tobruk, 8 Commando was disbanded, and it was in the Middle East in January 1942 that Mallaby joined SOE. At a loose end, he had been detailed as an Italian-speaker to bring back to Cairo SOE's first batch of Italians recruited in East Africa. Soon, and as a corporal (a commission would come in August 1943), he was on the SOE payroll and escorting groups of Italians from camp to camp around the Middle East. In Palestine, taking the opportunity to share their training, he received repeated instruction in the specialist techniques taught at SOE's para-military school on the slopes of Mount Carmel. He also learned to parachute and polished his wireless operating skills.

When Mallaby volunteered to replace Bruno Luzzi the following January, he seemed a perfect substitute. 'There is no doubt that our new man is in every respect a much more satisfactory proposition,' Cairo told London.[7] Hearing of the switch, Cecil Roseberry agreed: 'a 22-lander [Briton] can be taken more fully into our confidence and can be regarded more completely as our own advance agent'.[8] Roseberry would also be impressed by the sound of Mallaby's character. 'To take the place of a casualty is one thing, but to volunteer to fill the place of one who has lost his nerve requires an unusual measure of determination.'[9] Jock McCaffery would write of hearing from someone who had known Mallaby 'that he possessed the kind of courage known as the cold, two o'clock in the morning type. But his appearance prompted a Swiss friend who met him later to say that one of the great strengths of England lay in its being full of fresh-faced pleasant youngsters like Dick, who were capable of going out and doing the man-sized jobs that he did.'[10]

Eventually, after yet more postponements, Cairo began to look for another way into Italy. Thought was briefly given to a blind drop into France from where Mallaby would make for Switzerland and enter Italy from there. Major Jacques de Guelis, an experienced agent attached to SOE's 'Massingham' base near Algiers, pointed out that for this to succeed Mallaby would have to speak French fluently, 'otherwise the identity documents and the tightening of police controls would make the operation very dangerous'. Noting that Mallaby spoke only 'a little French with a foreign accent and physically looked Nordic', SOE wondered if he might pass as a man from Alsace.[11] By May 1943 thoughts had turned to parachuting him directly into Italy. By July he had been sent from Cairo to 'Massingham', the RAF having agreed to drop him in from North Africa.

Eventually a plan was worked out for Mallaby to be parachuted by night, alone, into the middle of Lake Como. Early in August he was issued with his equipment and documents. As well as a diving suit, a 'Mae West' life-belt and an inflatable K-type rubber dinghy, he was given a waterproof bag that contained the following: toiletries; spare clothes; a text for double-transposition coding (Giovanni Papini's patriotic polemic, *Italia mia*); a torch battery; some toy bricks and various other items. Many of these were not what they seemed at first glance. Hidden inside the hollowed-out battery and bricks were wireless crystals, over 100,000 lire, spare identity documents and microphotographs of his signal plans. A hemp washing line had a flexible wireless aerial running through it. A pullover had been treated with a reagent for uncovering secret writing: the reagent could be extracted by soaking the pullover in an appropriate solution. He was also issued with identity cards in the name of Aldo Guazzini and a cover story that he was studying agriculture in Florence; SOE considered the story 'extremely well thought out and sufficiently elastic' (having learned something of farming from his father's Tuscan estate, Mallaby had suggested it himself).[12] Under his diving suit he was to wear a set of real Italian civilian clothes. These had been sent back from Sicily by Malcolm Munthe's 'G Topo' team. For his feet he was given ordinary shoes, carefully weathered and patched, in preference to a pair of Italian army boots that London had originally produced.

He had no wireless set, the plan being for him to get his hands on one that McCaffery had sent to Trieste ten months before. Nor was he issued a weapon, save for a knife attached to the sleeve of his diving suit.

After he left for the airfield, SOE recorded that 'Olaf' – using the codename chosen for Mallaby due, no doubt, to his blond and blue-eyed looks – was 'quite clear' about his mission. His task was to make his way to Milan, where he would establish a wireless link between McCaffery's groups and 'Massingham' and instruct those Italians in sabotage techniques and the receipt of parachute drops. Mallaby was 'fully confident' of his wireless skills, SOE noted, while the hundreds of hours he had spent at the training school in Palestine had left him exceptionally well equipped to handle his other duties: 'Olaf has done some seven complete paramilitary courses and is therefore fully competent.'[13]

The spot in Lake Como selected for Mallaby's drop was 4.6 miles northeast of Como town and 1.2 miles southwest of the little lakeside commune of Pognano Lario: or, to be even more precise, under the second 'o' of 'Lake Como' on the 1:100,000 maps that SOE used. The immediate plan for when he hit the water was for him to inflate the dinghy, paddle ashore, use his knife to cut up his diving suit, the Mae West and the dinghy, sink the pieces in the lake, hide the rest of his kit, and set off in the morning for Como. Beyond Mallaby hitting the water, none of this happened, of course. When he parachuted from Alfred Ruttledge's Halifax at ten to three on the morning of 14 August 1943, the drop was clearly seen from the shore – as well as it being a moonlit night, the villages along the lakeside were packed with refugees from the recent Allied bombing of Milan – and Mallaby was picked up still afloat on the lake.

On 17 August, a Swiss newspaper published a story of the capture of a parachutist dropped from a British aircraft at Como. Enough proof filtered through over the next few days to convince Jock McCaffery in Berne and officers in London that the prisoner must be Mallaby. A long article in the Milanese paper *Il Secolo-La Sera,* which detailed the capture of a 24-year-old British parachutist speaking fluent Italian with a Tuscan accent, pretty much clinched it. '*UN PARACADUTISTA*', declared the front page, adding poetically: '*L'uomo caduto dal cielo fu tradito da un raggio di luna*': 'The man who fell from the sky was betrayed by a moonbeam.'[14]

'At first no one spoke,' McCaffery would recall of one dramatic press account of the standoff on the lake:

Then Dick, as he lay there in the water, asked them were they fishermen. Possibly nonplussed by the fluency of his perfect Italian, still no one spoke. And then, the newspaper informed its readers, this young man repeated his question, saying *in an annoyed tone of voice*: 'I asked you, are you fishermen?' It seemed absolutely incredible that in such a desperate situation any man could allow himself the luxury of being annoyed, but an enemy newspaper, which it still was, would hardly invent such a detail.[15]

Also reported was the ominous news that the captive was being held for trial by a military tribunal.

It is likely, of course, that Mallaby would have ended up in Italian hands sooner or later anyway, given the fact that the groups to which he was being sent were an enemy invention. Mallaby's instructions on landing were to make for a safe house in Como; if he found no one there, he should hitchhike to another in Milan or Genoa. Jock McCaffery had provided the addresses, which Mallaby had learned by heart. Both were known to SIM. The one in Como was the home of Enrico Cavadini, an agent of both SIM and the OVRA. The address in Milan was the SIM-provided flat used by Eligio Klein. 'We have good reason to place reliance on our end of the line,' Cecil Roseberry, blissfully unaware of the truth, had assured Cairo when Mallaby was first assigned to the operation. '[McCaffery] has given ample proof of [Klein's] bona fides and of his ability . . .'[16]

On top of that, McCaffery had sent letters to both Klein and

Giacomino Sarfatti, SOE's young Italian agent in Milan, warning them of Mallaby's imminent arrival. 'One of our colleagues – a trustworthy friend and gifted technician – ought to visit you on Saturday 14 [August] or in the days that follow,' Klein was told. 'Tito is his name . . . When you have done all that is necessary to accommodate him comfortably (and I know that I can count on you for this after you did the same so marvellously for Giacomo [i.e. Sarfatti]), give him the green suitcase which we sent a few months ago.'[17] The warning to Sarfatti was much the same: 'in a few days' time a colleague will be arriving. He will be known as Tito (his current name is Olaf).'[18] Both letters found their way rapidly into the hands of SIM. The quotes above come from copies among its records.

Once Mallaby had dropped into Italian hands and was being beaten up in Como's San Donnino prison, it did not take long for SIM to put the pieces together. 'Tito', SIM noted a week after Mallaby's capture, 'is none other than the parachutist who was sent to Lake Como on the night of 13 [August] and caught shortly after.' SIM also recorded that after 'repeated and stringent interrogation' in Como the prisoner had admitted to the name 'Olaf' and 'that his task was that of a radio operator for an extant group in Italy that was supposed to provide him with radio equipment (namely the one from Trieste contained in the green suitcase)'.[19] Within days, from both an Allied and Italian point of view, the fact that SIM had established Mallaby's identity would prove to be no bad thing.

⊙

'The Italian hope of independently negotiating a surrender was slim indeed,' Dwight Eisenhower would write in his memoirs, 'because throughout the Italian governmental structure Mussolini had permitted or had been forced to accept the infiltration of countless Germans, all of whom were ready to pounce upon the first sign of defection and to take over the Italian nation in name as well as in fact.'[20] That a channel for negotiation was ever established owed much to the personal actions and initiative of a short, dark man in a civilian suit who, incognito, left Rome by train on the evening of 12 August 1943 and, three days later, presented himself in neutral Madrid to Sir Samuel Hoare, the British Ambassador to Spain.

Ostensibly Hoare's visitor was Signor Raimondi, a member of a diplomatic party en route from Rome to collect a party of Italian officials arriving in Lisbon from Chile. His real name was Giuseppe Castellano and he was in fact a 49-year-old general in the Italian Army whose true mission, as he now disclosed, was to seek out Allied officials and discuss with them the possibility of removing Italy from the war. Castellano was an aide to General Vittorio Ambrosio, chief of Comando Supremo, the military Supreme Command, and it had been Ambrosio, with the knowledge of Badoglio and the King, that had put him on the train to Spain. Accompanying Castellano was an interpreter, Franco Montanari, a young English-speaking official from the Italian Foreign Ministry; he also had with him a letter of introduction from Sir D'Arcy Osborne, the British Minister in the Vatican, addressed to Hoare, stating that Castellano could speak for Badoglio. Otherwise he carried no credentials. It was a highly delicate mission that called for the strictest secrecy to prevent the Germans from discovering what was afoot and trying to stop it. 'I was not given any document which would confirm to the Anglo-Americans the official task entrusted to me,' Castellano later wrote. 'I started upon my trip entrusting myself solely to good fortune.'[21]

Castellano's appearance was not the first Italian peace feeler recently received by the Allies. The new Badoglio government had sent out two that month already. Before Mussolini's fall even a few Fascists had tried to sound out the ground, while the earliest approach from Badoglio – the one via Berne through the offices of Luigi Rusca – had come a year before Castellano set off. This approach was different, however. Castellano's instructions from his superiors in Italy were to tell the Allies about Italy's situation in general and suggest Allied landings on the coast north of the Rome. As he sat with Hoare in Madrid, however, he stated instead that Italy would accept the terms of unconditional surrender if it were allowed to change sides and fight the Germans with the Allies. These ideas, though they had never been discussed with Badoglio, were to prove essential in ensuring that talks progressed. As one historian has written, if Castellano had stuck to his original instructions 'he would have faced the same wall of [British] Foreign Office opposition, and the request for unconditional surrender prior to any discussion, as had all the other Italian emissaries'.[22]

Late on 15 August, after the general and his interpreter had gone, Hoare sent word of Castellano's proposal to London. From there it was forwarded immediately to Quebec where Churchill, Roosevelt and a host of senior British and American leaders and commanders were attending the Anglo-American 'Quadrant' conference. Reading Hoare's telegram, Anthony Eden, who was in Canada too, urged that the Allies should continue to call for the Italians to surrender unconditionally. Churchill and Roosevelt felt differently. Instructions were dispatched that night to Allied Forces Headquarters in Algiers for Eisenhower to send two of his senior officers, under conditions of extreme secrecy, to neutral Lisbon, where Castellano and young Montanari, continuing their travels, were shortly due to arrive.

By the afternoon of 18 August, Eisenhower had selected two of his 'most trusted staff officers'.[23] One was his chief of staff, Major General Walter Bedell Smith, later a director of the CIA; the other was his chief intelligence officer, Brigadier Kenneth Strong, who was British. 'Arrangements were accordingly put in hand to try to get them off by aeroplane at 2 p.m.,' reported Harold Macmillan, the future British Prime Minister, who was then the resident British minister attached to Eisenhower's headquarters:

Somehow the Mediterranean Air Command had to produce a British civilian aircraft to take the two officers from Gibraltar to Lisbon; somehow civilian clothes had to be obtained; somehow civilian papers had to be provided, for it was felt that if these two officers were to arrive openly in Lisbon the international press and the German Secret Service would be on to them in a moment. Fortunately both officers had common surnames and by juggling with the christian names and with the photographs, passable papers were provided before lunch time.[24]

Soon Bedell Smith and Strong were flying to Gibraltar. Next day they flew on to Lisbon. 'I shall never forget Bedell sporting an appalling Norfolk jacket which he had somehow purchased in Algiers and some grey flannel trousers which fitted him very ill,' Macmillan would write in his memoirs.

He had obtained some kind of dubious hat with a feather in it; but I persuaded him to remove this, saying that no British traveller of whatever class would walk about with this unusual decoration. Kenneth Strong did not find the civilian tailors of Algiers to his taste, and was similarly decked out in a very improbable costume. However, they got through.[25]

At half-past ten on the evening of 19 August, Castellano and Montanari were shown in to the drawing room of the British Embassy in Lisbon. Waiting for them were Bedell Smith, Strong, the British Ambassador and the American Chargé d'Affaires. 'The Ambassador introduced me to all of them,' Castellano wrote later; 'they all greeted me with a nod. No one offered to shake my hand.'[26] Discussions then began. 'Both our visitors were nervous,' Strong remembered.

Castellano, a small, dark-eyed and suave Sicilian, of about fifty years of age and with an intelligent and alert face but speaking no English, was obviously a man of importance, accustomed to authority. He carried on the talks with scarcely a reference to notes and he had a remarkable grasp of detail. He remained friendly throughout . . .
Montanari, whose mother was American, had been educated at Harvard and looked and behaved like an Anglo-Saxon, both in dress

and manner. He was, however, clearly the junior partner in the affair; he seemed to know little of military matters and Castellano seldom referred to him except on some minor political point. He scarcely volunteered a remark, looking extremely sad the whole time, but as an interpreter his translations were excellent.

Talks lasted through the night. Castellano stuck to his line that Italy would surrender unconditionally if permitted to change sides when the Allies attacked the mainland; he also asked to know Allied plans. 'That he was unable to obtain any concessions of importance was not a criticism of his ability,' Strong noted. 'Bedell Smith had no authority to depart one iota from his instructions.'[27] Those instructions were to make it quite clear that the Italians must agree unconditionally to a military armistice, though the precise terms might be modified depending on the degree of assistance forthcoming from the Italian Government and people. By the time the discussions ended at seven the following morning, Castellano, who had no authority to discuss the terms, had agreed to take them back to Rome.

Before the meeting broke up, Castellano had also agreed to try to establish from Rome a means of clandestine communication with the Allies so that this crucial contact could survive and develop. Ideally this would take the form of a secret wireless link; if that proved impossible, he would attempt to communicate instead with the British Legation in Berne. The Combined Chiefs of Staff in Quebec had identified this as a matter of such vital importance that they had instructed Eisenhower, even before Castellano's meeting in Lisbon, to ensure that such a link could be provided. Eisenhower had turned to Harold Macmillan. Macmillan then spoke to Lieutenant Colonel Douglas Dodds-Parker, the head of SOE's 'Massingham' base.[28]

Both Dodds-Parker and Leo Marks, a young coding expert working in London at the time, would later make a series of erroneous claims as to the part that they and SOE were to play in the Italian surrender. Dodds-Parker, in his memoirs, confused

Castellano with General Giacomo Zanussi, an entirely different Italian emissary dispatched from Rome at about this time.[29] Marks, in his memoirs, would appear to have modelled his own recollections on those of Dodds-Parker.[30] What really happened is that Eisenhower's request was forwarded to London where it landed in the lap of 'The Moke': Brigadier Eric Mockler-Ferryman. Six months earlier, Mockler-Ferryman had been head of Eisenhower's intelligence team for the campaign in Northwest Africa until he was sacked, unfairly, after the chaotic American defeat at the Kasserine Pass. Sent home in apparent disgrace and seemingly fated for a job in London with the Boy Scout movement, Mockler-Ferryman had been snapped up instead by SOE and put in charge of its operations in Northwest Europe. Now, in Baker Street, he put his mind to meeting Eisenhower's request. Speed, he knew, was paramount: Castellano, to maintain his visiting diplomat's cover, would have to return soon to Rome. One idea, very briefly entertained, was to send out Max Salvadori and a first-class wireless operator and have them return with Castellano to Italy. This was dropped in favour of Cecil Roseberry securing in London a secret SOE signals plan, flying with it to Lisbon, and handing it to Castellano, who would also be given an SOE wireless set and instructions in how to use it.

The first hiccup was quick in coming. Roseberry received Mockler-Ferryman's instructions late in the afternoon of 18 August. He dropped everything and acted immediately but found that there was no senior officer still at work in SOE's London signals office. The only officer present declared that he could not possibly issue a signals plan until he had been formally informed that a project had been both approved and allotted a codename. Bluffing, Roseberry assured him that it had been approved with the codename 'Monkey'. With his boxes ticked, the officer produced the plan. The 'Monkey' name would stick.[31]

Roseberry failed to catch that night's flight to Lisbon. Then the next night's was cancelled. He finally flew the night after that, on the evening of 20 August, and reached Lisbon early the following morning. By then Bedell Smith and Strong had finished talking to Castellano and already returned to Algiers, but the two Italians were still there. On Baker Street's instructions, the SOE office in Lisbon handed over a wireless set for the pair to take back to Italy; SOE-designed, it was known as a B Mark II and fitted snugly into what Castellano would recall as an elegant leather suitcase. They also taught Montanari, Castellano's interpreter, how it worked; a wireless specialist on the Lisbon staff, Jack Robertson, acted as instructor. Roseberry arrived just in time to brief the Italians on the use of the 'Monkey' signals plan. He also helped arrange a simple double-transposition code based on the text of *L'omnibus del corso*, a 1941 novel by the Florentine writer Bino Sanminiatelli. The book was chosen after three copies were found in Lisbon: one for each end of the wireless link, plus a spare.

Roseberry, aware of reports reaching London that Dick Mallaby had been captured, also took the opportunity in Lisbon to try something else. Could he convincingly pretend to the Italians that the far-sighted British had dropped a wireless operator into Italy precisely for this eventuality, and try to persuade them to use a fully trained SOE wireless operator to work the Italian end of a link between Rome and Algiers? If Mallaby could be hauled out of prison and used like this, it might also save him from being shot. With all this in mind, Roseberry pointed out to Castellano that it was vital for the Italians to be 'certain' of any wireless operator.

[I] also laid great stress on the importance of the correct procedure when making contact ... [Castellano] was very impressed with this difficulty and asked how it could be solved. The following conversation took place:
'We cannot get such an operator.'
'I can give you one.'
'Where is he?'
'In Italy.'
'An Italian?'

'No. A British officer who entered your country by parachute so as to be available for just such an emergency.'

'Will he work for us?'

'Definitely no, unless he receives from you ... certain messages which he will know could not have emanated from anybody but me.'

'Where is he now?'

'In prison at Como; you captured him two [*sic*] days ago ...'

[Castellano] seemed rather doubtful as to whether a British officer who had been taken 'as a spy' would be approved by Badoglio. At this I pointed out that although a British subject, he was born [*sic*] in Italy, loved Italy, but was prepared to risk his life in an attempt to fight against Fascism, which was exactly what the mission themselves [Castellano and Montanari] had set out to do.[32]

Castellano agreed to use him. 'As soon as he crosses [the] Italian frontier General 'C' will telephone Rome saying no action must be taken against Olaf,' SOE recorded. He would also 'apply for the custody of Olaf' and seek to use him as his operator.[33]

Delayed by the late arrival of the Italian party coming from Chile, Castellano and Montanari eventually left Lisbon on 23 August. Embarking by train, the pair took with them the proposed armistice terms and, secreted in its neat leather case, their SOE wireless set, together with guidance regarding wavelengths and transmitting times and strict instructions that they had until midnight on 30 August to make contact. If nothing were heard, the Allies would assume that the Italian Government had not accepted the terms. With the Allied assault on mainland Italy now being prepared for early September, time was already very short.

In the hope of speeding Castellano safely back to Rome, orders were issued to the RAF to lay off bombing and strafing his likely route. Other than that, little more could be done on the Allied side except to make certain that any incoming messages from Castellano's set – if Rome proved willing and able to get it working – were heard, taken down and decoded. These tasks were given to the SOE signals station at 'Massingham', where a handpicked team of four young women of the First Aid Nursing Yeomanry, the well-heeled unit that did much of SOE's secret signals work, was assigned to handling the Monkey traffic if Rome ever came up on the air. 'To maintain total security we were kept incommunicado,' remembered one of the four, Patricia 'Paddy' Sproule, who had joined the FANYs in 1942.[34] The daughter of a British Army colonel, she had trained for coding and cipher work after finding, at five-foot-two, that she was too short to reach the pedals of an ambulance. The day after Castellano's departure from Lisbon was her nineteenth birthday.

While the SOE signals staff in Algiers waited and watched for any sign of life from Rome, they also waited, with growing anxiety, for a copy of *L'omnibus del corso*, the Italian book on which the Monkey transposition code was based. Castellano had taken one copy with him when leaving Lisbon. Cecil Roseberry had flown back to London with the other two, one of which had been quickly placed in the hands of another SOE officer detailed to fly with it, at once, to Algiers. The plan was for this officer to make immediately for a rendezvous at Algiers' Hotel Saint George on rue Michelet, home to Eisenhower's Allied Forces Headquarters, where he was to hand the book straight away to one of 'Massingham's' officers. London's chosen courier was Major Harold Meakin, a 41-year-old staff officer in SOE's Signals Section who, before the war, had run a little company in London making glass for optical instruments. With the book in his care, Meakin left London for Algiers on 24 August. It was expected that he would arrive next day. That day came and there was no sign of him. Nor was there any the next day. Nor did he show up the day after that. After a badly delayed journey, Meakin finally turned up, three days late, at six o'clock on the evening of 28 August. On the morning of 29 August, SOE operators manning the signals station at 'Massingham' heard a Morse key tapping from Rome.

⊙

Decoded using the text of *L'omnibus del corso*, the first full messages, which were received in Algiers on the morning of 30 August, carried news that 'Olaf' was free.[35] As SOE learned later, Mallaby, after being pulled from the lake, beaten up and quizzed, had been transferred from Como to Milan for further investigation by SIM, and then sent back to the cells in Como. But he had not remained in prison for long. On returning to Italy, Castellano had immediately instructed that Mallaby be sent to him.

Concerned that he might suspect an Italian trap if asked by his captors to work a wireless set on their behalf, Cecil Roseberry had primed Castellano with certain messages and facts that would, he hoped, convince the young man that SOE was genuinely involved. These included Mallaby's real name and rank, plus 'a covert hint to communicate with us in his own code to prove to us that he was working without restraint'.[36] Castellano would remember that Mallaby, being 'completely in the dark', had still taken some convincing before agreeing to co-operate.[37] When Mallaby finally said he would help, the Italians then installed him on the top floor of the Palazzo Vidoni, the Rome headquarters of the Comando Supremo. There, with the assistance of a senior Italian wireless operator by the name of Baldanza, he began coding and sending the outgoing Monkey messages and receiving and decoding the signals received.

Major Luigi Marchesi, an Italian officer into whose care he had been placed, would later recall that Mallaby had also been helped by a team of three young Italian sergeants: Otello Griffoni, Luciano Del Col and Mario Della Corte. One or two published accounts have made the romantic claim that Mallaby transmitted from the sixteenth-century Palazzo del Quirinale, the official residence of the Italian king, but there is no evidence to support this. In fact, Mallaby became so concerned that German direction-finding techniques might pick up his transmissions that at one point, together with his Italian team, he was moved to an apartment in the city's outskirts. The apartment turned out to be in close proximity to a staff office of the German Red Cross.[38]

When Rome began sending, 'Massingham' spotted from the style of Morse-keying that at least two operators in Rome were taking turns to transmit. That one of these was Mallaby was confirmed when, in response to a reply from Algiers, he sent a message using the original code that SOE had given him prior to his parachute drop. As Algiers began to send more signals and a regular dialogue developed, Mallaby – realising that he, too, knew people at the opposite end – managed to add some personal messages to the outgoing traffic drafted by Badoglio's staff. 'Give my love to Mary Blondie and Miss Grinville [sic],' reads one of them. 'Wish I were with you.'[39] 'Mary Blondie' was Mary McIntyre, Douglas Dodds-Parker's blonde secretary at 'Massingham'. 'Miss Grinville' was Christine Granville, a Polish SOE agent – her real name was Krystyna Skarbek – much written about since the war; Mallaby had been her wireless instructor, and the two had become friends.[40]

'I recollect vividly my tremendous relief,' wrote Kenneth Strong of hearing that signals had been received over the Monkey link. 'The conversations in Lisbon had not failed. Our confidence in Castellano was justified.'[41] Justified, too, had been the faith invested in SOE's ability to provide a secure, rapid and regular way of keeping in contact with Rome. But Badoglio and Eisenhower's only channel of communication would also prove vital, for the coming negotiations with Rome were to become very far from straightforward.

⊙

'They do not want to humiliate us,' Castellano had reported on returning to Rome, pointing out that 'the formula of unconditional surrender' had been changed to 'Armistice Terms' and that there was now 'an entire change of attitude favourable to us which must be held in great consideration'. But it was 'certain', he had added, 'that the diplomatic phase, that is, the one which intended to make known the conditions of the country and which asked for Anglo-American intervention before any action on our part, is now definitely over. General [Bedell] Smith's decisive attitude was an indication of this trend since he permitted no further discussions.' As Castellano also put it: 'today it is only General Eisenhower who speaks'. Convinced that the Italians had little room to manoeuvre, he had therefore been stunned and disgusted to find few of his superiors in Rome ready to accept the Allies' terms. These men included Badoglio, whom Castellano seems to have considered an indecisive old fool afflicted by 'a softening of the brain aggravated by ill breeding', and Raffaele Guariglia, Badoglio's new Minister of Foreign Affairs.[42]

A good sense of the tension and dithering – and mudslinging – in senior Italian circles can be found in Castellano's diary. In this, he gave his frustration full vent:

The 27th of August . . .

I briefly related the events of my trip and I read the armistice terms. The Marshal [Badoglio] behaved like an imbecile. Guariglia objects stating that we cannot ask for an armistice because if we did the Germans would butcher us. He would like to see the Anglo-Americans invade Italy without any assistance being offered on our part (thusly conducting ourselves as cowards) . . .

The 28th of August . . .

Guariglia criticizes my doings [in Madrid and Lisbon] and affirms that I should not have alluded to military co-operation. (Then what would have been my reason for having gone?) Ambrosio defends me. Guariglia does not want to accept [the Allied terms], saying that we cannot ask for an armistice at the moment of the landing but only after the landing had taken place and after the Anglo-Americans are entrenched in Italy. [To Ambrosio] I repeat that in this situation with an imbecile at the head of the government and with a coward as Foreign Minister, no headway can be made . . .

The 29th of August . . .

As soon as I arrive at the office I go to see Ambrosio to tell him that according to my way of thinking, it is necessary to go above Badoglio's head . . .

At eleven, I accompanied Ambrosio to the Quirinale Palace. The King, through [the Minister of the Royal Household, Duke Pietro] Acquarone, states that the head of the government will decide first [on what action to take] and then he will give the last word.

Badoglio, Ambrosio and Guariglia hold a meeting in a private room. A few minutes later they go to see the King. Upon coming out, Ambrosio made a sign to the effect that the answer had been negative. He then beckoned me to join him and Badoglio. They asked me what procedure would have to be followed in order to give a reply [to the Allied demand for acceptance of the armistice terms] which would neither be yes or no. I answered that I had agreed with [Bedell] Smith only upon a definite yes or no.

Badoglio picks up his hat and kicks me out . . . stating that these are 'questions of government' and that I 'Mister Castellano' should depart. I am dumbfounded.[43]

On 31 August, and in line with a plan proposed in Lisbon and confirmed by messages over the Monkey link, Castellano, still acting as Rome's delegate, flew from the Italian mainland to Sicily to resume discussions. His aircraft, a three-engined Savoia-Marchetti, was met by Allied fighters and escorted safely to the ground. Waiting for him among the olive trees at Cassibile – a little town near Siracusa where the commander of all Allied forces in Sicily, General Sir Harold Alexander, had his tented headquarters – were Bedell Smith and Strong. Both were now back in uniform. Neither was amused to find that Castellano had been authorised by Badoglio to sign an armistice only on the condition that the Italian Government should be informed where, and in what strength, the Allies would land in Italy.

That condition was immediately dismissed. 'We had already decided that for security reasons we could not give the Italians precise information,' Kenneth Strong recalled:

We could only keep impressing on Castellano that we intended to land in force; that whatever he said or did Italy was doomed to become a battlefield; [and] that we would declare an armistice before we landed but that we could not give any exact information of our intentions and plans until shortly before the landing took place.

Told to return immediately to Italy and secure a final decision, Castellano left that night. 'All our nerves were on edge,' Strong wrote, 'and we could do nothing but wait.'[44]

On the morning of 2 September, Castellano flew again to Sicily. Again he was found to lack the authority to sign the armistice terms. 'The situation was becoming ridiculous,' remembered Strong. 'The invasion was due to take place in a few days' time and many of our plans were based on reaching some kind of agreement.' The highest-ranking officer in Sicily at the time, General Alexander, now entered the arena, 'booted, spurred and bemedalled' for the occasion. When the Italians told him that they were unable to sign the terms, Alexander 'burst into a torrent of angry words'. He indicated, 'in Hitlerian manner, that his sorely tried patience was at an end,' and delivered 'a sound lecture on the disgraceful manner in which they were endangering not only our own military operations but even the future of Italy'.[45] Castellano, via Monkey, dispatched a chaser to Rome. 'The Commander-in-Chief, Allied Forces, will not discuss any military matters whatever unless a document of acceptance of the armistice conditions is signed,' his message began. 'As operations against the Peninsula will begin very shortly with landings, this signature is extremely urgent . . .'[46]

Finally, over the Monkey link on the afternoon of 3 September, a message was heard from Badoglio authorising Castellano to sign. An hour later, seated at a wooden camp table in an army tent in an olive grove close to Cassibile, he and Bedell Smith duly signed the agreed armistice terms.

'We picked branches from the trees to keep as mementos of the occasion,' Strong recalled. 'General Rooks produced a bottle of whisky; we drank out of rather dirty glasses and Bedell Smith,

Castellano, Montanari and I had our photographs taken.'[47] The most famous photograph of the events at Cassibile demonstrates how SOE had helped with the negotiations in another way. In the centre of the shot, between a seated and signing Bedell Smith and the short and sturdy frame of a black-suited Castellano, stands a young British officer in the uniform and forage cap of the Queen's Royal Regiment. This is Captain Edward 'Teddy' de Haan. Twenty-three years old, he had lived in Milan for ten years as a boy, spoke Italian fluently, and, when war broke out, had been a hotel manager's apprentice at the Savoy, Fortunato Picchi's old employer. Joining the army, de Haan had transferred to SOE in 1942 and was manning the Italian desk at 'Massingham' when suddenly summoned to Sicily and given the job of Allied interpreter for the talks with Castellano.

With the ink barely dry on the documents signed at Cassibile, discussions continued, still in conditions of great secrecy, as Allied officers and Badoglio's delegates sought to prepare for the main invasion of Italy and ensure that the Germans were not alerted too soon to what was coming. Although two British divisions landed on Italy's toe on the night of 3 September, Rome had agreed that news of the armistice would stay secret until Eisenhower revealed it to the world in a radio broadcast on the eve of Operation Avalanche, the main Allied invasion of southern Italy, timed for 9 September: the moment when troops of the US Fifth Army would go ashore at Salerno. Talks were 'very intricate', Eisenhower recalled. 'They involved the still strong Italian fleet, the remnants of the Italian air forces, and Italian ground forces throughout the peninsula and in the Balkans. Above all they involved the feasibility of a surrender while the Germans so closely dominated the entire country.'[48] On 7 September, when General Maxwell Taylor was sent secretly to Rome to coordinate plans with senior Italian officers, he discovered such a state of fear, inaction and confusion among them that a planned parachute drop near the city by the US 82nd Airborne Division had to be scrapped.

Helping to speed this planning and problem solving, the Monkey channel continued to hum. In Rome, Dick Mallaby and his Italian assistants were still coding, decoding, sending and receiving. In Algiers, behind the locked doors of a suitably isolated washroom and 'working 24 hours a day in [eight-hour] shifts – two girls on and two off,' Paddy Sproule and her young FANY colleagues continued to code and decode.[49] As SOE recorded later:

The 'Monkey' link was used to arrange the ex-filtration of technical experts, of members of the [Italian] Army, Navy and Air Force staffs to give details of defences; the infiltration of General Taylor to Rome to report on the possibilities of an airborne landing; the surrender of the [Italian] fleet, and in fact all the innumerable details which were necessary to ensure the implementation of the Armistice terms and the maximum degree of success in the contemplated landing at Salerno.[50]

On 8 September, Badoglio reported in another Monkey message that, given the growing presence of German forces around Rome, an immediate announcement of an armistice was impossible: 'it would provoke occupation of the capital and violent assumption of government by the Germans'.[51] A furious Eisenhower personally dictated an immediate reply. 'I intend to broadcast the existence of the armistice at the hour originally planned,' he said. 'If you or any part of your armed forces fail to co-operate as previously agreed I will publish to the world [the] full record of this affair. Today is X-day and I expect you to do your part.'[52] Transmitted over Monkey, that message reached Badoglio barely an hour before Eisenhower went on the air. 'This is General Dwight D. Eisenhower, Commander in Chief of the Allied forces,' he began, on schedule, at six-thirty that evening. 'The Italian government has surrendered its armed forces unconditionally. As Allied Commander in Chief, I have granted a military armistice.'[53] Badoglio duly followed it with his own broadcast an hour or so afterwards. The armistice took immediate effect.

When they heard Badoglio speak, very few Italian soldiers, of any rank, had known that an end to hostilities was being negotiated or had been told how to react if it came. Nor did Badoglio's broadcast call on them to fight the Germans, even though Hitler's forces were now present in Italy in rapidly increasing strength: King Vittorio Emanuele would formally declare war on Nazi Germany only on 13 September. Nevertheless, to all Italian troops manning garrisons across Italy, including those occupying foxholes and machinegun nests above beaches where the Allies might land, it was quite clear that Badoglio was telling them to stop fighting. On the morning of 9 September, when Allied forces began going ashore on the beaches at Salerno, they met solid German resistance, but Italian guns – save for those of a few diehard Fascists – were silent.

⊙

On the afternoon of 8 September 1943, Foreign Secretary Anthony Eden addressed an assembly of representatives of Allied nations at the Foreign Office in London. Italy had surrendered, Eden told them. He read out Eisenhower's announcement, which at that moment had still to be broadcast, and briefly explained that talks in Lisbon and Sicily had led to the signing of an armistice five days before. 'He then asked the representatives whether they wished to ask any questions,' the Iraqi Chargé d'Affaires told Baghdad afterwards. 'One of them asked him whether the Germans were aware of what had happened. The Minister said that he thought they knew, and for that reason had concentrated part of their forces near Rome.'[54]

It is true that German forces across the Mediterranean had been preparing themselves for an Italian capitulation. It is true, too, that German officials in Italy had felt that such a collapse was imminent. By the end of August, Major Herbert Kappler, the chief SS liaison officer in Rome, was telling Berlin that he believed Badoglio would step aside or conclude a separate peace 'in 10 days at the latest'.[55] It is also the case that, when the announcement came, the German military command in Italy reacted rapidly. Rome was swiftly dominated. Italian units were disarmed. Strong German reinforcements were quickly rushed into place to meet the Allied soldiers landing at Salerno; they would prove formidable opposition. Indeed, the days that Badoglio spent dithering over the armistice conditions may well have lost the Allies a good many military advantages. Nevertheless, it is clear today from declassified British intercepts of enemy signals that the negotiations had been conducted so securely that, for both of Italy's former allies, Germany and Japan, news of them still came as a shock.

'Of late', the Japanese Ambassador in Berlin, Hiroshi Ōshima, told Tokyo after Eisenhower and Badoglio had announced the armistice, the German Government had felt that 'sooner or later such a thing would occur', but 'the skill with which this affair had been planned was amazing'. Even on 8 September, when the German Ambassador in Rome, Rudolf Rahn, had a private audience with the King, 'the latter had said that since the downfall of Mussolini a feeling of confidence had been wanting between Germany and Italy but that this would gradually change for the better, and he would exert his efforts to this end . . . Rahn then saw Badoglio, and the latter spoke on the same lines.' That evening the armistice was announced. When the German General Headquarters telephoned Rahn and told him,

Rahn went so far as to state positively that such a thing could not possibly be so. However, at 7 o'clock [the Italian] Foreign Minister [Raffaele] Guariglia notified Rahn that Italy had been compelled to sue for peace with the United States and Britain. Rahn said that this was nothing short of treachery, and violently reproached Guariglia, but nothing could be done.[56]

'In view of the rapidity and great skill with which Italy's capitulation was carried out,' Ōshima continued next day, it may be said to be increasingly clear now that negotiations with Britain and America had been in progress for some considerable time ... Through what channel the negotiations were carried on is not yet clear, but it is suspected that ... the Vatican acted to some extent as intermediary. In the meanwhile the Badoglio Government very adroitly concealed these proceedings and tried to delude the Japanese and Germans with their lies up to the very last moment – a breach of faith on its part which one can only view with disgust.[57]

Abject apologies followed from Shirokuro Hidaka, the Japanese Ambassador in Rome. 'I realised that Badoglio and Company would probably be glad to get out of the war while saving Italy's face,' Hidaka told Tokyo, 'and I tried to do my humble best to prevent this; but the fact that . . . I failed to see through Badoglio's treachery and missed the opportunity of taking suitable action was a blunder for which I can offer no excuse. Consequently I respectfully await your instructions.'[58]

Though it was only a tiny cog in the Allied military machine and had become involved more by luck than by design, SOE had contributed to Hidaka's humiliation. It had not been established with a view to handling peace negotiations, and recognition of the importance of Dick Mallaby's role must acknowledge that his involvement came only after carefully laid plans had gone badly wrong. Nevertheless, such a rapid and reliable means of clandestine communication could not have been fashioned if the Allies had had to resort to more conventional and less adaptable channels, or if SOE had lacked able and imaginative officers in London, sound technical expertise, and a good man on the ground. An in-house history of its Italian operations concluded accurately at the end of the war:

SOE's part in assisting the carrying out of the Armistice terms was undoubtedly responsible in no small measure for the shortening of the Italian war at this vital stage, and equally may be regarded as one of our major contributions to the Mediterranean campaign.[59]

14

'Inglese Ignoto'

By 8 September 1943, of the eight trained SOE agents who had worked clandestinely on Italian soil, only one had returned to Allied lines. This was Max Salvadori, whose impressive drive along Sicilian roads packed with retreating Italian troops had lasted only a few hours anyway. Of the other seven, SOE knew by the Armistice that two of them were dead. One was Fortunato Picchi, who had parachuted into Italy with the Colossus party in 1941. The other was Antonio Gallo, who had gone ashore on Sicily in 1942. Rome had named both men when broadcasting news that they had been caught and shot. Of the remaining five, three were still missing. Branko Nekić, who had been put through the German lines in Sicily in August 1943, was one of those. Confirmation of his capture and news of his execution would come a few weeks later. The other missing agents were Gabor Adler and Salvatore Serra, the team sent into Sardinia in January 1943. Lastly there were two agents that SOE thought were safe: Dick Mallaby and Giacomino Sarfatti. Mallaby was thought to be in Rome and under the protection of Badoglio's government. Sarfatti was believed to be at liberty in Milan, though nothing had been heard of him for a fortnight.

Long after dark on the evening of 10 September 1943, a young man walked into a café in Chiasso, the Swiss customs town on the border with Italy. His shoes were covered in mud and his trousers were torn and bloody. When the last customer had left he approached the woman running the place and explained that he was an Englishman, a civilian, who had escaped from internment in Italy. He had made it across the frontier, he said, and wanted to get in touch with the nearest British consul. The café-owner fed him, found him a bed for the night, changed his Italian money and gave him a pair of her husband's trousers. Next morning, following her advice, he caught a train to Lugano and contacted the British vice-consul.

The young man who crossed the border that night was Giacomino Sarfatti, the Italian wireless operator who had been living in Milan since the previous December. Until the Armistice, SIM had continued to keep him under its gaze, monitoring his correspondence with McCaffery, permitting him to use his wireless set, and generally allowing him to believe that he was free and life was good. So far as Sarfatti had been aware, the chief danger he had faced in Milan was from Allied bombing. In August, when air raids on Italy were reaching their peak, an incendiary bomb smashed through the roof of the next-door flat. He helped put out the fire with water from his bath, having kept it full for just such an emergency.

According to one Italian account given to British interrogators, by the summer of 1943 SIM had been wondering whether it might be time for Sarfatti's arrest. Had he been hauled in a few months earlier, Sarfatti might well have ended his days in Forte Bravetta with his back to a firing squad. Aware that he was Italian and had returned to Italy as an enemy agent, SIM possessed more than enough evidence to make a death sentence a formality. As it was, with Mussolini gone, Fascism finished, and Italy's surrender apparently imminent, SIM seems to have decided instead to encourage him gently, through Eligio Klein, to go home. In early September, advised by Klein that the air raids were making Milan far too dangerous and that he really ought to return to Switzerland, Sarfatti left the city and headed north. On 10 September, opposite Chiasso, he scouted the frontier for a suitable crossing point. Evading an Italian patrol, he made a break for it later that evening. He shredded his trousers and buttocks getting through the barbed wire, then fell into a ditch, but got across.

Sarfatti made contact with Jock McCaffery a few days later. At that moment both men remained wholly oblivious to the fact that Sarfatti's nine-month stint in Milan had been controlled entirely by SIM. Much later, when Sarfatti finally learned that Klein had been a plant, he reflected that the latter had certainly been strange. He noted Klein's 'complete lack of morality, of political principles or of principles of any kind', his 'amazing tendency to lie and to enlarge everything', and his habit of 'contradicting himself even in the course of the same conversation ... I also noticed that he had very little or no courage, as I was able to find out during alarms and air raids. At the same time he seemed so sure of himself in what he was doing. The two things did not seem to fit well together.' The fact that he had failed to rumble that Klein was really an enemy agent, Sarfatti felt, was because

I was handicapped by two things: (a) [by] my age (22 at the time) and my very little experience of life and men generally; [and] (b) by the fact that I had been repeatedly told both in London and Berne that I could trust [Klein] and rely completely on him. I was actually told he was a wonderful man and that I was going to be quite safe as long as he was looking after me.[1]

After eight days in Lugano, Sarfatti left Switzerland to return to what was now German-occupied northern Italy. He made it across the border, no thanks to the local smuggler employed to assist him who managed it so badly that Sarfatti was caught by a Swiss patrol. Sarfatti got away by saying that he was trying to escape into Switzerland, whereupon the patrol sent him back to where they believed he had come from: Italy. Sarfatti was to remain in northern Italy for another year. Through no fault of his own, it was a period in which his training, qualities and skills went largely to waste. For a while he stayed in Milan. Since he had no papers, no friends and no wireless set, there was little for him to do except take up his old routine. In January 1944 he moved to a village in the Val Camonica and took up with a poorly supported partisan movement called the Fiamme Verdi. Still he had no wireless set, so he worked instead couriering around messages and propaganda. In July, after news reached him that a wireless operator was needed in Milan, he joined a new group and at last got his hands on a set, which he used to keep the partisans in contact with others elsewhere. At first he worked in the city. Later he moved to Veniano, near Como, and it was there, at one o'clock in the morning on 19 August 1944, that the house in which he was operating was raided. Abandoning the wireless set, Sarfatti made it on to the roof, where he entangled himself in electrical wires before deciding to jump into the street. Hurting his feet when he hit the ground, he staggered off into the night in pain but unseen. For ten days he eked out an existence in a wood, nursing his nerves and feet and surviving on peaches, grapes and cupped handfuls of pond-water. In October 1944 he returned to Switzerland.

'Had bad luck in the field,' was the accurate opinion of the SOE officer who debriefed him a fortnight later. Sarfatti was 'full of determination', he added, and, 'in spite of his quiet reserved manner, clearly has plenty of go and courage'.[2] The war ended before Sarfatti could be given another opportunity to prove himself, but sight should not be lost of the risks he had run and the strain he had endured during eighteen months in enemy territory. Jock McCaffery would remember that in Berne he had thought often of Sarfatti 'living literally in the shadow of death ... Men get high decorations on the battlefield for valour of a lower order.'[3]

Giacomino Sarfatti survived the war. He went back to his agricultural studies, but in Italy, not Reading. In 1948 he graduated with a degree in agricultural sciences and began a distinguished academic career, studying, teaching and writing about society, science and the environment.[4] He died in 1985. At the end of his career he was Professor of Botany at the University of Siena. Today its Department of Environmental Sciences is named after him.

⊙

The night after Sarfatti crossed into Switzerland, a four-man SOE team boarded a British troopship in Sicily and sailed for the southern Italian port of Taranto. Going ashore on 12 September, they had orders to requisition a local vehicle or two and make a dash for Brindisi, on Italy's heel, thirty-odd miles away. It was a dangerous time to be driving around southern Italy. British forces, including the 1st Airborne Division, had landed, unopposed, at Taranto on the afternoon of 9 September, but German ambushes and roadblocks were met as they pushed inland, with one burst of machinegun fire fatally wounding the division's commanding officer, Major-General George Hopkinson. The SOE party, which included young Teddy de Haan, who had acted as interpreter during the Armistice talks in Sicily, appreciated the risks. Procuring a car and a three-wheeled van, they set off with their wireless set lying on a bed of straw in the back, with two of the party, a pair of SOE signals NCOs, one of them a West Indian wireless operator from British Guiana, sitting either side of it with a box of matches and a can of petrol.[5] Later that day they drove into Brindisi on the heels of a machinegun-toting jeep patrol of Popski's Private Army, a specialist raiding and reconnaissance unit that was spearheading the Allied advance. Although the Germans had gone, de Haan and his team did find Dick Mallaby.

Four days earlier, Mallaby had been in Rome. Within hours of the announcement of the Armistice and as German troops began to secure control, he had then been attached to a party of elite Italians making a break for the Allied lines. Among them were Marshal Badoglio and several of his senior officers, together with the Italian king, queen and crown prince. Mallaby took with him his wireless set and was accompanied by the Italian operators with whom he had been working the Monkey link. First stop was Pescara, on the Adriatic. Next, after passing long German convoys thundering in the opposite direction, was the port of Ortona. There the party was ferried out to a waiting Italian corvette, the *Baionetta*, and sailed for Brindisi, docking there in the afternoon of 10 September. Installed with his set and assistants on the upper floor of one of the towers of Brindisi's massive Swabian Castle, Mallaby settled down again to sending and receiving signals between Badoglio and the Allies. He was still operating the link when de Haan, whom he knew, drove in to the port. Hearing that an SOE team had arrived at the Internazionale Hotel, Mallaby, according to a later account, turned up in the foyer, 'anxiously scanning the faces of the throng and revelling in the new-found thrill of seeing British uniforms once more'. He was still in civilian clothes and the hotel porter refused to let him in, whereupon the resulting altercation caused heads to turn and an SOE officer recognised him.[6]

Mallaby carried on working the Monkey link until it was closed down a few days later. After that he joined the headquarters of No. 1 Special Force, a new unit responsible for SOE operations supporting the military campaign in Italy. One job was to work as an instructor to Italian wireless operators provided by SIM, which was now working hand-in-hand with SOE, for future missions in the German-occupied north. Cecil Roseberry wrote later that rumours of Mallaby's exploits 'created a spirit of emulation among his students'.[7]

Mallaby's accomplishments received official recognition when, in December 1943, it was announced in the *London Gazette* that he had been awarded the Military Cross. No further details were published. War Office records reveal that he had originally been put forward for an immediate award of a higher decoration, the Distinguished Service Order. The recommendation explained that he had 'dropped alone into Lake Como by parachute' and found himself 'in conditions of unexpected difficulty which were a severe test of his courage'. Praising his conduct in captivity where he was first 'kept in handcuffs and beaten', it concluded that, but for his 'exceptional coolness, perseverance and devotion to duty' while operating the Monkey link, the Allied landings on the Italian mainland might have been made with Italy still an enemy.[8]

Wireless instructing kept Mallaby in a safe staff role for several months. In July 1944 he was briefly able to do something more active, driving north with another officer to contact partisans in the town of Macerata, in the Marche, from which the Germans had recently retreated. During this trip Mallaby drove over to his childhood home at Asciano, near Siena. To mutual surprise and delight, he arrived, unheralded, to find his father and stepmother safe and well. Back in southern Italy in September, by when SOE was dropping increasing numbers of its missions into German-occupied northern Italy to work with local partisans, Mallaby was eventually earmarked for a mission to Milan. When this was aborted, another plan was drawn up, this time to send him into northern Italy to establish fresh wireless communications in Milan and generally improve them across the north.

To get Mallaby into Milan, it was decided that he should go overland via the Swiss border, which seemed to offer the least problematic route. With this in mind, he was flown from southern Italy to liberated Lyons in eastern France; next, he crossed clandestinely from France into Switzerland. Then, on the evening of 13 February 1945, Mallaby left Berne for Lugano aboard a slow overnight train, travelling third class to keep a low profile. With him were two young Italian priests and an Italian wireless operator, all of whom would accompany him into Italy. Next day they took a car from Lugano to a point fairly close to the frontier, picked up a pair of smugglers en route, and, at about nine that evening, struck off on foot with the smugglers leading the way. An hour later they crossed into Italy. Four hours after that, after a nasty little journey in ordinary shoes through deep snow, they reached the Italian village of Carlaccio and the home of one of the smugglers. Around dawn on 15 February, leaving their guides behind, Mallaby and his companions set off again, this time for Milan, walking to Menaggio, on Lake Como, where they tried to hire a car but ended up renting a boat and crossing the lake to Varenna. From Varenna they managed to hitch a lift to Lecco in a lorry carrying nails and odds and ends. It was in Lecco that things went wrong.

Having eaten little and slept even less, the four men entered a restaurant and sat together at a table. Then two soldiers came in: a pair of Italian NCOs of the Brigate Nere, a Fascist military force still loyal to Mussolini. (Rescued from Italian captivity by a crack force of German paratroops in September 1943, Mussolini was now leader of the collaborationist Repubblica Sociale Italiana in German-occupied northern Italy.) Mallaby's party stood up to leave. The two soldiers stopped them. One of the priests was told to turn out his pockets. 'As one might have expected,' reads a later SOE report, 'his pockets were full of a mass of compromising papers; every sort of travel permit and identity document was produced as well as lots of little notes with names and addresses and messages from [partisan] liberation committees.' Before long, everyone's pockets were empty and the two Brigate Nere NCOs were demanding an explanation. 'All the members of the party had solemnly stated that they did not know one another. When, however, three of their identity cards were put together and all found to bear the same civilian address, this proved too much for the NCOs and they were all placed under arrest.'[9] Soon the four were occupying cells in the Brigate Nere barracks in Lecco.

At this point Mallaby decided to embark on an extraordinary bluff. 'At 2200 hrs on the 15th,' reads a subsequent report sent personally by the Brigate Nere commander in Como to no less a personality than Mussolini, 'Captain [Bricoli], commanding the 5th Company of this Black Brigade based on Lecco, brought me a British Captain named Richard Tucker.' This British officer had been captured at Lecco, the report explained, and now wished to speak to 'a senior officer only'. The report also explained that Tucker (who was Mallaby) had declared that he was the personal emissary of Field Marshal Sir Harold Alexander, Supreme Allied Commander in the Mediterranean, and had been sent secretly to Italy on a vitally important and highly confidential mission to speak to Marshal Rodolfo Graziani, Mussolini's Minister of Defence in the Repubblica Sociale Italiana.[10]

'I immediately telephoned to General [Edoardo] Facduelle [chief of staff of the Brigate Nere] that someone must discuss this matter urgently with Marshal Graziani,' the Como commander added in his report:

I was assured that a conversation would be requested in my name that night. I then reported to Captain Richard Tucker that I had arranged for him to meet Marshal Graziani. The Captain gave me his word of honour that he would not try to escape, but I told him that he would be placed under surveillance as he had been arrested by us and not reported of his own free will.[11]

The following day, Mallaby was taken under escort from Como to Milan and delivered to General Facduelle. Facduelle then telephoned Graziani's headquarters on Lake Garda and, that evening, set off with Mallaby to see him. They arrived late, the drive being made without headlights to avoid being strafed by Allied aircraft, and Mallaby was allowed to get a few hours' sleep in the comfort of a lakeside villa. Next day, 17 February, when Mallaby was driven to Graziani's headquarters, it transpired that the Marshal had decided not to see him, since his headquarters was crawling with Germans and he did not want them finding out what was afoot. Mallaby was taken instead to another headquarters, this one in nearby Volta Mantovana. Here he was finally interviewed. His interrogator was the Italian colonel in charge of the Servizio Informazioni Difesa, Graziani's intelligence service. This man was not unfamiliar with dealing with captured enemy agents. His name was Candeloro De Leo. As a SIM officer in Sicily two years before, De Leo had interrogated Antonio Gallo and Emilio Zappalà and built the case against them that led to their execution.

'My true name is Richard Tucker,' begins the Italian transcript of what Mallaby told De Leo. 'I was born 26 April, 1919 at Ceylon ...' He went on to give De Leo a more or less honest account of his youth and schooling in Tuscany, choosing only to say that his father was now in England when really he was still in Italy. He gave an accurate version of his early soldiering in the Commandos and at Tobruk. Where he was more deceptive was in saying nothing about SOE or his earlier mission. Instead he told De Leo that he had worked as an interpreter at Allied headquarters in Cairo from early 1942 until June 1943; then at Allied headquarters in Algiers from June until September 1943; then, again as an interpreter, for the Allied Military Mission in Brindisi and Caserta for twelve months after that. In September 1944 he had come under Alexander's direct command, Mallaby said, and in December he had been asked if would be willing to carry out a mission to northern Italy. 'I accepted the mission, but asked to know its objectives,' Mallaby told De Leo. 'I was received by Marshal Alexander in person who told me that the mission was in the interests of Italy.'[12]

Still bluffing, Mallaby now related to De Leo the instructions that Alexander, he said, had given him personally. With documents provided by the British Legation in Berne, Mallaby was to enter northern Italy via Switzerland as Alexander's personal emissary and present himself to Ildefonso Schuster, Cardinal Archbishop of Milan, with a view to securing an introduction to Marshal Graziani; the three men with whom he had been caught in Lecco had been helpers assigned to getting him over the border and into Milan and introducing him to the Cardinal. Then, once Mallaby was standing before Graziani, he was to tell him that Alexander wished to employ Graziani's forces in a way that would help 'avoid useless bloodshed by the Allied and Republican forces on the one hand, and partisan and Republican forces on the other'.[13] More specifically, Mallaby was to establish a response to Alexander's proposal that Graziani's men should neither impede the progress of the Allies nor attack the partisans, but rather stop the Germans from scorching the earth as they withdrew and help maintain public order once they had gone. Finally Mallaby was to say that Alexander was prepared to receive Graziani, or a representative, at Allied headquarters for further talks. Telling De Leo all of this, Mallaby added that he was not permitted to discuss the proposals but had been authorised by Alexander to return with a reply.

When the Allies captured him a few weeks later, De Leo was himself interrogated. To judge from his responses, he had believed Mallaby's story. He recalled assuring 'Tucker' that he could speak to him freely 'as the personal representative of Graziani'. De Leo added that he had then passed Alexander's proposal to Graziani 'who strongly approved of the idea, but did not dare to make a direct reply to the offer'. Instead, De Leo said, Graziani had referred the matter to Mussolini, who was then living on Lake Garda, whereupon Mussolini had informed the Germans, to whom 'Capt Tucker' was then handed over.[14]

Mallaby was indeed given to the Germans. On 26 February he was removed to Verona where he was interrogated again, this time by the SS, though his questioner was apparently 'quite cordial'. Quizzed in detail about all aspects of his mission, Mallaby stuck to the story that he had given De Leo, stressing, so SOE learned later, that he was merely a low-ranking staff officer at a large headquarters 'and that, on account of his junior rank and his age, he had merely been charged with opening a link and putting forward certain generalised suggestions'.[15] That night, with the interrogation over, Mallaby was moved again. This time he was taken by car to a private villa at Fasano on the shores of Lake Garda. Escorted inside, he found himself talking to General Karl Wolff, commander of all SS forces in Italy.

Wolff spoke to Mallaby for two hours. 'The General started

off rather coldly but very politely,' SOE recorded later. It was 'impossible', Wolff said, to discuss anything with Mallaby until 'his identity and the authenticity of his mission' could be confirmed. Mallaby 'pretended to be very surprised and aggrieved at this attitude and said to the General that it was in the very nature of things that he had nothing with him to prove his identity as a British officer. This attitude appeared to impress General Wolff, who hastily reassured [Mallaby] and said that he was, of course, perfectly willing to accept the word of a British officer and that they had better get down to business.' Mallaby repeated Alexander's proposals as he had presented them to De Leo and the SS. Wolff said that he had already agreed with Cardinal Schuster not to blow anything up as his forces withdrew. He added that he had also arranged with Graziani for Italian forces to pull out 'shoulder to shoulder' with the Germans.[16]

Then Wolff subjected Mallaby to a half-hour monologue about 'how the finest chivalrous ideals of medieval knighthood found their modern expression in the German S.S., and that the S.S. are now the only people in Germany who are in a position to see that any agreement made with the Allies is carried out'. That done, he told Mallaby that he 'offered himself to the Allies as a link between any person or group, military or civilian, in Germany with whom the Allies wished to establish contact. He went on to say that anyone could see that the Germans had lost the war and that some sort of end would have to be put quite soon to the present conflict. He said also that he was a personal friend of Hitler and [Field Marshal Albert] Kesselring and therefore might be useful.' To this, Mallaby repeated his story about Alexander's offer to receive representatives and extended it to include Wolff. The General replied that he would prefer to send Mallaby back with a message for Alexander, making him first give his 'word of honour' that he would return with Alexander's reply. Wolff's message, evidently aimed at shoring up his anticommunist credentials, was to the effect that, if the Allies stopped supplying arms to communist partisans in northern Italy, he would permit non-communist Italian guerrillas to move freely into Allied territory if they wished. Wolff finished up with a 'long winded account of his own important position' and, by the end of the interview, was 'very friendly'.[17]

The same evening, Mallaby was taken back to Verona. On 28 February, after five hours in a German bomb shelter as Allied bombs dropped on the town, he was driven by fast car to a villa close to Como where, with the assistance of the local SS commander, arrangements were made for his safe dispatch back into Switzerland. At seven that evening he crossed the border. In Chiasso he reported to the Swiss frontier post. Internment followed and lasted longer than expected. Ten days passed before Mallaby was finally delivered to the British Legation in Berne and able to report to Jock McCaffery.

'Dick appears to have put up a good show,' Cecil Roseberry remarked when he read a report of Mallaby's latest adventures. 'The last time he got free it was one chance in a million and this time it was one in a thousand. He will think these things are easy!'[18] But Mallaby may have done more than skilfully fashion his own escape. On 2 May 1945, secret negotiations between Karl Wolff and Allen Dulles, the chief OSS man in Berne, culminated in the unconditional surrender of all German forces in Italy, the first major German capitulation to the Western Allies. The first talks between Dulles and German emissaries from Italy seem to have started in Lucerne on 3 March. Wolff himself arrived in Lugano on 8 March when he began to take part personally. Today, the story of those negotiations, known as Operation 'Sunrise' and sometimes as Operation 'Crossword', is well known. Most of the credit for their success is rightly placed at Dulles's door. What has not been adequately recorded is the identity of a shadowy English officer who flits through contemporary documents and post-war books as 'Tucker', 'Mallaby', 'Drucker', 'Wallaby', and even 'Tucker-Wallaby', and whose 'clever ruse', as Dulles described it, may well have encouraged Wolff to believe that Allied officials wished to talk.[19]

When the war ended, Dick Mallaby was on the Allied side of the lines. SOE had shifted its Italian headquarters to Siena by then and he was there when news arrived on 8 May of Germany's surrender. In August he left SOE. A few months after that, he married Christine Northcote-Marks, a FANY coder who had worked on the SOE signals staff in Algiers and Italy. With the war over the couple went to live in England where Mallaby studied engineering at the University of Southampton and they began to raise a family. Returning to Italy in the early 1950s, they settled eventually in Verona where Mallaby worked for NATO. His youngest son remembers that his father never spoke about his wartime experiences despite the fact that, in Verona, the family lived for twenty years just yards from where Mallaby had been questioned by the SS in February 1945. Mallaby died in Verona in 1981 at the age of sixty-two, and is buried on his father's estate in Tuscany.

⊙

Overlooked by the Alps, Turin, in northwest Italy, was one of Italy's last cities to be liberated in 1945. The first Allied soldiers to reach it were Brazilian reconnaissance troops, whose armoured cars drove in at the end of April. American infantrymen were not far behind. There was little resistance. Most of the German and Fascist forces had already pulled out and the city was in the hands of Italian partisans. It was in Turin on 4 May that one of the agents whom SOE had put into Sardinia in 1943 suddenly appeared, alive and well, out of the partisans' ranks. It was Salvatore Serra.

After reporting to Turin's new military authorities, Serra was rapidly returned to the SOE fold. Soon he was in Siena at SOE headquarters. He was also under arrest: the reports of SIM officers who had switched sides after the Armistice meant that officers there were very aware that Serra had apparently assisted the Italians in the arrest of other agents in Corsica. Then he was questioned. The officer who quizzed him was Peter Cooper, a young Italian-speaking British officer who was working as an interrogator for SOE's security section.

Serra began at the beginning. First he described his capture. Hours after paddling ashore that January night in 1943, he and Gabor Adler had met a local shepherd. This man, after giving them food and water, slipped off to fetch some soldiers and Carabinieri. Immediately arrested, the two agents were held for the rest of the day in the old coastal watchtower of San Giovanni di Sarrala and then sent to Cagliari, the Sardinian capital. There, Serra said, he had been stripped naked, bound hand and foot, beaten and questioned, but had refused to talk. At one point the Italians took him back to where he and Adler had been arrested; Serra was beaten and kicked and told to explain every detail of the landing. Twice he was threatened with execution; on one occasion a priest was brought along. Every morning he received an injection that gave him a high temperature.

He and Adler had been quickly separated, Serra said. His Italian interrogators told him that Adler was an Italian agent, was co-operating fully, and had confessed everything. Then Serra had found himself talking to a Sicilian sent from Rome. He described this man as 'short; well built; rather bald; fingers covered with rings and jewels'. Between beatings, this man gave Serra two choices. He could follow Adler's 'good example' and collaborate, which would secure his life if not his freedom. Or he could refuse, in which case he would be 'shot out of hand'. (Later, reading Peter Cooper's report of Serra's debriefing, another officer scribbled next to that passage: 'This man is almost certainly Col. Faga.')[20] Eventually, Serra said, the Italians flew him to the mainland and locked him up in Regina Coeli.

Serra then tried to explain what he had done for the Italians in Corsica. Cooper recorded in his report:

[Serra] was escorted into a room [in Ajaccio] where a young French lieutenant was sitting surrounded by Italian officers and carabinieri. [He] was made to sit down in front of the officer who was then asked if he knew [him]. The Frenchman answered that he did. There then followed about 10 minutes [of] rapid conversation in French which [Serra] failed to understand. The Frenchman had been one of the students who had been in training with him in Algiers. [Serra] had then had no idea who he was or where he would be sent. He was, in fact, extremely surprised to see him in Corsica.

After that, Serra said, he had been flown back to Rome and imprisoned again. Later that year, after the Germans took control of Rome, he was moved from Regina Coeli to a prison in Mantua. In 1944 he was shifted to a civilian internment camp at San Martino di Rossignano, near Alessandria. From there he escaped, to spend the last months of the war fighting alongside local partisans.[21]

Cooper, who was already familiar with aspects of the story from SIM reports and other records, was not convinced that Serra was telling him the whole truth. He thought Serra's account of his arrest was probably accurate and that 'his bitterness over his treatment at the hands of the Italians after his capture is rather too real to be assumed'. He also felt sure that Serra would at first have refused to talk: as a Carabiniere deserter, his 'first and most natural instinct' would probably have been 'the stubbornness of a renegade' in the face of old comrades. But when confronted with the proffered alternatives – collaboration or death – Serra 'must have made some sort of promise, although he denies promising anything concrete'. Serra's account of his time in Corsica was very doubtful, Cooper thought. 'It is quite likely that the incident at which [Serra] claims he was identified by a French officer was actually the reverse of the truth.'[22]

However, Cooper went on, even if Serra had gleaned 'a few odd details from the indiscretions of French students in training', he would have had minimal knowledge of SOE work on Corsica. 'Probably [Serra] was asked to do this one case of identification.

Possibly there were one or two others at most ... It is hard to believe that [he] was in a position to do more than this and very hard to think that [he] would have had sufficient information on plans and movements to have anyone picked up.' Also, Cooper stressed, 'it must be recorded that he was almost certainly subjected to fairly extreme duress'. Serra's suspicion that Adler was already collaborating, 'added to his physical miseries and the threat of being shot,' had probably caused him to make 'some sort of confession and some sort of agreement to collaborate'.[23]

A few months later, Serra was released from arrest, discharged from SOE and returned to civilian life. No hard evidence had been produced to condemn him. There was also a degree of sympathy for his fate after capture. A final analysis of the case felt that he had not been really cut out for the situation that arose when he and Adler landed, but 'once he was with the partisans and able to fight as he understands, he appears to have done a good job'. It also acknowledged, accurately, 'that he was recruited at a time when recruiting was extremely difficult, and when the best material was not to be had,' and that he had undertaken 'a highly dangerous operation voluntarily, and was well aware at the time of the risks'.[24]

⊙

When he reappeared in Turin, Serra had no recent news of Gabor Adler. The last time he had seen him, he told Peter Cooper, was in Regina Coeli on the day of the Italian Armistice. Another man whom SOE, in 1945, was able to question about Adler was Cesare Faccio, the SIM officer who had shared his mess with him in Sardinia and driven him around the island. Faccio, who was now working for the Allies, could not help either, save for giving assurances that 'Armstrong', as he called him, was likely to have been in Rome in September 1943 and had not been ill treated or shot: a statement that suggests that the Italians had felt that Adler, like Serra, had co-operated enough to escape the attentions of a firing squad.[25] By 1945, however, SOE knew more than Serra and Faccio about Adler's time in Rome.

Allied forces had reached the city on 4 June 1944. Since landing on the mainland nine months before, the advance had been slow and bloody. By the end of 1943 it had more or less ground to a halt, held south of Rome by the Germans' well-defended Winter Line. In January 1944, in an ambitious attempt to outflank it, British and American forces had then made fresh landings at Anzio and Nettuno on the coast west of Rome. Three months later, those forces had barely moved: vicious German resistance still had them pinned to the beaches. Only in May, after a series of major assaults along a rugged front running west from Monte Cassino to the sea, did Allied troops in the south finally break the German lines and resume the push north, while a simultaneous advance at Anzio at last ended the stagnation there. By then Rome had been declared an 'open city'. That meant the occupying forces had declared they would not defend it, in return for which, they hoped, their attackers would not assault it but simply march in. American soldiers from the Anzio bridgehead were the first to get there, reaching Rome as the last Germans withdrew through the city's northern outskirts. Soon, tens of thousands of Allied soldiers had flooded into the city and Allied flags were flying from all principal buildings. Among the liberators were a handful of SOE personnel, one of whose immediate tasks was to follow up the stories that Gabor Adler had once been imprisoned in the city.

Peter Cooper carried out the investigation. He began his inquiries on the afternoon of 3 August 1944 when he arrived at the gates of Regina Coeli to inspect its surviving files. Leafing through these, he found a record of Adler's arrival on 29 April 1943. He also turned up Adler's statement that his name was Giovanni Armstrong, that he was British, and that he had been born in Gibraltar in 1919. The files confirmed that Adler had been held at SIM's disposal until the Armistice. After that the prison had come under German control. A final document stated that

Adler had been moved to the feared fourth wing, the section that the Germans used for holding political prisoners, in October 1943. Here the files ended. '[T]he Germans,' noted Cooper, 'were careful to take away all their own records with them.'[26]

Cooper then began to search in Rome for ex-inmates who might have known Adler in prison. One man he eventually found was the unfortunate Eugenio Paladino, the Italian businessman whom Jock McCaffery had put in touch with Eligio Klein in 1942, a step that had led to his arrest and a thirty-year prison sentence for military espionage. Paladino explained that he had first encountered 'Lieut. John Armstrong' when the guards had allowed Paladino to share with other inmates some of the food that his family was delivering to him; he added that Adler had confided his codename to him as well as a contact telephone number in London: these details Paladino had written on the wall of his cell.[27] After the Germans moved Adler to the fourth wing, however, Paladino had not seen him again.

Another man who had known Adler in Regina Coeli was Renato Traversi. In a written account that finally reached Cooper via the Swiss authorities, Almerico Bonetti, Traversi's brother-in-law, recounted that Traversi had been released in October 1943 after five-and-a-half years' imprisonment and had arrived home anxious to arrange the escape of a fellow inmate, 'a valorous British officer, Major [sic] Armstrong, who had been arrested in Sardinia'. With Bonetti on board, a bold rescue had then been planned: with others' help, including that of a few prison staff, and brazenly dressed in German uniforms, they would drive a truck to the gates of Regina Coeli and request that Adler be released into their care. But the plan had been betrayed and Renato Traversi re-arrested; after a spell at the hands of German interrogators in the notorious Gestapo headquarters on Via Tasso, he ended up again in Regina Coeli, where Bonetti, his brother-in-law, was eventually able to visit him. 'He told me of the tortures he had undergone at Via Tasso and to which these barbarians had submitted him to obtain the names of those involved,' Bonetti wrote in his account; 'He was very worried about Armstrong.' (Three months after Traversi's re-imprisonment, Bonetti was invited to the prison mortuary to inspect the corpses of the latest prisoners executed by the Germans. Among these he found his brother-in-law's body. 'It was very difficult to recognise Renato amongst the 10 dead bodies, as their clothes had been changed. I finally had to examine the bodies themselves, and eventually identified my poor Renato from the socks he was wearing, and which I had sent him during his detention.')[28]

Renato Traversi's arrest may well explain why the Germans moved Adler to the political prisoners' wing: Adler's pseudonym appears to have been among the names tortured out of Traversi at Via Tasso.[29] To judge from the memories of Amedeo Strazzera-Perniciani, who had spent months working at Regina Coeli with a commission dealing with prisoners' welfare, it seems that Adler, too, was taken to Via Tasso and subjected to similar treatment. In 1946, Strazzera-Perniciani published a book about Regina Coeli's recent history that described 'John Armstrong' as a tall young man with a 'sturdy constitution' whom the Germans left with a broken nose, multiple bruises to his face, a wound to the arch of his left eyebrow, a cut right ear, and heavy bruising elsewhere.[30] 'Strazzera[-Perniciani] knew Armstrong [*sic*] quite well,' Peter Cooper discovered when he spoke with him in Rome in 1944. 'He formed a good opinion of him. He describes him as inclined to be silent, but always cheerful.' Strazzera-Perniciani, who seems not to have told Cooper about Adler's brutal treatment or injuries, did assure him that Adler was still in Regina Coeli 'up to the last day before the arrival of the Allies in Rome'. But he did not know, he said, if Adler 'was carried off by the Germans' when they evacuated the city or if had managed somehow to escape. 'Strazzera had always assumed that Armstrong had got out, and rejoined the Allies as soon as they arrived. He expresses surprise that he has not reported.'[31]

Confirmation that Adler had been in Regina Coeli at the beginning of June 1944 came from another former inmate, Louis Ingram Leslie, an Englishman caught by the Germans in January 1944 who had apparently lived for years in Rome under the protection of influential friends. Deciding that he was a British agent, the Germans had locked up Leslie in Regina Coeli's fourth wing. 'Leslie's connection with Armstrong started on the first afternoon of his imprisonment,' recorded Cooper after they spoke:

He was sitting alone in his cell when Armstrong was shown in and asked him if there was anything which he could do for Leslie. The net result of this question was that later on in the afternoon a pair of prison sheets and a table appeared in Leslie's cell . . . From time to time, up to the first week in March, Armstrong and Leslie visited each other's cells between 1 p.m. and 7 or 8 p.m. . . . . Armstrong was on extremely good terms with all the guards . . .

At the beginning of March the 4th wing of Regina Coeli became very overcrowded, and so Leslie was moved into Armstrong's cell, No. 461 . . .

When Leslie first arrived in Armstrong's cell, he said that Armstrong's morale was very high, and that he had been very ill with dysentery, from which he had by that time recovered. It appears that whilst he was ill the German commandant of the prison, who was a 200% Nazi, and the only man whom Armstrong had failed to impress, stated that 'It did not really matter if Armstrong died, as it would save everyone a great deal of trouble.' Leslie described Armstrong at this time as a very powerful muscular man, but still a little weak from his illness. He had the build of a professional pugilist.

Cooper also heard from Leslie that 'Armstrong vouchsafed little information about himself, but little by little the story came out.' Adler's mother, Leslie recalled, 'about whom he talked a great deal, was Spanish. His father was a Scot, and was dead. Before the war he lived in Gibraltar, travelling to the UK at the outbreak of the war. He was called up almost immediately.' Adler's capture, Leslie remembered him saying, had come during 'a commando raid' on

Sardinia when he and his men had accidentally been left behind on the beach; after that, he had been imprisoned in Sardinia and in a regular prison camp near Chieti, in the Abruzzo, before escaping at the time of the Armistice; recaptured by the Germans a fortnight later, Adler had then been imprisoned in Rome as a suspect spy. (Cooper, well aware of Adler's real history, noted: 'It appears that Armstrong never completely trusted Leslie'.) The last time that Leslie saw Adler was on the afternoon of 2 June, Cooper recorded. 'Both were together in their cell when a warder entered and called Leslie's name, telling him to pick up his things quickly. Leslie asked if he was going to be sent to Germany, to which the warder replied that he did not know.'[32] Leslie was taken away and escaped soon afterwards.

A week after speaking with Leslie, Cooper interviewed in his office in Rome a young woman called Neda Solic. She had recently started work in the city on propaganda broadcasts for the Allies, but from January to June 1944 she had been a prisoner in Regina Coeli. 'The interest of the girl for us is that she knew Armstrong,' Cooper recorded, 'and was probably one of the last people to see him.' Solic, according to Cooper's notes of the interview, was twenty-one, 'an ardent communist, and a follower of Tito'. She was Croatian, spoke a host of languages, and had been arrested during a clandestine mission to Italy for the Yugoslav partisans. She also struck Cooper as 'extremely self-possessed . . . and spoke with great clarity and firmness. She showed a regard for detail, and seemed sure of everything she said.' Her story seemed 'of more than average reliability'.[33]

Solic told Cooper that, at Regina Coeli, Adler had been 'more or less free to move about within the Wing for a certain period (1 or 2 hours) each day'. It was then that she had first seen him, passing along the corridor, 'and as she speaks English she says that they exchanged a few words every now and then. He did not, however, tell her his story, apart from the fact that he was a British officer.' Cooper's report goes on:

The real story begins on the 2nd June '44 when the Germans were preparing to evacuate the prison. At 17.30 hrs. after supper, [Solic], who was under sentence of death, was taken to Via Tasso to be shot ... 10 minutes after they arrived in Via Tasso, Armstrong was brought in, with all his personal belongings, and guarded by SS men. The guard said to [her], 'This man is English. You are forbidden to speak to him.' They were put up against the wall, and the guards went into the next room.

For some reason they decided to risk talking, which they did very quietly in undertones, and slowly, word by word. In the end the whole story came out. He was using Italian, which, according to [her], he spoke with difficulty, and with a very bad accent. When pressed to describe the accent she said, 'He only seemed to know some Sardinian dialect.' She said to him that she had seen him in Regina Coeli, and also exchanged a few words. He said that he recognised her too. He went on to say that he was a British officer who had been in a PW camp in Sardinia. He had succeeded in escaping from there, but had subsequently been recaptured. He was then accused by the Italians of being a spy. Armstrong was wearing a grey green jacket, but he opened it to show her that he was wearing the uniform of a British officer (khaki). He did not tell her for exactly how long he had been in Regina Coeli, but commented that he had been there longer than she ...

At 1800 hrs. they were all taken to the cells separately. At 21.30 hrs. 80 former prisoners from Regina Coeli were called for. [Solic] was the only woman among them. All had their hands tied. The roll was called ... Armstrong's name was called with the others. An officer then made them a little speech, saying that they would be taken straightaway to Verona, where they would have to work. If they attempted to escape on the journey, they would be shot on the spot. They were then sent back to their cells once more.

At 2200 hrs. they were assembled once more, and the party was loaded on to trucks. [Solic] IS POSITIVE THAT ARMSTRONG WAS ON ONE OF THE TRUCKS [capitalised in original]. That was the last she saw of him. She herself was removed from the party at the last minute.[34]

In a subsequent interview, Solic corrected herself, assuring Cooper that it was on 3 June that she and Adler had been removed from Regina Coeli and taken to Via Tasso. But she remained 'quite positive' that Adler was among the eighty-strong party that boarded trucks that evening to be transported to northern Italy.

The whole party was seen going out of the courtyard prior to getting on the trucks, which were waiting outside ... After a certain amount of commotion had gone on, it was realised that there were not enough trucks for the whole party, and some people were brought back ... about a dozen or fifteen ... [who] filed back through the courtyard and passed Nedda [*sic*] in the corridor, and went into the prison. Once again, Nedda is sure that Armstrong was not among them. She therefore assumed that Armstrong had left.

Solic added that about three hours later, at half-past midnight on the night of 3–4 June, she had watched as 'a special party of 13 or 14 was assembled in the courtyard [with] ... their hands tied behind their backs. The party was taken out of the courtyard, and presumably got on the trucks.' One man, 'although he had his hands bound ... decided that he had nothing to lose and jumped off ... He managed to escape, although the Germans fired several shots after him.' This man's name was Marcelo Guarcini and Solic told Cooper that she had spoken to him since. Although he had not known Adler, Guarcini had said that no one matching his description had been among the little party on that final truck. 'Nedda herself,' Cooper ended his report, 'is quite adamant in her belief that Armstrong is not dead.'[35]

A short walk from the Coliseum, Via Tasso is a quiet street of modest apartments built in the 1930s. Inside No. 145 today is the Museo Storico della Liberazione di Roma, a museum dedicated to commemorating the city's liberation in 1944 and the work of the Italian Resistance. It occupies the floors that housed the headquarters of the Gestapo during the Nazi occupation. Windows, fittings and decor are exactly as they were seven decades ago. Cell walls remain covered in prisoners' graffiti. '5882820 SSM J LLOYD

BRITISH ARMY,' reads one message scratched into the plaster. 'CONDANNATO A MORTE' says another.

Above that last inscription is a signature: 'S.Ten A. Paladini'. An Italian artillery officer who had joined the partisans after the Armistice and later worked as an agent for the American OSS, Lieutenant Arrigo Paladini had been caught in May 1944. Though condemned to death, he was not in fact executed. On the night of 3–4 June, when the Germans were busily evacuating Via Tasso and putting prisoners into trucks, Paladini climbed into one that failed to start, whereupon he was returned to his cell. Hours later, the last Germans left and he found himself free.

By the time that Cooper heard Neda Solic's account of that night at Via Tasso, many in Rome knew the fate of the 'special party' she had seen assembling in the yard and from which Marcelo Guarcini had managed to escape. A few hours after the truck had driven away, farm workers in open countryside north of the city saw a German convoy draw to a halt by the side of the road at a spot called La Storta. Then they watched as a group of men with their hands tied behind them were taken under guard from one of the trucks and led to a nearby barn. 'In the evening, at dusk, they made them leave the barn,' remembered one of the workers, a thirteen-year-old boy at the time. 'They made them fall in line with their hands tied behind their backs and tied together with a long rope . . . There was a German guard for every three prisoners. At the head of the line was an officer.' The Germans led them towards a cluster of concealing trees. 'I was there, I had climbed a tree to see . . . As they went, one of the prisoners said, "Now you are taking us to die!"' The prisoners were lined up. Then, 'one by one . . . starting from the left,' they were shot. 'Everything lasted no more than three minutes.'[36]

When the Germans had gone, the bodies of fourteen men, all shot through the back of the head, were recovered and transferred to Rome where they were taken to the mortuary of the city's oldest hospital, the Ospedale Santo Spirito, and laid out for visitors to identify. The first public announcement of their fate appeared in *Il Messaggero* on 8 June. Three days after that, a funeral service was held in the sixteenth-century Church of the Gesù, on Via degli Astalli, with all fourteen coffins at the high altar. Burials followed in Rome's Campo Verano cemetery. Thirteen corpses had been identified by then. All thirteen were those of men who had been among the 'special party' assembled at Via Tasso. They included Bruno Buozzi, a leading trade unionist and socialist politician. The coffin containing the fourteenth body recovered from La Storta had a placard attached. It stated simply that he was an unknown *'soldato inglese'*.[37]

Among those who came to identify the bodies was Marcelo Guarcini, the man who had managed to leap from the truck that night and run off. Neda Solic would tell Cooper that she had spoken to Guarcini afterwards. Guarcini claimed to have identified every one of the dead as having been on the truck from which he escaped, 'and Armstrong was certainly not present among these people'.[38] Another man who visited the mortuary was Owen Snedden, a young Roman Catholic priest from New Zealand who, in 1940, had found himself stranded in the Vatican when Italy entered the war. Latterly he had helped to conceal and feed Allied ex-prisoners on the run around Rome. To Peter Cooper he described how he had gone to the Santo Spirito hospital to see if the 'unidentifiable body' was that of a British escapee whom he had known. The custodian of the mortuary refused to let Snedden see the corpse. Snedden persisted, Cooper recorded, and 'eventually a second custodian took pity on him and unscrewed the coffin of the unidentifiable body. Snedden says that it was impossible to recognise any features, but that he was of the opinion that the body was slightly taller and a little more robust than that of [the escapee].' Talking afterwards with the friendlier of the two custodians, 'Snedden was informed that on 3rd June two Englishmen were in Via Tasso. One of them had been there all the time, and this was quite definitely [the escapee]. The other had been brought from some other place on 2nd or 3rd June, and it was generally understood that this second Englishman had come from Regina Coeli.'[39]

Cooper, closing his investigation in September 1944, felt that the 'only credible eyewitnesses' to Adler's fate during the final thirty-six hours before Rome's liberation were Louis Leslie, his cellmate in Regina Coeli, and Neda Solic, who had been with him in the courtyard in Via Tasso. 'The situation at the moment is therefore that Adler is likely to have been taken to Northern Italy by the Germans, and may, therefore, still be alive.'[40] By the summer of 1945, however, with the war in Europe over and all prisons and concentration camps liberated, there was still no news of him. For officers tasked with accounting for SOE's missing and dead, this did not look good. It was not possible to be definite (there had been 'much conflicting evidence' as to his fate in those last hours, one officer noted, 'and it is not possible to say with certainty what happened') but it now seemed 'fairly certain' that he had been among the party removed from Via Tasso and subsequently shot at La Storta. 'Most probably he is dead, but this conclusion can only be reached by a process of conjecture, and by eliminating other alternatives.'[41]

In December 1945, a letter was sent to Gabor Adler's mother in Budapest explaining that 'it is greatly feared, in view of the absence of any news of him since the cessation of hostilities, that the chances of this officer being alive are now extremely remote'.[42] The following month, her reply reached London. Written in English and carefully typed, it survives among SOE's files. It also reveals that her missing boy had at least been spared the ordeals of the Holocaust that had overtaken the rest of his family later in the war. 'First of all may I express my thanks to you for taking so much trouble about my sad case,' the letter began.

The tragic fate of my son, Gabor Adler, has achieved to brake [*sic*] a mother's heart that had already been severely tried by all the tragedies that preceded this. Now I have no more children left, for my elder son, who would now be 30 years of age, was carried away by the German gangsters and I have never heard of him since. Both were extraordinary boys, intelligent, cultured, speaking seven languages. They were the only hope and aim of my life. Now I am all alone without any support. My husband died, all my relatives, my 91 years [old] mother included, were deported and none of them came back . . . I have got nothing but a room in a flat that belongs to strangers.

Adler's mother went on to explain that she had a surviving relative in England – 'my brother's daughter, married to a British subject' – and asked for a travel permit to get there, 'with special permission to pass through Italy and remain there until I have personally searched for my son. As I speak Italian perfectly I would be quite capable of making the necessary investigations. Even if I were only capable of establishing without any doubt the circumstances of his disappearance, I would be satisfied with that.'[43] It is unclear from the files whether any support was forthcoming for her appeal for help. She did travel to Italy, however. For the last years of her life she lived in Rome, where she died, aged eighty-eight, in 1976. She is buried in the Cimitero Flaminio, which lies a few miles north of the cemetery at Verano where the remains of the fourteenth body found at La Storta are interred.

Today there seems little doubt that the fourteenth body was that of Gabor Adler. Nothing was heard of him again after June 1944. No other convincing candidate has been proposed for the unidentified body recovered from La Storta. Neda Solic may have seemed a solid eyewitness, but perhaps, in the confusion and terror of that night at Via Tasso, she had simply failed to see him among the special party from which Marcelo Guarcini managed to escape; or perhaps Adler had been shifted to their truck only after it began its journey. Guarcini, too, who never knew him anyway, may have simply failed to spot him. And Father Snedden's difficulty in discerning the features of a man shot at close range through the back of the head may suggest that Guarcini, when inspecting the dead laid out in Santo Spirito, could not have been certain that Adler was not among them.

A monument stands today at La Storta recording the killings of 4 June 1944. For years, thirteen plaques on surrounding trees carried the names of all but one of the dead. The inscription on a fourteenth plaque read '*Inglese Ignoto*'. Only in 2007, after the release of SOE records, were wartime British sources compared to Italian ones and the conclusion drawn that, in all probability, the 'Unknown Englishman' had been Gabor Adler.[44] In 2009, the Mayor of Rome unveiled a fresh memorial finally to commemorate the 24-year-old Hungarian Jew who had hidden his true identity so completely.

15

'Foreign agent'

Days after the announcement of the Italian Armistice, Cecil Roseberry was asked to write a report about SOE's contribution to the war against Italy. Submitting it at the end of September 1943, he prefaced his account with the caveat that 'after 20 years of suppression' no 'strong coherent opposition' existed within Italy's borders. He then highlighted the following: the outstanding success of the vital wireless link between Algiers and Rome during the armistice negotiations; the work done outside Italy with exiled members of Giustizia e Libertà; the handling of the early contact with Badoglio through Luigi Rusca and Berne; the subsequent insight into intentions and machinations in Rome courtesy of contacts like Filippo Caracciolo and Adriano Olivetti; and the effort made to stimulate the growth and activity of the Partito d'Azione.[1]

Roseberry also drew attention to the success had from Switzerland in encouraging and supplying Jock McCaffery's 'action groups' in Italy. 'Throughout two and a half years,' he asserted with confidence, 'we have had lines into Italy which not only enabled us to send in and bring out representatives of the various groups, but enabled us to keep the action parties supplied with explosive and incendiary material.' The groups were made up of men of diverse backgrounds and had done excellent work, he added. 'They included members of the steel workers' federation, electrical workers, dockers, railwaymen, garage hands, and cells were formed in the services,' and they had carried out 'a continuous series of fires, explosions and derailments'. Some had waged 'a systematic campaign of slashing the tyres of commercial and military lorries'. Some had attacked goods trains. One had specialised in 'liquidating isolated German soldiers'.

Five wireless sets had been sent into Italy with a view to future operators picking them up and working them. 'Our own wireless operator [Giacomino Sarfatti] had [also] been maintained in a town in northern Italy for nearly a year.'[2]

'I consider that [Roseberry] has done exceptionally well,' wrote Colin Gubbins, SOE's new chief, in a covering note when he passed Roseberry's report to Lord Selborne, its minister. 'When he took over the section [in late 1941] practically nothing had been achieved, but by his persistence and technical skill he surmounted the most difficult obstacle of breaking the crust (ably assisted by [McCaffery] in Switzerland) and from that moment has gone from strength to strength.'[3] Copies of the report were sent as well to the War Office and the Chiefs of Staff.

A few weeks later, Roseberry was in southern Italy, in the Adriatic port of Brindisi, attached temporarily to a British military mission liaising with Badoglio's staff, when SIM officers who had just switched sides began talking about their earlier work against the Allies. It was then that the first indications emerged that SOE's successful record from Switzerland had been nothing of the sort. 'Intimate details' from SIM, Roseberry told London in an immediate telegram, had revealed that an Italian agent named Eligio Klein, codenamed 'Giusto', had been deceiving the British in Berne; a courier codenamed 'Elda' had been in on it, too. As a consequence, all operations into Italy through these two had been under SIM surveillance and control.[4]

When word was dispatched to SOE's outpost in Berne, care was taken to break the news gently to Jock McCaffery. A few weeks earlier he had ended up in a Lugano clinic suffering from nervous exhaustion from overwork and 'cerebral commotion' from a spot of concussion, and he was still a sick man. Unsurprisingly his first reaction to the report was one of shock and disbelief. Had Edmund Schwerdt been involved, he asked. Had Almerigotti/Klein been 'a willing double-crosser or a dupe'? Why had nothing happened to young Giacomino Sarfatti whom he had recently seen after his safe escape to Switzerland? Why had SIM said nothing about the Tigrotti, his other main anti-Fascist group?[5]

Gradually SIM disclosed more details to Roseberry. Since its officers had fled Rome in a hurry, there were no documents and the story emerged 'little by little in conversation'. In time, however, the ghastly scale of the deception took greater and convincing shape:

The head of the Wolves and Almerigotti had been deliberately planted . . . Pin-points [for supply drops] and addresses had all been supplied by the chief co-ordinating officer of SIM in Rome . . . [Sarfatti's] reception and safe housing had all been arranged by SIM . . . Rusca had not been planted: his activities had come to light as all messages conveyed by certain couriers had been opened and photographed . . .

The SIM officers with whom he was talking also assured Roseberry that it had kept the OVRA, the Italian police and the Germans 'entirely ignorant' of this counter-subversion work. He noted, too, that they were vague about some details, 'but their inability to remember might be due to their fear that the British might take reprisals'.[6] Certainly SIM did not tell Roseberry everything. All knowledge of the Tigrotti was denied, which encouraged SOE to believe that that group, at least, had been genuine. It would take much longer to discover the Tigrotti's true colours, which SIM had in fact known all about. Only in the spring of 1945, when the British got their hands on its architect, the sleek and wily Luca Osteria, did SOE hear that it had been the victim of an equally devious and effective deception by the OVRA.

Playing down the significance of the Italians' success, Roseberry would later make the interesting argument that the reports of supposed sabotage, true or not, had still usefully boosted SOE's prestige and profile among senior British commanders. He also claimed that no serious damage had been done: a claim that made its way into W. J. M. Mackenzie's Cabinet Office history of SOE, generally considered today to be the most authoritative published account of its history available, written in 1946 with privileged access to files otherwise kept secret for more than fifty years. Certainly, in terms of men and material lost, SOE's failure to spot the Italians' ruse bore little comparison to the infamous deception in Holland, for example, where it was tricked into dropping dozens of Dutch agents straight to the Germans, who then killed almost all of them, or to ruses in France, where it was similarly deceived by the Germans and, as a consequence, lost more agents. Nevertheless, it was far from correct to claim, as Mackenzie did, that 'no harm was done to the real [Italian] resistance'.[7]

Controlling Berne's links into Italy had allowed SIM and the OVRA to identify and neutralise genuine anti-Fascists in Italy, such as Luigi Rusca, Eugenio Paladino, the two Yugoslav students in Milan – whose ultimate fate remains obscure – and the Yugoslavs' circle of sympathisers. It had also meant that the British expended their energies in pointless directions, which may have meant, too, that SOE became so absorbed in channelling support to the likes of Eligio Klein and the Tigrotti that it failed to consider adequately other avenues that could have proved authentic. Little effort appears to have been made to contact and work with communists inside Italy, for instance. The communists were few in number; they were active nevertheless.

Possibly SOE may also have missed an opportunity by not thoroughly investigating the potential of Gioacchino Malavasi, a Milanese lawyer whom Lauro Laurenti, the Italian businessman recruited by its Cairo office in 1942, claimed to have contacted during one of his trips to Italy from Istanbul. SOE had always been suspicious of Laurenti. 'He wanted 8,000,000 lire,' Roseberry would recall after the war, referring to a sum that Laurenti had requested to fund 'some fantastic scheme for a movement headed jointly by [Luigi] Federzoni (fascist) and [Alcide] De Gasperi [Prime Minister of Italy, 1945–53, who had sheltered from Fascism in the Vatican] with the Pope's blessing . . . I refused to consider it. I felt – and still believe – [that Laurenti] was an agent of S.I.M.'[8] Malavasi, though, had indeed been a solid anti-Fascist with good Catholic and socialist contacts, just as Laurenti had described him; co-founder in 1928 of a Catholic opposition group, Guelfo d'Azione, he had been sentenced in the 1930s to five years' imprisonment for spreading subversive propaganda.[9] Then again, greater effort at exploring Malavasi's possibilities might merely have led to more trouble; by the summer of 1942, Jock McCaffery, on London's instructions, had already asked Eligio Klein to make discreet 'enquiries' about Malavasi 'and if possible find some suitable means of contact'.[10]

In fact, if the British had had more contacts, greater resources and better means of delivery, it is quite possible that more stores and personnel would have been channelled into Italian hands. As it was, there were several close calls. Before Andrew Croft and his SBS colleagues buried four wireless sets on a headland near Portofino in August 1943, SOE had planned that one of its Italian wireless operators, Giulio Koelman, would go ashore, too, and attach himself to the Tigrotti. When Koelman's confidence began to wobble, SOE ruled him out and wondered if two of its hardened anti-Fascists, Alberto Tarchiani and Alberto Cianca, should land instead. In the end it was decided that those two old hands – both pushing sixty, they were codenamed 'the elderlies' – would be too conspicuous in enemy territory and more useful on the Allied side of the lines.

Another plan that summer had been to land four Italians near Genoa: two prominent members of Giustizia e Libertà, Aldo Garosci and Leo Valiani, plus an associate of Emilio Lussu's, Dino Gentili, and a wireless operator called Binetti who had fought in Spain. The plan was for them to go ashore from a submarine, collect one of the wireless sets buried near Portofino, and then make their way to Trieste, the supposed base of one of McCaffery's groups. Another plan, to drop Valiani and Binetti by parachute at a spot north of Udine, reached the point where McCaffery was instructed to tell Eligio Klein to prepare to receive the pair and take them to a safe house. Those plans, too, failed to come off, after Binetti, the wireless operator, damaged his knee while parachute training. SOE had also wondered if a sabotage instructor and one or two more wireless operators should follow Dick Mallaby into northern Italy and work with the Tigrotti.

One man briefly in the frame for that last mission was Branko Nekić, who was destined instead to be caught and killed by the Germans in Sicily. Given that Mussolini fell in July 1943 and his successors were inclined to seek peace, there is a danger of over-speculating about the fate of agents who might have been captured by the Italians that summer. It should be noted, though, that Italy's authorities had been executing enemy agents as a matter of course when Giacomino Sarfatti arrived in Milan in December 1942. Probably Sarfatti owed his life to the SIM decision that he should be watched, not arrested.

Acknowledgement of the efficiency of Mussolini's secret police and counter-espionage set-up is essential to understanding a good many of SOE's troubles as it tried to target Italy, just as the strength of that skilled system of suppression helps explain why the regime had been so secure from domestic opponents for so long. Important to acknowledge, too, is the fact that Italy at war was a thoroughly dangerous environment for anti-Fascists contemplating rebellion. As SOE eventually learned from experience, opposition elements inside Italy 'felt, quite rightly, that the time had not come when they could run risks by coming into the open'. Anti-Fascists outside, meanwhile, 'were loathe [sic] to become too deeply implicated in active opposition [and] they were not yet in the state of mind where they would willingly become technical traitors'.[11]

It is pertinent to note that SOE encountered near-identical troubles trying to work into Nazi Germany. SOE's X Section was responsible for German operations and found itself confronted, as one officer put it, with 'a stupendous task'.[12] A report drawn up in 1945 explains:

It must be realized that the operation of secret agents in the heart of the enemy country – especially when this involves the carrying out of sabotage – where 100% of the population can be considered as hostile, is an infinitely more difficult and dangerous task than similar work in friendly countries occupied by the enemy, such as France, Belgium, Holland, etc. It must also be appreciated that as there was no Allied secret organisation established in Germany at the outbreak of the war, and as at that time at least there were practically no sympathisers with the Allied cause among Germans, it was not possible to supply reception committees, safe houses or reliable contacts to any agents willing to carry out operations . . .

Furthermore, the possible field of recruitment of suitable agents was from the outset extremely restricted and was practically confined to refugees from Nazi oppression or anti-Nazi individuals among interned enemy aliens or Prisoners of War. The possible use of the latter, however, was very much restricted by the necessity of observing the Geneva Conventions. As to the former, i.e. refugees from Nazi oppression, a large percentage of them were of the Jewish race and appearance, which would handicap them from the start, and, in addition, most of them had not lived recently in Germany and were therefore not cognisant of the ways of life pertaining in that country in war time.[13]

By the end of 1943, X Section had dispatched just two agents to Germany. As late as July 1944, it was still reporting that there were 'no active resistance groups in Germany such as existed in the Occupied territories: nor were these likely to emerge unless the German Armed Forces suffered a decisive defeat'. Undoubtedly there were 'potential oppositional elements' and 'minor acts of sabotage had been carried out', but such elements were 'mostly inactive and unorganised' and 'at present primarily interested in preserving their own lives and ensuring some kind of existence for themselves in the future'.[14]

Interestingly, X Section, faced with this desperate situation, considered the capture of its agents to be part and parcel of its goal of discomfiting the enemy:

It was always our conviction that if we sent into Germany a limited number of sabotage agents of which a certain number were bound to be caught, the Germans, whose mentality never changes, would immediately deduce that agent activity was taking place on a large scale and act accordingly. This meant that they were bound to extend still further their already over-expanded Security Services.[15]

Certainly SOE's experience in Italy showed that an agent's capture in enemy territory could lead to achievements that far outstripped anything he might have been capable of accomplishing had he managed to remain free. Probably the propaganda value of the fate of Fortunato Picchi, executed after being caught with the Colossus party in 1941, was far more useful to the Allied cause than his work as an interpreter. The potential to contribute to deception schemes is neatly demonstrated by the success had in exploiting the capture of Gabor Adler and Salvatore Serra in Sardinia in 1943. The usefulness of Dick Mallaby as a prisoner speaks for itself. Although SOE files do not suggest that anyone was dispatched deliberately into Fascist Italy or Nazi Germany as a pawn to be caught, such successes, fortuitous and unpredictable though they were, underline the potential worth to any war effort of having capable agents (and even incapable ones) at large in enemy territory.

◉

Cecil Roseberry's assessment of SOE's pre-Armistice Italian record was based purely on the information available to him when he sat down to write it. Had he known more, he might have included the contribution made by Gabor Adler's wireless set to two major Allied deception schemes in the Mediterranean that summer. And if he had written the report a little later, Roseberry might even have included a discovery made in January 1944 after the Allied landings at Anzio that revealed another instance of SOE having inconvenienced the Italians, albeit inadvertently, while Mussolini had been in charge.

When Allied soldiers secured and searched Anzio's neigh-bouring town of Nettuno, documents found in its police station included a months-old Italian report carrying the following urgent warning: 'Informing all concerned of a projected attempt on the life of the Duce . . . alleged to be sponsored by the British.'[16] The would-be assassin was reputed to be an Italian, Luigi Mazzotta, once of the 24th Artillery Regiment, who had left Lecce for Africa in 1935 and, after leaving the army, set himself up in Addis Ababa as a tailor. Hearing of this, SOE immediately recognised Mazzotta as one of its Italian volunteers from East Africa. Mazzotta, in fact, had come as close as any agent to being sent into enemy territory to be deliberately caught: it was he that Roseberry had proposed to drop into Sardinia as a way of implying that the British still believed that Gabor Adler and Salvatore Serra were free.

SOE was never quite sure how the assassination plan had reached the Italians. Clearly there had been a leak somewhere but it all seemed very garbled: Mazzotta had never been earmarked for the mission to kill Mussolini. 'It was a companion of Mazzotta's who was to make this attempt on the Duce's life,' one officer noted. 'His name was Di Giunta. He was, however, indiscreet to such an extent that it was found necessary to dispose of him before he went into the field.' Perhaps Mazzotta, 'who is extremely boastful,' had proved similarly indiscreet: 'He must have known well what Di Giunta's mission in the field was, owing to Di Giunta's indiscretions.' Perhaps, while training in Palestine, Mazzotta had bragged that he was going to have a crack at killing Mussolini, and his boast somehow found its way to Italy. There was also the possibility that Emilio Zappalà, the MI6 agent captured in Sicily with SOE's Antonio Gallo, had said something to his interrogators. 'Zappala knew very well that it was Di Giunta who was to make the attempt on the Duce's life, but he may have made the confusion on purpose.'[17] Ultimately it proved impossible to discover exactly what had happened.

The full worth of another aspect of SOE's pre-Armistice work took time to emerge, too. This was the important post-Armistice pay-off of its efforts, before September 1943, at helping Italians who were hostile to Fascism. Once Italy was fighting for the Allies and half the country was German-occupied, Italian anti-Fascism lost its anti-national character, and several men with whom SOE had closely co-operated went on to make significant contributions both to the anti-German struggle and to Italy's recovery. For example, 'the elderlies' – Alberto Tarchiani and Alberto Cianca – landed at Salerno with Malcolm Munthe and assisted with his search for new recruits; both men also joined the Giustizia e Libertà-backed Partito d'Azione. In 1944, Tarchiani, who went ashore with Munthe at Anzio, too, became Minister of Public Works in Badoglio's short-lived government; and later that year, when Ivanoe Bonomi became Prime Minister, he went to the United States as Italy's Ambassador, a post he would hold for ten years. Cianca, who also served as a minister under Bonomi, saw out the war as a minister in Alcide De Gasperi's first government. Aldo Garosci and Leo Valiani, who had almost been dropped into Italian hands in the summer of 1943, both did good work behind the German lines: Garosci in Rome, after the British sent him in by parachute; Valiani across the north, after being put through the German lines at Salerno. Valiani ended up in Milan working with the most senior members of the partisan leadership, the Comitato di Liberazione Nazionale. After the war, both Garosci and Valiani, who had also become members of the Partito d'Azione, mixed politics with successful careers as journalists and historians. Then, of course, there were the ex-POWs and recruits from East Africa and Canada who would go into German-occupied territory on dangerous SOE missions to work with partisan bands, or would assist at training schools and signals stations.

Another old friend who did important work with the Italian Resistance was Emilio Lussu, of whom the British had heard little – save for the occasional message – since putting him ashore in southern France in August 1942. When Fascism fell, Lussu made his way into Italy with his wife, Joyce, and proceeded to Rome. Shortly after the Allied landings at Salerno, Joyce set out to cross the front line in the hope of regaining contact. Intercepted by Allied soldiers, she was locked up close to the battlefield while inquiries were made into her story.

After three days she was told she had a visitor. 'It will be one of those Intelligence Officers, I thought with irritation,' she later wrote. 'But when the captain entered in his dusty battledress, a khaki beret on his fair hair, I threw my arms around his neck and greeted him noisily in Italian so shrill that the footsteps of several sentries could be heard rushing up the stairs.'[18] 'I had not seen her since I was in France a few days before the fall of Paris,' her brother, Max Salvadori, would recall. 'The officer who took me to her room was visibly astonished . . . We have different names, I am in British uniform under an assumed name and she is an Italian who has crossed the lines . . . how the hell did we know each other so well?'[19] Soon afterwards, Joyce returned to enemy territory and made it safely to Rome, where she and Lussu helped organise anti-German resistance until the city's liberation. The Lussus, too, joined the Partito d'Azione and, after the war, remained active in politics: Emilio later joined the Socialist Party and became a senator; Joyce devoted herself especially to anti-colonial causes.

Max Salvadori – or Max Sylvester as he had been commissioned in the British Army – had landed with Malcolm Munthe's party at Salerno. At the end of 1943, while engaged in the ever-hazardous task of running agents through the front lines, he escaped with light wounds while trying to recover one of their bodies from the middle of a minefield. The following January, again with Munthe, he landed at Anzio and took over the mission when Munthe was wounded. Later, Salvadori assisted for a while with covert naval operations along Italy's Adriatic coast. In June 1944 he was a member of SOE's little spearhead team that reached Rome on the day the city fell to American soldiers. Shortly afterwards, asked by Harold Macmillan to participate in the newly formed Italian Government, he refused, seeing his work with the Italian Resistance as unfinished. The recommendation for Salvadori's Military Cross, awarded later that year, praised his 'great daring and gallantry' and his 'calmness, cheerfulness, and contempt for danger'.[20]

Salvadori parachuted into the snow-bound hills of German-occupied northern Italy in February 1945. It was a dangerous time to be there. Within weeks, two British colleagues were dead – one killed by accident and the other in an ambush – and Salvadori was in Milan, pursuing an active clandestine life despite an ever-present risk of detection. He stayed there, playing a prominent liaison role with the partisan leadership, until the city's liberation. 'Major Salvadori was warned against entering Milan until the situation was quieter,' read the recommendation for his DSO, which he received a few months later. 'However he insisted on entering the city to investigate the situation and to assist the remaining members of the Resistance.'[21] The Milanese later made him an honorary citizen.

Salvadori left SOE in August 1945. 'A PROFESSOR TURNS COMMANDO' declared a story in the *New York Post* when he visited to see his family that summer. 'It is hard to imagine Lt. Col. Max Salvadori M.C. of the British Army in the role of a college professor, which is what he was before the war. But in a Commando uniform, as he was seen in New York the other day, with a paratrooper's wings on his right sleeve, the tall, lanky, blond, blue-eyed Anglo-Italian was thoroughly in character...'[22] During the same trip, he was also under FBI surveillance. 'The subject and his wife boarded the 11:30 to Washington and seated themselves in a coach, which was the third car from the end of the train,' reads one report. 'The subject was wearing a British Lt. Colonel's uniform, khaki shirt, overseas cap, wide canvas belt, and carrying two brown leather bags and a military canvas bag similar to a gas mask container.

His wife was wearing a gray and white print dress, and black hat.'[23] Finally satisfied that he was engaged in nothing subversive, the FBI soon stopped watching him and, in December, closed its investigation. Ten years later, two additions were made to his file. One was a *New York Times* report that President Eisenhower had praised a lecture by Salvadori on how the United States should be seen from abroad.[24] The other was a subsequent *Newsweek* profile, explaining how Eisenhower's endorsement had 'catapulted into fame' this 'obscure college professor'.[25]

Demobilised from the British Army in 1945, Salvadori had worked briefly in Paris for UNESCO and NATO, but then returned permanently to the United States and a full-time career in academia, settling at Smith College, Massachusetts, where he became Professor of History and taught until his retirement. He also wrote, particularly about liberal democracy, and worked hard to maintain the memory of the anti-Fascist struggle and its relevance to the contemporary world. 'Count Salvadori belonged to a privileged family but his sympathies were always for exploited peasants and workers,' read a local newspaper editorial when, shortly before his death in 1992, a study-day was held in his honour in Porto San Giorgio in the Marche, where his family had had their home. 'He himself put it slightly differently,' says Salvadori's *Times* obituary, 'claiming to be just "an old-fashioned Radical – in the British sense"'.[26]

The memoirs of John Verney, a British officer of the Special Boat Squadron who parachuted into Sardinia in 1943 to raid enemy airfields, contain a criticism often levelled at units engaged in behind-the-lines work. Verney would recall a British general at the War Office grumbling that 'irregular formations and private armies' served only 'to offer a too-easy, because romanticized, form of gallantry to a few anti-social irresponsible individualists, who sought a more personal satisfaction from the war than that of standing their chance, like proper soldiers, of being bayoneted in a slit-trench or burnt alive in a tank'. Verney agreed. If he and his colleagues had been keen to drop into Sardinia, 'it was for the adventure itself rather than for its military significance'.[27]

There were certainly men and women employed by SOE whose motives matched Verney's. As Max Salvadori had judged from reports coming out of German-occupied Yugoslavia in 1944, there were plenty of young British SOE officers 'to whom the war is a big adventure and politics too puzzling to bother with'.[28] But these characteristics were hardly those of a man like Salvadori. Nor, indeed, can they be applied to many of the men, often forgotten in books like this one, who sat quietly behind desks at headquarters in roles that were not adventurous at all. Cecil Roseberry, for example, whom senior officers would praise as 'a shrewd political observer ... hard-working and extremely conscientious', dedicated himself passionately to Italian matters until the end of the war, yet barely left London.[29] In Berne, recovered from his illness and the shock of SIM's revelations, Jock McCaffery, too, stayed at his post until the end, doing well in complicated cross-border dealings with senior Italian partisans and being rewarded with an OBE.

It would also be hard to argue that the remarks made by Verney and his general can be applied to the motives of many of the recruits whom SOE selected to resist Mussolini. Only a few emerge from the files as adventurers, mercenaries or thrillseekers: Gabor Adler, perhaps; Giovanni Di Giunta, probably; two or three others, possibly. A man like Fortunato Picchi may have been naïve about the dangers, but his motivation for parachuting back into Italy appears to have been a selfless sense of duty to the British, coupled with genuine distaste for Fascism. And of those agents who volunteered to follow him, all, whether they were passionate anti-Fascists or drifting individualists, knew very well that they risked Picchi's fate if caught. Whether the British took adequate care with the lives of these volunteers is another matter.

Indeed these Italians risked more than their lives. Among SOE's papers survives a letter dated July 1947 from Signora Iacopina Pazzi of 'Prato, La Briglia n/153', addressed to the 'War Office, Whitehall, London'. Signora Pazzi was the mother of Fortunato Picchi. Writing in Italian, she outlined in her letter what little she had learned of his return to Italy. She said that she had heard that he had come back 'for the purpose of organizing Resistance nuclei'. She knew that he had been captured and shot. She had heard the BBC speak of him, 'praising his heroic deed', and was aware that an article published by Italians in London on the third anniversary of his death had proclaimed him to be '*il primo martire del 2° Risorgimento Italiano*': the first martyr to Italy's second Risorgimento. 'I am a poor old woman who cannot hope to live much longer but before dying I would like to know something about my son,' she wrote; 'to know whether, before leaving on that mission which was to cost him his life, he had left some word or message (or souvenir) for his mother far away.'[30] What she did not mention was how her family had suffered after her son's capture. Persecution by the regime had seen three of her children denied work. One son had felt compelled to volunteer to serve with the unenvied Italian contingent sent to fight on the Eastern Front. Another was denounced as a traitor and deported to Mauthausen concentration camp.[31]

Replying to the letter, the War Office broke the news to Picchi's mother that her son had left no message, while all his possessions had gone to Florence Lantieri, his landlady. But the War Office (more accurately, a department still dealing with outstanding SOE matters, SOE itself having been disbanded a year before) did seek to reassure her on one point. 'Please accept our sympathy in the loss of your son, who was very much respected in this country,' she was told; 'Fortunato Picchi was the first Italian to volunteer to return to Italy in the cause of her liberation.'[32]

That meant liberation from Fascism. But whether men like Picchi had really been loyal to Italy is a question that would endure long after the war. Italy's new authorities would refuse Picchi's mother's request for her son to be acknowledged as a patriot or partisan; their explanation was that he had been serving in the British Army when he parachuted into Italy and had not been fighting Nazis. In 1949, an Italian press article asked if Picchi was 'a traitor or a hero' and concluded that he was a bit of both.[33] It was exactly the stigma that Emilio Lussu and others had predicted for those who committed themselves unconditionally to a foreigners' war against their home.

Even Max Salvadori, after twenty years of spotless anti-Fascist work, experienced this sting in the tail. In June 1944, while Allied forces in Italy were battling their way north, Salvadori was at SOE's headquarters in Allied-occupied Bari when he heard that Polish frontline soldiers had reached Fermo, a hill town in the Marche close to Porto San Giorgio and his family's old home. Aware that his father had returned there from Switzerland in the mid-1930s, Salvadori, in his British officer's battledress, clambered into an army truck and set off, hoping to find his parents.

After Pedaso I knew every inch of the road: Torre di Palma, l'Ete, Santa Maria, Porto San Giorgio . . . The Rio, Capodarco on top of the hill, the Vallato, the pine avenue . . . Eleven years away from it all.

The light was failing. I got down from the lorry and waited a few minutes before going into the house. Emotion? Why not? Memories and images rushed through my mind: the long years in Switzerland, England, Africa, America; all my experiences before and during the war; efforts both successful and unsuccessful; fallen friends . . .

Someone was walking along the verandah. I opened the door and went up the dark stairs. I heard muttered words – they did not seem to be directed particularly towards me, but they were – it was my father's voice.

'*Agente straniero!*' – 'Foreign agent.'

Wrapped in a familiar black cloak, he passed me on the stairs and vanished into the gathering darkness. So that was my welcome home.

'Others might not be so outspoken, but might well have the same thought on seeing me in foreign uniform,' Salvadori reflected. 'And to think that for all these years I had dreamed of that moment.'[34]

Acknowledgements

First and foremost I would like to thank Christopher Woods, CMG, MC, an SOE officer during the Second World War and former SOE Adviser to the Foreign & Commonwealth Office. His knowledge of SOE's Italian exploits and readiness to share his writings and research have been of enormous benefit to me.

Tessa Stirling, CBE, and Sally Falk, Head and Deputy Head of Official Histories at the Cabinet Office, were consistently encouraging as the book was taking shape. Funding from the Gerry Holdsworth Special Forces Charitable Trust made possible a series of highly productive research trips to Milan, Rome, Sicily and Washington, DC. I am grateful to the Trustees and to the Trust's Secretaries, Nick Campling and Michael Martin, for their support.

Chris Grindall patiently summoned files to Admiralty Arch for me to see. Neil Slaughter of the National Archives kindly arranged space for me to work on more records at that end. Thank you to the staff of the Imperial War Museum, the Bodleian Library, the Churchill Archives Centre in Cambridge and King's College Archives in London. Robin Darwall-Smith helped me to navigate Douglas Dodds-Parker's papers at Magdalen College, Oxford. Susan Scott, Archivist at the Savoy, dug out documents concerning Fortunato Picchi.

I would also like to acknowledge the time and trouble taken by the Freedom of Information offices of the Federal Bureau of Investigation, the US Departments of the Army and Navy, the US Department of Defense, US Immigration and Customs Enforcement, and the Criminal Department of the US Department of Justice to respond so fully to my search for archive records relating to Max Salvadori and his time in the United States.

In Milan, Dr Tommaso Piffer, currently at Harvard, organised and accompanied me on a memorable search in wintry Carate Urio for traces of Dick Mallaby's impromptu arrival in August 1943. I would particularly like to thank Anna Maria Rusconi who did recall that strange event. Thank you to Dick Mallaby's youngest son, Richard, for chatting to me in Milan and for sharing information so freely; this included photographs that appear in these pages and a hot-off-the-press copy of Gianluca Barneschi's fine 2013 book, *L'inglese che viaggiò con il re e Badoglio: La missioni dell'agente speciale Dick Mallaby*. Gianluca, in turn, generously shared with me his detailed knowledge of Mallaby's life and wartime exploits. Andrea Torre, of Milan's Istituto Nazionale per la Storia del Movimento di Liberazione in Italia, assisted with research into Fortunato Picchi's fate and last letter.

In Rome, Simone Ferretti and colleagues of the Associazione CampotrinceratoRoma guided me around Forte Bravetta, where the Special Tribunal sent so many victims to be shot. I am also grateful to the staff of the Museo Storico della Liberazione on Via Tasso. Both they and the Associazione CampotrinceratoRoma do vital work in preserving the city's recent heritage. Thank you also to Mariapini Di Simone and the staff of Rome's Archivio Centrale dello Stato.

For help with research in Sicily I would especially like to thank Richard Brown, Honorary British Consul in Catania, for taking time to accompany me to Troina where, in the town archives, Angela Raffaela Caso, Rosalba Di Franco and Santina Monastra helped turn up details of Giovanni Di Giunta. Professor Rosario Mangiameli and Dr Giuseppe Boscarello, both of the University of Catania, made time to field questions. For her kindness in helping me actually to get to Sicily I am grateful to Marta Sobota.

Thank you, too, to the following: Gorazd Bajc, Paolo Campana, Felix Driver, the late John Earle, Mimmo Franzinelli, Steven Kippax, Judith Moellers, Claudia Nasini, Peter Pirker, Caitlyn

Schwartz, Blaz Torkar and Elke Zacharias. The late Margaret Jackson, MBE, shared with me her memories of Cecil Roseberry. Patricia Azarias, while carrying out her own research in the State Archives in Rome, generously undertook extra work on my behalf among the Special Tribunal records. For invaluable assistance in producing careful translations of Italian material, I am grateful to Fiamma Mazzocchi Alemanni, Rachel Donati and family, Lucian George and Duncan Stuart, CMG.

Permission to quote from the papers of Lieutenant-Colonel Julian Dobrski was granted by the Trustees of the Liddell Hart Centre for Military Archives, King's College, London. Thank you to Lisa McCaffery and Moira Durdin Robertson for permission to quote from the unpublished memoirs of their late father, Jock McCaffery.

At Faber, Julian Loose, Kate Murray-Browne and Hannah Marshall helped steer the text towards publication. Finally, thank you to Suzanne Bardgett, MBE, Gianluca Barneschi, Jim Daly, Alan Ogden, Nigel Perrin, Dr Tommaso Piffer, Mark Seaman, Donald Sommerville, Professor David Stafford and Christopher Woods for taking time to read my manuscript and provide vital commentary.

Notes

Prologue

1 E. De Selincourt (Revised by C. L. Shaver), *The Letters of William and Dorothy Wordsworth: The Early Years 1787–1805* (Oxford: OUP, 1967), pp. 34–5.
2 Sortie report: Operation 'Neck', TNA AIR 20/8350.
3 'Segnalazione – agenti nemici aviolanciate in abito civile', report by Comando Difesa-Territoriale Milano, 16 August 1943, TNA HS 6/872.
4 J. Gleeson and T. Waldon, *Now It Can Be Told* (London: Elek Books, 1954), pp. 125–6.
5 Author's interview with Anna Maria Rusconi, Carate Urio, 17 December 2010.
6 'The Mallaby Case', report by Captain P. Cooper, 1 August 1944, TNA HS 6/872.
7 'Cattura di un paracadutista nemico', report by Ufficio Protezione Impianti e Difesa Anti-paracadutisti, 14 August 1944, TNA HS 6/872.
8 Squadron Leader H. G. Crawshaw to Captain J. Dobrski, 2 July 1943, TNA HS 6/870.
9 Captain E. de Haan to Major C. Roseberry, 15 August 1943, TNA HS 6/870.
10 M. R. D. Foot, *SOE in France: An Account of the Work of the British Special Operations Executive in France, 1940–1944* (London: HMSO, 1966).
11 C. Cruickshank, *SOE in the Far East* (Oxford: Oxford University Press, 1983); C. Cruickshank, *SOE in Scandinavia* (Oxford: Oxford University Press, 1986).
12 M. R. D. Foot, *SOE in the Low Countries* (London: St Ermin's, 2001).
13 Report by Dame Barbara Salt, July 1969, TNA CAB 103/570. For more on the heritage and evolution of SOE official histories, see: R. Aldrich, 'Policing the Past: Official History, Secrecy and British Intelligence since 1945', *English Historical Review* (2004), 119/483, pp. 922–53; Christopher J. Murphy, 'The Origins of *SOE in France*', *Historical Journal* (2003), 46/4, pp. 935–52; and M. Seaman, 'A Glass Half Full: Some Thoughts on the Evolution of the Study of the Special Operations Executive', *Intelligence and National Security* (2005), 20/1, pp. 27–43.
14 D. Stafford, *Mission Accomplished: SOE and Italy, 1943–45* (London: The Bodley Head, 2011).

15 C. M. Woods, CMG, MC. A personal memoir of Captain Woods's work in German-occupied Italy is preserved in the archives of London's Imperial War Museum.

16 These consist principally of a mass of SIM '*controspionaggio*' files that fell into the hands of the American Office of Strategic Services at the end of the Second World War, copies of which survive today at the US National Archives at College Park, Maryland. The SIM archive in Italy, held in Rome in the Archivio dell'Ufficio Storico dello Stato Maggiore dell'Esercito, was temporarily opened to research a few years ago; during work on this book, however, it was closed for reordering. Other Italian documents drawn upon here are the files in Rome of the Special Tribunal, which was responsible for trying captured Allied agents (among other opponents of the regime); those records are available to readers at the Archivio Centrale dello Stato.

17 Christopher Woods and the Italian historian Mireno Berrettini are the principal writers who have sought before to explore SOE's overall record against Italy prior to September 1943. For Christopher Woods's work, see his articles 'SOE in Italy', in M. Seaman (ed.), *Special Operations Executive: A New Instrument of War* (London: Routledge, 2006), pp. 91–102, and 'A Tale of Two Armistices', in K. G. Robertson (ed.), *War, Resistance & Intelligence: Essays in Honour of M. R. D. Foot* (London: Leo Cooper, 1999), pp. 1–17. Full details of Mireno Berrettini's publications can be found in the bibliography, but his main work is *La Gran Bretagna e l'antifascismo italiano: diplomazia clandestina, intelligence, operazioni speciali, 1940–1943* (Florence: La Lettere, 2010). A brief chapter in Professor W. J. M. Mackenzie's in-house history of SOE, completed for the Cabinet Office in the late 1940s and published over fifty years later as *The Secret History of SOE: The Special Operations Executive 1940–1945* (London: St Ermin's, 2000), remains one of the few other accounts in print to touch on the topic of SOE's efforts against Fascist Italy. For accounts of SOE's work in Italy's overseas territories, W. E. D. Allen's *Guerrilla War in Abyssinia* (London: Penguin, 1943) and D. McNab's *Mission 101* (Sydney: Macmillan, 2011) both describe SOE-backed operations in Italian-occupied Abyssinia (Ethiopia). For a thorough study of SOE activity in Axis-occupied Albania, see my own *The Wildest Province: SOE in the Land of the Eagle* (London: Jonathan Cape, 2008), which draws heavily on SOE records and the stories of survivors.

18 Brigadier C. Gubbins to Lord Selborne, 22 December 1942, TNA HS 6/901.

19 Narrative of the work of SOE's Italian Section by Lieutenant-Colonel C. Roseberry, July 1945, TNA HS 7/58.

20 D. Eisenhower, *Crusade in Europe* (London: Heinemann, 1948), p. 202.

1 'Useless wishful thinking'

1   Information provided by the SOE Adviser to the Foreign & Common-wealth Office.
2   Recommendation for the award of the Distinguished Service Order, 26 April 1945, TNA WO 373/11.
3   M. Salvadori, *The Labour and the Wounds: A Personal Chronicle of One Man's Fight For Freedom* (London: Pall Mall Press, 1958), p. 12.
4   Quoted in 'Fascists and Their Critics: Assault on a Florence Professor', *The Times*, 11 April 1924.
5   Salvadori, *The Labour and the Wounds*, p. 16.
6   *Manchester Guardian*, 6 December 1929.
7   Other variations/suggestions include the Opera Volontaria di Repressione Antifascista and the Opera Vigilanza Repressione Antifascismo.
8   Salvadori, *The Labour and the Wounds*, pp. 46, 52.
9   Ibid. p. 93.
10 M. Canali, 'I cedimenti di Max Salvadori', *Liberal*, No. 27, December 2004/January 2005.
11 Ibid.
12 Salvadori, *The Labour and the Wounds* pp. 94–8.
13 M. Salvadori, 'With SOE in Italy: As I Saw It', undated note written for Christopher Woods, *c.* 1990, private papers of M. Salvadori (hereafter, Salvadori papers).
14 *The Times*, 1 November 1922.
15 It is possible that 'Mr Constable' was Kenneth Cohen, a retired naval officer recruited by Claude Dansey in 1937.
16 'David' (C. Dansey) to 'Peter' (M. Salvadori), 2 March 1938, Salvadori papers.
17 'Girl Beatrice. Report Re: Accident 26th August, 1938', Salvadori papers.
18 'David' (C. Dansey) to 'Peter' (M. Salvadori), 2 June 1939, Salvadori papers.
19 'David' (C. Dansey) to 'Peter' (M. Salvadori), 22 August 1939, Salvadori papers.
20 Telegram, 'David' (C. Dansey) to 'Peter' (M. Salvadori), 28 August 1939, Salvadori papers.
21 J. R. M. Butler, *History of the Second World War: Grand Strategy. Volume II: September 1939 to June 1941* (London: HMSO, 1957), pp. 12, 295.
22 'Secret War Diary of M.I.R. from September 3rd, 1939 to October 2nd 1940', TNA HS 8/263.
23 Handwritten manuscript by L. Grand, untitled and undated, TNA HS 7/5.
24 'D Section: Early History [of SOE] to September 1940', TNA HS 7/3.
25 Section D History, TNA HS 7/4.
26 'Propaganda in Italy in favour of the Allies', memorandum by

M. Salvadori, September 1939, Salvadori papers.

27 Ibid.

28 Minute by Sir Andrew Noble, 7 October 1939, TNA FO 371/23787.

29 K. Jeffery, *MI6: The History of the Secret Intelligence Service* (London: Bloomsbury, 2010), p. 423.

30 M. Canali, 'I cedimenti di Max Salvadori', in *Liberal* no. 27, December 2004/January 2005.

31 Ibid.

32 See, for example: M. Canali, *Le spie del regime* (Bologna: Il Mulino, 2004), and M. Canali, 'L'uomo che visse due volte: prima al servizio del Duce, poi di Sua Maestà', *Corriere della Sera*, October 2004.

33 M. Canali in *la Repubblica*, 5 July 2005.

34 P. Ross, writing on behalf of 'Mr Douglas' (Major Lawrence Grand), to 'Mr Sylvester' (M. Salvadori), 17 November 1939, Salvadori papers.

35 M. Salvadori to Miss Ross, 21 November 1939, Salvadori papers.

36 'Accounts for Journey November 29 to December 27, 1939', Salvadori papers.

37 M. Salvadori to 'Adriano', 6 December 1939, Salvadori papers.

38 'My meeting with an agent of the OVRA', report by M. Salvadori, sent under covering letter, M. Salvadori to 'Mr Douglas' (Major Lawrence Grand), 27 December 1939, Salvadori papers.

39 Ibid.

40 M. Salvadori to 'Mr Douglas' (Major Lawrence Grand), 27 December 1939, Salvadori papers. 'The account of your meeting was extremely interesting,' Section D replied. 'We are very glad that you have returned safely . . . As regards finance, I note that you will forward to me a cheque for £40, and that 120 French francs and a total of 500 Swiss francs will also be refunded to us . . .' P. Ross to M. Salvadori, 6 January 1940, Salvadori papers.

41 M. Salvadori to 'David' (C. Dansey), 25 April 1940, Salvadori papers.

42 Salvadori's papers shed little explicit light on his initial contact with the Italian Embassy in Washington, DC. However, his hostility to Fascism was so deep-rooted, and his contact with the devious Claude Dansey was so established and supportive, that it is hard to believe that his motives were different. It is not impossible, though, that that earlier move was a lone wolf initiative that he started himself and later shared with the British.

43 'Report by the Right Hon. Sir Percy Loraine, Bt., GCMG, on his Mission to Rome, May 2, 1939, to June 11, 1940', TNA FO 371/33232.

44 Ibid.

45 Quoted in W. Churchill, *The Second World War. Volume II: Their Finest Hour* (London: Cassell, 1949), pp. 107–8.

46 'Summary of a policy to be adopted by the pro-Allied propaganda in Italy', May 1940, Salvadori papers.

47 P. Hope to M. Salvadori, 23 May 1940, Salvadori papers.

48 'SOE Personnel: SOE History Sheet', TNA HS 9/134/4.

49 It is possible that Cianca was able to put this money to good use. According to Section D records, two clandestine printing presses were subsequently subsidised in Turin and Milan.

50 M. Salvadori to Mr Martin, 14 May 1940, Salvadori papers.

51 M. Salvadori to 'David' (C. Dansey), 2 June 1940, Salvadori papers.

52 'David' (C. Dansey) to 'Peter' (M. Salvadori), 6 June 1940, Salvadori papers.

2 'Pottering about'

1 'Report by the Right Hon. Sir Percy Loraine, Bt., GCMG, on his Mission to Rome, May 2, 1939, to June 11, 1940', TNA FO 371/33232.

2 M. Muggeridge (ed.), *Ciano's Diary 1939–1943* (London: Heinemann, 1947), pp. 263–4.

3 R. Lamb, *Mussolini and the British* (London: John Murray, 1997), p. 286.

4 J. Colville, *The Fringes of Power: Downing Street Diaries 1939–1955* (London: Hodder & Stoughton, 1985), p. 152.

5 Ibid.

6 'SOE: Early History to September 1940', TNA HS 7/3.

7 John F. Parke, 'Hamilton Ellis – An Appreciation', *Railway World*, September 1987.

8 C. H. Ellis to Mr Strauss, 9 June 1940, TNA HS 9/477/7.

9 'SOE: Early History to September 1940', TNA HS 7/3.

10 'Mr Hamilton Ellis', F. Strauss to Major L. Humphreys, 9 July 1940, TNA HS 9/477/7.

11 'SOE: Early History to September 1940', TNA HS 7/3.

12 Ibid.

13 W. J. M. Mackenzie, *The Secret History of SOE*, p. 754.

14 B. Pimlott (ed.), *The Second World War Diary of Hugh Dalton* (London: Jonathan Cape, 1986), p. 62.

15 SOE War Diary, TNA HS 7/211.

16 Basil Davidson, interview No. 8682, Imperial War Museum Sound Archive. 'We were totally amateurish – totally, one hundred per cent amateurish – and it couldn't have been otherwise,' Davidson adds in his interview. 'You can't suddenly create an effective organisation with the aims that SOE had, which were to support resistance and promote resistance in countries that might be occupied and, when they were occupied, to keep the links going and to help the people who were resisting.'

17 For more on British activities in Slovenia during and after this period, see: G. Bajc, 'Collaboration between Slovenes from the Primorska Region, the Special Operations Executive and the Inter-Services Liaison Department after the Occupation of Yugoslavia (6 April 1941)', *Annales: Series Historia et Sociologia*, 11/2, 2002, pp. 363–84;

G. Bajc, *Iz nevidnega na plan: slovenski primorski liberalni narodnjaki v emigraciji med drugo svetovno vojno in ozadje britanskih misij v Sloveniji* (Koper: Založba Annales, 2002); and J. Pirjevec, 'Britanska tajna organizacija na Slovenskem (1940–1941)', *Prispevki za nojejšo zgodovino* (2010), 40/1, pp. 323–30.

18 'Italian Information on English Terrorist action in Jugoslavia', 26 September 1940, TNA HS 5/895.

19 G. S. Frodsham to M. H. S. Everett, 17 May 1940, TNA BW 66/6.

20 *The Times*, 14 September 1940.

21 'Note on the death of G. S. Frodsham', A. Lawrenson to Colonel G. Taylor, 5 June 1945, TNA HS 9/546.

22 Ibid.

23 Ibid.

24 Section D History, TNA HS 7/4.

25 Telegram, A. R. Glen to B. A. Sweet-Escott, 16 September 1940, HS 5/895.

26 'Note on the death of G. S. Frodsham', A. Lawrenson to Colonel G. Taylor, 5 June 1945, TNA HS 9/546.

27 Section D History, TNA HS 7/4; telegram, A. R. Glen to B. A. Sweet-Escott, 16 September 1940, HS 5/895.

28 'Note on the death of G. S. Frodsham,' A. Lawrenson to Colonel G. Taylor, 5 June 1945, TNA HS 9/546.

3 'Garibaldi's curse'

1 'Crastinus' (Silvio Corio), 'Fortunato Picchi: Hero of "New Italy"', *New Times and Ethiopia News*, 26 April 1941.

2 'Subversive Activities in Relation to Strategy', first Chiefs of Staff directive to SOE, 25 November 1940, TNA CAB 80/56.

3 B. Pimlott (ed.), *The Political Diary of Hugh Dalton, 1918–40, 1945–60* (London: Jonathan Cape, 1986), pp. 173–4. For Dalton's later and less generous account of the meeting, see: H. Dalton, *The Fateful Years: Memoirs 1931–1945* (London: Frederick Muller, 1957), pp. 34–5.

4 G. Jebb, *The Memoirs of Lord Gladwyn* (New York: Weybright and Talley, 1972), pp. 104–5. Certainly Dalton's manner was not to everyone's taste. Within a month of arriving he had argued with and dismissed Lawrence Grand, the old Section D chief. Absorbed into SOE along with many of his personnel, Grand had found the transition to new management hard to take. Another who shared his unhappiness was Peter Hope, a young linguist whom Grand had instructed in May 1940 to set up an Italian sub-section for Section D; Hope left SOE in early 1941 to join MI5.

5 H. Hopkinson to G. Jebb, 25 November 1940, TNA HS 6/901.

6 B. Sweet-Escott, *Baker Street Irregular* (London: Methuen, 1965), p. 56.

7 Minute, Sir Frank Nelson to G. Jebb, 27 November 1940, TNA HS 6/901.

8 Note by H. Dalton on minute from Sir Frank Nelson to G. Jebb, 27 November 1940, TNA HS 6/901.

9 Pimlott, *The Second World War Diary of Hugh Dalton*, p. 113.

10 Minute, H. Dalton to G. Jebb, 19 December 1940, TNA HS 6/901.

11 Pimlott, *The Second World War Diary of Hugh Dalton*, p. 128. Even before Nelson's report reached him, a bristling Dalton had been unhappy with SOE's progress on Italy. In October he had been reminded by an SOE subordinate 'that the difficulty in Italy was that, when the balloon went up, we had no apparatus there at all'. Dalton, a vigorous opponent of pre-war appeasement policies, replied 'that I fully realised this and had openly stated as much in the Cabinet and elsewhere; we had been completely let down by the ineptitude of HM's previous Government, and of certain of their advisers in the Foreign Office and in the Embassy at Rome.' H. Dalton to G. Jebb, 5 October 1940, TNA HS 6/901.

12 Pimlott, *The Second World War Diary of Hugh Dalton*, p. 128.

13 Minute, H. Dalton to G. Jebb, 5 October 1940, TNA HS 6/901.

14 G. Thomas to P. Broad, 22 December 1940, TNA HS 6/901.

15 R. Leeper to Sir Orme Sargent, 2 January 1941, TNA HS 6/901.

16 Pimlott, *The Second World War Diary of Hugh Dalton*, p. 113.

17 Minute, H. Dalton to G. Jebb, 4 December 1940, TNA HS 6/901. Keyes had joined the Royal Navy in 1885. Since then, among other adventures, he had sailed anti-slavery patrols off the African coast in the 1890s, scaled the walls of Peking during the Boxer Rebellion in 1900, been naval chief-of-staff off the Dardanelles in 1915, led the Dover Patrol and daring raids on Ostend and Zeebrugge in 1918, sat in the House of Commons since 1934, and been in charge of the British mission to King Leopold III of Belgium, in spring 1940.

18 'Lt-Cdr George Martelli' (obituary), *Daily Telegraph*, March 1994.

19 P. Hope to Major L. Humphreys, 30 August 1940, TNA HS 8/305.

20 G. Martelli to Sir Frank Nelson, 5 December 1940, TNA HS 6/901.

21 H. Dalton to Sir Roger Keyes, 6 December 1940, TNA HS 6/901.

22 Sir Roger Keyes to H. Dalton, 7 December 1940, TNA HS 6/901.

23 G. K. Logie to Brigadier C. Gubbins, 2 January 1941, TNA HS 6/793.

24 'Colossus', undated note, TNA HS 6/783.

25 G. K. Logie to Brigadier C. Gubbins, 2 January 1941, TNA HS 6/793.

26 Report by Lance-Corporal J. K. Macalister, 13 February 1941, TNA HS 9/238/6.

27 Report by Lance-Corporal Searle, 28 January 1941, TNA HS 9/1218/2.

28 Report by J. Dobrski, 31 March 1941, TNA HS 6/884.

29 Report by J. Dobrski, 15 April 1941, TNA HS 6/884.

30 J. McCaffery, 'No Pipes or Drums' (unpublished memoir), Imperial War Museum.

31 J. Nicol, *Meet Me at the Savoy* (London: Museum Press, 1952), p. 42.

32 D. Tangye (ed.), *Went the Day Well* (London: Harrap, 1942), p. 208.

33 'Crastinus' (Silvio Corio), 'Fortunato Picchi: Hero of "New Italy"', *New Times and Ethiopia News*, 26 April 1941.

34 Tangye, *Went the Day Well*, p. 209.

35 'Crastinus' (Silvio Corio), 'Fortunato Picchi: Hero of "New Italy"', *New Times and Ethiopia News*, 26 April 1941.

36 Ibid.

37 Tangye, *Went the Day Well*, p. 210.

38 Ibid. pp. 210–11.

39 'Report on Picchi', by Lance-Corporal Searle, undated, TNA HS 9/1185/2.

40 'Report on Picchi', by Pilot Officer Roche, 27 January 1941, TNA HS 9/1185/2.

41 'Picchi, Fortunato,' TNA HS 9/1185/2.

42 Lieutenant-Colonel T. Pritchard to Brigadier B. Fergusson, 24 October 1946, TNA DEFE 2/1345.

43 A. Deane-Drummond, *Return Ticket* (London: Collins, 1953), pp. 13–14. Deane-Drummond was destined for a long and illustrious military career that would see him escape from a POW camp in 1942, land and again escape capture at Arnhem in 1944, and command the SAS in Malaya and Oman. He would retire as a major-general. He died in December 2012 at the age of ninety-five.

44 General Sir Hastings Ismay to Prime Minister, 8 January 1941, TNA PREM 3/100.

45 Prime Minister's inked annotation, 9 January 1941, on General Sir Hastings Ismay to Prime Minister, 8 January 1941, TNA PREM 3/100.

46 According to one account, an emotional Roger Keyes had paid a visit to Mildenhall earlier that day: X Troop paraded in the hangar where Keyes shook hands with every man and was overheard whispering 'A pity . . . a damned pity,' before surprising everyone by coming to attention and saluting *them*. R. Foxall, *The Guinea-Pigs: Britain's First Paratroop Raid* (London: Robert Hale, 1983), p. 48.

47 Deane-Drummond, *Return Ticket*, p. 21.

47 'Narrative of the Air Phase', in 'Operation COLOSSUS: Report Covering Period in Malta', 13 February 1941, TNA DEFE 2/153.

49 Ibid.

50 Minutes of Chiefs of Staff Meeting held on 13 February 1941, TNA CAB 79/9.

51 Sir Roger Keyes to W. Churchill, 13 February 1941, TNA PREM 3/100.

52 Comment (dated June 1941) by Sir Roger Keyes on the report of the commanding officer of HMS *Triumph*, quoted in Appendix XIV of the report on Colossus, November 1943, TNA DEFE 2/152.

53 Quoted in *The Times*, 15 February 1941. A few weeks later, the American military attaché in Rome reported that he had visited the imprisoned men, found them in excellent spirits, and heard their claim to have put the aqueduct out of action for several days. In time, via the Red

Cross, letters scribbled by members of Colossus began to reach family and friends. Several contained cryptic or coded comments about the operation. To escape the attention of the Italian censors, these comments were necessarily brief. Nevertheless, they suggested that the men had accomplished something. 'I know that the West Wing of the Old Hall was made untenable – no doubt the insurance will fit the bill,' Tag Pritchard wrote in June from an Italian POW camp, a statement interpreted in London as an allusion to repairable damage having been done to the aqueduct's western end. Quoted in Major M. Lindsay to Major D. Macfie, 26 June 1941, TNA DEFE 2/153. Several second-hand reports would also reach London from repatriated soldiers who had met men of the Colossus party in prison camps in Italy. The reports were oral and their accuracy varied. One returning medical officer reported that a Major Pritchett [*sic*] whom he had encountered in his camp had found his party's containers of 'pelican soup' to be particularly bulky to move around. He had misheard the word 'pemmican'. Appendix IX of report on Colossus, November 1943, DEFE 2/152.

54 Born in May 1919, George Robert Paterson had left Canada in 1937 and been studying forestry at the University of Edinburgh when war broke out. In September 1943, shortly after Italy's surrender, he escaped from a train taking him and other British prisoners to Germany. Joining a band of Italian partisans near Brescia, he worked to help other Allied fugitives reach the safety of neutral Switzerland until he was captured again in January 1944. After six months in an SS prison in Milan he escaped again and made his way to Switzerland. There he contacted SOE's Jock McCaffery and agreed to return to Italy as an SOE agent. In October 1944, while fighting alongside Italian partisans, Paterson was captured for the third time. Narrowly avoiding being shot on the spot, and after some brutal treatment and more imprisonment in Milan, he made his third escape in April 1945. For his work in Italy, Paterson received two Military Crosses.

55 'A narrative of the execution of the operation based on information given by Lt A. J. Deane-Drummond', Appendix XV in report on Colossus, November 1943, TNA DEFE 2/152.

56 Deane-Drummond, *Return Ticket*, p. 38.

57 Lieutenant-Colonel T. Pritchard to Brigadier B. Fergusson, 24 October 1946, TNA DEFE 2/1345.

58 Lieutenant A. Deane-Drummond, 'Report on Picchi', Appendix X in report on Colossus, November 1943, TNA DEFE 2/152.

59 'A narrative of the execution of the operation based on information given by Lt A. J. Deane-Drummond', Appendix XV in report on Colossus, November 1943, TNA DEFE 2/152.

60 Deane-Drummond, *Return Ticket*, p. 42.

61 Lieutenant A. Deane-Drummond, 'Report on Picchi', Appendix X on

report on Colossus, November 1943, TNA DEFE 2/152.

62 Foxall, *The Guinea-Pigs*, pp. 160–1.

63 Lieutenant-Colonel T. Pritchard to Brigadier B. Fergusson, 24 October 1946, TNA DEFE 2/1345.

64 'Interrogatorio dell'italiano catturato fra i paracadutisti inglesi', undated but *c.* mid-February 1941, TNA HS 6/884.

65 American Embassy in Rome to the Foreign Office in London, 18 October 1941, TNA DEFE 2/153.

66 A copy of Fortunato Picchi's last letter can be accessed through the website of L'Istituto nazionale per la storia del movimento di liberazione in Italia (National Institute for the History of the Liberation Movement in Italy): http://www.italia-liberazione.it/ultimelettere.

67 'The Project and Outline Plan', 2 January 1941, quoted in Appendix I in report on Colossus, November 1943, DEFE 2/152.

68 W. Churchill to General H. Ismay, 15 February 1941, TNA PREM 3/100.

69 *Evening Standard*, 14 February 1941.

70 *Evening Standard*, 15 February 1941.

71 *Sunday Pictorial*, 16 February 1941.

72 *The Times*, 17 February 1941.

73 Comment broadcast by radio from Berlin and quoted in the *Daily Telegraph*, February 1941. The Germans overlooked the fact that they had taken the idea of parachute troops from the Soviets.

74 *The Times*, 15 April 1941.

75 Note by Lieutenant F. Snow, undated (but 15 April 1941), TNA HS 9/1185/2.

76 *The Daily Express*, 16 April 1941.

77 *The Times*, 16 April 1941.

78 *Time*, 28 April 1941.

79 'Pentad', *The Remaking of Italy* (London: Penguin Books, 1942).

80 Tangye, *Went the Day Well.*

81 Nicol, *Meet Me at the Savoy* p. 44.

4 'Desperados' and 'Thugs'

1 'Italy', Sir Frank Nelson to F. T. Davies, 3 December 1940, TNA HS 6/885.

2 Captain Andrew Croft quoted in R. Bailey, *Forgotten Voices of the Secret War* (London: Ebury Press, 2008), p. 19.

3 'Note of Interview', TNA HS 9/518/5.

4 J. McCaffery, 'No Pipes or Drums'.

5 In December 1940, Martelli had felt that SOE might find 'perhaps 20 or 30' suitable candidates in Britain. G. Martelli to Sir Frank Nelson, 19 December 1940, TNA HS 6/885.

6 'Report on Recruiting of Italians', by G. Martelli, 9 January 1941, TNA HS 6/885. Martelli explained that the men he had interviewed 'fell into

two categories': '(a) Anglicised Italians with no interest in politics, most of them with family or business ties in this country, and not of the adventurous or idealistic type'; and '(b) Jewish refugees, most of them of the middle-class intellectual type – e.g. students, lawyers, teachers and doctors – who came to England after the passing of the racial laws in Italy (in 1938) and hoped to settle down peacefully in this country'. Men of both types had expressed themselves willing 'to do anything for England, but I received the impression that, with few exceptions, their apparent willingness derived from what they thought was expected of them, rather than from genuine enthusiasm'.

7 'I find that the great majority of the men here do not wish to go abroad or take any more active part in the war,' reads one frustrated report, drawn up in July 1941, after a visit to look through Italians in a Pioneer Corps camp outside London. 'It is better than internment for they enjoy the greater liberties and can get home quite often. I trust that it will be realised that I have had to waste a great deal of time contacting men who have proved themselves of this type and so useless for our requirements.' '270 Coy AMPC (Italians) Burnham Slough: Individual Reports', report by Lance-Corporal E. R. Saunders, 19 July 1941, TNA HS 6/888.

8 Sir Walter Monckton to G. Jebb, 24 April 1941, TNA HS 9/1185/2. For SOE, that reasoning missed the point. 'Surely the most disastrous aspect of the publicity given to the Picchi episode', wrote George Logie, then head of SOE's Italian desk, 'is that any Italians whom we may in future enlist from the Pioneer Corps or Internment Camps at once become marked men among their fellow pioneers or internees. If, for instance, we now recruit a man from the Pioneer Corps the whole of the rest of the Pioneer Corps will assume that he has gone for parachute training . . . Surely Sir Walter Monckton must realise that publicity such as this must endanger the lives of other trainees and their families in Italy.' G. K. Logie to D. L. J. Perkins, 6 May 1941, TNA HS 9/1185/2.

9 H. G. Crawshaw to D. L. J. Perkins, 17 June 1941, TNA HS 6/884.

10 'Report from Inverlair. 4.10.41', TNA HS 9/1218/2.

11 'Local Acting Unpaid L/Cpl Purisiol, R.', note extracted from report of 13 October 1942, TNA HS 9/1218/2.

12 Chief Instructor to Commandant, 30 April 1941, TNA HS 6/884.

13 'Report from O.C. STS No. 2', 22 March 1941, TNA HS 6/884.

14 Telephone message from Lieutenant-Colonel Munn, Commandant, Beaulieu Area, 29 April 1941, TNA HS 6/884.

15 Pilot Officer H. G. Crawshaw to D. L. J. Perkins, 17 June 1941, TNA HS 6/884.

16 'General Report' by J. Dobrski, 15 April 1941, TNA HS 6/884.

17 'Recruits', Pilot Officer H. G. Crawshaw to D. L. J. Perkins, 14 April 1941, TNA HS 6/884.

18 One of Thornhill's officers, the writer Christopher Sykes, would
    remember him as 'amiable, garrulous [and] indiscreet . . . an indefatig-
    able busybody'. Thornhill was also the man who would save the life
    of a depressed Orde Wingate, the future Chindit commander, while
    both were staying at Cairo's Continental Hotel in 1941. Hearing strange
    noises in the next-door room, Thornhill alerted the manager. They
    forced the door and found Wingate in a pool of blood, having stabbed
    himself in the throat with a hunting knife. 'When I hear a feller lock
    a door, I don't think anything about it,' Thornhill is said to have
    explained afterwards, 'and if I hear a feller fall down, that's his affair,
    but when I hear a feller lock his door and then fall down – it's time for
    action.' C. Sykes, *Orde Wingate* (London Collins, 1959), pp. 329, 331.
19 Some of this work had some success. 'Your leaflets fell on Bardia,'
    one captured Italian colonel told his interrogators. 'They have a very
    demoralising effect on the troops because they read them and come to
    the officers for explanation. We have no convincing arguments against
    the truth.' Quoted in H. Dalton to Prime Minister, 7 February 1941,
    TNA HS 3/189. It was one thing in 1940–1 to prove to Italian prisoners
    that they had lost a few battles; it was quite another to persuade them
    that the Axis would lose the war. Prisoners burned the leaflets handed
    around in the camps, while Thornhill's attempts to aim a pro-Allied
    newspaper at the 45,000 Italian civilians living in Egypt proved
    similarly ineffective. One plan was to take control of a local Fascist
    newspaper, the Italian-language *Il Giornale d'Oriente*, and reissue it
    as an anti-Fascist one. 'The paper was a complete failure,' recalled one
    of Thornhill's assistants. In its first week, sales 'fell from 2,200 to 300'.
    P. Vittorelli to E. Lussu, 26 March 1942, TNA HS 6/821.
20 'Memorandum on Anti-Italian Propaganda in the Middle East' by
    Colonel C. Thornhill and F. Stark, 15 August 1940, TNA FO 371/29936.
    For more on the Italian work of SO1 in the Middle East and the
    endeavour to raise a free Italian force, see: K. Federowich, 'Propaganda
    and Political Warfare: The Foreign Office, Italian POWs and the
    Free Italy Movement, 1940–43', in B. Moore and K. Federowich (eds),
    Prisoners of War and their Captors in World War II (Oxford: Berg,
    1996). Despite the creation of PWE, SOE would continue, in the Middle
    East, to draft and disseminate anti-Italian propaganda for months
    to come. By 1942, the responsible SOE department was known as the
    Directorate of Special Propaganda (DSP) and had the stated purpose
    of recruiting 'active supporters of the Allied cause' via propaganda
    that appeared not to emanate from any British source. Methods of
    dissemination included radio broadcasts, leaflets and rumours. The
    DSP set-up included a little Italian section that made radio broadcasts
    from Jerusalem and drafted leaflets and pamphlets for dropping by
    the RAF.
21 '[A]ll my intelligence officers are of [the] opinion that it is most unlikely

that sufficient Italians of the right calibre can be found in Egypt,'
Wavell telegraphed London. It would require 'time and care' to ensure
the reliability of any prisoners, while 'very few' of the Italian civilians
living in Egypt were of 'pronounced anti-Fascist opinion'. General
Sir Archibald Wavell to Chief of the Imperial General Staff, cipher
telegram, 23 December 1940, TNA WO 193/617.

22 D. Hart-Davis, *Peter Fleming: A Biography* (London: Jonathan Cape,
1974), p. 240.

23 War Office to General Sir Archibald Wavell, cipher telegram, 9 January
1941, TNA WO 193/617.

24 'Minute I', H. Dalton to G. Jebb, 23 January 1941, TNA HS 6/903.

25 'Minute II', H. Dalton to G. Jebb, 23 January 1941, TNA HS 6/903,
Although previously published accounts of Yak Mission have suggested
that Fleming's team was composed of half a dozen or so officers each
accompanied by his batman, contemporary paperwork indicates
that, by mid-March 1941, it had been authorised to become a force of
some size and substance, including seven officers, a sergeant-major,
a quartermaster sergeant, four drivers, two cooks, two clerks, three
signallers, a three-man detachment of Royal Engineers, and a thirty-
strong platoon of soldiers.

26 Cipher telegram, G. Pollock to SOE London, 21 March 1941, TNA
HS 3/197.

27 Hart-Davis, *Peter Fleming*, pp. 248–9.

28 'Italian Recruits from America', G. Taylor to G. Jebb, 4 December 1941,
TNA 6/905.

29 Quoted in 'Colonel Donovan', Sir Frank Nelson to G. Jebb, 8 February
1941, TNA HS 8/118.

30 Copy of cipher telegram, H. Dalton to General Sir Archibald Wavell,
5 April 1941, TNA HS 3/146.

31 A thirteenth volunteer had accompanied the party across the Atlantic.
This was Charles Formosa, a 32-year-old Maltese from Canada who
had been working until recently for the Enemy Aliens Department of
the Royal Canadian Mounted Police. A British citizen, Formosa had
refused to associate with Italians and insisted on travelling separately
from the others. Unlike them, he was also willing to be trained at once.
In the end, SOE felt he was unsuitable for its work but sent him to
Malta and found him a job with the Maltese Police. TNA HS 9/527.

32 D. Garnett, *The Secret History of PWE: The Political Warfare Executive*
(London: St Ermin's Press, 2002), p. 139. Four of the party would be
assessed as doing particularly well in India. One was a trained doctor,
32-year-old Lucio Tarchiani, who had fought in France in 1940 and
been the outstanding member of the group from the start. The other
three were Americo Biasini, a lamp-maker in his early twenties; Luigi
Ceccarelli, a cook in his forties who had fought in the First World War;
and Albino Zattoni, aged about thirty, who had worked as a news-

paperman in the United States and fought in Spain. The rest of the party, however, were considered as unsatisfactory in India as they had been during their time with SOE. One, Osvaldo Forlani, the man who had tried to take five years off his age, vanishes from PWE's records in the summer of 1942. It was thought that he might have died in the hot weather. For a detailed study of the party and its work in India, see K. Federowich, "'Toughs and Thugs': The Mazzini Society and Political Warfare amongst Italian POWs in India, 1941–43', *Intelligence and National Security*, Vol. 20, No. 1, March 2005, pp. 147–72.

33 Information provided by the SOE Adviser to the Foreign & Commonwealth Office.

34 Ibid.

35 Statement on the Ingrao case sent by SOE to MI5 under note dated 7 March 1942, KV 2/3172.

36 H. N. Sporborg to Sir Charles Hambro, 15 May 1943, TNA HS 6/887. Ingrao made his offer to the SOE-sponsored Mazzini Society, threatening them with 'revelations' but saying he would 'settle the matter' for $2,500. Cipher telegram, SOE New York to SOE London, 24 May 1943, TNA HS 6/887. Days later, when asked in New York by Count Carlo Sforza how much money he would consider as adequate recompense for his alleged wrongs, Ingrao upped his figure to £100,000.

37 *Chicago Sunday Tribune*, 12 September 1943.

38 Report by J. Hale, 7 September 1943, TNA KV 2/3712.

39 Tarchiani, who had made his way to the United States after fleeing Paris as the Germans marched in, was also the father of Lucio Tarchiani, the most impressive of the twelve-strong Italian party sent from New York to London in 1941. Helped by British funds, the Mazzini Society's main vehicle was a weekly newssheet, the *Mazzini News*, with a modest circulation that began in February 1941 at 2,000 copies and by October had grown to 5,000, while its most capable members toured the country giving talks.

40 'Interim Report on Italians in the U.S.A.', 31 December 1941, TNA HS 8/42.

41 Cipher telegram, SOE New York to SOE London, November 1941, TNA HS 8/88; report, SOE New York to SOE London, 19 November 1941, TNA HS 8/88; cipher telegram, SOE New York to SOE London, 19 November 1941, TNA HS 8/88; 'I. B.' to 'Drew-Brook', 19 November 1941, TNA HS 8/88.

42 Major F. M. G. Glyn to M. Coit, 4 January 1942, TNA HS 8/88.

43 Section 3 ('J. D. P.') to Sections 2 and 35A, 23 December 1941, TNA HS 8/88.

44 Cipher telegram, SOE New York to SOE London, 27 December 1941, TNA HS 8/88.

45 Section 35A ('I. B.') to Section 3 ('J. D. P.'), 24 December 1941, TNA HS 8/88.

46 Report ('Max William Salvadori, with alias Emmett Williams') by E. P. O'Neil (FBI field office, San Antonio, Texas), 25 February 1942, quoting letter dated 20 February 1942 from L. T. McCollister (Border Patrol, McAllen, Texas), Bureau file 100-893, FBI Archives.

47 Ibid.

48 Report ('Max William Salvadori') by W. J. Goodwin (FBI headquarters, Washington, DC), 11 July 1941, quoting undated letter from L. T. McCollister (Border Patrol, McAllen, Texas), Bureau file 100-2769, FBI Archives.

49 *British Security Coordination: The Secret History of British Intelligence in the Americas 1940–45* (London: St Ermin's Press, 1998), p. 435. See also H. Montgomery Hyde, *The Quiet Canadian: The Secret Service Story of Sir William Stephenson* (London: Hamish Hamilton, 1962), pp. 228–9.

50 'Peter' (M. Salvadori) to 'David' (C. Dansey), 14 November 1940, Salvadori papers. This was also a game, as Salvadori told Dansey, that had managed to secure him an Italian passport from the Italian Embassy in Washington, DC, 'which may enable me to get in touch with unfriendly people: is there anything I can do in making use of it?' One course of action, Salvadori thought, might be to 'make the attempt to go back to the Old Country [i.e. Italy]. It would be impossible for me to say what exactly I could achieve there and how long I could stay, but perhaps it would be worth trying.' Another could be to 'go to some country which is not the Old Country. I would prefer it because I could remain with my family.' In the end, it seems, Salvadori had little need of the passport.

51 'Report on XX's Trip', Salvadori papers.

52 Ibid.

53 Handwritten note by M. Salvadori, 14 August 1980, Salvadori papers.

54 'Report on XX's Trip', Salvadori papers.

55 Report ('Max Salvadori alias Paleotti'), 21 July 1941, attached to letter from P. E. Foxworth (FBI office, New York) to the Director (FBI headquarters, Washington, DC), 8 October 1941, Bureau file 100-12404, FBI Archives.

56 Letter ('Re: Max William Salvadori. Internal Security – I'), J. Edgar Hoover (FBI headquarters, Washington, DC) to Special Agent in Charge (FBI headquarters, Washington, DC), 3 June 1941, Bureau file 100-23064-1, FBI Archives.

57 Letter ('Re: Max William Salvadori. Internal Security – I'), S. K. McKee (FBI headquarters, Washington, DC) to the Director (FBI headquarters, Washington, DC), 4 April 1942, Bureau file 100-2769, FBI Archives.

58 Report ('Max William Salvadori, with aliases Dr Massimo Salvadori-Palleotti, Dr Massimo Salvadori, Dr M. Salvadori-Pallotti' by P. P. Schneider (FBI headquarters, Washington, DC), 4 April 1942, Bureau

file 100-2769, FBI Archives.

59   Report by Corporal E. Beaumont, 9 July 1943, TNA HS 6/882.
60   Report by Corporal E. Beaumont, 16 July 1943, TNA HS 6/882.
61   Vetere was from Montreal and had worked before the war as a clerk. Peter Lizza was a shoemaker from Toronto and the only one of the six to speak fluent Italian, his parents having taken him, when he was two, to live in Italy for a few years. Frank Fusco was a pre-war welder from Niagara Falls. The remaining three of that six-strong Canadian party went on to work at SOE headquarters and training schools. Another Italian-Canadian, a labourer and hotel worker called Frank Misericordia, was trained as a wireless operator and would have gone into action but for illness. Recruited in Ottawa in 1941 at the older-than-average age of thirty-five, Misericordia was a married father of four who had been in Canada for twenty years but remembered southern Italy well. Training reports glowed with praise: 'one of the best shots that has ever been trained at this school . . . intelligent and conscientious . . . has shown aptitude, concentration and great keenness . . . happy, likeable and helpful . . . extremely keen to go to Italy and to do any work . . . has a deep hatred of the regime'. Quoted in report entitled 'Frank', 17 April 1943, TNS HS 9/1042/1. Passed fit for work as an agent, Misericordia refrained from disclosing to SOE that he suffered from a bad heart until, in 1944, he became so ill that he was incapable of concealing it. By then, SOE had already made a series of attempts to land him behind the enemy lines by boat. 'On no less than five occasions he was taken within reach of land,' SOE recorded, 'but each time something outside his control went wrong; engine failed, oars broke, patrols observed on the beach, etc . . . It is not difficult to conceive that being keyed up on five occasions for a hazardous enterprise accentuated his heart trouble.' Lieutenant-Colonel C. Roseberry to Flight Lieutenant J. L. Day, 18 May 1944, TNA HS 9/1042/1.
62   Information provided by the SOE Adviser to the Foreign & Common-wealth Office.
63   R. Maclaren, *Canadians Behind Enemy Lines 1939–1945* (Vancouver: University of British Columbia Press, 1981), p. 174.
64   'Italy', Sir Frank Nelson to G. Jebb, 15 October 1941, TNA HS 6/885.

5 'A mass of difficulties'

1   E. Lussu, *Sardinian Brigade* (New York: Knopf, 1939), pp. 122–3.
2   J. Lussu. *Freedom has no Frontier* (London: Michael Joseph, 1969), p. 10.
3   Information provided by the SOE Adviser to the Foreign & Common-wealth Office.
4   Ibid.
5   Ibid.

6   Ibid.

7   Ibid.

8   Ibid.

9   SOE War Diary, TNA HS 7/265.

10 'Lussu's Plan', G. Jebb to F. Nelson and H. Dalton, 13 November 1941, TNA HS 6/907.

11 Information provided by the SOE Adviser to the Foreign & Commonwealth Office.

12 Ibid.

13 Cipher telegram, L. H. Mortimore to Major L. Humphreys, 19 December 1941, TNA HS 6/907.

14 *Hansard*, HC Debates, Volume 377, Column 1017.

15 SOE War Diary, TNA HS 7/265.

16 Note by C. M. Woods on conversation with Leo Valiani, May 1989, Woods papers; Stafford, *Mission Accomplished*, p. 13.

17 Author's interview with Margaret Jackson, MBE, wartime personal assistant to General Sir Colin Gubbins, 28 October 2012.

18 C. Roseberry to Brigadier C. Gubbins, 27 January 1942, TNA HS 6/907.

19 C. Roseberry to Brigadier C. Gubbins, 10 February 1942, TNA HS 9/621/7.

20 G. Jebb to Sir Frank Nelson, 11 February 1942, TNA HS 6/907.

21 C. Roseberry to Brigadier C. Gubbins, 10 February 1942, TNA HS 9/621/7.

22 Information provided by the SOE Adviser to the Foreign & Commonwealth Office.

23 'Notes on conversation between M. [Brigadier C. Gubbins] and Simon [E. Lussu]', 14 February 1942, TNA HS 6/907.

24 Minute by G. Jebb, 16 February 1942, TNA HS 6/907.

25 Minute by H. Dalton, 18 February 1942, TNA HS 6/907.

26 Information provided by the SOE Adviser to the Foreign & Commonwealth Office.

27 Ibid.

28 Ibid.

29 Hambro had achieved a lot with his life by then and his opinions commanded respect. In 1917, as a very young lieutenant on the Western Front, he had won a Military Cross for a display of 'conspicuous gallantry' when taking prisoners, rescuing wounded, and shooting four of the enemy with his revolver (*The London Gazette*, No. 30466, Supplement, 8 January 1918, p. 612). Between the wars, while a thirty-year-old banker in the City, he had been made a director of the Bank of England. Joining SOE in 1940, he had been knighted the following year for overseeing, among other things, the successful smuggling from Scandinavia of vital ball-bearing supplies.

30 Sir Charles Hambro to Lord Selborne, 14 May 1942, TNA HS 6/907.

31 Information provided by the SOE Adviser to the Foreign & Commonwealth Office.

32 Ibid.
33 Ibid.
34 Minute, G. Jebb to Sir Frank Nelson, 6 March 1942, TNA HS 6/907.
35 SOE War Diary, TNA HS 7/232.
36 Information provided by the SOE Adviser to the Foreign & Common-wealth Office.
37 Ibid.
38 'History of Italian Activities of SOE, 1941–1945', TNA HS 7/58. Earl Brennan, head of the Italian desk of the Office of Strategic Services in Washington, DC, was another who would think Lussu a man of the highest potential. Brennan wrote to Bill Donovan, the head of OSS, in August 1943 that Emilio Lussu 'is sometimes referred to as "the uncrowned king of Sardinia"' and 'is the greatest single factor which will contribute to the success of operations in Sardinia. In fact I am satisfied that with Lussu's co-operation a well-conceived and well-operated Sardinian plan cannot fail to be successful.' E. Brennan to General William J. Donovan, 'Emilio Lussu (Emilio Dupont)', 24 August 1943, NARA, RG 226, Entry A1-211, Box 14.
39 Information provided by the SOE Adviser to the Foreign & Common-wealth Office.
40 Ibid.
41 'Lussu's Plan', G. Jebb to F. Nelson, 13 November 1941, TNA HS 6/907.
42 A. Tarchiani to M. Ascoli, 26 June 1944, TNA HS 6/881.
43 A. Tarchiani to M. Ascoli, 3 August 1944, TNA HS 6/881.
44 Information provided by the SOE Adviser to the Foreign & Common-wealth Office.
45 'History of Italian Activities of SOE, 1941–1945', TNA HS 7/58.
46 SOE War Diary, TNA HS 7/262.

6 'More or less a suicide job'

1 E. Newby, *Love and War in the Apennines* (London: Hodder & Stoughton, 1971), p. 14.
2 Captain G. Simpson, 'HMS Una: Patrol Report No. 9 (Including Operation "Why Not"), 9–19 August 1942', 5 September 1942, TNA ADM 236/42.
3 The 48-year-old Hayhurst-France had been a cavalry officer in the First World War, when he had won a Military Cross for galloping along the front to gauge the enemy's strength by being shot at. He had been farming in Essex before he was recalled to service in 1940 and recruited by SOE.
4 SOE Malta to SOE Cairo, 16 August 1942, TNA HS 3/134.
5 Captain G. Simpson, 'HMS Una: Patrol Report No. 9 (Including Operation "Why Not"), 9–19 August 1942', 5 September 1942, TNA ADM 236/42.

6   Newby, *Love and War in the Apennines*, p. 13.

7   Ibid. p. 16.

8   Captain G. Simpson, Remarks on Patrol Report, 5 November 1942, TNA ADM 199/1226.

9   Monthly Log of HM Submarine *Una*, October 1942, TNA ADM 173/17696.

10 Lieutenant C. Norman, Patrol Report, 26 October 1942, TNA ADM 199/1226.

11 Captain G. Simpson, Remarks on Patrol Report, 5 November 1942, TNA ADM 199/1226.

12 'Note on Italy', by Major F. Carver, 18 August 1942, TNA HS 6/889.

13 SOE War Diary, TNA HS 7/237.

14 'GI (b) Report No. 1', Captain O. Gallagher to Major T. G. Roche, 13 June 1944, TNA HS 8/874.

15 Note by Corporal Beaumont, 11 June 1943, TNA 9/1334/4.

16 'Dr Franco Mola', character reference by Major A. Kennedy, 13 December 1944, TNA HS 9/1048/2.

17 H. Boutigny to C. M. Woods, May 1989, private papers of C. M. Woods (hereafter, Woods papers).

18 H. Seton-Watson to T. Masterson, 13 March 1942, Dobrski papers, LHCMA, KCL.

19 'Dr Ulisse Francesco La Terza', TNA HS 9/888/6.

20 Sergeant L. Norris to B7 (Italian Section, SOE Cairo), 1 December 1942, TNA HS 6/896.

21 Ibid.

22 'Draft letter to Gibraltar', 16 December 1942, TNA HS 9/888/6.

23 Cipher telegram, SOE Cairo to SOE London, 7 December 1942, TNA HS 6/896.

24 'Contact with Italy', Z Section (Cairo) to London, 26 March 1942, TNA 6/821; Major F. Carver to Major J. Pearson, 14 May 1942, TNA HS 6/821.

25 Major J. Pearson to Major F. Carver, 7 June 1942, TNA HS 6/821; Major C. Roseberry to Captain J. Dobrski, 22 October 1942, TNA HS 6/821.

26 Ibid.

27 Cipher telegram, Major C. Roseberry to SOE Cairo, 15 May 1942, TNA HS 6/821.

28 L. A. G. Harrop to Major F. Carver, 16 September 1942, TNA HS 6/821.

29 'Report on Psychological Examination of Maltese [*sic*] Student Group', by Major A. Kennedy, 23 October 1942, TNA HS 6/890.

30 Major F. Carver ('Edmund') to London, 16 June 1942, TNA HS 6/889.

31 'Dareme, Pierre Edouard @ [*sic*: 'alias'] Tridondani', report by Captain C. E. Morton, 28 April 1943, TNA HS 9/1483/8.

32 Major F. Carver ('Edmund') to London, 15 August 1942, TNA HS 9/1483/8.

33 Major C. Roseberry to Captain J. Dobrski, 11 September 1942, TNA HS 9/1483/8.

34 Comment by Lance-Corporal Hodson, 13 May 1943, TNA HS 9/1483/8.

35 Tridondani is buried under the name 'Edouard Fredpudan' in field 1A, row 12, grave H. Information from the Salzgitter Memorial Museum archives. I am grateful to Elke Zacharias of the Arbeitskreis Stadtgeschichte e.V study group for her time and assistance in helping me to unearth this information.

36 Major C. Roseberry to Captain J. Dobrski, 19 August 1942, TNA HS 6/889.

37 Ibid.

38 Captain J. Dobrski to SOE London, 8 September 1943, TNA HS 6/889.

39 Major C. Roseberry to Brigadier C. Gubbins, 2 August 1942, TNA HS 6/889.

40 SOE War Diary, TNA HS 7/262.

41 A. Gallo ('Salvatore Mellis') to 'Signor Comandante', 16 July 1942, TNA HS 6/889.

42 L. Mazzotta, responses to questionnaire, 28 May 1944, TNA HS 9/1013.

43 Translation of quotation in M. Franzinelli, *Guerra di spie: i servizi segreti fascisti, nazisti e alleati, 1939–1943* (Milan: Mondadori, 2004), p. 121.

44 Sicily: ISO(S) Handbook, 1943, TNA WO 220/403.

45 Captain P. Cooper to Commander J. Senter, enclosing translations of extracts from a report made by Colonel Mario Bertacchi, 7 August 1944, TNA HS 6/816.

46 Translation of report by Major C. De Leo, 12 November 1942, B.851, F.11993, Records of the Special Tribunal, Archivio Centrale dello Stato, Rome.

47 Ibid. Given the fact that the documents with which Zappalà was caught included British identity cards carrying his photograph and the same cover-name ('Nerces Kenapian') that he had used in East Africa, it is not impossible that the account he gave De Leo and these apparent proofs had been prepared for the event of him falling into Italian hands.

48 Translation of quotation in Franzinelli, *Guerra di spie*, pp. 122–3.

49 Translation of report by Major C. De Leo, 12 November 1942, B.851, F.11993, Records of the Special Tribunal, Archivio Centrale dello Stato, Rome.

50 Ibid.

51 *The Washington Post*, 29 November 1942.

52 See, for example: 'Alleged Saboteurs Executed in Italy', *The Spokesman Review*, 3 December 1942.

53 SOE War Diary, TNA HS 7/262.

54 Ibid.

55 Narrative of the work of SOE's Italian Section by Lieutenant-Colonel C. Roseberry, July 1945, TNA HS 7/58.

56 DNI Memorandum, 4 December 1941, p. 121, TNA ADM 223/851.

57 K. Jeffery, *MI6: The History of the Secret Intelligence Service, 1909–1949* (London: Bloomsbury, 2010), p. 497. Keith Jeffery's few lines on MI6 operations against Fascist Italy make no mention of Zappalà and Gallo.

58 The news was widely published. '2 Spies Executed, Rome Says', reported *The New York Times*. 'London, Nov. 10 (U.P.) – An Italian propaganda broadcast from Rome said today that two men who had landed from a British submarine a month ago to act as spies and saboteurs had been executed. They were identified as Mario [*sic*] and Eugenio [*sic*] Zaccaria of Fiume and were said to have confessed.' *The New York Times*, 11 November 1942. To judge from Italian and SOE records, Amaury and Egon Zaccaria were the two Italian agents whom one MI6 'case-officer' – quoted in Keith Jeffery's *MI6* – would remember as a 'very happy go lucky' pair of ex-POWs who were put ashore on the Tuscan coast in 1942 and never heard of again. Jeffery's text implies that the pair may simply have absconded and gone home. Jeffery, *MI6*, p. 497. Italian sources, however, including reports of the brothers' interrogation, show that the two men should be recorded as committed anti-Fascists who died in the service of the British. For more on the Zaccaria brothers, see: Franzinelli, *Guerra di spie* and G. Peluso, 'Sbarchi a Cuma: Le spie venute dall'Oriente', *Pozzuoli Magazine*, 18 December 2011.

59 Keith Jeffery refers to this agent in *MI6*, stating that the ruse was spotted in time for A Force, a British organisation created to deceive the enemy through imaginative acts of counter-intelligence and subterfuge, to exploit it as part of a 'brilliantly successful deception operation' in the run-up to the Allied invasion of Northwest Africa in November 1942. This success, Jeffery says, was achieved by 'sending the agent "questions and warnings" which implied that Sicily was to be the target rather than North Africa'. Jeffery, *MI6*, p. 497. However, A Force's own records clearly state that MI6 learned of Rossi's capture only in February 1943.

60 'Lilou: Report by Dr V', February 1944, TNA WO 169/24902.

61 'Servizio Informazione Difesa', TNA WO 204/11953.

62 Note by Maresciallo Lo Scalzo, 2 November 1942, in the notebook of Hauptmann Dr Wilhelm Meyer, covering period 22 June 1942 to end July 1943, TNA WO 204/964. The same note refers to the Italians receiving stores and more money dropped by parachute on the occasion of 'the last full moon'.

7 'Rather a scatterbrained project'

1 See, for example, the allegations of Luigi Carissimi-Priori, a former partisan and commander of the political bureau of the Como police, who claimed to have investigated Mussolini's death in 1945, in R. Festorazzi, *Mussolini–Churchill: le carte segrete* (Rome: Datanews, 1998).

2   See, for example, F. Andriola, *Mussolini–Churchill carteggio segreto*
    (Casale Monferrato: Piemme, 1996), and L. Garibaldi, *Mussolini:
    The Secrets of His Death* (New York: Enigma Books, 2004).

3   Garibaldi, *Mussolini*, p. 64. For the latest theorising about Churchill's
    holiday habits, see: R. Festorazzi, *Mistero Churchill: Settembre 1945:
    che cosa cercava sul Lario lo statista inglese? Perché si celava dietro
    l'identità del colonnello Warden?* (Pietro Macchione, 2013).

4   See, for example, Robert L. Miller's introduction to Garibaldi,
    Mussolini, pp. ix–xviii.

5   This is based on a claim made by Bruno Giovanni Lonati, a former
    partisan commander, who, in 1994, declared that he had killed
    Mussolini and had done so at the request of a mysterious British agent
    called John who had personally executed Petacci. Bruno Giovanni
    Lonati, *Quel 28 aprile. Mussolini e Claretta: la verità* (Milan: Mursia,
    1994). Peter Tompkins, a former OSS agent and veteran journalist,
    reasserted Lonati's story in print and claimed to have identified 'John'
    as 'Captain Malcolm Smith, alias Johnson, an officer of the British
    Field Security Service [*sic*]'. P. Tompkins, *Dalle carte segrete del Duce:
    Momenti e protagonisti dell'Italia fascista nei National Archives di
    Washington* (Milan: Marco Tropea, 2001), p. 354. Tompkins again
    repeated Lonati's claims in a documentary broadcast on Italian
    state television in 2004 when the allegation of SOE involvement
    was apparently made explicit. See R. Owen, 'Mussolini killed "on
    Churchill's orders by British agents"', *The Times*, 28 August 2004.

6   Sir Winston S. Churchill quoted in E. G. to Miss Smith, 7 July 1952,
    TNA PREM 11/686. The book to which Churchill was referring was
    the second volume of his history of the Second World War. See W. S.
    Churchill, *The Second World War. Volume II: Their Finest Hour*
    (London: Cassell, 1949), pp. 107–8.

7   See Garibaldi, *Mussolini*, pp. 35–41.

8   Frances Saunders, *The Woman Who Shot Mussolini* (London: Faber
    and Faber, 2010), pp. 309, 225.

9   'Copy of case book entries regarding the Hon. Violet A. Gibson',
    TNA MH 79/262.

10 C. Hibbert, *Benito Mussolini: A Biography* (London: Longmans, 1962),
    p. 77.

11 'History of Emilio [*sic*] Recchioni, of 37 Old Compton Street, Soho',
    22 June 1917, TNA HO 144/18949; 'Copy of Special Branch report dated
    June 15th 1915', TNA HO 144/18949.

12 Minute on Special Branch report, 11 June 1929, TNA HO 144/18949.

13 Report by the Metropolitan Police, 24 April 1934, facsimile reproduced
    in P. Concetti and C. Muzzarelli Formentini, *Max Salvadori: Una vita
    per la Libertà* (Fermo: Andrea Livi Editore, 2008), p. 9.

14 See, for example, S. Pugliese, *Carlo Rosselli: Socialist Heretic and
    Antifascist Exile* (London: Harvard UP, 1999), pp. 187–8.

15 Salvadori, *The Labour and the Wounds*, p. 66.

16 Ibid.

17 Information provided by the SOE Adviser to the Foreign & Common-wealth Office.

18 SOE War Diary, May 1942, TNA HS 7/232.

19 Ibid.

20 Born in Edinburgh, the thirty-year-old Pearson was a six-foot-three Scot, an old boy of Winchester College and a Cambridge graduate, who, before the war, had spent seven years working for Stewarts & Lloyds, a steel manufacturer. SOE files dating from about this time describe him as one of London's best young senior officers, 'really first class . . . but of course with very little knowledge outside our particular work'. 'Major J. S. A. Pearson', Lieutenant-Colonel J. Kennedy to War Office, 10 August 1942, TNA HS 9/1159. Colin Gubbins considered him 'a good sound officer with a clear head & plenty of initiative'. Comment by Major General C. Gubbins on Special Confidential Report, 3 January 1943, TNA HS 9/1159.

21 SOE War Diary, May 1942, TNA HS 7/232.

22 'Five Fascists', *Time*, 6 September 1943.

23 Bosworth, *Mussolini's Italy: Life under the Dictatorship* (London: Allen Lane, 2005), pp. 129, 153.

24 'Black Farinacci', *Time*, 4 February 1929.

25 SOE War Diary, May 1942, TNA HS 7/232.

26 H. Fornari, *Mussolini's Gadfly: Roberto Farinacci* (Nashville, Tenn.: Vanderbilt University Press, 1971), pp. 178–9.

27 F. Taylor (ed.), *The Goebbels Diaries 1939–41* (London: Hamish Hamilton, 1982), p. 127. Interestingly, the Nazis came to consider Farinacci to be a suitably pro-Nazi replacement for the *Duce*. 'The Fuehrer intends to use Farinacci for setting up an Italian counter-government,' Goebbels, his old admirer, recorded in his diary after Mussolini was deposed and Fascism fell in July 1943. Only when Farinacci flew in to speak to them did they have second thoughts. 'Farinacci has arrived,' Goebbels's diary continued. '[He] was received by Ribbentrop and then by the Fuehrer. He behaved very unwisely during these talks. The Fuehrer expected [that] he would express his profound regret at developments and at least stand unreservedly by the Duce. This, however, he did not do. His report to the Fuehrer consisted mainly in severe criticism of the Duce's personality and conduct . . . [T]hat clumsy fool Farinacci . . . [I]t is evident that we cannot use this man on any grand scale . . . Farinacci is a completely broken man.' L. Lochner (ed.), *The Goebbels Diaries* (London: Hamish Hamilton, 1948), pp. 324, 327–9.

28 SOE War Diary, May 1942, TNA HS 7/232.

29 'Descriptive Catalogue of Special Devices and Supplies', TNA HS 7/28.

30 SOE War Diary, May 1942, TNA HS 7/232. Plenty of surviving

documents refer to that surgery in the context of Di Giunta's mission. Jimmy Pearson would describe Di Giunta as 'the fellow who had the facial operation and was going to do a job of work in Italy'. Major J. Pearson to Major C. Roseberry, 5 August 1942 TNA HS 6/821. A few weeks later he referred to Di Giunta's 'job of work' as 'the scheme for the gentleman who had the facial operation'. Major J. Pearson to Major C. Roseberry, 16 September 1942, TNA HS 6/821.

31 SOE War Diary, June 1942, TNA HS 7/234.
32 Ibid.
33 Ronald Turnbull, SA 26754, Sound Archive, Imperial War Museum. Probably of African origin, the ones now given to Di Giunta had been flown from London to Cairo for use by officers there as they saw fit, though it appears that the stones were doled out rarely. 'Cairo have not yet used one single diamond of those I have sent out,' complained a Baker Street finance officer that autumn, '& I have some really good ones waiting for a proper home.' Captain F. Snow to Major J. Pearson, 13 September 1942, inked annotation to Lord Glenconner to Major J. Pearson, 7 September 1942, TNA HS 3/122.
34 Entry, 18 February 1943, War Diary of No. 321 POW Camp, TNA WO 169/6768.
35 Major J. Pearson to Major C. Roseberry, 16 September 1942, TNA HS 6/821.
36 SOE War Diary, May 1942, TNA HS 7/232.
37 M. Seaman, Introduction to *Operation Foxley: The British Plan to Kill Hitler* (London: PRO, 1998), pp. 28–9.
38 Birth and family registers, Troina town archives.
39 Ibid.
40 'Register of deleted records', Troina town archives.
41 Author's interview in Troina, 7 November 2012.
42 'Register of deleted records', Troina town archives.

8 'An ideal subversive organisation'

1 G. Taylor to G. Jebb, 'Italy', 8 December 1941, TNA HS 6/901.
2 H. Seton-Watson, 'SOE Work in Southern Italy and Sicily', 17 February 1942, Dobrski papers.
3 'Appreciation of Situation in Sicily as in November 1942 with a view to Subversive Operations in that Country', Dobrski papers, KCL.
4 P. Dixon to Captain F. C. Benn, MI3c, War Office, 3 February 1941, TNA HS 6/901.
5 Cipher telegram, SOE Cairo 'to ACSS only' [London], 22 November 1941, HS 6/901.
6 SOE War Diary, TNA HS 7/226.
7 Decades after the war, many authors and historians still adhered to the story that imprisoned members of the US-based Mafia had been

instrumental in crucially smoothing the Allied conquest of Sicily in the summer of 1943. These mobsters, according to one writer, 'saw collaboration as a means of winning personal favour and freedom as well as of helping their compatriots to throw off the restricting shackles of fascism'. The most famous Mafia boss alleged to have helped was 'Lucky' Luciano, 'whose insignia – a yellow handkerchief marked with the letter L – fluttered from the allied invasion tanks as they headed, per instructions, for the small town of Villalba and Don Calogerò [sic] Vizzini, head of the Sicilian mafia. Thanks to Vizzini and the orders sent through his chain of command, Sicily was occupied almost bloodlessly within days.' A. Jamieson, 'Mafia and Political Power 1943–1989', International Affairs, 10/13, 1990, p. 13. A glance at the casualty figures and at the cemeteries in Sicily is enough to demonstrate that the battle was in fact very far from bloodless (American, British and Canadian forces lost more than 20,000 men killed and wounded as they cleared the island; Axis losses were even higher), while consensus is growing that no evidence exists of any American deal with the Mafia over Sicily or, for that matter, any decided plan for securing Mafia assistance with the invasion. Though still widely believed, the tale of advancing tanks adorned with 'L'-embroidered handkerchiefs is emblematic of post-war Mafia-themed mythology. 'The endless retellings of the episode have painted a thick crust of apocryphal conviction over it,' John Dickie has written, 'blurring its detail in some places, building up hardened swirls of pure invention in others. Most historians now dismiss it as fable.' J. Dickie, Cosa Nostra: A History of the Sicilian Mafia (London: Hodder, 2007), p. 237. This is not to say that there was no co-operation. The Office of Naval Intelligence does seem to have sought intelligence and contacts from the American Mafia and, in July 1943, a four-man ONI team accompanying the landings did get in touch with a few repatriated Sicilian-American criminals whose names had been passed along by contacts in New York. 'They were extremely co-operative and helpful because they spoke both the dialect of that region and also some English,' remembered Paul Alfieri, one of the team's officers. R. Campbell, The Luciano Project, The Secret Wartime Collaboration of the Mafia and the US Navy (New York: McGraw-Hill, 1977), p. 176. It would be hard to argue, however, that the ONI team and its local Sicilian-American contacts, which did gather some useful naval intelligence along the coast, had any discernible impact on the more decisive campaign inland. 'By far the larger contribution was provided by the US Army Counter-Intelligence Corps,' as Tim Newark has written, 'who had eighty agents on the ground throughout the fighting. However, there is no evidence whatsoever of any kind of alliance between them and the Mafia in Sicily before or during the campaign.' T. Newark, 'Pact With the Devil?', History Today, 57/4, 2007.

8   See, for example, Campbell, *The Luciano Project*; S. Lupo, 'The Allies and the Mafia', *Journal of Modern Italian Studies*, 2:1, 1997, pp. 21–33; M. Finkelstein, *Separatism, the Allies and the Mafia: The Struggle for Sicilian Independence 1943–1948* (Cranbury: Lehigh University Press, 1998); T. Newark, *The Mafia at War: Allied Collusion with the Mob* (London: Greenhill Books, 2007); E. Costanzo, *The Mafia and the Allies: Sicily 1943 and the Return of the Mafia* (London: Greenhill Books, 2007).

9   SOE War Diary, TNA HS 7/226.

10 SOE War Diary, TNA HS 7/265.

11 SOE War Diary, TNA HS 7/226.

12 Today, serious historians of organised crime in the United States doubt some of the tales of the *Unione Siciliana*'s criminality. For brief modern studies, see, for example: D. Critchley, *The Origin of Organized Crime in America: The New York City Mafia, 1891–1931* (Oxford: Routledge, 2009), pp. 46–50, 208–10; and J. Fentress, *Eminent Gangsters: Immigrants and the Birth of Organized Crime in America* (Lanham, MD: University Press of America, 2010), pp. 112–13.

13 M. Salvadori, 'Reply to questionnaire concerning political conditions in Sicily', 15 July 1942, Salvadori papers.

14 'Appreciation of Situation in Sicily as at the end of December 1942 with a view to Subversive Operations in that Country', Dobrski papers, KCL.

15 Ibid.

16 M. Corvo, *The OSS in Italy, 1942–1945: A Personal Memoir* (New York: Praeger, 1990), p. 22. After the Sicily landings took place, however, OSS did begin to work with local Mafia members.

17 Dobrski had joined SOE in London in the summer of 1940. Born Giulio Giuliano Augusto Dobrski in Genoa in 1901, he was the son of an Italian-Irish mother and a father whose forebears had left Poland for Italy in the late eighteenth century. Brought up in Italy, France, Belgium, Switzerland and Spain, Dobrski spoke fluent Italian, French and English, had a degree from the University of Lyons and had served for two years as a junior officer in the Italian Army before coming to Britain in 1928, working thereafter in the City as a director of Lyons Silks Limited. Naturalised British in August 1939, he joined SOE with an introduction from René Pleven, a future French Prime Minister with whom he had been at school. Dobrski spent several months working in London on Italian matters, helping look for likely agents in various corners of the British Isles and keeping an eye on Italian students during training. Later, as a commissioned British Army officer with the name of Julian Anthony Dolbey, he was sent to the Mediterranean where he helped run an SOE office on Malta before eventually taking charge of Cairo's Italian desk. 'Very much a man of the world,' reads a short report on him from 1941. 'Quick and capable mind. Rather argumentative.' Comments of the commandant of the Beaulieu training

area, 25 September 1941, TNA HS 9/437/4.

18 Author's interview in Troina, 7 November 2012.

19 'List of Members of the Mafia', 6 August 1942, Dobrski papers, KCL. An alternative explanation might be that the two *marchesi* could have been involved in some way with another secret society active in Sicily: the Freemasons.

20 Ibid. Another name apparently provided by Di Giunta was that of a lawyer called Villa, said to be 'Chief of the Rome region'.

21 The testimony of Antonio Calderone, a former member of *Cosa Nostra* from Catania, provides rare and interesting insight into the history and workings of the Mafia in eastern Sicily. According to Calderone, who had been born in 1935 and became one of the most important repentants – or *pentiti* as they are known – after his arrest in 1986, *Cosa Nostra* in Palermo had authorised the creation of the first Mafia 'family' in Catania, by a group of 10 to 15 *uomini d'onore* ('men of honour'), in 1925. P. Arlacchi, 'Mafia: The Sicilian Cosa Nostra', *South European Society and Politics*, 1/1, 1996, p. 77. The next family was apparently created only in the 1950s. Calderone describes the Ferraras, to whom he also refers as the 'Cavadduzzi' and whose forebears included a certain 'man of honor . . . nicknamed "Cavadduzzo"', as an established criminal family, 'a real clan', which rose to become part of 'the cream of the Catanian Mafia'. P. Arlacchi, *Men of Dishonor: Inside the Sicilian Mafia: An Account of Antonio Calderone* (New York: William Morrow & Co., 1993), pp. 45, 65, 118. For more on post-war Ferrara/Cavadduzzo criminality and Mafia activity in Catania in general, see: C. Fava, *La mafia comanda a Catania 1960–1991* (Rome/Bari: Laterza, 1991).

22 'List of Members of the Mafia', 6 August 1942, Dobrski papers, KCL.

23 This was in a famous report by Ermanno Sangiorgi, chief of the Palermo police, in 1900. S. Lupo, *History of the Mafia* (New York: Columbia University Press, 2009), p. 213.

24 SOE War Diary, TNA HS 7/237.

9 'Things seem to be going according to plan . . .'

1 J. McCaffery, 'No Pipes or Drums'.

2 'Interference with Italian Railway Communications: Extracts from Paper prepared by Railway Research Service, dated 30 August 1940', TNA HS 6/1010.

3 Minute, Prime Minister to Secretary of State for Air and the Minister of Economic Warfare, 26 January 1941, TNA HS 6/1010.

4 J. McCaffery to Sir Frank Nelson, 27 March 1941, TNA HS 6/1006.

5 Information provided by the SOE Adviser to the Foreign & Commonwealth Office.

6 J. McCaffery to Sir Frank Nelson, 27 March 1941, TNA HS 6/1006.

7   Information provided by the SOE Adviser to the Foreign & Common-
    wealth Office.
8   'Work into Germany from Switzerland', by R. [*sic*] Jellinek, *c.* 1945,
    TNA HS 7/145.
9   Information provided by the SOE Adviser to the Foreign & Common-
    wealth Office.
10 J. McCaffery to Sir Frank Nelson, 24 April 1941, TNA HS 6/1006.
11 J. McCaffery to Sir Frank Nelson, 27 March 1941, TNA HS 6/1006.
12 J. McCaffery to Sir Frank Nelson, 24 April 1941, TNA HS 6/1006.
13 'Report from JQ', 9 October 1941, TNA HS 6/1005.
14 This was the story that Silone told in January 1943 to G. M. Mayer,
    an associate of Allen Dulles, the newly arrived representative in
    Switzerland of the OSS. Silone 'spoke very bitterly about John
    McCaffery (Assistant Press Attaché, British Legation, Bern)', Mayer
    noted. Memorandum, G. M. Mayer to Mr A. W. Dulles, 8 January 1943,
    NARA RG 226, Entry 125, Box 8, Folder 124, (Bern – OSS).
15 Handwritten note, undated (but probably *c.* February 1943), NARA
    RG 226, Entry 125, Box 8, Folder 124.
16 Note by C. M. Woods on conversation with Peter Jellinek, June 1992,
    Woods papers.
17 J. McCaffery to Sir Frank Nelson, 24 April 1941, TNA HS 6/1006.
18 SOE War Diary, TNA HS 7/262.
19 J. McCaffery to SOE London, 17 April 1942, TNA HS 6/1005.
20 J. McCaffery to G. K. Logie, 30 January 1941, TNA HS 6/884.
21 Report by J. Dobrski, 15 April 1941, TNA HS 6/884.
22 Lieutenant-Colonel S. H. C. Woolrych to Commandant, 30 April 1941,
    TNA HS 6/884.
23 Captain P. Cooper to Ensign M. Sample, 5 September 1944, TNA
    HS 9/1311.
24 SOE War Diary, TNA HS 7/230.
25 Captain P. Cooper to Ensign M. Sample, 5 September 1944, TNA
    HS 9/1311.
26 Cipher telegram, Major C. Roseberry to SOE Cairo, 4 June 1942,
    TNA HS 9/1311.
27 Cipher telegram, Major C. Roseberry to SOE Cairo, 10 June 1942,
    TNA HS 9/1311.
28 'Brief read by Rossi,' 2 October 1942, TNA HS 9/1311.
29 G. Sarfatti to Flight Lieutenant H. G. Crawshaw, October 1942, TNA
    HS 9/1311. Written when he and his companions were about to embark
    on the last sea-bound leg to France, Sarfatti's letter also provides an
    interesting glimpse of how Odette Sansom was seen by some of her
    peers. '[T]he three women, except the eldest one, have been rather
    annoying on the whole,' he wrote. 'The youngest one [Sansom] is
    enough to drive anybody crazy. Anyhow she gets nice and sick quite
    easily, so she will be quiet.' Cecil Roseberry passed a copy of that

note to Maurice Buckmaster, head of SOE's F Section. Buckmaster underlined the penultimate sentence and wrote: 'We thought so too!!' M. Buckmaster, pencil annotation to C. Roseberry to M. Buckmaster, 12 November 1943, TNA HS 9/1311.

30   SOE War Diary, TNA HS 7/262.

31   Cipher telegram, SOE Berne to SOE London, 19 December 1942, TNA HS 9/1311.

32   Information provided by the SOE Adviser to the Foreign & Commonwealth Office.

33   SIM report No. 82385, 27 August 1943, NARA RG 226, Entry 174, Box 229, Folder 66 (1350).

34   P. Jellinek to C. M. Woods, 12 May 1992, Woods papers.

35   Petitioner's statement, 5 September 1934, TNA J 77/3332/1751.

36   'Report from JQ', 2 October 1941, TNA HS 6/1005.

37   SOE War Diary, TNA HS 7/221.

38   SOE War Diary, TNA HS 7/222. Roseberry had even wondered in London whether McCaffery should be replaced. He had been reading the files, he explained in October 1941, and had noted that 'results so far achieved were disappointing'. This could be due to 'McCaffery's policy of advancing slowly', Roseberry thought, but his channels appeared 'to be capable of development . . . [He] had not done enough in recruiting individuals or in establishing safe houses.' SOE War Diary, TNA HS 7/221.

39   By the end of the year, McCaffery was being instructed by London 'that SOE material could be used in Italy by Pellegrini, [the] Tigrotti or anybody else, without restriction as to targets'. SOE War Diary, TNA HS 7/224. In February 1942, on the eve of the momentous first delivery of a suitcase of stores to Milan, McCaffery told London that he wanted more time to ensure that every link in the chain was secure. London told him to press on. Risks were 'always attendant on such operations', he was told, while 'a start must be made and moreover the Tigrotti might lose confidence if the opportunity were missed'. SOE War Diary, HS 7/265.

40   SIM reports, 7 and 27 March 1941, NARA RG 226, Entry 174, Box 201, Folder 8 (H) (1292).

41   '2-Schwerd [sic]', undated note, NARA RG 226, Entry 174, Box 224, Folder 55 (D).

42   SIM summary report on the British 'I.S.' (Intelligence Service) in Switzerland, with covering note dated 14 August 1941, NARA RG 226, Entry 174, Box 202, Folder 10 (G) (1294).

43   SIM report No. 81924, 26 October 1941, NARA RG 226, Entry 174, Box 220, Folder 48 (K). Schwerdt's excesses may help explain why several Italian reports describe him as 'old' and one estimated his age at fifty when he was still only thirty-nine. '1.65m tall, wrinkled bony face, thick reddish eyebrows, reddish-blond hair mixed with grey,'

one report adds. 'He has stated that he is divorced and has children in London. He plays the piano a lot, also composes music and is writing a novel.' SIM report No. 82283, 9 June 1943, NARA RG 226, Entry 174, Box 221, Folder 49 (A).

44 SIM report No. 81175, 21 February 1942, NARA RG 226, Entry 174, Box 220, Folder 48 (K).

45 Ibid.

46 Annex No. 3 to SIM report No. 81175, 21 February 1942, NARA RG 226, Entry 174, Box 220, Folder 48 (K).

47 SIM report No. 81175, 21 February 1942, NARA RG 226, Entry 174, Box 220, Folder 48 (K).

48 'Preliminary Interrogation Report on Osteria, Ugo Luca, Alias Parodi, Giovanni', 15 March 1945, TNA HS 6/823.

49 'Translation of a report (undated) made to Rossi [J. McCaffery] by Ugo', TNA HS 6/823.

50 Ibid.

51 Ibid.

52 This was not the only curious incident that came to the attention of the British and could have justified deeper investigation. Possibly the most significant was a warning passed along by MI6 in London to SOE in July 1942 that the Tigrotti were 'in the hands of the Fascists'. SOE War Diary, TNA HS 7/262. When SOE asked for the source of that information, MI6 replied simply that it came from a report received from France. Available files suggest that little if any effort was expended in exploring the report further.

53 'Translation of a report (undated) made to Rossi [J. McCaffery] by Ugo', TNA HS 6/823.

54 SOE War Diary, TNA HS 7/238.

55 'Translation of a report (undated) made to Rossi [J. McCaffery] by Ugo', TNA HS 6/823.

56 Cipher telegram, J. McCaffery to SOE London, 12 May 1943, TNA HS 6/901.

57 SIM report No. 81126, 22 March 1944, NARA RG 226, Entry 174, Box 208, Folder 23 (1307). On behalf of the British, Cavadini delivered suitcases of explosives and other supplies to a socialist lawyer in Chiasso called Giuseppe Borella whose activities the OVRA was controlling. These supplies included, to quote from Italian documents, 'packets of inert gunpowder to sabotage train wagons and switchblades to cut car tyres'. SIM, too, appears to have run Cavadini for a while. Eventually, however, Italian counter-espionage officers came to doubt his loyalty and had him arrested. By then the Wolves had successfully requested a drop of stores into Lake Garda. SOE agreed to arrange it and six watertight containers were duly dropped from an RAF Halifax flying from Blida, in Algeria, on the night of 15/16 July.

58 'Interrogation report on Klein, Eligio', 11 June 1945, TNA HS 6/809.

59 SIM report, 31 March 1942, NARA RG 226, Entry 174, Box 178, Folder 28 (1243).

60 'Interrogation report on Klein, Eligio', 11 June 1945, TNA HS 6/809.

61 Interrogation report on Eligio Klein, 15 October 1945, NARA RG 226, Entry 215, Box 4.

62 Information provided by the SOE Adviser to the Foreign & Commonwealth Office.

63 SOE War Diary, TNA HS 7/262.

64 'Elenco del materiale contenuto nei recipienti metallici lanciati dall'aereo nemico la notte dal 13 al 14 aprile 1943 sul Lago di Viverone (Vercelli)', 18 April 1943, NARA RG 226, Entry 174, Box 236, Folder 5 (1361).

65 A. Croft, *A Talent for Adventure* (Hanley Swan, Worcs: Self Publishing Association, 1991).

66 'Report on Operation "Burrow"', by Captain A. R. McClair, included in 'H.M. Submarine "Seraph" – Report on Patrol', 15 September 1943, TNA ADM 199/1345.

67 SOE War Diary, TNA HS 7/232.

68 SIM report No. 81539, 19 May 1942, NARA RG 226, Entry 174, Box 237, Folder 6 (B) (1362).

69 SIM report, 2 June 1942, NARA RG 226, Entry 174, Box 237, Folder 6 (B) (1362).

70 'Azione di doppio gioco verso l'I.S. (Elda–Giusto)', SIM report No. 33408, 31 December 1942, NARA RG 226, Entry 174, Box 221, Folder 49 (A).

71 'Azione di doppio gioco verso l'I.S. (Elda–Giusto)', SIM report No. 33122, 26 December 1942, NARA RG 226, Entry 174, Box 221, Folder 49 (A).

72 'Relazione' by E. Klein ('Almerigotti'), 30 December 1942, NARA RG 226, Entry 174, Box 221, Folder 49 (A).

73 Ibid.

74 'Azione di doppio gioco verso l'I.S. (Elda–Giusto)', SIM report No. 33122, 26 December 1942, NARA RG 226, Entry 174, Box 221, Folder 49 (A).

75 'Azione "E–G"', SIM report 2087, 12 February 1943, NARA RG 226, Entry 174, Box 221, Folder 49 (A).

76 Ibid.

77 'Part 2. Mission E/G', 11 August 1944, TNA HS 9/9/3.

78 Interrogation report of Eligio Klein, 15 October 1945, NARA RG 226, Entry 215, Box 4.

10 'As much alarm as possible'

1 Report by Leading Seaman F. R. Taylor, TNA HS 6/877.

2 McGeoch's report also explains the submarine's temporary dis-

appearance: '0540 [hours]. Boat had not returned, but it was necessary to dive for the dawn.' Patrol Report, 25 January 1943, TNA ADM 199/1838.

3   Interrogation report on Salvatore Serra, 27 May 1945, TNA HS 9/1343/1.
4   History Sheet, TNA HS 9/1343/1.
5   C. Mackenzie to SOE London, 16 February 1942, TNA HS 9/1343/1.
6   Report by F. Jackson, 10 March 1942, TNA HS 9/1343/1.
7   Report by Corporal Morris, 25 March 1942, TNA HS 9/1343/1.
8   Report by Corporal Saunders, 2 April 1942, TNA HS 9/1343/1.
9   Report by Corporal Saunders, 10 April 1942, TNA HS 9/1343/1.
10 Report by Corporal Saunders, 30 April 1942, TNA HS 9/1343/1.
11 Report by Corporal Saunders, 22 May 1942, TNA HS 9/1343/1.
12 Report, 22 June 1942, TNA HS 9/1343/1.
13 Report, 5 July 1942, TNA HS 9/1343/1.
14 Report, 16 August 1942, TNA HS 9/1343/1.
15 Report, 25 September 1942, TNA HS 9/1343/1.
16 Report by Sergeant Garvin, 19 February 1942, TNA HS 9/9/3.
17 Report by Sergeant Garvin, 6 March 1942, TNA HS 9/9/3.
18 Report by Sergeant Garvin, 26 February 1942, TNA HS 9/9/3.
19 Report by Sergeant Garvin, 6 March 1942, TNA HS 9/9/3.
20 Note by Major C. Roseberry to Major-General J. H. F. Lakin, 23 November 1942, TNA HS 9/9/3.
21 L. Valiani, *Tutte le strade conducone a Roma* (Bologna: Il Mulino, 1983), p. 30.
22 SOE War Diary, HS 7/236.
23 Interview with I. McGeoch, SA 9859, Imperial War Museum.
24 'Appendix 'O' to Patrol Report M.3 of the Commanding Officer, H.M. Submarine "P.228"', undated, by Lieutenant I. McGeoch, TNA ADM 199/1344.
25 Major C. Roseberry to 'D/Navy', 10 February 1943, TNA HS 6/877.
26 Appendix 'O' to Patrol Report M.3 of the Commanding Officer, H.M. Submarine "P.228"', undated, by Lieutenant I. McGeoch, TNA ADM 199/1344.
27 Major C. Roseberry to 'D/Navy', 10 February 1943, TNA HS 6/877. Three months later, on its sixth patrol, by then renamed *Splendid*, *P.228* became one of the forty Royal Navy submarines lost in the Mediterranean (and one of ten destroyed between November 1942 and May 1943) when it was depth-charged off Capri and forced to the surface. As the attacking German destroyer set about finishing the job, its gunfire killed eighteen of McGeoch's forty-eight-strong crew as they emerged from the conning tower and jumped into the sea. Ian McGeoch, *An Affair of Chances: A Submariner's Odyssey 1939–44* (London: Imperial War Museum, 1991).
28 Message No. 1 to Moselle, 22 February 1943, in 'Copy of Messages to and from Avocat', TNA WO 169/24902. 'Moselle' was the SOE

codename for the wireless link to Adler's set. 'Avocat' was the mission's codename.

29 Letter of 12 January 1943 quoted in 'Extract from "Section II – Part I – Parachutists"', August 1944, TNA HS 9/9/3.

30 'Activities of Italian Counter-Espionage prior to September, 1943 – Source: Col. Mario Bertacchi', July 1944, TNA HS 9/9/3.

31 'Interrogation Report on Faccio, Cesare', 19 March 1945, TNA HS 9/1343/1.

32 Ibid.

33 'Interrogation Report on Sergeant Major Silvestri', 17 February 1945, TNA HS 6/877.

34 'Annex Nr. 1' to 'Report on a mission performed in Sardinia from July to September 1943', 23 September 1943, NARA RG 226, Entry 190, Box 90, Folder 32.

35 'Interrogation Report on Sergeant Major Silvestri', 17 February 1945, TNA HS 6/877.

36 Ibid.

37 'Part 1. Action S/A', 11 August 1944, TNA HS 9/9/3.

38 Message No. 3 from Moselle, received 26 February 1943, in 'Copy of Messages to and from Avocat', TNA WO 169/24902.

39 'Moselle', Major Phillips to Colonel Nicholls, 27 February 1943, TNA HS 6/877.

40 'Second Interrogation of Prisoner of War Bergadano', 8 March 1943, TNA HS 6/877.

41 Extract from CSDIC report, 4 March 1943, TNA HS 6/877.

42 Extract from CSDIC report, 3 March 1943, TNA HS 6/877.

43 Cipher telegram, Major C. Roseberry to Massingham, 26 February 1943, TNA HS 6/877.

44 SOE War Diary, TNA HS 7/262.

45 Message No. 12 to Moselle, 28 April 1943, in 'Copy of Messages to and from Avocat', TNA WO 169/24902.

46 Message No. 20 from Moselle, received 1 May 1943, in 'Copy of Messages to and from Avocat', TNA WO 169/24902.

47 Message No. 21 from Moselle, received 7 May 1943, in 'Copy of Messages to and from Avocat', TNA WO 169/24902.

48 'Minutes of the 37 Committee Meeting held on Friday, 14.5.43', TNA WO 169/24888.

49 SOE War Diary, TNA HS 7/263.

50 'Minutes of the 37 Committee Meeting held on Friday, 7.5.43', TNA WO 169/24888.

51 Message No. 23 to Moselle, 3 June 1943, TNA WO 169/24902.

52 Message No. 25 to Moselle, 11 June 1943, TNA WO 169/24902.

53 Message No. 23 from Moselle, received 12 May 1943, in 'Copy of Messages to and from Avocat', TNA WO 169/24902.

54 Message No. 28 from Moselle, received 8 June 1943, TNA WO 169/24902.

55 Message No. 30 from Moselle, received 30 June 1943, TNA WO 169/24902.
56 Cipher telegram, Major C. Roseberry to Massingham, 6 May 1943, TNA HS 6/877.
57 Report by Major A. Kennedy, 20 October 1942, TNA HS 6/890.
58 Report by Lieutenant F. Basett, 15 April 1943, TNA HS 9/1013.
59 SOE War Diary, TNA HS 7/263.
60 Cipher telegram, Major C. Roseberry to SOE Algiers, 11 May 1943, TNA HS 6/877.
61 Sortie report, 16/17 July 1943, TNA AIR 20/8352.
62 A Force Narrative War Diary, 1 January to 31 December 1943, TNA CAB 154/3.
63 'You should now speed up your plans for the organisation of local sympathisers,' read one in early August. 'It is imperative that you keep in constant touch with us from now onwards,' added another the next day. Messages No. 33 and 35 to Moselle, 4 and 5 August 1943, in 'Moselle Traffic', TNA WO 169/24902. Algiers also sent a 'questionnaire' designed to draw 'Italian smoke'. 'Minutes of 40 Committee Meeting held on 13th Aug. 1943', TNA WO 169/24888. 'We urgently require further information on the following points,' Sardinia was told. 'What areas are forbidden to civilians? Which beaches suitable for large scale operations are mined or wired? What other means of defence are there? By what strength of troops are the beaches held? Description of any fixed coastal defences including type and calibre of weapons. State of alertness on all defences . . .' Message No. 36 to Moselle, 5 August 1943, in 'Moselle Traffic', TNA WO 169/24902.
64 Cipher telegram, SOE London to SOE Algiers, 14 June 1943, TNA HS 6/877.
65 Message No. 34 to Moselle, 4 August 1943, in 'Moselle Traffic', TNA WO 169/24902.
66 'Minutes of 40 Committee Meeting held on 27.8.43', TNA WO 169/24888.
67 Message No. 42 to Moselle, 30 August 1943, in 'Moselle Traffic', TNA WO 169/24902.
68 Message No. 44 to Moselle, 3 September 1943, in 'Moselle Traffic', TNA WO 169/24902.
69 Message No. 45 to Moselle, 6 September 1943, in 'Moselle Traffic', TNA WO 169/24902.
70 'Part 1. Action S/A', 11 August 1944, TNA HS 9/9/3.
71 A Force Narrative War Diary, 1 January to 31 December 1943, TNA CAB 154/3.
72 Abwehr Operational Material, No. 832, 13 August 1943, TNA CAB 154/77.
73 Abwehr Operational Material, No. 833, 13 August 1943, TNA CAB 154/77.

74 'Annex Nr. 1' to 'Report on a mission performed in Sardinia from July to September 1943', 23 September 1943, NARA RG 226, Entry 190, Box 90, Folder 32.

75 Lieutenant-Colonel C. Roseberry to Commander J. Senter, 6 March 1945, TNA HS 6/877.

76 A Force Narrative War Diary, 1 January to 31 December 1943, TNA CAB 154/3.

77 'Activities of Italian Counter-Espionage prior to September, 1943 – Source: Col. Mario Bertacchi', July 1944, TNA HS 9/9/3.

78 'Interrogation Report on Faccio, Cesare', 19 March 1945, TNA HS 9/1343/1.

79 'Interrogation Report on Sergeant-Major Silvestri', 17 February 1945, TNA HS 6/877.

80 Ibid.

81 Cipher telegram, Major C. Roseberry to Squadron Leader H. G. Crawshaw, 12 May 1943, TNA HS 6/877.

82 Information provided by the SOE Adviser to the Foreign & Commonwealth Office.

83 Messages Nos. 2 and 3 from Moselle, received 22 and 26 February 1943, in 'Copy of Messages to and from Avocat', TNA WO 169/24902.

84 Message No. 2 to Moselle, sent 27 February 1943, in 'Copy of Messages to and from Avocat', TNA WO 169/24902.

85 'Activities of Italian Counter-Espionage prior to September, 1943 – Source: Col. Mario Bertacchi', July 1944, TNA HS 9/9/3.

86 Ibid.

87 'Interrogation report on Sergeant-Major Silvestri', 17 February 1945, TNA HS 6/877.

88 Sources agree that Scamaroni committed suicide, but James Hutchison, an RF Section officer who investigated his death, felt the more lurid stories were untrue. In October 1943, Hutchison travelled to Corsica 'and during my visit there I made numerous enquiries as to the fate of my friend Scameroni [sic]. There is no doubt that he committed suicide in prison, but it was by hanging himself and the stories of extreme torture are probably exaggerated. I interviewed and obtained this information from his uncle and aunt who had seen his body.' Pencil annotation in 'RF Section History 1943–1944', Volume Two, TNA HS 7/124. I am grateful to Nigel Perrin for bringing this to my attention.

89 M. Cobb, *The Resistance: The French Fight Against the Nazis* (London: Simon & Schuster, 2009), pp. 189–90.

90 Report by Corporal Mangeolles, 23 April 1942, TNA HS 9/690/3.

91 'Sea Urchin', report by C. H. Harmer to Colonel Robertson, 11 April 1943, TNA KV 6/12.

92 'They have been taken and have "sold me",' Hellier is alleged to have said. 'I've waited 24 hours before speaking, hoping everyone would get clear, and now in my turn I have "sold" everything.' 'RF Section

History 1943–1944', Volume Two, TNA HS 7/124.

93 V. Sias, *Il controspionaggio italiano in Sardegna e Corsica (1943)* (S'Alvure, 1991).

11 'The Explosive Topo Lads'

1   'Action in Corsica, Sardinia, Sicily and Italy', Major General W. Smith to Commanding Officer ISSU-6, 9 February 1943, TNA WO 204/10240.
2   'Special Operations Executive Directive for 1943', Chiefs of Staff memorandum, 20 March 1943, TNA CAB 80/68.
3   SOE War Diary, TNA HS 7/237.
4   Corvo, *OSS in Italy*, p. 73.
5   SOE War Diary, TNA HS 7/264.
6   H. Hargreaves, interview No. 12158, IWM Sound Archive. Another of Munthe's wireless operators remarked forty years later that 'if he turned up tomorrow looking for my services, I'd follow him without hesitation'. 'Brief Record', by D. A. MacDonell, Woods papers.
7   Ibid.
8   Report by Major M. Munthe, March 1944, Woods papers.
9   SOE War Diary, TNA HS 7/264.
10 Report by Major M. Munthe, March 1944, Woods papers. In his memoirs, Munthe would write – incorrectly – that he and his team landed with the Camerons on the opening day of the invasion. M. Munthe, *Sweet is War* (London: Duckworth 1954), p. 162.
11 Report by Major M. Munthe, March 1944, Woods papers.
12 Ibid.
13 'Brief record', by D. A. MacDonell, Woods papers.
14 Report by Major M. Munthe, March 1944, Woods papers.
15 H. Hargreaves, interview No. 12158, IWM Sound Archive.
16 Munthe, *Sweet is War*, p. 162.
17 Report by Major M. Munthe, March 1944, Woods papers.
18 Ibid.
19 Unpublished reminiscences of Captain Peter Cooper, 1985, P. M. Lee papers, Imperial War Museum.
20 In all and at various times, five volunteered their services. Three of these, Leo Valiani, Renato Pierleoni and Giuseppe Petacchi, went on to undertake important operations in Italy after the Armistice.
21 'Notes on American Organisations and Personnel', 1943, TNA HS 7/76.
22 Information provided by the SOE Adviser to the Foreign & Commonwealth Office.
23 Salvadori, *The Labour and the Wounds*, pp. 145–6.
24 A moving account of Arthur Galletti's short life, drawing on two trunks' worth of correspondence with his wife, has been published by their daughter, Annette Moat: *On Two Fronts: A Soldier's Life of Travel, Love and War* (Long Riders' Guild Press, 2007).

25 Major C. Roseberry to P. Dixon, 21 July 1943, TNA HS 6/879.

26 'Nekic, Branko', comments dated May 1942, TNA HS 9/1091.

27 SOE War Diary, TNA HS 7/268.

28 SOE War Diary, TNA HS 7/237.

29 SOE War Diary, TNA HS 7/264.

30 Munthe, *Sweet is War*, p. 164.

31 Information provided by the SOE Adviser to the Foreign & Commonwealth Office.

32 H. Hargreaves, interview No. 12158, IWM Sound Archive.

33 Salvadori, *The Labour and the Wounds*, p. 155.

34 Report by Major M. Munthe, March 1944, Woods papers.

35 Salvadori, *The Labour and the Wounds*, p. 159.

36 M. Salvadori to C. M. Woods, 25 February 1990, Woods papers.

37 Report by Major M. Munthe, March 1944, Woods papers.

38 Ibid. Today it is apparent that 'Professor Canepa' was Antonio Canepa, a strident Sicilian separatist who had been appointed Professor of the History of Political Thought at the University of Catania in 1937. Drawing on sources that include the travel-writer Norman Lewis's *The Honoured Society: The Mafia Conspiracy Observed* (London: Collins, 1964), some post-war studies of Canepa, who was killed in a shoot-out with the Sicilian police in June 1945, have claimed that he was in contact with British Intelligence before the Sicily landings and, with some of his students, co-operated with a British raiding party on an attack on the German airfield at Gerbini in June 1943. There is even a claim that he may have made three trips to London. See Finkelstein, *Separatism, the Allies and the Mafia*, pp. 21–2. So far as SOE is concerned, it seems from its records that the first it ever heard of Canepa was from Munthe's 'wizened' journalist in July 1943.

39 Report by Major M. Munthe, March 1944, Woods papers.

40 Ibid.

41 Ibid.

42 Salvadori, *The Labour and the Wounds*, p. 156.

43 'Brief record', by D. A. MacDonell, Woods papers.

44 A. R. Cooper, *The Adventures of a Secret Agent* (London: Frederick Muller, 1957), p. 191.

45 Report by Major M. Munthe, March 1944, Woods papers. The enterprising Gallegos had been the first SOE officer to set foot in Sicily. Briefed to requisition any available local craft that might be suitable for SOE use, he had contrived on 10 July to hitch a lift on a landing craft from Tripoli to Malta, which the tired Canadian crew were glad to allow him to navigate but omitted to tell him about the mine-swept approach to Malta's Grand Harbour. He then secured a passage from Malta to Siracusa on a motor-torpedo-boat, arriving on 16 July. Although he had to return to Malta the next day, his time ashore was sufficient for him to find a rat-infested schooner, the *Gilfredo*, which in

subsequent months and with an SOE crew was to see valuable service ferrying arms and men all over the Mediterranean.

46 Report by Major M. Munthe, March 1944, Woods papers.
47 Ibid.
48 Ibid.
49 SOE War Diary, TNA HS 7/264.
50 Report by Major M. Munthe, March 1944, Woods papers.
51 'Moro, Attilio', note by Sergeant E. Saunders, undated but *c.* 1945, TNA HS 9/1062/4.
52 Ibid.

12 'Big and serious stuff'

1 Cipher telegram, SOE Algiers to SOE London, 6 July 1943, TNA HS 6/800.
2 Ibid.
3 Interview with Commander Richard Gatehouse, Imperial War Museum Sound Archive, Ref. No. SA 12213.
4 See, for example, M. Hastings, *All Hell Let Loose: The World at War 1939–45* (London: HarperPress, 2011), p. 365.
5 Narrative of the work of SOE's Italian Section by Lieutenant-Colonel C. Roseberry, July 1945, TNA HS 7/58.
6 Prime Minister to Lord Selborne, 1 May 1944, TNA HS 8/281.
7 'Armistice and Post-War Committee', Lord Selborne to Prime Minister, 27 April 1944, TNA HS 8/281.
8 Mackenzie, *The Secret History of SOE*, p. 395.
9 For SOE's success at securing foreign currency, see: Christopher J. Murphy, 'SOE's Foreign Currency Transactions', *Intelligence and National Security*, 20/1, March 2005.
10 Lieutenant-Colonel C. Roseberry to D/HIS.1, 25 July 1945, TNA HS 7/58.
11 Bosworth, *Mussolini's Italy*, p. 384.
12 P. Morgan, *The Fall of Mussolini: Italy, the Italians and the Second World War* (Oxford: Oxford University Press, 2007), p. 85.
13 Cipher telegram, J. McCaffery to SOE London, 2 September 1942, TNA HS 6/778.
14 Information provided by the SOE Adviser to the Foreign & Commonwealth Office.
15 'General Annibale Bergonzoli', 13 September 1943, TNA HS 6/778.
16 Cipher telegram, General Sir Archibald Wavell to War Office, 24 March 1941, TNA FO 371/29936.
17 Minute by V. Cavendish-Bentinck, 11 April 1941, TNA FO 371/29936.
18 Cipher telegram, General Sir Archibald Wavell to War Office, 9 April 1941, TNA FO 371/29936.
19 Minute by P. Dixon, 13 May 1941, TNA FO 371/29936.
20 Information provided by the SOE Adviser to the Foreign & Commonwealth Office.

21 'Memo from SOE Berne dated 5th January 1943', TNA HS 6/777.

22 Cipher telegrams, SOE London to J. McCaffery, 13 January 1943,
TNA HS 6/824.

23 Sir Orme Sargent to Sir Charles Hambro, 21 January 1943,
TNA HS 6/777.

24 Roseberry added that 'Badoglio, the son of a Piedmontese yeoman,
would have been surprised at this description of himself.' Narrative of
the work of SOE's Italian Section by Lieutenant-Colonel C. Roseberry,
July 1945, TNA HS 7/58.

25 Foreign Office to the Prime Minister, 17 February 1943,
TNA PREM 3/242/9.

26 Prime Minister to the Secretary of State for Foreign Affairs, 13 February
1943, TNA PREM 3/242/9.

27 Sir Orme Sargent to Sir Charles Hambro, 20 March 1943,
TNA HS 6/901.

28 According to Professor F. H. Hinsley, the War Cabinet's continued
insistence on the principle of no-undertakings-before-negotiations
had 'put an end' to that Italian approach. This was either because
'the Italian offer had not been genuine' or because the British
'stipulations' 'had proved unacceptable to the Italians'. F. H. Hinsley,
*British Intelligence in the Second World War: Its Influence on Strategy
and Operations. Volume III, Part I* [London: HMSO, 1984], p. 102n.
Professor W. J. M. Mackenzie, in his long-classified Cabinet Office
history of SOE, stated too that 'this was sufficient to break off
discussions'. Mackenzie, *The Secret History of SOE*, p. 540. But in fact,
from inspection of SOE records, it seems that Jock McCaffery did not
have the opportunity to report the fresh position to Rusca before his
line to him from Berne went down.

29 SOE War Diary, TNA HS 7/262.

30 J. McCaffery ('M') to L. Rusca ('Vulp'), undated but December 1942,
NARA RG 226, Entry 174, Box 221, Folder 49 (A).

31 SIM report No. 81372, 30 March 1943, NARA RG 226, Entry 174,
Box 221, Folder 49 (A).

32 SIM report No. 7098, 'Azione "E–G"', 3 April 1943, NARA RG 226,
Entry 174, Box 221 Folder 49 (A).

33 G. Bonsaver, *Censorship and Literature in Fascist Italy* (Toronto:
University of Toronto Press, 2007), p. 235.

34 Major C. Roseberry to Captain J. R. M. Senior, 24 September 1943,
TNA HS 6/780.

35 'SOE & Italy', by Major C. Roseberry, 28 September 1943,
TNA HS 6/901.

36 Roseberry's regret is echoed by Mackenzie's Cabinet Office history of
SOE: 'a rising in Italy timed to follow swiftly on the fall of Tunis [in
May 1943] would have made an immense difference to the whole aspect
of the war . . . The balance of arguments lay very even, and the decision

taken [to dismiss Badoglio's approach] was certainly one of crucial importance.' Mackenzie, *The Secret History of SOE*, pp. 540–1.

37 Information provided by the SOE Adviser.

38 Covering letter to 'An Italian Policy', Sir Charles Hambro to the Foreign Office, 9 December 1942, TNA HS 6/901.

39 'An Italian Policy', 9 December 1942, TNA HS 6/901.

40 Later, Roseberry would claim to understand the grounds for that policy. As he put it, 'It is difficult for us to think always along the same lines as the Foreign Office, seeing that whereas they are necessarily concerned with the situation after [Allied] occupation, we are only concerned with operations which will hasten the day and ease the operations leading to [Allied] occupation.' C. Roseberry to Brigadier E. Mockler-Ferryman, 28 June 1943, TNA HS 9/1119/7. But there was more to it than that, as Mackenzie acknowledged in his history of SOE. For example, 'the political risks of negotiation were obvious': the Anglo-American commitment to the policy of 'unconditional surrender' was seen as crucial to convincing the Soviet Union that a coalition with the Western Allies was worth it. Mackenzie could have added that public opinion in both Britain and the United States demanded nothing less. Certainly he was right to mention that this policy 'meant that no serious attempt could be made to corrupt or seduce any part of the governing oligarchy in Germany or Italy'. He was also right to acknowledge 'the technical difficulties of mustering sufficient forces for a landing and providing them with air cover while Sicily was still in enemy hands,' which made it impossible for the Allies to offer the Italians much military support or any hope of Allied landings until late August. Mackenzie, *The Secret History of SOE*, pp. 538, 541. Mackenzie was on less solid ground when implying – as many have done – that an alternative policy would have made a difference. Stephen Ambrose, Eisenhower's official biographer, put that claim at perhaps its most extreme. In Ambrose's opinion, 'Because the Allies were unwilling to abandon Roosevelt's unconditional-surrender formula, deal once again with a fascist like Darlan, or even move quickly, the Italian campaign was long, slow, bloody and sterile . . . The bill for the delay was paid at in blood at Salerno, Anzio and Cassino.' S. Ambrose, *The Supreme Commander: The War Years of General Dwight D. Eisenhower* (New York, Doubleday, 1970), pp. 235, 253.

41 Report by Political Warfare Bureau, 1944, TNA WO 204/10917.

42 Cipher telegram, J. McCaffery to SOE London, 17 April 1943, TNA HS 6/904.

43 Ibid.

44 Cipher telegram, J. McCaffery to SOE London, 29 April 1943, TNA HS 6/904.

45 Information provided by the SOE Adviser to the Foreign & Commonwealth Office.

46 Cipher telegram, J. McCaffery to SOE London, 30 June 1943,
    TNA≈HS 6/904.
47 Cipher telegram, SOE London to SOE Berne, 30 June 1943,
    TNA HS 6/904.
48 Cipher telegram, SOE London to SOE Berne, 10 July 1943,
    TNA HS 6/904.
49 McCaffery got as far as having a British passport made out for La
    Malfa, but he was persuaded by Mussolini's fall that he was better off
    returning to Italy to watch events unfold.
50 Cipher telegram, J. McCaffery to SOE London, 15 June 1943,
    TNA HS 6/904.
51 Ibid.
52 Major C. Roseberry to Major-General C. Gubbins, 17 June 1943,
    TNAHS 9/1119/7.
53 Cipher telegram, SOE London to SOE Berne, 17 June 1943,
    TNA HS 9/1119/7.
54 Ibid.
55 Cipher telegram, SOE Berne to SOE London, 19 June 1943, TNA
    HS 9/1119/7. Olivetti told McCaffery that the idea of a committee 'had
    been suggested to him by [Egidio] Reale to whom Dulles had sent him
    before seeing me to [authenticate his] . . . bona fides'. Reale was an
    Italian lawyer and prominent anti-Fascist who had been living in exile
    in Switzerland since 1926.
56 Cipher telegram, J. McCaffery to SOE London, 3 July 1943,
    TNAHS 6/904.
57 Cipher telegram, SOE London to SOE Berne, 5 July 1943,
    TNAHS 9/1119/7.
58 Cipher telegram, SOE Berne to SOE London, 15 July 1943,
    TNA HS 9/1119/7.
59 Telegram, Berne to Foreign Office, 27 July 1943, TNA HS 9/1119/7.
60 Since Mussolini had fallen on 28 July, the Foreign Office considered
    Olivetti's proposals to be 'largely out of date'. Sir Alexander Cadogan
    to Sir Charles Hambro, 31 July 1943, TNA HS 9/1119/7.
61 SIM report No. 13736, 'Azione "E-G"', 30 June 1943, NARA RG 226,
    Entry 174, Box 224, Folder 55 (B).
62 SOE's plan had in fact been drawn up to meet a request from the
    RAF for help in targeting the Luftwaffe. It called for five agents, all in
    civilian clothes, to be dropped by parachute with the aim of ambushing
    in Brittany a busload of enemy aircrew. These airmen belonged to a
    Heinkel unit spearheading raids on Britain. SOE's plan was to kill
    them as they drove from their billets to the airfield. 'I think that
    the dropping of men dressed in civilian clothes for the purpose of
    attempting to kill members of the opposing forces is not an operation
    with which the Royal Air Force should be associated,' Portal wrote to
    SOE; 'there is a vast difference, in ethics, between the time-honoured

operation of the dropping of a spy from the air and this entirely new scheme for dropping what one can only call assassins.' In the end, Portal was talked round and SOE's men went in by parachute, but the enemy airmen changed their routine and the attack never came off. M. R. D. Foot, *SOE in France* (London: HMSO, 1966), p. 153. Portal's objections to the ethics of covert assassination are also interesting in view of the fact that he also became a leading advocate of area bombing, the deliberate tactic of targeting cities and their civilian inhabitants as a means of attacking the enemy's morale and workforce.

63 Sir Charles Portal to the Prime Minister, 13 July 1943, TNA FO 954/17.
64 See, for example: 'How Bomber Harris planned Dam Buster raid on Mussolini', *Daily Express*, 12 March 2010; 'Dambusters hero wanted to bomb Mussolini', *Scotsman*, 11 March 2010; and 'Britain planned Dambusters assassination of Mussolini', *Daily Telegraph*, 12 March 2010.
65 A. Eden to the Prime Minister, 14 July 1943, TNA FO 954/17.
66 'Chiefs of Staff Committee: Review of SOE Activities for Period 12 April 1943 to 10 May 1943', TNA HS 8/245.
67 'Memoranda on Musso's [*sic*] desk', TNA AIR 20/5383.
68 Ibid. Only an assessment of the situation in Turin expressed any dismay with this growing dissent. 'While a really limited number of people [here] follow with interest the developments of the war situation, realising that the future and the very life of the Nation is at stake in this conflict, the greater part of the population shows openly indifference, only seeing in the necessary war sacrifices a limitation of personal liberty, and only caring for its own selfish well-being, showing a most deplorable lack of interest in what is happening to the country. But both of them agree on blaming the Regime for having brought the nation to the present critical situation, because it did not prepare the armed forces and the nation in time for this war, that political circles and propaganda presented as unavoidable.'
69 Salvadori, *The Labour and the Wounds*, pp. 154–5.
70 'Fall of Mussolini', report by the Joint Intelligence Sub-Committee, 27 July 1943, TNA PREM 3/242/11A.
71 D. Eisenhower, *Crusade in Europe* (London: Heinemann, 1948), pp. 202–3.

13 'The man who fell from the sky'

1 'Attempts at Recruiting Volunteers for Italy', 17 October 1941, TNA HS 6/888.
2 D. L. J. Perkins to P. Broad, 16 May 1941, TNA HS 6/901.
3 D. L. J. Perkins to Sir Frank Nelson, 24 July 1941, TNA HS 6/901.
4 R. Lamb, *War in Italy 1943–1945: A Brutal Story* (London: John Murray, 1993), p. 15.

5 'Report on Psychological Examination of Maltese [sic] Student Group', by Major A. Kennedy, 20 October 1942, TNA HS 6/890.

6 Major C. Roseberry to Captain J. Dobrski, 5 January 1943, TNA HS 6/871.

7 Captain J. Dobrski to Major C. Roseberry, 15 February 1943, TNA HS6/871.

8 Major C. Roseberry to Captain J. Dobrski, 5 January 1943, TNA HS 6/871.

9 'The Olaf Story', by C. Roseberry, 28 September 1943, TNA HS 6/775.

10 J. McCaffery, 'No Pipes or Drums'.

11 SOE War Diary, TNA HS 7/262.

12 Captain J. Dobrski to Major C. Roseberry, 2 July 1943, TNA HS 6/869.

13 Captain E. de Haan to Major C. Roseberry, 15 August 1943, TNA HS 6/870.

14 *Il Secolo-La Sera*, 18 August 1943, reproduced in G. Barneschi, *L'inglese che viaggiò con il re e Badoglio: La missioni dell'agente speciale Dick Mallaby* (Gorizia: LEG, 2013).

15 J. McCaffery, 'No Pipes or Drums'.

16 Major C. Roseberry to Captain J. Dobrski, 19 January 1943, TNA HS 6/869.

17 J. McCaffery ('To.') to E. Klein, 12 August 1943, NARA RG 226, Entry 174, Box 221, Folder 49(A).

18 J. McCaffery ('Tomaso') to G. Sarfatti ('Giacomo'), 12 August 1943, NARA RG 226, Entry 174, Box 221, Folder 49(A).

19 SIM report, 'Azione "E–G"', 20 August 1943, NARA RG 226, Entry 174, Box 221, Folder 49(A).

20 Eisenhower, *Crusade in Europe*, p. 202.

21 'Diary of Giuseppe Castellano, General, Italian Royal Army', RG 226, Entry 210, Box 358, WN#14052.

22 E. Aga Rossi, *A Nation Collapses: The Italian Surrender of September 1943* (Cambridge: Cambridge University Press, 2000), p. 74.

23 Eisenhower, *Crusade in Europe*, p. 202.

24 Report, H. Macmillan to the Prime Minister, 20 September 1943, TNA PREM 3/249/5.

25 H. Macmillan, *The Blast of War 1939–1945* (London: Harper and Row, 1968), p. 381.

26 'Diary of Giuseppe Castellano, General, Italian Royal Army', NARA RG 226, Entry 210, Box 358, WN#14052.

27 K. Strong, *Intelligence at the Top: The Recollections of an Intelligence Officer* (London: Cassell, 1968), pp. 146–7.

28 The use of an alternative wireless link with Rome was also considered. In 1943, British security officers had caught in Tunisia an Italian wireless operator who had been left behind to work a clandestine set in hills near Tripoli. Persuaded to work for the British, he was used by A Force, the deception specialists, to send back to Italy false troop

movements in advance of the Sicily landings. At the beginning of
August, on the instructions of Eisenhower and London, that channel,
which the British codenamed 'Llama', was then considered as a means
of securing a reliable link to Rome. This was a time when a number
of Italian commanders in the Eastern Mediterranean were trying to
contact the Allies with a view to seeking peace, and Allied officers
were anxious to ascertain if they spoke with Rome's authority and
were secure. Eventually a message was sent to Rome over the 'Llama'
link informing the Italians that their operator had been captured
and offering the link as a means of 'direct and secret communication
between the British and Italian General Staffs'. The Italians replied
accepting the offer but warned that the ciphers were not secure. In the
end, Castellano's arrival in Lisbon overtook these dealings. 'Historical
Record of Deception in the War Against Germany and Italy', TNA
CAB 154/100. Some official records of the 'Llama' episode remain
heavily redacted. See, for example: 'A Force Narrative War Diary,
1st Jan to 31st Dec 1943', TNA CAB 154/3.

29 D. Dodds-Parker, *Setting Europe Ablaze: Some Account of
Ungentlemanly Warfare* (Windlesham: Springwood Books, 1983),
pp. 136–41.

30 L. Marks, *Between Silk and Cyanide: The Story of SOE's Code War*
(London: HarperCollins, 1998), pp. 358–62, 379–80. Marks, whose
memoirs, though entertaining, are shot through with invention,
claimed to have upgraded Dick Mallaby's emergency signal plan
for the purposes of Monkey. That is not what happened. Monkey
was a brand new double-transposition signal plan issued to Cecil
Roseberry in London, then passed to Castellano in Lisbon to take
with him back to Rome, to be used with Bino Sanminiatelli's novel,
L'omnibus del corso. Mallaby had gone into Italy with three different
plans: 'Maraschino Orange', to be used in communications with
'Massingham'; 'Maraschino', to be used, if necessary, to communicate
with London; and 'Pallinode', which had been a code originally
prepared for Bruno Luzzi and the mission to Trieste. When Mallaby
opened up from Rome and made contact with 'Massingham', he
used Maraschino Orange to confirm his identity and then continued
with Monkey, save for the occasional message dealing with personal
matters. The last messages passed in the Monkey code were sent in
mid-September; thereafter, new plans were used.

31 Narrative of the work of SOE's Italian Section by Lieutenant-Colonel
C. Roseberry, July 1945, TNA HS 7/58. His encounter with the signals
office was an 'interesting instance', Roseberry reflected, 'of how
internal regulations aimed at ensuring smooth and proper working,
could, unless circumvented in emergency, delay, hamper, or even
prevent the carrying out of a vital project.'

32 'The Olaf Story', by C. Roseberry, 28 September 1943, TNA HS 6/901.

'A very good one too,' wrote Lord Selborne on the copy given to him to read the day after Roseberry wrote it.

33 Cipher telegram, Major C. Roseberry to 'Massingham', 25 August 1943, TNA HS 6/779. This was not the only plan afoot to secure Mallaby's release. When SOE first heard of Mallaby's capture, thought was given immediately to his rescue. From Switzerland, Jock McCaffery sent word to one of his supposed confidants in Italy, Enrico Cavadini, the head of the Wolves, to see what he could do about helping Mallaby escape. In Rome, Sir D'Arcy Osborne, the British Minister to the Holy See, asked the Vatican to help with a prisoner exchange: SOE felt that two Italian saboteurs of the elite San Marco Regiment, captured recently in Libya trying to sabotage British aircraft, might make a suitable swap. 'Please intervene unofficially in any way you think most effective,' Osborne was told from London. 'We are most anxious to ensure that he is not shot out of hand.' Cipher telegram, Foreign Office to The Holy See, 26 August 1943, TNA HS 6/872. Three days later, Luigi Maglione, the Vatican's Cardinal Secretary of State, informed the British Minister that Mallaby was 'all right and will probably be brought to Rome on August 30th'. Cipher telegram, SOE London to Massingham, 30 August 1943, TNA HS 6/872.

34 D. Williams, 'An Interview with Miss Paddy Sproule', *FANY Gazette* (1999). The three other FANYs were Leonora Railton, Sue Rowley and Barbara Tims, with a FANY officer, 29-year-old Lieutenant Margaret 'Peg' Todd, responsible for the Ops Room.

35 Wireless message, 'Massingham' to SOE London, 30 August 1943, TNA HS 6/779. On 29 August, 'Massingham' and Rome had only exchanged over Monkey one or two standard 'Q' code messages to establish contact. One of the first proper messages sent to Rome over Monkey informed the Italians that General Zanussi, the other Italian general whom Rome had sent to Lisbon, had endorsed the proposals put to Castellano; Zanussi had left Italy before Castellano's return and, like him, had no secure means of reporting on his activities, thus leaving Rome unaware of his progress. These proposals were the so-called 'Short Terms', which had been agreed under pressure from Eisenhower's headquarters in Algiers for an urgent military armistice document, and had been presented to Castellano with a personal communication from Churchill and Roosevelt. They contained a proviso that full political, economic and other conditions would be submitted at a later date. Although the full surrender terms, known as the 'Long Terms', had received top-level Allied agreement, it was feared in Algiers that, if these were transmitted to the Italian Government before they had accepted the Short Terms, the conclusion of a military armistice could be badly delayed. Later, Zanussi was flown to Algiers, where Douglas Dodds-Parker met him, and then flown to Sicily to be present for the final negotiations.

36 'The Olaf Story', by C. Roseberry, 28 September 1943, TNA HS 6/901.
37 G. Castellano, *Come firmai l'armistizio di Cassibile* (Milan: Mondadori, 1945), p. 123. Gianluca Barneschi's fine account of Mallaby's life and wartime missions draws on a brief memoir, unpublished and incomplete, that Mallaby wrote after the war. In this, Mallaby recalled that he had been brought to Rome and held at first in Regina Coeli prison, before being taken out again, put in a car, and driven through the city. Still with no idea as to what it was all about, he feared they might be taking him to be shot. On reaching the Palazzo Vidoni, home of the Comando Supremo, he was ushered into the presence of Castellano and Montanari. Barneschi, *L'inglese che viaggiò con il re e Badoglio*, p. 148.
38 Ibid. p. 157.
39 Wireless message, Monkey to 'Massingham', 4 September 1943, TNA HS 6/779.
40 For more on Christine Granville, see M. Masson, *Christine* (London: Hamish Hamilton, 1973), and C. Mulley, *The Spy Who Loved: The Secrets and Lives of Christine Granville* (London: Macmillan, 2012).
41 Strong, *Intelligence at the Top*, p. 155.
42 'Diary of Giuseppe Castellano, General, Italian Royal Army', NARA RG 226, Entry 210, Box 358, WN#14052.
43 Ibid.
44 Strong, *Intelligence at the Top*, pp. 156–7.
45 Ibid.
46 Quoted in report, H. Macmillan to the Prime Minister, 20 September 1943, TNA PREM 3/249/5.
47 Strong, *Intelligence at the Top*, p. 158.
48 Eisenhower, *Crusade in Europe*, p. 205.
49 D. Williams, 'An Interview with Miss Paddy Sproule', *FANY Gazette* (1999).
50 'History of Italian Activities of SOE, 1941–1945', TNA HS 7/58.
51 Wireless message, Monkey to Massingham, 8 September 1943, TNA HS 6/779.
52 Wireless message, General D. Eisenhower to Marshal P. Badoglio, 8 September 1943, quoted in A. Chandler (ed.), *The Papers of Dwight David Eisenhower: The War Years Volume III* (Baltimore: Johns Hopkins Press, 1970), p. 1402.
53 Quoted in S. Ambrose, *Eisenhower: Volume One: Soldier, General of the Army, President-Elect, 1890–1952* (New York: Simon & Schuster, 1983), p. 260.
54 Intercepted signal, Iraqi Chargé d'Affaires in London to Minister for Foreign Affairs in Baghdad, 9 September 1943, TNA HW 12/292.
55 Intercepted signal, Rome to Berlin, 30 August 1943, TNA HW 19/237.
56 Intercepted signal, Japanese Ambassador in Berlin to Tokyo, 9 September 1943, TNA HW 12/292.

57 Intercepted signal, Japanese Ambassador in Berlin to Tokyo, 10 September 1943, TNA HW 12/292.

58 Intercepted signal, Japanese Ambassador in Berlin to Tokyo, 23 September 1943, TNA HW 1/2036.

59 'History of Italian Activities of SOE, 1941–1945', TNA HS 7/58.

14 'Inglese Ignoto'

1 Report by G. Sarfatti, November 1944, TNA HS 9/1313.

2 'Impression of Source', 2 November 1944, TNA HS 9/1313.

3 J. McCaffery, 'No Pipes or Drums'.

4 A selection of Sarfatti's academic writings between 1948 and 1983, collected and compiled by his son, was published in 2011. See G. Sarfatti, *Sogni necessari. Ambiente, agricoltura, scienza e società* (Borgo San Lorenzo: All'insegna del giglio, 2011).

5 Accompanying de Haan were Captain Freddie White, Sergeant Edward Archibald Case and Corporal Ken Royle. Hailing from Georgetown, British Guiana, the 37-year-old Case was a highly skilled wireless operator who had worked before the war for the West Indian General Post Office. 'He could operate a morse key at phenomenal speeds,' remembered Jack Wolstenholme, an SOE officer who ran an SOE signals office in Monopoli, near Bari, where Case later worked. J. Wolstenholme to C. M. Woods, 30 April 1992, Woods papers. Case was also the holder of the Military Medal, awarded for his work with a small SOE team during the Allied landings in Algeria in November 1942.

6 J. Gleeson and T. Waldron, *Now It Can Be Told* (London: Elek Books, 1954), p. 132.

7 Narrative of the work of SOE's Italian Section by Lieutenant-Colonel C. Roseberry, July 1945, TNA HS 7/58.

8 Recommendation for an award of the Distinguished Service Order, 28 October 1943, TNA WO 373/94.

9 'Interrogation report on Capt. Richard Mallaby', 12 April 1945, TNA HS 6/873.

10 Paolo Porta to 'Duce', February 1945, TNA HS 6/873.

11 Ibid.

12 'Interrogation', 18 February 1945, TNA HS 6/873.

13 Ibid.

14 'Detailed Interrogation Report of Foschini, Vittorio, and De Leo, Candeloro', 15 September 1945, NARA RG 226, Entry A1-215, Box 4, Folder WN#26042.

15 'Interrogation report on Capt. Richard Mallaby', 12 April 1945, TNA HS 6/873.

16 Ibid.

17 Ibid.

18 Lieutenant-Colonel C. Roseberry to Lieutenant-Colonel R. T. Hewitt, 17 March 1945, TNA HS 6/873.

19 Bradley F. Smith and Elena Aga Rossi, *Operation Sunrise: The Secret Surrender* (New York: Basic Books, 1979), p. 68.

20 'Interrogation report on Serra, Salvatore', 27 May 1945, TNA HS 9/1343/1.

21 Ibid. These claims were quickly checked. Interviewing ex-internees from San Martino, SOE heard two Englishwomen describe Serra as 'a very mysterious man'. He had arrived from a prison in Mantua, they said, and had not only claimed to be English but also to know their cousins in Staines. He had also 'refused to be photographed when anyone was taking snaps'. A Chilean priest remembered Serra's claim to be a British Army officer and recalled that he had later escaped and joined a band of Italian partisans, the 42nd Brigata Patria; the priest had actually seen Serra with the brigade and had 'a very high opinion of his courage, resourcefulness and devotion to the patriotic cause'. Appendix A to 'Interrogation report on Serra, Salvatore', 27 May 1945, TNA HS 9/1343/1. The commander of that brigade confirmed for SOE that Serra had escaped from internment in November 1944 and joined the partisans, and had claimed to be an Eighth Army major. He added that Serra had done useful work (gathering information on local enemy and friendly forces and assisting in the rescue of two downed American airmen), but had also seemed somewhat odd. A British major called Leach was working with nearby partisans, but Serra had seemed anxious to avoid meeting him. As the partisan commander explained: 'there were many favourable opportunities for a meeting and it seemed strange to everyone that an officer of the 8th Army should have no wish to meet a colleague'. Appendix B to 'Interrogation report on Serra, Salvatore', 27 May 1945, TNA HS 9/1343/1. According to SOE records, Major D. G. Leach commanded its 'Erwood' mission in the Alessandria area from March to May 1945.

22 'Interrogation report on Serra, Salvatore', 27 May 1945, TNA HS 9/1343/1.

23 Ibid.

24 Ibid.

25 'Interrogation Report on Faccio, Cesare', 19 March 1945, TNA HS 9/1343/1.

26 Captain P. Cooper to Major P. Lee, 3 August 1944, TNA HS 9/9/3.

27 'Translation by A.M.212 [Captain P. Cooper] made July 44 of statement by Paladino, Eugenio', TNA HS 9/9/3.

28 A. Bonetti to 'the Swiss Legation in charge of Foreign Embassies to be forwarded to the British Embassy', translated 12 August 1944, TNA HS 9/9/3.

29 Gian Paolo Pelizzaro, 'Il Cerchio si Chiude', *Storia in Rete*, 2009.

30 A. Strazzera-Perniciani, *Umanità e eroismo nella vita segreta di*

Regina Coeli (Rome: Azienda Libraria Amato, 1946), quoted in
Gian Paolo Pelizzaro, 'Il Cerchio si Chiude', *Storia in Rete*, 2009.
SS-Obersturmbannführer Herbert Kappler, in Rome at the time,
would later tell British interrogators that he learned of Adler's presence
as a result of the plot to free him, and confirmed that the Germans
had interrogated him. SOE observed from Kappler's testimony that
Adler 'appears to have admitted to having been a British agent, but in
general told a cover story . . . including [the claim] that he was English'.
Kappler also claimed that no further action had been taken against
Adler. 'Adler, Gabriele, alias Armstrong, John, alias Bianchi, Gabriele',
attached to note from Captain A. M. Baird to Lieutenant-Colonel T. G.
Roche, 25 August 1945, TNA HS 9/9/3.

31 Captain P. Cooper to Major P. Lee, 3 August 1944, TNA HS 9/9/3.

32 'Report on Conversation with Louis Ingram Leslie', 16 August 1944,
TNA HS 9/9/3.

33 Report by Captain P. Cooper, 23 August 1944, TNA HS 9/9/3.

34 Ibid.

35 'Statement made by Nedda Solich [*sic*] to AM.212 [Captain P. Cooper]
on 17 September 1944 concerning John Armstrong', TNA HS 9/9/3.

36 Quoted in Gian Paolo Pelizzaro, '14 colpi alla nuca in 3 minuti',
Storia in Rete, 2009.

37 'Interim report on the Adler case', by Captain P. Cooper, 23 September
1944, TNA HS 9/9/3.

38 'Statement made by Nedda Solich [*sic*] to AM.212 [Captain P. Cooper]
on 17 September 1944 concerning John Armstrong', TNA HS 9/9/3.

39 'Report of a conversation with Father O. Snedden', 15 August 1944,
TNA HS 9/9/3.

40 'Interim report on the Adler case', by Captain P. Cooper, 23 September
1944, TNA HS 9/9/3.

41 'Adler, Gabriele, alias Armstrong, John, alias Bianchi, Gabriele',
attached to note from Captain A. M. Baird to Lieutenant-Colonel T. G.
Roche, 25 August 1945, TNA HS 9/9/3.

42 Major A. Butler to Mrs Irma [*sic*] Adler, 20 December 1945, TNA
HS 9/9/3.

43 Mrs Samu [*sic*] Adler to Major Butler, 21 January 1946, TNA HS 9/9/3.

44 The detective work of Italian researchers proved especially important
in this regard: Marco Patucchi, a journalist for *La Repubblicca*, in
articles published in 2007–8; Gian Paolo Pelizzaro, who published his
detailed findings in a series of articles for the journal *Storia in Rete*
in 2008–9; and Aladino Lombardi, writing in *Patria Indipendente*
in 2009. Among his discoveries, Pelizzaro traced Neda Solic, then in
her eighties and living in Rome. Shown a picture of Adler, she told
Pelizzaro that this was the man she remembered as having been with
her in Via Tasso. Research in Rome also located the remains of the
fourteenth victim at La Storta in 'box 5' in the section for 'political

victims' in the cemetery at Verano ('riquadro 5, vittime politiche, Cimitero Monumentale del Verano'). A. Lombardi, 'Finalmente ha un nome il quattordicesimo assassinato a La Storta', *Patria Indipendente* (2009), p. 31.

15 'Foreign agent'

1 'SOE & Italy', by Lieutenant-Colonel C. Roseberry, 28 September 1943, TNA HS 6/901. Some of Roseberry's claims to success were rather overdone. He was wrong, for example, to say in his report that the Partito d'Azione had caused the strikes in northern Italy in the spring of 1943.

2 Ibid.

3 'SOE & Italy', Major-General Colin Gubbins to Lord Selborne, 4 October 1943, TNA HS 6/775.

4 SOE War Diary, TNA HS 7/263.

5 Ibid.

6 Ibid.

7 Mackenzie, *The Secret History of SOE*, p. 541.

8 Lieutenant-Colonel C. Roseberry to Miss Close, 5 January 1948, TNA HS 8/430.

9 For more on Malavasi, see Paolo Trionfini, 'L'antifascismo cattolico di Gioacchino Malavasi. Note per una biografia politica dell'ultimo guelfo', *Bollettino dell'Archivio per la storia del movimento sociale cattolico in Italia*, 35/3, 2000, pp. 171–213; and Paolo Trionfini, *L'antifascismo cattolico di Gioacchino Malavasi* (Rome: Edizioni Lavoro, 2004).

10 SOE War Diary, TNA HS 7/262.

11 'History of Italian Activities of SOE, 1941–1945', TNA HS 7/58.

12 'SOE History: German and Austrian Section: 1940–1945', by Lieutenant-Colonel R. H. Thornley, 1 October 1945, TNA HS 7/145.

13 'Operations into Germany from the UK mounted by the German Section', by Major W. Field-Robinson, TNA HS 7/145.

14 'SOE History: German and Austrian Section: 1940–1945', by Lieutenant-Colonel R. H. Thornley, 1 October 1945, TNA HS 7/145.

15 'Operations into Germany from the UK mounted by the German Section', by Major W. Field-Robinson, TNA HS 7/145.

16 Quoted in 'Luigi Mazzotta alias Gino Cover', 29 May 1944, TNA HS 6/893. The report contained a physical description: 'Height 1m.77, chest 0.86, wavy brown hair, long face, round chin, brown eyes, regular eyebrows, rosy complexion, defective teeth, age about 30, slim, low forehead.' SOE reports conflict as to whether this description related to Mazzotta or Di Giunta.

17 Ibid.

18 J. Lussu, *Freedom Has No Frontier*, p. 143.

19 Salvadori, *The Labour and the Wounds*, pp. 166–7.

20 Recommendation for the award of the Military Cross, 29 September 1944, TNA WO 373/11.

21 Recommendation for the award of the Distinguished Service Order, 26 April 1945, TNA WO 373/11.

22 *New York Post*, 20 July 1945.

23 Quoted in report ('Max William Salvadori, with aliases, Dr Massimo Salvadori-Paleotti, Dr Massimo Salvadori, Dr M. Salvadori-Palleotti, Col. Pallavicini') by Special Agent Joseph T. Genco, 7 August 1945, Bureau file 100-12404, FBI Archives.

24 'Foreign-Born Professor Hailed By President for Lecture in U.S.: Salvadori of Smith Singled Out for His Interpretation of Country Abroad', *New York Times*, 22 March 1956.

25 'Meet the Professor', *Newsweek*, 2 April 1956.

26 'Max Salvadori', *The Times*, 29 August 1992.

27 J. Verney, *Going to the Wars: A Journey in Various Directions* (London: Penguin, 1958), pp. 136–7.

28 Salvadori, *The Labour and the Wounds*, p. 198.

29 Information provided by the SOE Adviser to the Foreign & Commonwealth Office. Signed off from SOE in August 1945, Roseberry died, aged eighty, in 1971.

30 Signora Iacopina Pazzi to the War Office, 8 July 1947, TNA HS 9/1185/2.

31 A. Affortunati, *Di morire mon mi importa gran cosa. Fortunato Picchi e l'Operazione 'Colossus'* (Prato: Pentalinea, 2004), pp. 106–7. The brothers sent to Russia and Mauthausen managed to survive.

32 The War Office (MO1 SP) to Signora Iacopina Pazzi, 1 August 1947, TNA HS 9/1185/2.

33 Affortunati, *Di morire mon mi importa gran cosa*, pp. 141–6.

34 Salvadori, *The Labour and the Wounds*, pp. 189–90.

Sources and Bibliography

Archives

Archivio Centrale dello Stato, Rome
Records of the Special Tribunal

Balliol College, Oxford
Papers of Colonel B. A. Sweet-Escott

Bodleian Library, Oxford
Papers of Stephen Clissold

British Library of Political and Economic Science, London
Papers of Baron Dalton of Forest and Frith

Churchill Archives Centre, Churchill College, Cambridge
Papers of Sir Alexander Cadogan
Papers of Lord Gladwyn

Federal Bureau of Investigation, Washington, DC
Bureau files relating to Max Salvadori

Franklin D. Roosevelt Library, Hyde Park, New York
Roosevelt Office Files

Imperial War Museum (Department of Documents), London
Papers of Major J. S. H. Clissold
Papers of Major-General Sir C. McV. Gubbins
Papers of Major P. M. Lee

Imperial War Museum (Sound Archive), London
Lieutenant-Colonel Basil Davidson (Sound Archive interview No. 8682)
Commander Richard Gatehouse (Sound Archive interview No. 12213)
Harry Hargreaves (Sound Archive interview No. 12158)
Vice-Admiral Sir Ian McGeoch (Sound Archive interview No. 9859)
Ronald Turnbull (Sound Archive interview No. 26754)

Istituto Nazionale per la Storia del Movimento di Liberazione in Italia, Milan
Copy of last letter of Fortunato Picchi

Liddell Hart Centre for Military Archives, King's College, London
Papers of Lieutenant-Colonel Count J. A. Dobrski

Magdalen College, Oxford
Papers of Sir Douglas Dodds-Parker

National Archives (NARA), College Park, Maryland
Office of Strategic Services records (RG 226) (including extensive SIM records)
William J. Donovan records (Microfilm series 1642)

The National Archives (TNA), London
Government archives (with class-marks):

Admiralty
  Submarine Logs (ADM 173)
  War History Cases and Papers, Second World War (ADM 199)
  Naval Intelligence Division and Operational Intelligence Centre:
    Intelligence Reports and Papers (ADM 223)
  Submarine War Patrol Reports, Second World War (ADM 236)
Air Ministry
  Records of the Air Historical Branch (AIR 20)
British Council
  Registered Files, Yugoslavia (BW 66)
Cabinet Office
  Chiefs of Staff Committee: Minutes 1939–1946 (CAB 79)
  Chiefs of Staff Committee: Memoranda 1939–1946 (CAB 80)
  London Controlling Section: Correspondence and Papers (CAB 154)
Foreign Office
  Political Departments: General Correspondence 1906–1966 (FO 371)
Home Office
  Registered Papers, Supplementary 1868–1959 (HO 144)
Ministry of Defence
  Combined Operations: Records (DEFE 2)
Ministry of Health
  Confidential Registered Files (MH 79)
Prime Minister's Office
  Operational Correspondence and Papers 1937–1946 (PREM 3)
  Correspondence and Papers, 1951–1964 (PREM 11)
Security Service
  Personal Files (KV 2)
  List Files (KV 6)

Special Operations Executive
  Africa and Middle East Group: Registered Files 1938–1969 (HS 3)
  Western Europe: Registered Files 1936–1992 (HS 6)
  Histories and War Diaries: Registered Files *c*. 1939–1988 (HS 7)
  Headquarters: Records (HS 8)
  Personnel Files (HS 9)
  Registry: Italian Section Agent Particulars Nominal Index (HS 15)
Supreme Court of Judicature
  Divorce and Matrimonial Causes Files (J 77)
War Office
  British Forces, Middle East: War Diaries, Second World War (WO 169)
  Directorate of Military Operations: Files concerning Military Planning,
    Intelligence and Statistics (WO 193)
  Middle East Forces: Military Headquarters Papers, 1936–1946 (WO 201)
  British Military Missions in Liaison with Allied Forces: Military
    Headquarters Papers, 1938–1952 (WO 202)
  Allied Forces, Mediterranean Theatre: Military Headquarters Papers,
    1941–1948 (WO 204)
  Directorate of Civil Affairs: Files, Reports and Handbooks (WO 220)
  Recommendations for Honours and Awards for Gallant and
    Distinguished Service (Army) (WO 373)

Papers in private hands
Memoirs (unpublished) of J. McCaffery
Papers of M. Salvadori
Papers of C. M. Woods

Town archives, Troina, Sicily
Birth and Family Registers
Register of 'Deleted' Records

Newspapers, Periodicals

*Corriere della Sera, The Daily Express, The Daily Telegraph, The Evening
Standard, The Guardian/Manchester Guardian, Hansard, The London
Gazette, The New Times and Ethiopia News, The New York Post, The New
York Times, Patria Indipendente, la Repubblica, The Scotsman, The Spokes-
man Review, The Sunday Pictorial, Time, The Times, The Washington Post*

Books

Aga Rossi, Elena, *L'inganno reciproco. L'armistizio tra l'Italia e gli anglo-
  americani del settembre 1943.* Ministero Beni Att. Culturali, 1993
____, *A Nation Collapses: The Italian Surrender of September 1943.*
  Cambridge: Cambridge University Press, 2000

Affortunati, Alessandro, *Di morire mon mi importa gran cosa. Fortunato Picchi e l'Operazione 'Colossus'*. Prato: Pentalinea, 2004

Allan, S., *Commando Country*. Edinburgh: National Museums of Scotland, 2007

Ambrose, S., *Eisenhower: Volume One: Soldier, General of the Army, President-Elect, 1890–1952*. New York: Simon & Schuster, 1983

——, *The Supreme Commander: The War Years of General Dwight D. Eisenhower*. New York, Doubleday, 1970

Amé, Cesare, *Guerra segreta in Italia, 1940–1943*. Rome, 1954

Andriola, F., *Mussolini–Churchill carteggio segreto*. Casale Monferrato: Piemme, 1996

Angioni, Giulio, *Emilio Lussu e i sardi, in Il dito alzato*. Palermo: Sellerio, 2012

Anon., *British Security Coordination: The Secret History of British Intelligence in the Americas, 1940–45*. London: St Ermin's Press, 1998

Arlacchi, Pino, *Men of Dishonor. Inside the Sicilian Mafia: An Account of Antonio Calderone*. New York: William Morrow & Co., 1993

Atkinson, Rick, *The Day of Battle: The War in Sicily and Italy, 1943–1944*. London: Macmillan, 2007

Badoglio, Pietro, *Italy in the Second World War: Memories and Documents*. Westport, Connecticut: Greenwood Press, 1976

Bailey, R., *Forgotten Voices of the Secret War*. London: Ebury Press, 2008

——, *The Wildest Province: SOE in the Land of the Eagle*. London: Jonathan Cape, 2008

Bajc, G., *Iz nevidnega na plan: slovenski primorski liberalni narodnjaki v emigraciji med drugo svetovno vojno in ozadje britanskih misij v Sloveniji*. Koper: Založba Annales, 2002

Barneschi, G., *L'inglese che viaggiò con il re e Badoglio: La missioni dell'agente speciale Dick Mallaby*. Gorizia: LEG, 2013

Battaglia, Roberto. *The Story of the Italian Resistance*. London: Odhams, 1957

Beevor, Antony, *Crete: The Battle and the Resistance*. London: Penguin, 1992

Beevor, Jack, *SOE: Recollections and Reflections, 1940–1945*. London: The Bodley Head, 1981

Bennett, Gill, *Churchill's Man of Mystery: Desmond Morton and the World of Intelligence*. London: Routledge, 2007

Berrettini, Mireno, *La Gran Bretagna e l'antifascismo italiano: diplomazia clandestina, intelligence, operazioni speciali, 1940–1943*. Florence: La Lettere, 2010

Bonsaver, G., *Censorship and Literature in Fascist Italy*. Toronto: University of Toronto Press, 2007

Bosworth, R. J. B., *The Italian Dictatorship: Problems and Perspectives in the Interpretation of Mussolini and Fascism*. London: Arnold, 1998

——, *Mussolini*. London: Bloomsbury, 2010

——, *Mussolini's Italy: Life under the Dictatorship*. London: Allen Lane, 2005

Butler, J. R. M., *History of the Second World War: Grand Strategy, Volume II: September 1939–June 1941.* London: HMSO, 1957

____, *History of the Second World War: Grand Strategy, Volume III, Part 2: June 1941–August 1942.* London: HMSO, 1964

Campbell, R., *The Luciano Project, The Secret Wartime Collaboration of the Mafia and the US Navy.* New York: McGraw-Hill, 1977

Canali, M., *Le spie del regime.* Bologna: Il Mulino, 2004

Carboni, Giacomo, *Memorie segrete, 1935–1948: Più che il dovere.* Florence, 1955

Cascioli, Ferruccio, *Eroi della resistenza in Roma 1943–1944.* Florence: CEG, 1967

Castellano, Giuseppe, *Come firmai l'armistizio di Cassibile.* Milan: Mondadori, 1945

____, *La Guerra Continua.* Milan: Rizzoli, 1963

Chandler, A. (ed.), *The Papers of Dwight David Eisenhower: The War Years Volume III.* Baltimore: Johns Hopkins Press, 1970

Churchill, W. S., *The Second World War. Volume II: Their Finest Hour.* London: Cassell, 1949

____, *The Second World War. Volume V: Closing The Ring.* London: Cassell, 1951

Clark, M., *Modern Italy, 1871–1982.* London: Longman, 1984

Cobb, Matthew, *The Resistance: The French fight Against the Nazis.* London: Simon & Schuster, 2009

Concetti, P., and Muzzarelli Formentini, C., *Max Salvadori: Una vita per la Libertà.* Fermo: Andrea Livi Editore, 2008

Colville, J., *The Fringes of Power: Downing Street Diaries 1939–1955.* London: Hodder & Stoughton, 1985

Cooper, A., *Cairo in the War 1939–1945.* London: Hamish Hamilton, 1989

Cooper, A. R., *The Adventures of a Secret Agent.* London: Frederick Muller, 1957

Corner, P., *The Fascist Party and Popular Opinion in Mussolini's Italy.* Oxford: Oxford University Press, 2012

Corvo, Max, *The OSS in Italy, 1942–1945: A Personal Memoir.* New York: Praeger, 1990

Costanzo, E., *The Mafia and the Allies: Sicily 1943 and the Return of the Mafia.* London: Greenhill Books, 2007

Critchley, D., *The Origin of Organized Crime in America: The New York City Mafia, 1891–1931.* Oxford: Routledge, 2009

Crosswell, D. K. R., *Beetle: The Life of General Walter Bedell Smith.* Lexington: University Press of Kentucky, 2010

Croft, A., *A Talent for Adventure.* Hanley Swan, Worcs: Self Publishing Association, 1991

Dalton, Hugh, *The Fateful Years: Memoirs 1931–1945.* London: Frederick Muller, 1957

Deakin, F. W., *The Brutal Friendship.* London: Pelican, 1966

____, *The Last Days of Mussolini*. London: Pelican, 1966

Deane-Drummond, A., *Arrows of Fortune*. London: Leo Cooper, 1992

____, *Return Ticket*. London: Collins, 1953

De Blasio Wilhelm, Maria, *The Other Italy: Italian Resistance in World War II*. New York: Norton & Co., 1988

Delzell, Charles, *Mussolini's Enemies: The Italian Anti-Fascist Resistance*. Princeton: Princeton University Press, 1961

Dickie, J., *Cosa Nostra: A History of the Sicilian Mafia*. London: Hodder, 2007

Dilks, D. (ed.), *The Diaries of Sir Alexander Cadogan 1938–1945*. London: Cassell, 1971

De Selincourt, E. (Revised by Shaver, C. L.), *The Letters of William and Dorothy Wordsworth: The Early Years 1787–1805*. Oxford: OUP, 1967

Dodds-Parker, Douglas, *Setting Europe Ablaze: Some Account of Ungentlemanly Warfare*. Windlesham: Springwood Books, 1983

Duggan, Christopher, *The Force of Destiny: A History of Italy since 1796*. London: Allen Lane, 2007

Dulles, A., *The Secret Surrender*. London: Weidenfeld & Nicolson, 1967

Ehrman, J., *History of the Second World War: Grand Strategy. Volume V: August 1943 to September 1944*. London: HMSO, 1956

Eisenhower, D., *Crusade in Europe*. London: Heinemann, 1948

Fava, C., *La mafia comanda a Catania 1960–1991*. Rome/Bari: Laterza, 1991

Federowich, K., and Moore B., *The British Empire and Its Italian Prisoners of War, 1940–47*. Basingstoke: Palgrave Macmillan, 2002

Fentress, J., *Eminent Gangsters: Immigrants and the Birth of Organized Crime in America*. Lanham, MD: University Press of America, 2010

Festorazzi, R., *Mussolini–Churchill: le carte segrete*. Rome: Datanews, 1998

Finkelstein, M., *Separatism, the Allies and the Mafia: The Struggle for Sicilian Independence 1943–1948*. Cranbury, PA: LeHigh University Press, 1999

Foot, M. R. D., *Resistance: An Analysis of European Resistance to Nazism*. London: Eyre Methuen, 1976

____, *SOE in France: An Account of the Work of the British Special Operations Executive in France 1940–1944*. London: HMSO, 1966

____, *SOE: The Special Operations Executive 1940–1946*. London: BBC, 1984

Fornari, H., *Mussolini's Gadfly: Roberto Farinacci*. Nashville, Tenn.: Vanderbilt University Press, 1971

Foxall, R., *The Guinea-Pigs: Britain's First Paratroop Raid*. London: Robert Hale, 1983

Franzinelli, M., *Guerra di spie: i servizi segreti fascisti, nazisti e alleati, 1939–1943*. Milan: Mondadori, 2004

____, *I tentacoli dell'OVRA: agenti, collaboratori e vittime della polizia politica fascista*. Turin: Bollati Boringhieri, 1999

Gallegos, Adrian, *From Capri to Oblivion*. London: Hodder & Stoughton, 1960

Garibaldi, L., *Mussolini: The Secrets of His Death*. New York: Enigma Books, 2004

Garland, Albert N., and Smyth, Howard M., *United States Army in World War II: The Mediterranean Theater of Operations: Sicily and the Surrender of Italy*. Washington, DC: Government Printing Office, 1965

Garnett, David, *The Secret History of PWE, 1939–45: The Political Warfare Executive*. London: St Ermin's Press, 2002

Garosci, Aldo, *Storia dei fuoriusciti*. Bari: Laterza, 1953

Gilmour, David, *The Pursuit of Italy: A History of a Land, its Regions and their Peoples*. London: Allen Lane, 2011

Gleeson, J., and Waldron, T., *Now It Can Be Told*. London: Elek Books, 1954

Grose, Peter, *Gentleman Spy: The Life of Allen Dulles*. London: André Deutsch, 1995

Gwyer, J. M. A., *History of the Second World War: Grand Strategy, Volume III, Part 1: June 1941–August 1942*. London: HMSO, 1964

Hart-Davis, Duff, *Peter Fleming: A Biography*. London: Jonathan Cape, 1974

Hastings, Max, *Finest Years: Churchill as Warlord, 1940–45*. London: HarperPress, 2009

____, *All Hell Let Loose: The World at War 1939–45*. London: HarperPress, 2011

Hibbert, C., *Benito Mussolini: A Biography*. London: Longmans, 1962

Hinsley, F. H., *British Intelligence in the Second World War: Its Influence on Strategy and Operations. Volume I*. London: HMSO, 1979

____, *British Intelligence in the Second World War: Its Influence on Strategy and Operations. Volume II*. London: HMSO, 1981

____, et al., *British Intelligence in the Second World War: Its Influence on Strategy and Operations. Volume III Part 1*. London: HMSO, 1984

____, et al., *British Intelligence in the Second World War: Its Influence on Strategy and Operations. Volume III Part 2*. London: HMSO, 1988

Holland, J., *Malta: An Island Under Siege 1940–1943*. London: Phoenix, 2004

Holmes, D., *Ignazio Silone in Exile: Writing and Antifascism in Switzerland 1929–1944*. Aldershot: Ashgate, 2005

Howard, M., *History of the Second World War: Grand Strategy, Volume IV: August 1942–September 1943*. London: HMSO, 1972

____, *The Mediterranean Strategy in the Second World War*. London: Weidenfeld & Nicolson, 1968

Hunt, David, *A Don at War*. London: Frank Cass, 1990

Jakub, Jay, *Spies and Saboteurs: Anglo-American Collaboration and Rivalry in Human Intelligence Collection and Special Operations, 1940–45*. London: Macmillan, 1999

Jebb, G., *The Memoirs of Lord Gladwyn*. New York: Weybright and Talley, 1972

Jeffery, K., *MI6: The History of the Secret Intelligence Service, 1909–1949*. London: Bloomsbury, 2010

Killinger, C., *Gaetano Salvemini: A Biography*. London: Praeger, 2002

Knox, MacGregor, *Hitler's Italian Allies: Royal Armed Forces, Fascist Regime, and the War of 1940–43*. Cambridge: Cambridge University Press, 2000

____, *Mussolini Unleashed 1939–1941: Politics and Strategy in Fascist Italy's Last War*. Cambridge: Cambridge University Press, 1982

Kogan, Norman, *Italy and the Allies*. Cambridge, Mass.: Harvard University Press, 1956

Lamb, Richard, *War in Italy, 1943–1945: A Brutal Story*. London: John Murray, 1993

____, *Mussolini and the British*. London: John Murray, 1997

Leake, E., *The Reinvention of Ignazio Silone*. Toronto: University of Toronto Press, 2003

Lochner, L. (ed.), *The Goebbels Diaries*. London: Hamish Hamilton, 1948

Lonati, Bruno Giovanni, *Quel 28 aprile. Mussolini e Claretta: la verità*. Milan: Mursia, 1994

Lupo, S., *History of the Mafia*. New York: Columbia University Press, 2009

Lussu, Emilio, *Diplomazia clandestina: 14 giugno 1940–25 luglio 1943*. Florence: La Nuova Italia, 1956

____, *Enter Mussolini: Observations and Adventures of an Anti-Fascist*. London: Methuen & Co., 1936

____, *Sardinian Brigade*. New York: Knopf, 1939

Lussu, Joyce, *Freedom has no Frontier*. London: Michael Joseph, 1969

Luzi, Alfredo, and Muzzarelli Fromentini, Clara (eds), *Max Salvadori: L'uomo, il cittadino*. Fermo: Andrea Livi Editore, 1996

Macintosh, C., *From Cloak to Dagger: An SOE agent in Italy 1943–45*. London: William Kimber, 1982

Macintyre, Ben, *Operation Mincemeat: The True Spy Story that Changed the Course of World War II*. London: Bloomsbury, 2010

Mackenzie, W. J. M., *The Secret History of SOE: The Special Operations Executive 1940–45*. London: St Ermin's Press, 2000

Mack Smith, Denis, *Italy: A Modern History*. Ann Arbor: University of Michigan Press, 1959

____, *Mussolini*, London: Weidenfeld and Nicolson, 1981

Macmillan, Harold, *The Blast of War 1939–1945*. London: Harper and Row, 1968

____, *War Diaries: Politics and War in the Mediterranean, July 1943–May 1945*. London: St Martin's Press, 1984

Maclaren, R., *Canadians Behind Enemy Lines 1939–1945*. Vancouver: University of British Columbia Press, 1981

Mallett, Robert, *Mussolini and the Origins of the Second World War, 1933–1940*. London: Palgrave Macmillan, 2003

Marchesi, L., *Come siamo arrivati a Brindisi*. Milan: Bompiani, 1969

____, *Dall'impreparazione alla resa incondizionata. 1939–1945 memorie di un ufficiale del comando supremo*. Milan: Mursia, 1993

____, *Per la libertà. Il contributo militare italiano al servizio informazioni alleato (dall'8 settembre 1943 al 25 aprile 1945)*. Milan: Mursia, 1995

Marks, Leo, *Between Silk and Cyanide: The Story of SOE's Code War*. London: HarperCollins, 1998

McGeoch, Ian, *An Affair of Chances: A Submariner's Odyssey 1939–44*. London: Imperial War Museum, 1991

Moat, Annette, *On Two Fronts: A Soldier's Life of Travel, Love and War*. Long Riders' Guild Press, 2007

Molony, C. J. C., *History of the Second World War: The Mediterranean and Middle East, Volume V: The Campaign in Sicily, 1943 and the Campaign in Italy, 3rd September 1943 to 31st March 1944*. London: HMSO, 1973

Montgomery Hyde, H., *The Quiet Canadian: The Secret Service Story of Sir William Stevenson*. London: Hamish Hamilton, 1962

Morgan, Philip, *The Fall of Mussolini: Italy, the Italians, and the Second World War*. Oxford: Oxford University Press, 2007

____, *Italian Fascism: 1915–1945*. London: Palgrave Macmillan, 2004

Moseley, R., *Mussolini's Shadow: The Double Life of Count Galeazzo Ciano*. London: Yale University Press, 1999

Muggeridge, M. (ed.), *Ciano's Diary 1939–1943*. London: Heinemann, 1947

Munthe, Malcolm, *Sweet is War*. London: Duckworth, 1954

Murphy, Christopher J., *Security and Special Operations: SOE and MI5 During the Second World War*. London: Palgrave Macmillan, 2006

Newark, T., *The Mafia at War: Allied Collusion with the Mob*. London: Greenhill Books, 2007

Newby, E., *Love and War in the Apennines*. London: Hodder & Stoughton, 1971

Newnham, M., *Prelude to Glory: The Story of the Creation of Britain's Parachute Army*. London: Sampson Low, Marston & Co., 1948

Nicol, J., *Meet Me at the Savoy*. London: Museum Press, 1952

Nitti, Franceso Fausto, *Escape: The Personal Narrative of a Political Prisoner who was Rescued from Lipari, the Fascist Devil's Island*. New York: Putnam, 1930

Ogden, A., *A Spur Called Courage: SOE Heroes in Italy*. London: Bene Factum, 2011

'Pentad', *The Remaking of Italy*. London: Penguin Books, 1942

Petersen, N. H. (ed.), *From Hitler's Doorstep: The Wartime Intelligence Reports of Allen Dulles 1942–1943*. University Park, Pa: Pennsylvania State University Press, 1996

Pimlott, Ben, *Hugh Dalton*. London: Jonathan Cape, 1985

____, *The Political Diary of Hugh Dalton 1918–40, 1945–60*. London: Jonathan Cape, 1986

Pimlott, Ben (ed.), *The Second World War Diary of Hugh Dalton*. London: Jonathan Cape, 1986

Playfair, I. S. O., *History of the Second World War: The Mediterranean and Middle East. Volume I. The Early Success Against Italy (to May 1941)*. London: HMSO, 1954

____, *History of the Second World War: The Mediterranean and Middle East. Volume II. The Germans Come to the Help of Their Ally, 1941.* London: HMSO, 1956

____, *History of the Second World War: The Mediterranean and Middle East. Volume III. British Fortunes Reach Their Lowest Ebb.* London: HMSO, 1960

Playfair, I. S. O., and Molony, C. J. C., *History of the Second World War: The Mediterranean and Middle East. Volume IV. The Destruction of the Axis Forces in Africa.* London: HMSO, 1966

Pugliese, S., *Bitter Spring: A Life of Ignazio Silone.* New York: Farrar, Straus and Giroux, 2009

____, *Carlo Rosselli: Socialist Heretic and Antifascist Exile.* London: Harvard UP, 1999

____, *Desperate Inscriptions: Graffiti from the Nazi Prison in Rome.* Boca Raton, Fla.: Bordighera, 2002

Pugliese, S. (ed.), *Fascism, Anti-Fascism, and the Resistance in Italy: 1919 to the Present.* Lanham, MD: Rowman & Littlefield, 2003

Read, A., and Fisher, D., *Colonel Z: The Life and Times of a Master of Spies.* London: Hodder & Stoughton, 1984

Richards, Brooks, *Secret Flotillas. Volume II: Clandestine Sea Operations in the Mediterranean, North Africa and the Adriatic, 1940–44.* London: Frank Cass, 2004

Rigden, Denis, *Kill the Führer: Section X and Operation Foxley.* Stroud: Sutton, 2002

Salvadori, M., *The Labour and The Wounds: A Personal Chronicle of One Man's Fight for Freedom.* London: Pall Mall Press, 1958

____, *Resistenza ed azione. Ricordi di un liberale.* Bari: Laterza, 1951

Santoro, Lorenzo, *Roberto Farinacci e il Partito Nazionale Fascista 1923–1926.* Soveria Mannelli: Rubbettino, 2008

Saunders, Frances, *The Woman Who Shot Mussolini.* London: Faber and Faber, 2010

Schreiber, G., Stegemann, B., Vogel, D., *Germany in the Second World War. Volume III: The Mediterranean, South-east Europe, and North Africa 1939–1941.* Oxford: Clarendon Press, 1995

Seaman, M., Introduction to *Operation Foxley: The British Plan to Kill Hitler.* London: PRO, 1998

Sias, V., *Il controspionaggio italiano in Sardegna e Corsica (1943).* S'Alvure, 1991

Simpson, William, *A Vatican Lifeline: Allied fugitives, aided by the Italian resistance, foil the Gestapo in Nazi-occupied Rome, 1944.* London: Leo Cooper, 1995

Smith, Bradley F., and Aga Rossi, Elena, *Operation Sunrise: The Secret Surrender.* New York: Basic Books, 1979

Sogno, E., *Guerra senza bandiera.* Milan: Mursia, 1970

Srodes, J., *Allen Dulles: Master of Spies.* Washington, DC: Regenery, 1999

Stafford, David, *Britain and European Resistance: A survey of the Special Operations Executive, with documents*. London: Macmillan, 1983

___, *Camp X: Canada's School for Secret Agents, 1941–45*. Toronto: University of Toronto Press, 1986

___, *Mission Accomplished: SOE and Italy 1943–1945*. London: The Bodley Head, 2011

Strazzera-Perniciani, A., *Umanità e eroismo nella vita segreta di Regina Coeli*. Rome: Azienda Libraria Amato, 1946

Strong, Kenneth, *Intelligence at the Top: The Recollections of an Intelligence Officer*. Cassell: London, 1968

Sweet-Escott, Bickham, *Baker Street Irregular*. London: Methuen, 1965

Tangye D. (ed.), *Went the Day Well*. London: Harrap, 1942

Taylor, F. (ed.), *The Goebbels Diaries 1939–41*. London: Hamish Hamilton, 1982

Tompkins, P., *Dalle carte segrete del Duce: Momenti e protagonisti dell'Italia fascista nei National Archives di Washington*. Milan: Marco Tropea, 2001

Trevelyan, Raleigh, *Rome '44: The Battle for the Eternal City*. London: Secker & Warburg, 1981

Trionfini, Paolo, *L'antifascismo cattolico di Gioacchino Malavasi*. Rome: Edizioni Lavoro, 2004

Valiani, Leo, *Tutte le strade conducono a Roma*. Bologna: Il Mulino, 1983

Vento, A., *In silenzio gioite e soffrite. Storia dei servizi segreti italiani dal Risorgimento alla guerra fredda*. Milan: Il Saggiatore, 2010

Verney, J., *Going to the Wars: A Journey in Various Directions*. London: Penguin, 1958

Waterfield, G., *Professional Diplomat: Sir Percy Loraine of Kirkharle*. London: John Murray, 1973

West, Nigel, *Secret War: The Story of SOE, Britain's Wartime Sabotage Organisation*. London: Hodder & Stoughton, 1992

Wilkinson, Peter, and Astley, Joan Bright, *Gubbins and SOE*. London: Leo Cooper, 1993

Woodward, Sir Llewellyn, *History of the Second World War: British Foreign Policy in the Second World War. Volume I*. London: HMSO, 1970

___, *History of the Second World War: British Foreign Policy in the Second World War. Volume II*. London: HMSO, 1971

Wylie, Neville, *Britain, Switzerland, and the Second World War*. Oxford: Oxford University Press, 2003

___, *European Neutrals and Non-belligerents during the Second World War*. Cambridge: Cambridge University Press, 2002

Articles, Book Chapters, Theses

Arlacchi, P., 'Mafia: The Sicilian Cosa Nostra', *South European Society and Politics* 1/1, 1996

Aldrich, R., 'Policing the Past: Official History, Secrecy and British Intelligence since 1945', *English Historical Review* 119/483, 2004

Bajc, G., 'Collaboration between Slovenes from the Primorska Region, the Special Operations Executive and the Inter-Services Liaison Department after the Occupation of Yugoslavia (6 April 1941)', *Annales: Series Historia et Sociologia* 11/2, 2002

Barneschi, G., 'Misteri, equivoci e ambiguità del tragico settembre 1943: Le radiotrasmissioni dell'agente speciale Dick Mallaby, l'inglese che viaggiò con il re e con Badoglio', *Nuova Storia Contemporanea* 3, 2013

Bernabei, A., 'The London Plot to Kill Mussolini', *History Today* 49/4, 1999

Berrettini, M., 'Diplomazia clandestina: Emilio Lussu ed Inghilterra nei documenti dello Special Operations Executive', Introduction to Lussu, E., *Diplomazia Clandestina*. Online edition, 2009

____, 'Lo "Special Operations Executive" e la missione di Filippo Caracciolo', *Nuova Storia Contemporanea* 1, 2008

____, 'Set Europe Ablaze! Lo Special Operations Executive e l'Italia 1940–1943', *Italia Contemporanea* 252–253, 2008

____, 'To set Italy Ablaze!' Special Operations Executive e i reclutamenti di agenti tra Enemy Aliens e Prisoners of War italiani (Regno Unito, Stati Uniti e Canada) ', *AltreItalie* 40, 2010

Blatt, Joel, 'The Battle of Turin, 1933–1936: Carlo Rosselli, Giustizia e Libertà, OVRA and the Origins of Mussolini's Anti-Semitic Campaign', *Journal of Modern Italian Studies* 1/1, 1995

Campbell, A. E., 'Franklin Roosevelt and Unconditional Surrender', in Langhorne, E., *Diplomacy and Intelligence during the Second World War: Essays in Honour of F. H. Hinsley*. Cambridge: Cambridge University Press, 1985

Canali, M., 'I cedimenti di Max Salvadori', *Liberal* 27, December 2004/ January 2005

____, 'L'uomo che visse due volte: prima al servizio del Duce, poi di Sua Maestà', *Corriere della Sera*, October 2004

Delzell, Charles, 'The Italian Anti-Fascist Resistance in Retrospect: Three Decades of Historiography', *Journal of Modern History* 47/1, 1975

Dodds-Parker, D., 'SOE and Military Operations in Italy', in *No. 1 Special Force and Italian Resistance: Proceedings of the Conference held at Bologna, 28–30 April 1987*. Bologna: Cooperativa Libraria Universitaria Editrice Bologna, 1990

Federowich, Kent, 'Propaganda and Political Warfare: The Foreign Office, Italian POWs and the Free Italy Movement', in Moore, B., and Federowich, K. (eds), *Prisoners of War and their Captors in World War II*. Oxford: Berg, 1996

____, '"Toughs and Thugs": The Mazzini Society and Political Warfare amongst Italian POWs in India, 1941–43', *Intelligence and National Security* 20/1, March 2005

Fucci, Franco, 'La beffa del Terzo Fronte', *Storia illustrata* 281, April 1981

Jamieson, A., 'Mafia and Political Power 1943–1989', *International Affairs*, 10/13, 1990

Lombardi, Aladino, 'Finalmente ha un nome il quattordicesimo assassinato a La Storta', *Patria Indipendente*, 27 September 2009

Lupo, S., 'The Allies and the Mafia', *Journal of Modern Italian Studies* 2/1, 1997

Murphy, Christopher J., 'The Origins of SOE in France', *Historical Journal* 46/4, 2003

____, 'SOE's Foreign Currency Transactions', *Intelligence and National Security* 20/1, March 2005

Newark, T., 'Pact With the Devil?' *History Today* 57/4, 2007

Pelizzaro, Gian Paolo, '14 colpi alla nuca in 3 minuti', *Storia in Rete*, 2009

____, 'Il Cerchio si Chiude', *Storia in Rete*, 2009

Peluso, G., 'Sbarchi a Cuma: Le spie venute dall'Oriente', *Pozzuoli Magazine*, 18 December 2011

Pirjevec, J., 'Britanska tajna organizacija na Slovenskem (1940–1941)', *Prispevki za nojejšo zgodovino* 40/1, 2010

Seaman, M., 'A Glass Half Full: Some Thoughts on the Evolution of the Study of the Special Operations Executive', *Intelligence and National Security* 20/1, 2005

Trionfini, Paolo, 'L'antifascismo cattolico di Gioacchino Malavasi. Note per una biografia politica dell'ultimo guelfo', *Bollettino dell'Archivio per la storia del movimento sociale cattolico in Italia* 35/3, 2000

Wales, T. C., 'The "Massingham" Mission and the Secret "Special Relationship": Cooperation and Rivalry between the Anglo-American Clandestine Services in French North Africa, November 1942–May 1943', *Intelligence and National Security* 20/1, March 2005

Williams, D., 'An Interview with Miss Paddy Sproule', *FANY Gazette*, 1999

Williams, D. M., 'Italy Through the Looking Glass: Aspects of British Policy and Intelligence Concerning Italy, 1939–1941', Doctoral thesis, University of Toronto, 1997

Willams, M., 'Mussolini's Secret War in the Mediterranean and the Middle East: Italian Intelligence and the British Response', *Intelligence and National Security* 22/6 December 2007

Woods, Christopher, 'A Tale of Two Armistices', in K. G. Robertson (ed.), *War, Resistance & Intelligence: Essays in Honour of M. R. D. Foot*. London: Leo Cooper, 1999

____, 'SOE in Italy', in M. Seaman (ed.), *Special Operations Executive: A New Instrument of War*. London: Routledge, 2006

Wylie, Neville, 'SOE and the Neutrals', in M. Seaman (ed.), *Special Operations Executive: A New Instrument of War*. London: Routledge, 2006

Index